Also by Gerald Posner

Mengele: The Complete Story
Warlords of Crime: Chinese Secret Societies: The New Mafia
The Bio-Assassins
Hitler's Children
Case Closed: Lee Harvey Oswald and the Assassination of JFK
Citizen Perot: His Life and Times
Killing the Dream: James Earl Ray and the Assassination
of Martin Luther King, Jr.

MOTOWN

MOT

GERALD POSNER

OWN

MUSIC, MONEY, SEX, AND POWER

RANDOM HOUSE
NEW YORK

Title page photo montage courtesy of Peter Benjaminson

Library of Congress Cataloging-in-Publication Data
Posner, Gerald.
    Motown: music, money, sex, and power / Gerald Posner.
      p. cm.
    Includes bibliographical references and indexes.
    ISBN 0-375-50062-6
    I. Motown Record Corporation. 2. Sound recording industry—United States. 3. Gordy,
Berry. 4. Sound recording executives and producers—United States—Biography. I. Title.
ML3792 .P37 2003
781.644'09774'34—dc2I   2002069768

Printed in the United States of America on acid-free paper
Random House website address: www.atrandom.com

9 8 7 6 5 4 3 2

First Edition

BOOK DESIGN BY MERCEDES EVERETT

To the only number-one hit in my life,
my eternal partner, Trisha

Sources and Acknowledgments

The idea of writing a history of Motown came from a friend, the journalist Fredric Dannen, whose book about CBS Records, *Hit Men: Power Brokers and Fast Money Inside the Music Business* (Times Books, 1990), was a bestseller. While researching *Hit Men*, Dannen kept hearing astonishing tales about Motown. But fearing that another book about the music industry might pigeonhole him as a writer, Dannen went on to other subjects. Motown, meanwhile, lay fallow.

When I finally started some research in 1997, I understood why Dannen thought that a journalist who was not necessarily a music writer should tell Motown's story. The music was vital, of course, but what was most fascinating was the cast of characters—the extended family of artists and musicians—who brought about this once-in-a-generation venture.

My research on Motown was hampered somewhat by my own previous work, much of which has been investigative. When word spread in the music industry about this project, many assumed I was most interested in uncovering dirt and buried skeletons. All the major Motown stars I contacted wanted the right either to review the manuscript prior to publication or to have veto power over what I used from interviews with them. Two asked for money. Since none of those conditions was acceptable, unfortunately it meant that most of them, including Berry Gordy, refused repeatedly to talk to me.

Nearly two dozen key figures spoke to me only under the condition of complete anonymity. They had different reasons for not wanting to be identified. Some still work in the music business and fear the possible wrath of Gordy, one of the industry's legendary figures. Others are bound by court settlements that mandate they not talk about their cases. Some were constrained by nondisclosure agreements they had signed as part of their employment, either for Motown or for some of the artists or executives personally. A few were still involved in residual litigation with Motown. And finally, some were concerned that they had no control over my depictions or conclusions; I did not make any guarantees since I did not know where the research would lead.

One person wavered for several years over whether to cooperate. This source even met my wife, Trisha, and me several times while deciding. After we assumed the last long stretch of silence meant *no*, we received a telephone call from this person only weeks before the manuscript was finished. The information helped answer an otherwise puzzling question.

During the past four years, I have occasionally received plain brown envelopes in the mail. They always had no return addresses. They usually contained copies of old internal Motown memorandums, documents, sales records, financial documents, or personal letters between some of the principals herein. I never discovered who sent those care packages, or whether they came from several people.

My preference is always to list all my sources, but I also promised anyone who spoke to me that, even if their reasons for anonymity were ones with which I did not agree, I would respect them. In balancing those requests with my desire for documentation, I trust that what follows provides a comprehensive account of the publicly available information on which this book is based.

The material presented is the result of four years of research through documents in public and government archives, as well as in private collections; dozens of interviews; and many published books and articles. (Whenever a person told me a story similar to one they had described earlier in print, I always quote from the early, printed source, believing that a person's earliest recollections tend to be more accurate, given the frailties of memory.)

The most important source of information turned out to be the archives of the Wayne County Court in downtown Detroit, which hold the files of almost every major Motown lawsuit over the decades. As readers of this book will discover, few relationships between the label and its artists, producers, songwriters, and executives did not eventually end up in court. The history of the label is interspersed between the legal filings and the motions for stays and dismissals.

Entering the basement archive is like stepping back to the early 1960s, when Hitsville was just coming to be. There are worn linoleum floors, faded green walls, and four antiquated computers atop some simple Formica desks. Fluorescent lamps cast a bluish light. Wires dangling from the ceiling raise doubts about the thoroughness of the last fire inspection in this place where paper is king.

A wooden counter separates visitors from the literally hundreds of vintage metal file cabinets holding the county court's history. The stacks of cardboard boxes piled precariously behind the counter and bursting with documents are evidence of how the files have outgrown their space. More than twenty of those creaky file cabinets are filled with just the litigation between Gordy and his top songwriting team, the Holland brothers and Lamont Dozier.

The Wayne County files were critical because many of them contain depositions in which scenes, characters, and even dialogue help re-create the early days at Motown. In some instances, the court records confirmed stories I had read or heard. In other cases, they provided information not available elsewhere. Many of the exhibits are copies of artist contracts. Others provide the conclusion to a story, such as the case that has the "supplemental agreement" giving the moving details behind Flo Ballard's dismissal from the Supremes.

Important legal cases are also in the archives of other jurisdictions, most in Los Angeles Superior Court. There is the enormous file of the many lawsuits between Motown and the Jacksons. A thirty-page memo from Berry Gordy, for instance, not only lays out how Motown signed the band but also recounts some of his telephone conversations with the boys' father, Joe Jackson. Gordy also discusses the group's contracts, their royalty arrangement, and how much he felt the Jacksons still owed to Motown. Statements like Gordy's, made under oath and much closer in time to the actual events than his autobiography—written eighteen years later—carry considerable credibility. Attached to the same litigation are the extensive depositions of each of the Jackson 5. Also there is a revealing statement (another thirty pages) of Ralph Seltzer, the Motown vice president who negotiated the original deal that brought the Jacksons to the company. The sworn statements include Motown executive Suzanne de Passe's twenty-five-page declaration and that of Richard Arons, Joe Jackson's attorney, among many others. In the same court files are copies of letters between Berry Gordy and Joe Jackson covering everything from the group's deteriorating relationship with the label to Jermaine Jackson's marriage to Gordy's daughter Hazel.

Divorce proceedings of the principal players often provide an intimate look at their personal lives, contrasted to what was happening in the business during the same period. All the court cases are in the public record (with the exception of certain sealed documents and files from the *Holland-Dozier-Holland v. Motown* litigation), and the primary ones relied upon are listed in the bibliography.

Almost as important as the court archives is the E. Azalia Hackley Collection, housed at Detroit's main public library, a comprehensive collection of African-American music history, including early articles about Motown as well as company promotional materials. Many interviews with artists and others involved in Motown, as well as studies and private papers, are also maintained in Detroit at the City-County Building's record room, the Motown Historical Museum, the archives of *The Detroit News,* the Burton Historical Collection at the Detroit Public Library, and the Charles H. Wright African-American Museum.

In any matter in which I have relied on a published source, either a book or an article, I always tried to confirm independently the accuracy of that information. For example, in her book, *Berry, Me, and Motown,* Raynoma Gordy Singleton, Gordy's second wife, claims she was one of three original board members when Motown was incorporated. The other two, according to her, were Berry and his sister Esther. Years later, Gordy summarily dismissed Raynoma's claim, telling the television program *Hard Copy* that she "wasn't even there" when the company was formed. After obtaining copies of the amended articles of incorporation and the certificate of merger and amendments of Motown Record Corporation, I determined that Raynoma was indeed an original member of the board of directors.

One other instance, out of literally several dozen, is the seemingly simple issue of whether Joe Jackson was represented by legal counsel when he negotiated the Jackson 5 contract with Motown. Jackson long claimed that no lawyers helped him. Ralph Seltzer, Motown's lead negotiator, in court documents does not contradict that. The original seven-page contracts for each of the group's five members, dated July 26, 1968 (copies of which I obtained), show no reference to an attorney for the Jacksons. The same is true of the group's nine-page recording contracts dated March 11, 1969. However, in a 1976 sworn statement by Alan Croll, a Motown attorney, Croll contended that Joe Jackson was in fact represented by outside counsel named Jack Richardson. It seemed then to be a matter of determining whose credibility was better. But in a further check on Jack Richardson, I discovered he was not an attorney but simply a family friend who often traveled with the Jacksons. So, a week of research resolved the issue in the same way it had already been reported in many magazines and books.

In other situations, I used census records, private files of a music magazine that prefers not to be named, transcripts of press conferences and television and video specials, and private notes maintained by former Motown workers, all to verify information used from published accounts.

Also, many of the quotations from the artists and executives are from interviews in Detroit papers from the early 1960s. This was before Motown was world famous, when the artists had not yet become stars, and those very early interviews sometimes offer better insights into what was really going on than do the more practiced answers given for the hundredth time.

However, this book was ultimately possible because some people went out of their way to accommodate my many requests for information and research. I am indebted to them, especially in the instances in which they endured repeated demands, often at inconvenient hours and on short notice. There were many who helped me who did not want to be acknowledged, but among those who were willing I am especially indebted to Barney Ales, Phil Jones, and Tom Noonan for their detailed recollections and wonderful perspective on Motown during its heyday. Noonan, in particular, helped at a critical juncture by providing the telephone numbers for several dozen hard-to-reach interviewees, as well as unrestricted access to his remarkable collection of early Motown photos. Adam White, of Universal Music International, knows more about Motown than any other person, including probably Berry Gordy himself. Adam generously agreed to read a draft manuscript, and his insight and attention to detail spared me from many stumbles and errors. And Carol Kaye and Glenn Letsch had fascinating information, which they generously shared, about Motown in Los Angeles. Lawrence Schiller had some wonderful stories about his experiences working with Gordy on *Lady Sings the Blues.* Brian Cahill at Caesars Palace in Las Vegas was always agreeable in trying to arrange interviews with Motown's stars as they passed through there.

Specials thanks on the documentation are due to Barbara Martin of the Detroit Public Library; Mark Silverman, editor, and Linda Culpepper and Pat Zacharias at the *Detroit News* Library; Gwen Priestley at Motown; Lynne M. Glover of the Wayne County Court; Leslie M. Jackson of the Motown Historical Museum; and the staff of the E. Azalia Hackley Collection of Black Music, Dance, and Drama of the Detroit Public Library. Steve Goldberg, Esq., in Los Angeles and David Ness in London were always willing to follow up on the most tenuous leads and invariably returned with wonderful information. Author and journalist Peter Benjaminson was always willing to share his own voluminous research on the label, and his wonderful sense of humor was always welcome.

I have, as with my last four books, been spoiled by the great publishing operation at Random House. Editorial assistant Dominique Troiano never tired of my many requests. Art director Daniel Rembert again designed a great cover. Laura Goldin did the impossible by making the legal review a pleasure. Tim Mennel's diligence as a copy editor helped streamline the manuscript. My friend Beth Pearson again spent many hours fine-tuning the text and pushing me with her insightful questions and comments. Bob Loomis, my dear friend and editor, is a joy to work with. He makes each book a cooperative venture, and his probing questions and fine editing have made this a much better book than the draft I originally submitted. My only hope is that he never retires.

Those lucky enough to know my wife, Trisha, understand that it is not hyperbole to say there would be no book without her. She is my indefatigable partner, not only a dream of a spouse but also an author in her own right as well as the collaborator on all my work. Trisha does every interview with me, spends months sifting through documents in libraries and private collections, and helps on everything from the first draft through all the revisions. Maybe one day I shall finally be successful in convincing her that her name belongs on the front cover as much as mine.

Contents

Introduction

November 28, 1979. Berry Gordy had imagined his fiftieth birthday would be different. For the great-grandson of a slave who had moved from the Ford assembly line to founding Motown Records—the most successful music label of the 1960s—the day should have been a milestone. But where were his stars, the people he had taken from ghettos and made into household names: Diana Ross, once one of his lovers; the mercurial Michael Jackson; his old friend Smokey Robinson? There had been no calls, cards, or telegrams. Instead, Gordy was in Las Vegas with his man Friday, Billy Davis, and Mira Waters, another young starlet in a seemingly endless procession of women he dated.

He sat and brooded in the cavernous marble Jacuzzi of his garish Caesars Palace suite. The life-size plaster busts of Roman emperors ringing the sprawling bathroom seemed to mock him, and with some cause. While he had created the hottest record company in decades—a singular success of black entrepreneurship in an industry long dominated by whites—there were serious problems. The early acts that had fueled Motown's success— Mary Wells, the Temptations, the Miracles, the Marvelettes, Martha and the Vandellas, the Four Tops, the Supremes—had been only partially replaced with new acts such as Gladys Knight and the Pips and Rare Earth. It had been a decade since Motown made music history by having five singles in the top ten in a single week.

The Jackson 5 had briefly promised salvation, but he had lost them to

CBS Records in a savage but ultimately futile struggle with Joe Jackson, the stars' strong-willed father. Gordy often boasted that Michael Jackson would have still been stuck as a cute act in Gary, Indiana, if he had not crafted him into an international star. The Jacksons could not write a great song if their lives depended on it, he contended, and he had given them four consecutive number-one hits. He relished telling about the night in 1968 when he threw a coming-out bash for them at his Detroit mansion. That had been some place—three stories crammed with marble and gold leaf, a marble-floor ballroom with enormous chandeliers, a bowling alley, an Olympic-size swimming pool, a pub filled with English antiques, and a private theater serviced by a secret underground tunnel. Gordy chuckled at the memory of Joe Jackson and his sons walking through the mansion with their mouths open. And when Joe stopped in front of the painting of Gordy dressed as Napoleon Bonaparte, he was humbled.

"Jesus. What can I say?" Jackson muttered. "Black people actually live like this? I just can't believe that this kind of thing is possible."

Now Jackson had taken his sons to CBS. Well, Gordy's contract with them was clear: Motown owned the name *Jackson 5*, and if they wanted it back, they would have to fight for it.

The Temptations were little better, also just leaving Motown. He had given them hit after hit. There was no loyalty anymore, he fumed. The top acts followed the money, and Gordy simply refused to get into bidding wars.

The new singers—and even stalwarts such as Ross, Stevie Wonder, and Marvin Gaye—were selling fewer records and dropping off the charts faster. Some had even started asking pointed questions about Motown's restrictive contracts and grumbling about royalty payments and the label's accounting.

It was so much easier in the beginning. Stevie Wonder was a skinny, blind ten-year-old when Gordy discovered him alternately pounding on bongos and playing a harmonica. When he first saw the Primettes, they were four rail-thin high school girls. Their a cappella version of the Drifters' "There Goes My Baby" wasn't great, but their extreme self-confidence contrasted sharply with their whiny voices. Before they finished school, he had the foresight to sign them as the Supremes.

There was the time he was leaving the 20 Grand, Detroit's hottest nightclub, and a light-skinned black girl with enormous doe eyes sang to him in the middle of the crowd. He instantly loved that raspy voice. "What's your name?" he had asked. "Mary . . . Mary Wells," she stammered.

Or how about that sixteen-year-old wanna-be songwriter who initially appeared to have more enthusiasm than talent? Smokey Robinson—and his group, the Matadors—had blossomed under Gordy's tutelage. When they were ready, Gordy released their first album, under their new name, the Miracles. Who else would have tolerated the youngster's daily intrusions at the studio?

What about Motown's movies? He had produced two hits—*Lady Sings the Blues* and *Mahogany*—against great odds and strong opposition from film-industry insiders. He still relished the day he grabbed control of the *Mahogany* set and forced the imperious British director, Tony Richardson, to storm off in a pique. But the movies had boosted Motown's prestige, not its profits. And then there was the previous year's release of *The Wiz.* He should not have let Ross talk him into giving her the role of Dorothy. Everyone knew she was too old for it, but she wouldn't take no for an answer.

And there were more pressing problems. He still had trouble shaking the rumors that organized crime had muscled into the company and that he was just a figurehead. He was tired of hearing it. There were silly stories of mysterious shootings, runaway gambling debts, loan-shark beatings, and even a rumor that a close friend of his had supposedly gone to jail in his place on a tax rap. There was not—he frequently assured his closest associates—a stick of evidence.

Gordy never thought fifty would feel like this. His body seemed to be on the same slide as the company. There was a thick roll of fat around his stomach. His once muscular arms were now soft and flabby. Even his trademark beard failed to hide a double chin.

He jumped out of the Jacuzzi and almost ran into Waters, who had returned from the casino. She was ready to join him in the tub, but he wasn't in the mood and surprised her with the ferocity with which he pushed her away.

"Let's play craps," he mumbled, almost more to himself than to her. "I feel lucky."

"We need some of that Gordy luck," said Waters.

In the casino, the pit bosses knew Gordy well. He was a heavy roller who was serious about gambling. Tonight he seemed distracted, playing only halfheartedly. In a couple of hours, he had lost twenty-five thousand dollars and was fighting a migraine. It was enough. Gordy returned the next morning to Los Angeles. When he arrived at his Sunset Boulevard office, his longtime accountants, brothers Sidney and Harold Noveck, were waiting. They had flown in unexpectedly from Detroit, and Gordy immediately sensed something was amiss. Though neither brother was naturally gregarious, a particular gloom now accompanied them.

"We have distressing news," Harold said softly.

"Like what?" asked Gordy.

"Well," Sidney broke in, "you're insolvent. . . . I've been telling you all along, over and over again, Mr. Gordy, you're spending too much. You've simply got nothing left."

CHAPTER 1

Detroit Dreaming

BERRY GORDY JR. WAS THE SEVENTH OF EIGHT CHILDREN, BORN IN Detroit on Thanksgiving Day, November 28, 1929, just at the onset of the Great Depression. His father was the son of freed Georgia slaves who had become sharecroppers of a 168-acre patch of barren farmland that had yielded barely enough to keep the family going. Twenty-three children were born there, but fourteen died at or shortly after birth. Those who survived were tough. The mulatto Berry Gordy Sr.—his own father was the child of a slave and her white plantation owner—was a short, wiry man who did not get to high school until he was twenty-two because his family could not spare him from the backbreaking farming.

Berry Gordy Sr. was thirty—mature by local standards—when he married Bertha, a short, cute nineteen-year-old schoolteacher of African and Indian descent. In 1922, three years into their marriage, Gordy made a deal that changed their lives—he sold a load of the farm's timber stumps for $2,600, a small fortune in rural Georgia. As word of the sale spread, the family worried that local whites might rob Gordy, so he traveled to Detroit, where his brother had recently moved, to cash the check. Once there, he never returned. Bertha and their three children joined him a month later.

The promise of assembly-line jobs in auto plants had lured many southerners to Detroit since the mid-1800s. The Motor City's population boomed 1,200 percent during a fifty-year period that ended with the Great War. Ford was the first to break the racial barrier when it began hiring black workers in 1914. During the Roaring Twenties, Detroit had become America's fifth-largest city and its second-fastest-growing. And although Jim Crow laws were still widely entrenched and the city largely segregated, to many southern blacks Detroit offered genuine possibilities for progress.

Berry Gordy Sr.'s start was not auspicious. Shortly after arriving, he used his share of the $2,600 windfall as a deposit on a cramped two-story home. It looked like a decent buy—at $8,500—until the Gordys moved in and discovered it was falling apart. Rotting plasterboard was hidden by fresh wallpaper, and bursting pipes had been concealed under duct tape. In the small space, the Gordys eventually had eight children who shared only three beds. Berry Jr. slept with his sister Gwen. The house was rat-infested, and the children often piled into the kitchen and watched in horror and fascination as their father killed giant rats. Once, a rat jumped from the oven onto Berry Sr.'s face, leaving him blood-covered and the children screaming in terror.

For several years, Berry Sr. hustled through a string of odd jobs and frequently rented an empty lot where he sold everything from ice to coal, wood, Christmas trees, watermelons, and old car parts. Finally, he landed a gig as an apprentice plasterer for black contractors and in a year earned a union card. He then found steady work and saved enough to launch his own businesses. He not only started a carpentry shop but also bought the neighboring Booker T. Washington Grocery Store, as well as a print shop.

When Berry Jr. was six, his family sold their decrepit house and moved to a better, two-story commercial building on the city's east side. (Years later, when Berry Jr. was a successful music mogul, he bought the street signs that marked the corner where their original home had been and planted them in his California backyard.)

Racial strife in Detroit worsened as Berry Jr. grew up. World War II saw almost two hundred defense plants open in the Motor City, and despite Franklin Roosevelt's Fair Employment Practices Committee, almost one third refused to hire blacks. Poor whites flooded the city to fill new jobs, upsetting longtime black residents. In June 1943, white workers at a Packard plant went on strike when three blacks were hired to work next to them. Tensions boiled over a couple of weeks later, leading to three days of race riots and a bloody police response. Thirty-four people were killed, most of them black, and almost half by the police.

But the Gordys tried to steer clear of all this. Political discussions were not tolerated at the dinner table. Gordy's parents had different concerns, ones shared by many middle-class black families: their energies were channeled into commerce, education, and discipline. Berry's mother, Bertha, raised her eight children and still found time to study retail management at Wayne State University, as well as take business courses at the University of Michigan. She earned a degree from the Detroit Institute of Commerce and later was one of three founders of a life insurance company that specialized in residents of black neighborhoods. Berry's father worked long hours and was frugal. The Gordys had a simple philosophy: family loyalty and hard work were the keys to happiness. The Gordy kids would start working in the family's grocery store once they were tall enough to reach over the countertop. "There is strength in unity," Bertha used to tell her children.

Both parents were strict disciplinarians, praising their children generously for good accomplishments but also meting out corporal punishment for transgressions. Serious infractions brought out an ironing cord that Berry Sr. wielded with little restraint, giving whippings that, Berry Jr. later said, "you didn't forget." Junior's worst beating came once after his parents discovered that he had stolen some money from one of his older brothers.

But the tough discipline and emphasis on hard work paid off. Loucye, one of four daughters, was a typical product of the family's mantra. She was the first black woman to become the assistant property officer at the nearby Fort Wayne army reserves. Her sisters, Esther, Anna, and Gwen, worked equally hard. The older Gordy sons were no different, with Fuller and George dutifully carrying out tough assignments in the family's construction and printing ventures. However, the Gordy work ethic somehow seemed to dissipate when it came to the youngest sons, Robert and Berry. Both disliked manual work. A childhood family friend, Artie King, recalled the two brothers as "the two laziest guys in the world." Robert preferred playing records in the basement and spending evenings at a local dance club, the Sedan. Berry also liked music, scribbling out a few rough songs and even winning a local talent contest for his "Berry's Boogie," a lively piece inspired by Hazel Scott's popular "Boogie Woogie."

Berry hung out on nearby Hastings Street, a colorful neighborhood through street filled with drunks, prostitutes, blues bars, poolrooms, a theater, and a half-dozen greasy spoons. During the day, the street was crammed with Orthodox Jews looking for goods to sell in pawnshops. At nights, hustlers—pimps, numbers runners, and gamblers—controlled the area. To Berry, Hastings Street offered something his family lacked: excitement. And he couldn't understand why his father worked so hard to earn a barely decent living when numbers runners worked less and had thick stacks of cash.

CT's, a busy barbecue joint, was also the local numbers headquarters. Berry was six when he played war, his first card game on the streets. Soon, the undersized kid moved from pitching pennies to craps, then to black-jack, and finally to poker. Although his parents were strictly against gambling, young Berry loved it and hid his new passion. He admired the flashy clothes and the sparkling Cadillacs that were the envy of the neighborhood. But he invariably lost to streetwise teenagers. The Hastings Street pawnshops got to know Berry when he was only fourteen. He brought them everything from suits to watches to raise money for more gambling. It was also along Hastings that Berry Jr. lost his virginity, paying a couple of dollars to a streetwalker for a few minutes in a dingy tenement.

With dreams of fast money and with little respect for formal education, Berry was, unsurprisingly, a poor student. He became a class clown to deflect attention from his failure to keep up with his classmates. Since he usually brought home report cards filled with D's and F's, his parents congratulated him when he managed to pull a C. To impress his teachers, Berry memorized the alphabet backward and raced through it for anyone who would listen. His parents and siblings were among the few who knew it was a memory trick and that he had basic problems reading. "I was so far behind the rest of the class," he later recalled, "I just knew I had to be dumb."

Berry's school problems and his fascination with street hustlers angered his father. He considered his son lazy and lacking self-control, citing his tendency to sleep late, run perpetually behind schedule, and be a bed wetter until he was ten. Although Berry knew he was seen as a problem child, it did not reduce his own mighty self-esteem. He considered himself "the chosen one" and reminded his siblings that he was the one named after their father.

His father tried to instill discipline by placing him on contracting jobs. Berry hated having to get up early on cold mornings, knocking out dirty ceilings, sucking in dust, and feeling constantly tired. Soon, his father had him sell Christmas trees. But again, he scraped by on the bare minimum. When he complained, his father lectured him about how rough times had been in the South and how lucky the children were to have the opportunities available in Detroit. His father's stories of hard work did not impress him.

Berry was anxious to find easier work away from his family. He and two friends set up a shoeshine stand outside the city's largest department store. After that failed, he went door to door in white neighborhoods hawking the city's largest black newspaper, the *Michigan Chronicle*. During that venture, he dabbled in something he really liked: music. Berry had a friend with a decent voice accompany him on his rounds. His friend sang "Danny Boy," and if the family had a piano Berry banged out some rough chords or tried a chopped-up version of "Boogie Woogie." Their "touring" ended when they failed to make any newspaper sales after a couple of months.

If the family's work ethic failed to impress Berry, he was also unmoved by their religious devotion. At the Bethel AME Baptist church, preachers consistently roused the packed house in frenzied services. Sometimes one of the worshipers would feel the Holy Spirit and start shaking, occasionally even speaking in tongues. Most considered these moments special, but Berry found them only amusing.

Instead, he reserved his enthusiasm for boxing at neighborhood gyms. It was a sport that appealed to many local blacks because the Brown Bomber—heavyweight champ Joe Louis—had learned to box in Detroit. Sugar Ray Robinson had also been born there. In the 1930s and 1940s, boxing was the only professional sport in which blacks earned top money. It tempted Berry Jr.—as it had briefly his brothers Robert and Fuller—as a quick escape from the drudgery of his father's twelve-hour days.

He thought of himself as "Killer Gordy." At five foot six and 112 pounds, he was nonetheless a scrappy boxer who could take a hit and stand his ground. Working with weights, he bulked up to 125 pounds and the featherweight class. By then, he was sixteen and had fifteen fights—twelve wins—under his belt. He was certain that his fortune was not far off. So when he was kicked out of a music class, he abruptly quit school and turned pro, earning $150 a fight. He didn't initially tell his parents, since he knew they would be furious. He left the house daily pretending that he was going to school. Instead, he went to the gym. When his parents uncovered the deception, they were devastated but failed to change his mind.

In 1948, when he was eighteen, he traveled to California, where he had three matches against two talented Mexican fighters. He won two. But after returning to Detroit, his career stalled as he began slacking off in his training.

As he grew frustrated, Gordy increasingly toyed with music as possibly offering fast fame and fortune. Some days he told friends he wanted to be like Sugar Ray Robinson, and on the next Nat King Cole was his idol. Young Gordy liked jazz, particularly Dizzy Gillespie, Miles Davis, and Charlie Parker. He hung out at the Club Sudan on weekends and then squeezed into the packed Greystone Ballroom and Gardens on Mondays, the only day the club—run by the Jewish Purple Gang, which had controlled liquor and graft in Prohibition-era Detroit—allowed blacks. Gordy loved those evenings, only plagued that he was awkward with girls. Nothing he said came out right.

When Gordy learned that Frankie Carle, a celebrated Hollywood bigband leader, was holding a local amateur night, he thought he might have found a way out of boxing. At the Michigan Theatre, he performed his "Berry's Boogie." Later, he dubbed his own performance "sensational" and bragged about wowing the judges and audience. Still, he lost to a five-year-old prodigy named Sugar "Chile" Robinson. When Gordy's friends teased him about being beaten by a child, he earnestly told them that Robinson was a midget who had won by playing with his knuckles.

In August 1950, Gordy was twenty. In his brief boxing career, he had won thirteen of his nineteen professional bouts. He had finished a tough day of training at the Woodward Avenue Gym when, exhausted, his muscles throbbing, he plopped onto a bench near the back wall. As he wiped the sweat from his face, he glanced up and noticed two posters plastered on the far wall. He walked over to them. One advertised a "Battle of the Bands" between Duke Ellington's outfit and Stan Kenton's. The other announced a fight between two promising boxers.

He stared at both for a few minutes. The fighters, who were in their early twenties, looked like they were fifty, and the bandleaders, who were much older, seemed younger. He thought that whereas fighters were getting physically beaten, the musicians could perform nightly and never get hurt.

Gordy was all too pleased to abandon his morning runs, the punching bag workouts, the sparring rounds, the hundreds of aching sit-ups, and, most of all, the recommended sexual abstinence before a fight.

"The war that had been raging inside me," he later wrote in his autobiography, *To Be Loved,* "music versus boxing—was finally over."

CHAPTER 2

Sliding into Music

AFTER HANGING UP HIS GLOVES, GORDY SURPRISED HIS FAMILY BY working hard on a newfound love for songwriting. Those closest to him weren't certain whether he was motivated only by the lure of fast money or whether music was a true calling, but there was little denying his enthusiasm. "If he would have worked like that on any of my jobs," said his father, "I could have had a lot more work."

Gordy spent his time in the rear of his family's print shop, and he constantly barraged the three shop workers with new lyrics. They were too polite to insult the boss's son but tried staying busy and avoided asking him how his songwriting was progressing. He seemed genuinely oblivious that most people ran away when he tried to corner them. Even his family humored him when he pleaded that they run a radio jingle he had written for the business: in order to stop his pestering, they let him put a one-minute commercial on the air—with Gordy himself singing and playing the piano. He was ecstatic and bragged to friends that listeners confused his voice with that of Nat King Cole. Not many believed him.

The Gordy family assumed that his songwriting mania was just a passing phase. It was easy to get caught up in the music fever that seemed endemic in Berry's neighborhood. "Detroit was a real music town," recalled Otis Williams of the Temptations. "You heard it everywhere, from radios and record players, outside the doors of clubs that kids like us were too young to enter legally, and from guys and girls standing out on the streets singing. It sounds like a scene out of a musical, but that's truly how it was."

"Detroit was jamming," confirmed Marvin Gaye, "Detroit was live."

Impassioned by the atmosphere, Gordy felt he had something to prove. He was soon sending songs to professional singers—Doris Day was the first—clipping magazine ads, and mailing twenty-five dollars to have his tape-recorded songs set as sheet music.

But a letter that arrived in the early spring of 1951 was not from a best-selling artist wanting to sing one of his songs—rather, it was a draft notice.

Army service was one area in which his own industrious father had shown no interest. When he had been drafted for service in World War I, he had faked illiteracy, complained about bad legs and poor eyes, and managed to get discharged after three months. Berry Jr. was not as successful in getting out of his service. Although he did not read or write well, Gordy tried deliberately giving incorrect answers on the induction center's IQ test. However, it turned out to be one of the few tests he ever passed.

Gordy tried to get into special services, the army's entertainment branch, but it turned him down since he did not have enough experience. Shuttling between bases in Michigan and Arkansas, Gordy amused himself by getting involved in almost every game of chance—from cards to dice to numbers. Most of the time, he ran short of money and borrowed from fellow soldiers.

He started boxing again and put together an impressive string of knockouts. And he received the equivalent of a high school diploma. Selected for leadership school, he seemed to be doing fine until, to his dread one night, he discovered that he had wet the bed. "It was a replay of days with Pop when I had to think fast." He quickly disposed of the sheets, and, to ensure the problem did not become a recurring one, he did not drink anything after 4:00 P.M. Only a few months later, when he was on a troopship steaming to Korea, he learned that bedwetting could have gotten him excused from the army. That he had not used it to get discharged was, he recalled, "some of the saddest news of my life."

When he arrived in Korea, Gordy initially was frightened by the strange surroundings. His attitude improved when he was transferred to the Third Artillery Division as a chaplain's assistant. But Gordy was not happy when he learned that his job included driving the chaplain to the front lines. There, Gordy played a portable organ and sang hymns as the chaplain said mass while battles raged nearby. (In an obvious overstatement, a 1965 Motown "fact sheet" boasted that from his tour of duty Gordy "still speaks fluent Korean.")

Gordy's service was completed without any incident or distinction. He was discharged in 1953 and quickly combined his desire to be his own boss with his fondness for music by borrowing seven hundred dollars from his father and brother George to open a record store, the 3D Record Mart—House of Jazz. Gordy's market research came from frequenting Detroit's jazz clubs. Considering himself cooler than he really was, he slicked his hair back with pomade, put on one of his two wildly colored suits, and headed out at night. He managed to see some leading artists who passed through Detroit, including Billie Holiday, Thelonious Monk, and Charlie Parker.

Since he thought jazz was a pure art form, Gordy was convinced that record buyers would flock to his store. And although he was evangelical in trying to persuade his customers that they should listen to only artists such as Miles Davis or Oscar Peterson, his timing was poor. While jazz was popular and had a certain snob appeal, many people—especially Detroit's large working classes—still liked the blues. When customers wanted Muddy Waters, B. B. King, and John Lee Hooker, Gordy didn't have them. It didn't take long for him to realize he was losing both customers and money and that he would not succeed if he ran his business as a school. He could not ignore the popularity of R&B. Even staid *Billboard*, the industry's bible, devoted an entire issue to R&B in 1954.

So Gordy started listening to blues artists—Fats Domino, Louis Jordan, the Midnighters, and Jimmy Reed, among others—and began appreciating the music. The more he listened, the more he liked the blues.

The clamor for records by blues artists meant there were often shortages of popular albums. However, Gordy found an outlet that was seemingly never out of stock, a place run by a Russian Jewish immigrant dubbed the Mad Russian. It was the first time Gordy had met anyone Jewish. He didn't know it was possible to be Russian and a Jew at the same time. (He knew so little about Jews that it wasn't until the 1960s that he learned about the Holocaust.) While he found the Mad Russian odd, Gordy became his friend and soon had a reliable source for the hottest albums.

One quiet day at the store, a childhood friend, Billy Davis, with whom Gordy had also served in the army, arrived with two young ladies. Gordy was attracted to one, Thelma Coleman, a light-skinned woman wearing a white nurse's outfit. Gordy, though nervous, managed some small talk before asking her out. She accepted. The two were quickly inseparable, and

Gordy's family hoped he might settle down. They were pleased when, only a few months after meeting, Berry and Thelma married.

But just as his personal life stabilized, his business sputtered. His emphasis on the blues came too late to make up for his early steep losses. Finally, in 1955, he closed the doors.

Gordy wanted to repay his father and brother their loans but had no desire to work for his family again. So he became a salesman for a local company, Guardian Service Cookware. Gordy's job was to prepare meals free of charge at social gatherings and then sell the company's line of pots and pans at exorbitant prices. Gordy closed deals quickly, fast-talking poor families into long installment-payment contracts for a $272 nine-piece cookware suite. He took his father along on one of his sales pitches, where he successfully sold the pots to a blue-collar worker struggling to keep a large family afloat. When they left, Gordy asked his father what he thought of his sales ability.

"I didn't like it," Berry Sr. told him glumly, shaking his head in disapproval. "I didn't like it at all."

Berry Jr. was stunned. The surprise was evident on his face.

"You sold that man something he couldn't afford," his father continued. "That poor man with all them little babies to feed, and you sold him pots he didn't even need. Same thing he could do with all of them, he could do with one or two."

Berry Jr. became defensive, claiming his customer had had a choice and that he had not forced him to buy the cookware.

"He loves his family, and you took advantage of that," his father said calmly. "You did a good sales job. You reminded me of that white real estate man who sold me my first house. I'm disappointed in you, son. Look into yourself, son. If you feel that was right, then it was. If you don't, then it wasn't."

Gordy later said his father's words that day hurt as much as any beating he had ever received. But it was a lesson about principle that he never forgot. He never sold another pot.

Quitting Guardian Service was easy. Figuring out what to do next was not. Thelma had become pregnant almost immediately after their marriage. Gordy, who desperately wanted a son, was ecstatic about the news. When the first child, a daughter named Hazel Joy, was born in August 1954, he was initially crestfallen. But the following year, in October, Gordy got his wish, a son, and named him Berry, too. Less than a year later, another son, Terry James, arrived.

Gordy was able to provide for his family largely because his father allowed him to move rent-free into an old apartment building he owned near the river. Without any overhead, and helped with food and toys for the children by Thelma's parents, Gordy decided to take another brief shot at songwriting. He was aware that both families denigrated his work as a lark, and they often asked why he did not hold a regular job. And he considered it demeaning that he relied on the generosity of his parents and in-laws to pay bills. "I had been called a bum for so long I thought maybe I was one."

Feeling the dismissive stares of his relatives, Gordy finally accepted a job his mother-in-law arranged for him at Ford. He was not excited about working at one of the big three automakers. Banned from civil-service positions because of discrimination, blacks often filled the lowest-paying jobs. It was difficult work where the on-the-job injury rate, and even the death rate, was remarkably high. Berry started at Ford in April 1955, assigned to the foundry, where he earned $86.40 weekly.

"You should be able to handle that job easily," his mother-in-law assured him. "It used to belong to a woman."

But Gordy immediately loathed the furnaces, noise, dust, smoke, and soot. Within an hour on his first day, he felt faint and had trouble understanding coworkers. He skipped lunch, unable to eat, and when his shift ended he ached so much that he barely was able to drive. "The foundry was hell, a living nightmare," he remembered. When Thelma greeted him at the door, proud of his first day, he immediately announced he wanted to quit.

"Think of all the trouble my mother went through," Thelma implored him. "You can't embarrass me like this."

But the next day, he told his supervisor he couldn't do the work, even if a woman had done it before. When he wasn't offered an easier job, he quit.

The families were furious. Yet Thelma's mother again threw herself into looking for work for him. This time she located an assembly-line job at the Lincoln-Mercury plant. Gordy liked it the moment he saw it—fastening upholstery and chrome strips to car frames that moved slowly along giant conveyor belts.

Gordy used his spare time to work on song melodies. To his family's delight, he also began saving some money. The only problem was that he was unable to shake his gambling interest and had joined a poker club. More often than not, he lost some of his weekly salary. One night, at his own house, he dropped three thousand dollars—all his savings—to two card sharks. When he discovered that he had been swindled he went to his brother George demanding a gun and wanting to track down the two con men. But his brother convinced him that if he was patient the men would likely return, since they probably considered him an easy mark. Sure enough, they did. This time, Gordy covered the tops of the marked cards and won back his own money plus another three thousand, nearly a year's salary on the assembly line. His family knew he was gambling regularly but had no idea that he was risking so much.

But there were more problems. Berry was an uninvolved husband, doing little at home with the children and Thelma. Nothing about family life seemed to energize him. His frustration over his stagnant songwriting career sometimes resulted in explosive temper tantrums that caused the children to cry and Thelma to cower in a corner. Late in 1956, Thelma had had enough and filed for divorce. In her papers, she charged that Gordy stayed out all night, often with other women, and that he was physically abusive to her. But shortly after filing her papers, she had to drop her lawyer and the proceedings when she ran out of money.

Berry and Thelma lived together in escalating tension. The number of his all-night forays increased. She was increasingly alone with the children. After two years at the factory and a year of heavy gambling on which he ran a streak of good luck, he had enough money for a deposit on a two-story house in a middle-class black neighborhood. But despite that, Gordy, now twenty-seven, was anything but settled. He was bored with his job and saw nothing but years of hard work that would end only in a mediocre pension. He was thirty-three years away from retirement.

Gordy's decision to quit his stable Lincoln-Mercury job for the uncertainties of freelance songwriting was again not well received by his wife or in-laws. He ignored the criticism and set about making sure no one would mistake him for an assembly-line laborer—he used some of his rainy-day savings to buy a silk suit and have his hair processed a slick, straight black. When Thelma and her parents called him a bum this time, he laughed and said that at least he was a happy one.

Gordy became a regular at local nightclubs, where he was again impressed with the flashy clothes, furs, and gaudy jewelry. His favorite spot was the Flame Show Bar, where his sister Gwen owned the photo concession and another sister, Anna, worked. Gordy's sisters were glamorous and popular. Anna was considered one of Detroit's most eligible women, and visiting musicians went out of their way to meet her. Both sisters took souvenir pictures at the club, while Gordy's brothers Robert and George worked in the darkroom. Gordy himself did not help out with the business but instead hung out near the bar, where singers performed on a small stage. There he saw leading blues vocalists such as Sarah Vaughan, Dinah Washington, and his favorite, Billie Holiday.

His sisters were only too happy to introduce Gordy to anyone who might help his career—they both hoped he would either quickly get lucky or disabuse himself of making a living as a songwriter. It was there that Gordy met local musicians Thomas "Beans" Bowles and showbiz veteran Maurice King, whose house band had worked with virtually every major black artist. Both Bowles and King would eventually be key elements of Motown's studio band.

Gordy's patience paid off. Anna introduced him to the club's owner, Al Green, who also managed several up-and-coming singers. One of those was Jackie Wilson, a flashy, athletic artist whose gyrating stage performances, coupled with his almost operatic delivery and unique combination of styles from both black blues singers and white crooners, had made him a star. Gordy had boxed with Wilson a decade earlier, but now Wilson had adopted a far more dramatic persona. He never went anywhere without makeup, and when he met Gordy he wore a thick pancake foundation, eyeliner, rouge, and, Gordy thought, possibly lipstick.

"I'm a songwriter," Gordy told Green enthusiastically.

"Well, that's great," said Green. "I have a music-publishing company and I'm always looking for new material. Stop by my office with some of your songs."

It was probably the best way to get rid of Berry, because he had developed an annoying reputation for carrying around sample tapes.

The next day, Gordy rushed over to Green's four-room Pearl Music Company. The first person he met, Roquel Billy Davis, liked his songs. (Davis was no relation to Berry's childhood pal Billy Davis.) Then Gordy was initially disappointed when he learned that Davis was only another songwriter. But since no one else was there, the two men sat in the front office and talked for hours. Although Davis had no hits, he had been in the business for several years, had songs recorded by decent artists, and had connections with Chicago's black-dominated Chess Records. When Davis suggested the two men write together, Gordy jumped at the chance. Gordy was soon writing songs that were recorded by many of Green's singers, though there still wasn't much money coming in.

At home, things were deteriorating. Thelma and Berry argued frequently in front of their children. With little income to show from his songwriting, Thelma ridiculed his efforts. One rainy spring day, the tension boiled over in what started as a trivial argument over whether Hazel Joy, who had a cold, should be allowed to go outside. Berry said no. Thelma wanted to take her out, and, after Thelma's mother arrived, the three adults got into a literal tug-of-war over Hazel. Moments later, Hazel was screaming and trying her hardest to pull away from her father. He could not help but see her reaction and was devastated that even his infant daughter rejected him. He let go, slouched down the hallway, walked into a tiny broom closest, and closed the door behind him. He stayed in the dark, brooding, for nearly an hour. He felt lost.

For a few days, both Berry and Thelma walked on eggshells, saying little to each other, trying to be nicer than they had in months. Then, less than a week later, the doorbell rang. When Gordy answered, he was served with divorce papers. Gordy withdrew into himself, not talking to Thelma for the rest of the day. But privately, he was relieved. He soon packed his bags and headed for Gwen's apartment, across the hall from where they had grown up. (It took another two years, until 1959, for the couple to divorce officially.)

When he arrived at Gwen's, Berry looked devastated. He was worried about losing his children and felt as though he had failed. Gwen tolerated none of his self-pity.

"So what?" she asked him when told of the divorce proceedings. "That's not the worst thing in the world."

He mentioned his children.

"What about them?" Gwen shot back. "You will always be the only father they will ever have. And they will always love you the same as we do."

Berry fell into his sister's arms, hugging her and sobbing at the same time. After he calmed, he sat in front of the piano. Instead of struggling with lyrics as he often did, on this night the words just flowed. Gwen looked over his shoulder. He was writing furiously about his children.

"My Cycle of Success"

THE MUSIC BUSINESS THAT GORDY HAD WANTED TO BREAK INTO in 1957 was racially segregated and dominated by a few large recording labels. The major ones—such as RCA and Decca—had so-called race records, on which they released songs by black singers, including almost all the early R&B greats, including Ruth Brown, Lloyd Price, the Orioles, Clyde McPhatter, the El Dorados, the Spaniels, and Little Willie John. Those records were usually played only on black radio stations, small operations whose signals were so weak that they often were not easy to find on the dial.

In the late 1940s, however, independent labels had started carving out niches with both black and white acts that the majors thought were not commercial enough. Shortly after Gordy left Thelma, Billy Davis introduced him to George Goldner, the somewhat eccentric owner of a New York independent label. Gordy watched Goldner direct a studio band during a recording and was impressed that a white man had so much rhythm. After that session, the fast-talking Gordy bragged to Goldner that he was great at writing tunes with catchy hooks and repetitive phrases. Gordy had barely finished his pitch when Goldner pulled out a crisp one-hundred-dollar bill and gave it to the startled Gordy.

"It's like a down payment in case we ever do business together," Goldner told him. Then he left. Gordy was elated. It was the first time someone had liked what he said about music enough to pay him.

Soon, he was pocketing up to fifty dollars daily to work on lyrics with singers including Erma Franklin, whose younger sister, Aretha, was a gospel singer, and Freda Payne, a teenager with a strong, moving voice. Record labels noticed Gordy and Davis—they sold their first song, "Jim Dandy Got Married," to Atlantic Records and LaVern Baker. For Chess Records, the pair, with Gordy's sister Gwen, wrote "All I Could Do Was Cry" (Etta James's version reached number two in 1960 on the R&B charts).

Gordy moved into a small apartment with his sister Loucye and a cousin, Evelyn Turk. Because the two women worked during the day, Gordy had the place to himself. There he furiously wrote lyrics that he belted out loudly, often with the television blaring in the background. It was just after this that Gordy and Davis placed a song—"Reet Petite"—with Al Green's star client, Jackie Wilson. Although Gordy was pleased to have someone of Wilson's stature record one of his songs, he held out little hope it would be a hit. Even the normally cocky Gordy considered "Reet Petite" "a so-so song."

But his intuition was wrong. Jackie Wilson's recording was terrific. It was released in October 1957 and reached number eleven on the R&B charts just two months later. One day, while working on lyrics, Gordy heard it on the radio. And a few minutes later when he turned on the television, Wilson was singing to millions of viewers on *American Bandstand.*

This kicked off what Gordy dubbed "my cycle of success." Suddenly he had an entourage of newfound "friends." Wilson was Detroit's most successful black entertainer, and Gordy was the most flamboyant member of his team. Although Gordy had no clue how much money he would make, he acted as though he was rich. He bought an elaborate wardrobe and picked up large tabs at bars and clubs. Unfortunately, his largesse was bigger than his income, and soon he was broke, playing in all-night card games to raise quick cash.

He kept pushing Wilson to record "To Be Loved," the song he had written the day Thelma had served him with divorce papers. When Wilson finally listened to it, he liked it and released it as a ballad. Other significant Gordy songs that Wilson recorded are "That Is Why (I Love You So)," "I'll Be Satisfied," and "Lonely Teardrops," which became Gordy's first R&B number one and his first tune to break into the top ten of the pop charts. Gordy retained some of their distinct elements—lyrics about relationships, the use of tambourines to boost the drumbeat, and a strong baritone sax—and later made them standard parts of Motown productions.

When Gordy went to one of Wilson's concerts in Flint, Michigan, the singer with the pretty-boy face and the upswept pompadour showed why he was nicknamed "Mr. Excitement." Swinging the jacket of his tightly fitted suit, he spun and jumped around the stage. When the show finished, Gordy watched jealously as women tried to jump Wilson as he fought to get to his dressing room.

Gordy dreamed of having Wilson's ability to attract women. He became a regular in the postshow dressing room crowd, telling the girls rejected by Jackie that he was a top songwriter. But women were still not impressed with the overly eager Gordy. At one show, Gordy sat next to a striking young woman and kept trying to get a date or at least her telephone number. When the show finished, she refused to allow Gordy to give her even a small kiss on the cheek. He was actually impressed that she was such a proper girl—until he arrived at the dressing room and saw her holding tightly on to Wilson, French-kissing him, her skirt pushed up around her waist. Gordy simply left.

When Al Green died unexpectedly, Nat Tarnopol, his junior partner, took over the business. Gordy and Tarnopol had become friends. Gordy hung out at his office and often borrowed his gold Cadillac to impress aspiring artists and girls. One day, he was working on lyrics in Tarnopol's office when the Matadors, a group of high school teenagers, arrived for an audition. There were four young men and one girl. Gordy sat quietly in the corner as they auditioned, and he thought they had some talent. But Tarnopol was unimpressed. They needed to sound more like the Platters, he told them, if they had any chance of making it.

"Come back after you've had some more practice," Tarnopol said, dismissing them.

The group seemed crushed, not even looking up as they left the office. Gordy followed them. He stopped the lead singer, a light-skinned black teenager (his grandmother had been white) with striking green eyes and reddish processed hair.

"Hey, I liked you guys a lot," Gordy said as nonchalantly as he could.

"You did?" asked the lead singer, somewhat incredulous.

They were from Detroit's blue-collar north end, a neighborhood the lead singer described as "the suave part of the slums": Ronnie White, small and wiry with thick glasses; Pete Moore, slightly nerdy and shy; Bobby Rogers, squat and acne-covered; and Claudette, a petite, shapely girl to whom Gordy was immediately attracted.

"And I'm William Robinson," said the thin seventeen-year-old lead singer, "but they call me Smokey. Who are you?"

When Gordy introduced himself, the group instantly recognized him as one of Jackie Wilson's songwriters. Gordy liked that.

"Who writes your songs?" Gordy asked.

"I do," said Smokey.

"Got any more?"

Smokey took out one of dozens of notebooks he usually carried with him. He was a bookworm who loved school, reading, and poetry. And he came from a home where the Victrola was never quiet, playing a steady stream of jazz, gospel, and dance music. It was there that he learned to adore Sarah Vaughan, whose music he found inspirational.

Smokey and the others followed Gordy back inside Tarnopol's offices.

"Sing your favorite song," Gordy told Smokey, who began softly singing the first song in his notebook. Gordy stopped him after a few lines and asked what the lyrics meant.

"They are about a boy and girl in love," Smokey said, surprised that it was not clear.

"Yes, but so what," continued Gordy, not giving the group any chance to say anything else. "Everybody's in love. What's different about your song? And you're rambling all over the place. Go ahead, do your next favorite song."

Smokey turned the page and started singing. That made Gordy a little nervous, since the notebook looked as though it contained more than a hundred songs. But he liked Smokey's passion, and he listened.

Gordy found problems with each of Smokey's songs, but instead of getting defensive Smokey seemed excited, asking Gordy repeatedly if he had time "for just one more."

After they made it through the entire notebook and Gordy had rejected all of them, he still told Smokey that he a talent for poetic, catchy lyrics. The problem was, said Gordy, that some songs had clever concepts that missed the point, others had good hooks but no story, and even the good stories weren't different enough to break out in a competitive field.

"Other than that, I liked 'em," said Gordy, chuckling. Smokey laughed even louder.

That was the beginning of their special relationship.

"When I met him," recalled Smokey, "he didn't have money, but he had direction. . . . And he had the balls to go after what he wanted. . . . Berry Gordy was street."

Their different talents served each other well. Gordy had a good ear for commercial songs, and Smokey needed his rough but enormous talent nurtured. "I had songs that went all over the place," Smokey later said. He began bringing new songs to Gordy, who kept rejecting them. But Gordy expected it was only a matter of time until the youngster wrote something that was good.

But there was another benefit in this new friendship for Smokey. He wanted a sense of family. His father, a truck driver, was a heavy drinker who had left when Smokey was three. And Smokey had been ten when his mother died at the age of forty-three from a cerebral hemorrhage. His aunt and uncle, already burdened with ten of their own children, helped raise Smokey, but his older sister, Gerry, was his legal guardian. Smokey admired the Gordy family closeness.

When Gordy offered to manage the Matadors, Smokey accepted immediately.

Smokey's breakthrough came in January 1958. Out of breath, he ran into an office where Gordy was working on lyrics with Billy Davis. Gordy had never seen him so excited. After Gordy led him into an empty room, Smokey looked around furtively to make sure no one else was there—it was as though he was about to impart a great secret.

"I got it, man," he whispered. "I really got it this time!"

Without waiting for Gordy, Smokey closed his eyes and softly started singing in his unmistakable falsetto. In the quiet room, Gordy thought his voice sounded its purest, "almost like a prayer." It took Smokey only a few lines of his song "Got a Job" before Gordy yelled for him to stop. He loved it. It was the natural followup, thought Gordy, to the current hit by the Silhouettes, "Get a Job" (so-called "answer records," trying to capitalize on another hit song's success, were common in the industry).

Smokey's song was almost ten minutes long. Over two weeks, they cut it to under three minutes. Gordy approached George Goldner, who agreed to release it on his small label, End Records. In Loucye's basement, accompanied by a local band, the Matadors practiced under Gordy's guidance. After a week, Gordy took them to the United Sound Studios in New York, where they laid down two songs, "Got a Job" and "My Mama Done Told Me," one of the songs Gordy had liked when he had first heard it in Tarnopol's office.

When they finished, Gordy had a final suggestion. He thought that since they had a girl in the group, they should change their name.

" 'The Matadors' sounds a little jive," he told them.

All of them wrote new names on small slips of paper and dropped them into a hat. The one that was drawn was Smokey's choice, the Miracles. And on Smokey Robinson's eighteenth birthday, February 19, 1958, the Miracles' first single was officially released. Gordy was listed as the producer and somehow had managed to get solo songwriting credit.

CHAPTER 4

Going Solo

GORDY AND DAVIS PUT TOGETHER A SMALL STABLE OF LOCAL singers to make demo tapes to show Jackie Wilson what their songs might sound like off the page. At United Sound Studios, they worked with singers who would later become key to Motown's growth, including the lanky six-foot-two David Ruffin (né Davis Ruffin) and the deep-voiced Melvin Franklin, both of whom would join the Temptations. Another of Gordy's singers was Eddie Holland, a good-looking teenager with a mellow tenor. Holland introduced Gordy to his look-alike brother, Brian, also a singer. The Hollands impressed Gordy because they wrote their own music and produced rough tapes in a makeshift basement studio. Gordy zeroed in on Brian, deciding that he had the same instincts and potential as Smokey Robinson.

One day at United Sound, Gordy was pestered by his brother Robert to record a song he had written, "Everyone Was There." Gordy liked the song, but the musicians thought it was too white-sounding. Furthermore, they were running out of studio time. Gordy relented but told his brother he had only twenty minutes. Robert cajoled the musicians into playing, and he sang the song himself. Gordy and the others were surprised. Robert's voice was remarkably good. Gordy gave Robert the stage name Bob Kayli and convinced the New York independent Carlton Records, a small but decent label, to release the single. It got some radio play and generated fair sales. In preparation for a promotion tour, Gordy helped Robert polish his stage act.

But Carlton canceled the tour after only three cities. Gordy went to see his brother to find out what went wrong. Robert had no idea and claimed his act was great.

A week later, Gordy got a chance to judge for himself when Robert was booked on Dick Clark's popular Saturday-night television program. Gordy remembered it well: "Bobby was right. He was great. But after the broadcast the record died altogether. The problem then became clear: people were shocked. This white-sounding record did not go with his black face. Bob Kayli was history."

It was a valuable lesson. Gordy knew that historically pop sold to whites and R&B mostly to blacks. But he also knew that the differences were diminishing, especially with the success of Elvis Presley. While critics debated whether Presley's music was really R&B or rock and roll, Gordy decided it was merely pop. Presley's first album sold more than one million copies. "Pop means popular," Gordy concluded, "and if that ain't, I don't know what is. I never gave a damn what else it was called." Despite his brother's failure, Gordy was determined to discover whether a black artist, singing a white-sounding pop song, could cross over.

But for the time being, Gordy and Davis had to be content with turning out R&B tunes. Although "Lonely Teardrops" was number one on the R&B charts for seven weeks, its sales were disappointing. A low royalty rate meant that the songwriting duo had little money for their efforts.

A financial statement Berry filed in 1959 in response to Thelma's request for additional alimony and child support buttressed his complaints about how little he earned. Despite hits with Jackie Wilson and Marv Johnson, who had a medium success with "My Baby-O," Gordy averaged fewer than thirty dollars weekly and, after expenses, netted under five dollars a week. His biggest royalty check was one thousand dollars for "Lonely Teardrops."

And this wasn't Gordy's only frustration. The songs he and Davis wrote were usually recorded on the A side of the single. That was the side people heard on the radio, asked for in stores, and flocked to buy. But Gordy noticed that the B sides of each hit record never carried their tunes. Instead, the singer's producer usually used one of his own songs or one written by a relative or close friend. Whatever was on the B side essentially got a free ride from the success of the A tune. Gordy was irritated that the B songwriters earned the same money he did but without making any contribution to the record's success.

He asked Nat Tarnopol why he couldn't also write the songs for the B side. Tarnopol dismissed the idea. Gordy wouldn't back down and gambled by saying that if he couldn't get the B sides he wouldn't write any longer for Jackie Wilson.

Tarnopol had a reputation as a penny-pincher. "Jackie is a star," he told Gordy. "You need him. He doesn't need you." Gordy knew it was true, but his pride was hurt by Tarnopol's flippant manner. Gordy walked out and went straight to Wilson, imploring him to change Tarnopol's mind. But Wilson wouldn't intervene. So after five straight hits, Gordy and Billy Davis parted ways with Jackie Wilson.

Davis and Gordy's sister Gwen, who often helped on the lyrics, were disturbed that Gordy had severed their highest-profile gig without consulting them. But it presented Gwen an opportunity for which she had been longing: to start her own record company, named after another Gordy sister, Anna. She worked feverishly on the new project, assuming Gordy would be part of it. Although Gordy worried that family partnerships were not easy, he couldn't initially bring himself to say no to Gwen. She made a deal with Chicago-based Chess Records for national distribution. Then, at a meeting with Gordy and Billy Davis, Gwen asked her brother to be the president of the new company. Davis, who by then was romantically involved with Gwen, had already agreed to be a partner. Gordy, however, surprised everyone by announcing that he did not want any partners.

After a few moments of strained silence, Davis started pleading with him, urging him to reconsider since it was "a chance of a lifetime." But Gordy was adamant.

"I really would be happier just being by myself," he said bluntly. To soften his no, he promised to write and produce for the new company. There was an uncomfortable silence for a few moments.

"Baby, we understand," Gwen finally said. "You've got to do what makes you happy."

CHAPTER 5

Smokey Dreams

ALTHOUGH GORDY WANTED TO BE INDEPENDENT, HE STILL MOVED his operations to Gwen's large multifloor apartment. It became a headquarters for Gordy family ventures. Gwen and Billy Davis ran Anna Records on the street level, next door to the print shop and cleaners run by her brothers Fuller and George. Pops and Mother Gordy lived on the top floor, next to Gwen.

From that building, in addition to writing and producing songs, Gordy also managed singers. The Miracles had a local hit with "Got a Job" and were popular in Detroit. Soon after its release, they were inundated with requests for live appearances. But their first date, at the Gold Coast Theatre in Pontiac, where many promising young acts played, was disastrous. The group's timing was off, they stumbled into one another onstage, and their banter with the audience was stiff. That bomb sent Gordy and the Miracles into a short but acute depression.

But he was determined to keep them doing live shows until they perfected it. One night in another dingy Pontiac, Michigan, club, a brawl broke out as the Miracles were lip-synching on top of the bar. As bottles and chairs flew and the Miracles cowered, Gordy ran to the end of the bar and frantically waved at them to follow him. They all dashed to Smokey's car. "We got out by the skin of our teeth," recalled Smokey. Inside the car, the band members complained bitterly about what had happened. They demanded to know why they had even been booked into such a place.

"A real manager wouldn't book us into no jive-ass joint like that," one groused. That started a laundry list of gripes. They had no costumes to wear and had no say in how their careers were developing. Usually, whenever there was a contentious issue between the band and Gordy, Smokey arbitrated. But he only sat silently on the front seat. Finally, in his soft voice, he spoke up.

"Yeah, man, you guys are right. It's not worth it."

Gordy's heart sank. "That hurt," he later remembered, "[and] probably more because Smokey said it." Gordy was quiet the rest of the trip back to Detroit and mumbled a quick good-bye when he was dropped off at his house. He wondered if the group was right. Maybe he wasn't cut out to be a manager.

He was moping, alone in his room, about the sudden turn of events, when Gwen knocked softly on his door. Smokey was downstairs, she announced, and wanted to talk. Gordy was apprehensive, but once he saw Smokey and heard what he had to say, any lingering doubts evaporated.

"We all know what you're trying to do for us," Smokey assured Gordy. "I'm sorry, man. We all are."

The two men sat on the floor and talked for hours, baring their souls. Gordy told Smokey about his ruined marriage, his fear of failure, and his fascination with gambling. Smokey talked about his difficulties with his family when he wanted to drop out of college to become a singer. Finally, Gordy admitted he had initially been attracted to the group because of Claudette, the Miracles' only woman member. Gordy had tried to date her, but she refused, telling him that she was dating Smokey.

Smokey grinned. "Yeah, I know. She told me all about it."

"In those early morning hours," Gordy later wrote in his autobiography, "Smokey and I made a little pact to never let anything come between us. But what was really developed that night was something more, much more—the beginning of a lifelong friendship."

Their bond meant that Gordy automatically considered Smokey for a role in each of his new musical ventures. So when he started his own music-publishing company—after a New York company that owed him royalties went bankrupt—Smokey became his first writer. Gordy called the company Jobete, a contraction of the names of his three children, Joy, Berry, and Terry. Shortly after that launch, Gordy and Smokey were together when the envelope arrived containing Gordy's producer's royalties for the hit "Got a Job." He eagerly tore it open and was startled to find a check for $3.19. They were speechless. Smokey broke the silence.

"You might as well start your own record label. I don't think you could do any worse than this."

Gordy agreed. He took the check and framed it. "We're going to re-member this motherfucker," Gordy said, " 'cause I don't intend to let it happen again."

Gordy figured he needed about a thousand dollars to pay for a record-ing, press an album, and package it with labels and sleeves. A local lawyer warned him that even so, his new business would be undercapitalized and doomed to failure. Berry was determined to prove him wrong. He vainly tried raising the seed money among acquaintances. Finally, he turned to his most reliable support system: his family. The Gordys had a fund, nick-named Ber-Berry after their mother (Bertha) and father (Berry), that oper-ated like a credit union. The fund required each family member to deposit ten dollars weekly and was established primarily to buy real estate. Gordy had been reluctant to approach the family, especially since getting a loan meant that everyone had to vote yes, something he thought impossible. But with no other options, he asked for a meeting.

As the Gordy clan sat around the dining table, they grilled Berry about his venture. His sister Esther asked the most difficult questions. It had been her idea to first organize the Ber-Berry fund for emergencies, and other sib-lings depended on her, a practical businesswoman, to be prudent with the money. Gordy made a heartfelt pitch, and he promised to repay the money with interest. When he finished, Gwen and Anna got up from their chairs and walked around the table in order to stretch their legs.

"Give him the money," Gwen said.

Anna agreed. "Give him a chance." Loucye, another sister, seemed in-clined to go along, but Esther sat, stern-faced. She seemed unmoved.

"Well, if you're so smart," she suddenly said, "why ain't you rich? You're twenty-nine years old, and what have you done so far with your life?"

Gordy, who had heard her ask him a similar question when he was younger, was surprised by her sharp tone.

"So what if I'm twenty-nine? I could be thirty-nine, forty-nine, or fifty-nine. So what? What's age got to do with it? So I haven't been a real success in my life. Big deal. Tomorrow could be a total turnaround. That's what's wrong with people; they give up their dreams too soon. I'm never going to give up mine."

"That's very nice," replied Esther, nonplussed. "But how are you going to pay it back?"

Gordy didn't answer. Instead, he looked at his mother and father, who had been sitting silently and observing their children during the meeting. His mother nodded to Gwen and Anna, letting them know she agreed that Berry should get the loan. Then his father, brothers, and Loucye said yes. With the family arrayed against her, Esther reluctantly said yes. Gordy got an eight-hundred-dollar loan. Esther wanted him to guarantee repayment. At her insistence, he had to go beyond the family's standard repayment form and agree that any of his future earnings would go first to pay off the loan.

"Esther had been tougher than I'd anticipated," Gordy later recalled. "But I knew right then, if I ever made money, she would be the one I'd get to watch it for me."

CHAPTER 6

"The Impostor of Success"

GORDY FLIPPED THROUGH OLD COPIES OF *CASH BOX* MAGAZINE looking for a catchy name for his label. He noticed that Debbie Reynolds's song "Tammy" had been a long-running number-one hit. Gordy figured that at least one million people were familiar with that name and decided he'd use it, even though that song was about as far away from Motown's eventual sound as one could possibly get. But he discovered the name was already trademarked. So he settled on Tamla.

Then he booked recording time at his favorite haunt, United Sound Studios, and set about producing his first release. Gordy chose "Come to Me," a song he had cowritten with Marv Johnson that sounded like it was straight out of the Jackie Wilson songbook. Thomas "Beans" Bowles, so nicknamed because he was six foot four and lanky like a string bean, was one of Detroit's best jazz musicians and was in the studio band. The backup singers were a group Gordy had met during the past year when he was wearing his producer hat. They were led by twenty-one-year-old Raynoma Liles, a striking, light-skinned woman who sported a popular blond, bobbed hairstyle. She was just over five feet tall and rail thin at ninety-five pounds, and she had a bubbly personality. Gordy helped the group choose the name Rayber Voices (a contraction of her first name and his own). The singers were Raynoma—who was a trained musician with perfect pitch—and Brian Holland, Robert Bateman, Sonny Sanders, and later Gwendolyn Murray. Raynoma, recently divorced and with a young child, hung around Gordy's apartment, helping him on everything from chord arrangements to writing lead sheets. Although she at first thought he looked like "a raggedy bum with a bad hairdo," she found something appealing about him, and it wasn't long before she had convinced herself that "Berry Gordy was going to be the great love of my life."

"Look," she told Gordy, "this working at Loucye's or Gwen's is ridiculous. Your sisters can't get a moment of privacy. And we shouldn't have to call a rehearsal quits if they're starting to cook, or always walk around on eggshells."

"You got a better plan, Ray?"

"Yeah, my place."

Ray lived with her three-year-old son in a tiny apartment in a quiet neighborhood. She had a piano and a Webcor tape recorder they could use to make demos.

"Oh," Ray cautioned, "no strings attached. It's purely a business proposition. You need a place to live, we need a place to work. Why not?"

Gordy liked the idea. The only drawback was that there was only one bed. They shared it by sleeping clothed and on opposite sides. Ray turned out to be a solid and nurturing partner. She had been a musical prodigy, played eleven instruments, and had studied musical harmony, composition, and theory. She encouraged Gordy's creativity while she handled the business's details. He was good to her son and soon had saved enough money so they could move to a larger and less cramped apartment.

Only two months into their relationship, Ray learned something that shocked her. Gordy had been mumbling one day, more to himself than to her. She asked him what he was saying.

"I've got to get out of this business," Gordy muttered.

"What business?"

His answer almost sounded like a groan: "I have a few girls."

Ray's eyes widened. "What do you mean 'a few girls'?"

"Down on John R," he said, "but I've got to get out. I can't do this."

Ray knew that one strip of John R Street was the red-light district, near Gordy's regular hangout, the Flame Show Bar. But she refused to believe that the man she had come to know fairly well could be a part-time pimp. She forced herself to appear nonchalant and just said casually, "Oh, yeah, well . . . ," hoping he might give her more information. And he did.

"I can't do what the motherfuckers down there do. They beat the women up, forcing them out on the street if they're sick or tired or pregnant. Heartless sons of bitches. They don't want to hear no sob stories. It's just 'Give me the money,' and if a girl gets uppity he kicks her ass. I can't do that shit. . . . But then on the other hand I've got so much riding on these acts, no money coming in, a ton of expenses—"

Without warning, Gordy kicked viciously at a chair, sending it flying across the small room. Then he looked at Ray, and for the first time smiled and said, "I'm just not cut out for it."

Ray felt numb, not sure what to do. Later that day, she went to John R Street and got a firsthand look at the streetwalkers. As she stared at the flashy cars driven by the pimps, she convinced herself that Gordy couldn't really be trading in girls since no self-respecting pimp would use a bus, as Gordy had to, for transportation.

The two never again spoke about the subject. Nor did Ray ever mention to Gordy what she did a week after that talk. The couple was virtually broke. There wasn't enough food for her baby, and the utility and telephone companies were threatening to cut off service. Roberta, a neighbor, traded sex for money, at nearly five times the rate of the John R streetwalkers. One day, she knocked on Ray's door and told her that a white man was coming by that evening. "Sugar, it's survival," Roberta told her. "There's no right or wrong about it. Ask Berry if that's not so—he should know. . . . Just once won't kill you."

In a book she wrote nearly thirty years later, *Me, Berry, and Motown* (a book that Gordy hated), Ray said she thought the suggestion was "insane." But still, that night she met the john, performed fellatio, and was paid seventeen dollars. When Gordy returned home, he saw the cash on the table but never asked where she got it. Ray says it was the only time she ever sold sex.

Not long after that, the couple launched their own music-publishing venture, the Ray-Ber Music Writing Company. And during the next month, while trying to sign singers and complete a demo, they also finally became lovers.

• • •

Meanwhile, Berry had decided to use twenty-year-old Marv Johnson to sing the lead track on his own song, "Come to Me." Gordy planted himself in the control room and overrode the engineer by emphasizing the bass and drums and lowering the instruments' level so that Johnson's voice stood out. It was Gordy's idea to move the smooth backup bass singer, Robert Bateman, to his own microphone. There were ten takes before Gordy had the sound he wanted. The song had simple lyrics set to a stock rock-chord progression. Gordy experimented with a snappy female chorus and instrumental anchors like a baritone sax and a tambourine. The result was, as one reviewer noted, a "clean R&B record that sounded as white as it did black."

Two days later, in the middle of a winter blizzard, Gordy and Smokey drove in a 1957 Pontiac convertible to Owosso, ninety miles outside Detroit. They were to pick up the first pressed Tamla singles. Twice along the nearly deserted but icy roadways the car slid onto the shoulder. Once they just missed an oncoming truck. A bulldozer had to pull them out of a ditch. "The road was a sheet of glass," Smokey later recalled. But the two were too excited to turn around. At the plant, and then in the car back to Detroit, they did not open the boxes of records. Once they were safely back home, they ripped open the first container. Gordy was beaming. "This was *my* box of twenty-five," he thought.

He then rushed from his apartment to drive to two local radio stations. Both broadcast "Come to Me" the day Gordy dropped it off. WLJB was white-owned, but its two black DJs, Bristol Bryant and "Frantic" Ernie Durham, had known Gordy from his record store. The station had a signal that reached as far as Cleveland, and, while its audience was primarily black, Durham promoted some records that got crossover play on white stations. The second station, WCHB, was black-owned and was new. Although its signal was weak, it had a large and faithful following.

Gordy had cut a record, pressed it, and got it local radio play but had little time to enjoy his progress. He was almost out of money. Since he paid only ten cents each to press a record, and it sold at retail stores for ninety cents, he thought there would be a large profit. But he quickly discovered that the distributor paid only thirty cents for each record and then sold it at a markup to retail stores—the stores kept any profits over that.

He was stumped until he received a call from Ernie Durham, telling him that United Artists wanted to buy his master recording and distribute it nationally. The next day, Gordy was on a plane to New York. There he signed a deal that let United Artists exclusively distribute and promote Marv Johnson, with the condition that he was the sole producer.

United Artists had the muscle to get "Come to Me" played everywhere. It reached number six on the R&B chart, and Gordy's star was again rising.

Coupled with his newfound success was the great personal news that Raynoma was several months pregnant. And while he did not want to upset her, according to her, Berry did wish to settle one piece of business between them. They had cosigned to form Tamla and Jobete. With Marv Johnson's success, Gordy was troubled that Ray's name was on the businesses—after all, it had been Ber-Berry money behind the recording. Shortly after the single became a hit, Gordy told Ray, "I've been thinking about how it looks, and, you said yourself, we're not some mom-and-pop operation. Well, that's how it looks now. And it would be just simpler to have it in one name. For tax reasons and all that. You know."

Ray recalled that she was "stunned. . . . My veins went icy and I felt as if the wind had been knocked out of me." But she only managed a weak "OK."

The next day at the City-County Building, she watched as Gordy signed new papers that put the business in his own name. Ray trusted him when he assured her, "It's just a formality. Nothing's going to change. You know that, whatever happens, I'm always going to take care of you." (Although Ray's parents, who referred to Gordy as "Little Napoleon," urged her to get the promised fifty-fifty split in writing, Ray bristled at the suggestion that Gordy might be anything but fair.)

•　　　•　　　•

At visits to United Artists' New York headquarters, Gordy was suddenly treated as a star producer. Marv Johnson did shows at the Apollo Theatre and Carnegie Hall, and Gordy bragged to everyone that he was Johnson's "manager." Soon, he signed a second artist, Rayber Voices singer Eddie Holland, to a long-term contract. Gordy thought the handsome Holland might follow in the Jackie Wilson groove. And Gordy also oversaw a group of budding songwriters, including youngsters like the streetwise William "Mickey" Stevenson (later nicknamed "Il Duce" inside Motown for controlling the rowdiest musicians) and Lamont Dozier, who had a short-lived performing career as "Lamont Anthony."

Gordy was so focused on his acquisitions that he was not fazed when Marv Johnson's second record, "I'm Coming Home," sold poorly. Holland's first Tamla release, "Merry-Go-Round," was also sold to United Artists for distribution, but it also bombed. However, Gordy was confident that future hits would make up for any flat period.

One of the people Gordy counted on was Smokey, who burst in one day with a song he desperately wanted Gordy to hear. Before Gordy could say hello, Smokey was singing the words to his tune "Bad Girl." The minute Gordy heard it, he thought it was in a class by itself and that Smokey had come into his own as a lyricist.

Gordy did not want to let Smokey get too big a head, so he told him the song was "a little crude." Smokey, who had been up all night working on it, visibly sagged. He was having problems with the song's bridge and asked Gordy to help smooth it out. Settling at the piano, in a couple of hours they had polished the song. Smokey said that Gordy should get credit for having cowritten it. Gordy weakly protested, but Smokey insisted.

Gordy turned his full attention to "Bad Girl." He thought it was so good that he wanted not only to produce it but to distribute it nationally. Less than a week after he first heard it, Gordy had worked out a deal to record at United Sound. He got a substantial discount for using the studio overnight, when it was otherwise closed. Gordy was so enthusiastic about the recording's beautiful melody and clever lyrics that he launched a new label for its release.

Multiple labels were something that became a Gordy trademark, as he eventually had thirty-nine, including Rayber, Melody, Rare Earth, and the short-lived Miracle label, with the catchy slogan, "If it's a hit, it's a Miracle." Some, like Gaiee, released only one single. Others—such as Soul and Gordy—survived decades. (Gordy was started hurriedly when he learned in 1962 that his first wife, Thelma, was about to launch her own record label. She settled on the mundane Thelma Records.)

But in searching for something catchy through which to release "Bad Girl," Gordy returned to his favorite method of combining a couple of names. Detroit had long been known as the Motor City because of the car industry. In place of *city*, Gordy substituted *town*, and a contraction of the two gave him Motown.

But his interest in label names faded fast when he realized that once again he had put too much money in cutting the song and not enough was left for national distribution. He took what little cash he had left and grabbed the next flight to United Artists in New York.

When he arrived at their Seventh Avenue headquarters, he was upset when he wasn't immediately buzzed through the outer office. No one greeted him with the "Good morning, Mr. Gordy" that he expected. "Probably a new receptionist," Gordy thought. When he announced himself to her and added that he was Marv Johnson's producer, she did not react. When she asked him to spell his name, he sensed he might be in trouble.

On the way to UA, Gordy had run into a couple of music-industry friends from Detroit. He wanted to impress them and invited them to join him. Now he kept nervously glancing at them. He leaned over the receptionist and whispered she was going to be in trouble unless she immediately called the sales department. She seemed briefly concerned, as though she might have been mistaken to treat him so cavalierly. She telephoned someone, spoke for a moment, and then slowly put down the phone. When she looked back to Gordy, she seemed confident. "I'm sorry, sir, they're all busy now. You'll just have to be patient. Why don't you have a seat, Mr. Gorney?"

Gordy left. He had underestimated how quickly his status had fallen with the poor sales of Marv Johnson's last record. He had learned a lesson about how fleeting fame could be in his business and promised himself that "never again would I allow myself to get psyched out by the impostor of success."

Dazed, Gordy made his way to the Brill Building, which housed many independent music companies. He dropped in on almost a dozen and tried in vain to find a distributor for his new recordings. Before the day was over, he had left for Chicago and the Chess brothers, Leonard and Phil. They were two Jewish Southside natives who had started a black record label when they noticed that market was poorly served. They recorded a number of arriving southern artists, including a group of blues guitarists who used electrical instruments. Among them were unknowns such as Chuck Berry and Bo Diddley, who appealed to white teenagers, and Muddy Waters and Howlin' Wolf, both of whom had large black followings. The Chess brothers had unwittingly recorded leading artists who fundamentally altered the blues.

They took "Bad Girl." Gordy didn't tell them everyone else had turned him down.

"Bad Girl" just broke into the bottom of the R&B charts. Again, a lot of venues wanted to book the Miracles. The one place the group wanted to perform more than any other was New York's Apollo. Gordy thought they were ready.

But the Miracles were almost canceled. Gordy and his groups did not use full arrangement sheets but rather relied on small chord sheets from which the studio musicians worked. The Apollo's house band thought the chord sheets were laughable and refused to play from them.

"Get lost," the Apollo's musical director screamed at Smokey. "Beat it. You can't be in no show without arrangements. Not at the Apollo."

Ray Charles, also on the bill, stepped in to save them. He urged the band to help the "kids just starting out," and he learned the songs from Smokey by ear. The Miracles, however, were rattled. And as they had a year earlier at the Gold Coast Theatre, they bumped into each other onstage and sang flat. This time, they had to endure the heckling that was a trademark of Apollo audiences. It was humiliating.

"We were pitiful, and I was petrified," recalled Smokey. "I memorized the back wall of the Apollo perfectly—every crack and paint blemish. I was too freaked to look at the audience."

After their performance, the Apollo's owner, Frank Schiffman, telephoned Gordy and demanded his money back.

In Detroit, the fiasco led Gordy's sisters, Gwen and Anna, to implore him to start an artist-development department so that acts could be better prepared when they went to perform. He dismissed the suggestion.

"All I care about is getting hit records," he told them curtly.

CHAPTER 7

Hitsville

AS HIS GROUPS GOT MORE EXPOSURE, GORDY BEGAN TO ATTRACT young women who hoped he might make them into recording stars. For the somewhat nerdy Gordy, who had been mostly clumsy and unsuccessful when it came to women, it was heady attention. He seemed to have trouble saying no to many, despite his relationship with Raynoma Liles.

Not only was Gordy a surrogate father to her first child, Cliff, but together they had a son, Kerry—Gordy's fourth child—born on June 25, 1959. They had been so certain it would be a girl, they had chosen the name Tamla, after their record label. But when it turned out to be a boy, they hurriedly took the name of a comic-strip character, Kerry Drake, from the local newspaper.

At the time, Gordy was not yet divorced from his first wife, Thelma, and Ray was still married as well. Ray suspected that Gordy was seeing other women, and it caused their worst arguments. But she grudgingly endured his overnight absences.

With the arrival of their son, the apartment suddenly seemed cramped. Ray hunted for a new home. She found a small, boxlike, two-story house at 2648 West Grand Boulevard, a middle-class, integrated neighborhood in central Detroit. The house had a picture window in front and a photo studio in the rear. (The previous occupant had been a photographer.) There was enough room for the family, and it was large enough to accommodate their growing business. Gordy and Liles bought it for twenty-five thousand dollars, putting three thousand down. The mortgage payments were $140 a month.

A couple of weeks after they moved in, a local club owner, George Kelly, visited. As he stood outside admiring the house, Kelly asked Gordy what he would call it. Gordy had been toying with a name for his new headquarters for days, but to no avail. But when Kelly asked him, he suddenly knew.

"Hitsville," he announced.

"You're joking," Kelly said, somewhat incredulously.

"No, I'm serious. That's the only name I can think of that expresses what I want it to be—a hip name for a factory where hits are going to be built. That's it—Hitsville."

Aside from being the birthplace of Nolan Strong and the Diablos' mid-1950s regional song "The Wind" and the 1959 tune "You're So Fine" by the Falcons, Detroit was not the city in which one would expect to find a Hitsville.

Gordy's new house needed a major overhaul, and everyone from relatives to singers pitched in. Gordy bought a used two-track recorder from local DJ Bristol Bryant and applied what he had learned in electronics in the military to set up a small studio. Gordy's father and his brother George plastered and sealed cracks and put up fresh Sheetrock. Ray used some discarded theater curtains to soundproof the studio, while Berry strung wires and set up microphones.

The house was soon completely transformed. The garage had become the recording studio and the first floor the business's small reception lounge and control room. Gordy and Ray, with the two boys, lived crammed between three floors of office supplies and recording accessories.

When it was almost finished inside, Gordy gathered a group of friends and family outside. He proudly placed a sign that stretched above the large picture window. It said simply, HITSVILLE, USA. Before long, in a front window, Gordy added a homemade poster that read THE SOUND OF YOUNG AMERICA.

Gordy started his company, coincidentally, the same year that Jim Stewart and his sister, Estelle Axton, mortgaged their home to launch Stax Records in Memphis, a black-dominated label whose big acts would eventually include Otis Redding and Isaac Hayes. Motown would come to represent an urbanized, lighter R&B sound, whereas Stax had a harder, almost blueslike intensity and rhythm on its records. Both operations were largely family affairs. "The Gordys were the tightest family I'd ever seen," said Marvin Gaye. "I never saw rivalry between them."

An upstairs bedroom became an office for Gordy's sister Esther. She had already worked with him for two years, doing simple secretarial work and helping to set tours for Marv Johnson and for the Miracles. At Motown, Esther was made a vice president and placed in charge of managing the label's artists. Esther's husband, George Edwards, a state legislator, found enough spare time from his public service to be Motown's comptroller. Berry's sister Loucye left her army reserves job for a vice president's title and responsibility for handling everything from album design to sales, billing and collection, and even the records' actual pressing. Gordy dubbed her catchall department, housed in a room adjacent to Esther, "manufacturing." "I couldn't believe we'd ever managed without her," recalled Raynoma. Loucye's husband, Ron Wakefield, a saxophonist who later toured with some Motown acts, came aboard later as a staff arranger.

Gordy's brother Robert quit the post office and became an apprentice engineer in the studio for sixty-five cents an hour. And while Berry's older brothers Fuller and George were busy running the family's construction and printing shops, they were also eventually drawn in. Berry Sr. suddenly saw that the son he had castigated as lazy and nonproductive had launched a venture that made the entire family proud. He became an unpaid consultant to it.

Liles's small office was on the building's main floor. Since she had the formal musical training that Gordy lacked, he relied on her as a jack-of-all-trades, helping on songwriting, occasionally singing backup, and also as a troubleshooter with the artists. (Eventually, some of them called her "Mother Motown.") Gordy, who hated sticky personal issues and confrontations, dealt with such problems by simply saying, "Go and talk to Ray." Gordy and Liles became the first officers of Tamla Records, as president and vice president. Soon, Ray's brother, Mike, who had a background in both music and accounting, helped create a payroll. And the company's first receptionist, a teenage aspiring songwriter, Janie Bradford—whom Raynoma remembered as having "a stupendous figure and a filthy mouth"—pitched in as well and ended up cowriting songs.

The lines of responsibility were loosely drawn, so everyone kicked in to help, mostly ignoring what someone's official title was. Hitsville provided a unique opportunity, and there was not only a sense of black pride but also the implied promise that fame and fortune were just ahead. Others in the black community—musicians, entertainers, and producers—dropped by to assist. Even the artists often did double duty. For instance, the Miracles did whatever they could when they weren't recording. Smokey helped other performers write lyrics. Bobby Rogers produced other artists. Pete Moore screened incoming songs from unsigned groups. Ronnie White helped Jobete arrange copyrights for its songs.

Eddie Holland had begun a singing career hoping to be the next Jackie Wilson. Berry would eventually produce ten singles for him with mixed results, and while he was good in the studio, he was terrible on the stage. "Performing wasn't for me," he admitted. After a disastrous outing at the Apollo, he finally abandoned his singing career. More than forty thousand dollars in debt, he had noticed that his brother, Brian, who had started writing songs for Tamla's first vocal group, the Santitones, had started making some money. So Eddie decided to join him.

Brian Holland, meanwhile, had become part of a loosely organized production team that often involved two singers, Freddie Gorman and Robert Bateman. Holland got into producing when one day Gordy literally shoved him into a control room, demanding, "What do you mean you're not an engineer? I need an engineer, and you're it!"

Eddie Holland discovered, much as another winning singer, Lamont Dozier, did, that his true talent lay in songwriting. Dozier had been a member of the Romeos and the Voice Masters and visited Motown in 1960 but was unimpressed and kept unsuccessfully pursuing his singing career for two years before returning for a job that paid only $2.50 a week plus royalties.

By 1962, the Holland brothers and Dozier became their own production team, called HDH inside Motown, and were on their way to becoming the most dominant songwriting and production team in the label's history.

Some fell into their jobs. In such an intimate environment, they could attract the owner's personal attention. For instance, Martha Reeves, an ambitious background singer and one of twelve children from a local family, was a thirty-five-dollar-a-week secretary. Smart and sultry, she hung in at Motown, dutifully doing her clerical duties, handling the complaints from the signed acts, and even baby-sitting Stevie Wonder, as she waited for her own chance to reveal her talents. "She was also bonkers for Berry," recalled Smokey Robinson. "Back then every female vocalist had a crush on Berry," replied Reeves.

Others weren't looking for their own recording careers but instead wanted to be songwriters. During a sweltering summer day in 1959, Gordy was in a particularly foul mood. As he walked through the hallway, Janie Bradford tried joking with him, only to be gruffly shunted aside. When she asked what was wrong, he told her about being stymied with a song. She asked what the song was about.

He told her that since most of the popular songs on the charts were about love, he had decided to write about something he needed most at that very moment: money.

"But won't people think that's all you care about?" Bradford asked.

"So what?" Berry replied. "Some will be shocked, some will think it's cute, some will think it's funny. I think it will make money."

He took Bradford to the piano and played some chords of his unfinished song. As he went along he really got into it, loudly singing the chorus, "Money, that's what I want. Yeah, yeah, that's what I want." Then suddenly Bradford blurted her own line, "Your love gives me such a thrill, but your love don't pay my bills, gimme some money, baby."

Berry stopped in midsong. He liked her line.

Barrett Strong, a rather shy and retiring artist, had been in an adjoining room listening to the work in progress. He came in uninvited, slipped next to Gordy on the piano bench, and started playing and singing the chorus. It was then that Gordy decided that Strong, who was actually one of Gwen Gordy's artists at Anna Records, had the right voice for this new song.

A few days later, Bradford, who thought she had just given Gordy a good line, was startled when he offered her 50 percent of the song for her contribution. As far as he was concerned, she had contributed the best verse and deserved half the profits.

"Money (That's What I Want)" was the first song cut at the Hitsville studio. The actual recording session lasted several days and was more like a party than a typical session. Because everything—the singer, band, and background singers—was recorded live, it had a raw feel to it, with an underlying beat derived from popular "twist" records. Gordy, who now owned the studio, had the luxury of not worrying about costs for the first time. Liles, who coordinated the backup singers, remembered there were forty takes. And when they finally had one they liked, they worked overnight to get the right mix. (Although Gordy claimed not to care any longer about studio costs, as the business became more polished, Gordy tried reducing most songs to one or two studio takes, less than an hour, and he succeeded for a few years before HDH again insisted on many takes.)

When Gwen Gordy heard the song a few days later, she loved it and wanted to release it on Anna Records, which was distributed nationally through Chess. Berry agreed, but in Detroit he released it on his own label, as Tamla 54027. (Although it was Tamla's eighth release, Berry picked a large number, hoping it would disguise how new and untested his label really was.)

"Money," with its driving rhythm-and-blues dance tune, was a strong hit, peaking at number two on the *Billboard* R&B chart. Listeners loved the constant piano riffs, the funky bass-drum groove, and the background tambourine. Gordy and Liles provided the catchy "That's what I want" chorus. "Money" was a blueprint to which many early Motown songs adhered.

But by early 1960, Berry had learned a lesson from his hasty decision to let Chess be the main distributor. In the three cities where Gordy worked directly with independent distributors ("indies"), he made more money than in all of the rest of the country combined. In all other cities, indies paid Chess, which then took its cut before paying Anna Records, which took another slice before sending the money to Gordy. "On my next record," said Gordy, "I knew I had to go for it by myself—national all the way."

Still, it did generate some necessary cash. Raynoma was ecstatic. She recalled "holding our first royalty check in awe. It was almost obscene, more than ten times the advance we had received from United Artists [the advance had been $3,000]. . . . The local distributors paid once a month and UA made quarterly payments from the national sales. It started pouring in, first slowly, then in a landslide." Gordy and Liles bought their first car, a 1959 white Pontiac convertible, for $3,500. When she wanted a 1959 VW nine-passenger bus, he also let her get that for another $1,900.

But despite a financial cushion, Gordy had slowly come around to Smokey Robinson's long-held view that he could get ahead only if he did everything himself. "It was not his goal to head up a major entertainment complex," said his sister Esther, "with recordings, films, and all these sorts of things. He just wanted to be a successful songwriter. . . . Motown is the result of one thing leading to another and Berry Gordy saying 'I'll do it my-self' when he could not get something done to his liking."

Gordy knew he needed to mimic the structure of large record compa-nies. At times he relied on his intuition and gambled on people he didn't know well. He looked for energy and a commitment to hard work. One of the departments he was missing was artists and repertoire (A&R), the divi-sion responsible for developing and nurturing the musical acts. One day William "Mickey" Stevenson showed up at Hitsville to audition as a singer. The fast-talking Stevenson, dressed in fashionable street clothes, did not impress Gordy with his voice. But Gordy did like him.

"Your singing is OK," Gordy told him, "but I just don't need another singer right now. What I really need is an A&R director. Can you do that?"

"Do a bear shit in the woods?" asked Stevenson as he broke into a big grin.

Gordy's instinct was good. Stevenson had a natural talent for dealing with artists, and he greatly influenced Gordy's own management style, mak-ing it more personal and far less structured than at traditional companies.

Also, unknown to Gordy when he hired him, Stevenson was a Detroit native who came from a showbiz family. He had been trying to get the city's black bourgeoisie to invest in a venture like Motown for several years. Stevenson was distrustful of white-owned independent labels and had ad-miringly watched Gordy's career since his time writing songs for Jackie Wil-son. He liked the Gordy family's entrepreneurial spirit and cohesiveness. Gordy, when he learned about Stevenson's commitment to black business advancement, felt even better about his choice.

Although Stevenson was hobbled with a poor voice, he had an ear for good artists. As one of his first jobs, he scoured Detroit's bars and lounges searching for musicians for Motown's house band. Many had jazz back-grounds. Stevenson inaugurated a jazz label called the Jazz Workshop, which placed local performers under long-term contracts both as recording artists and as staff players. This ensured that Motown was never short of musicians.

Eventually, the house band was called the Funk Brothers. It became a group that, the Temptations' Otis Williams later said, "must go down in history as one of the best groups of musicians anywhere." The band's composition changed over time, depending on who was in town and was available. The 280-pound piano-playing Earl Van Dyke was the titular bandleader, together with the cigar-smoking and wisecracking James Jamerson. Most critics give Jamerson, who had perfect pitch, credit for using his 1962 Fender Precision bass innovatively to help develop a distinct Motown sound. ("A genius," gushed Gordy.) Jamerson was strong-willed and often wanted the recording sessions to lapse into free-form jazz sessions—his strength—but Gordy would tell him to "stay in the groove." The highly strung, often stoned, and perpetually late Benny "Papa Zita" Benjamin on drums ("The higher Benny was, the better he played," said Van Dyke) and the wild-eyed Jamerson were crucial to the sound, and they were also Gordy's personal favorites. However, many fans have their own favorites, from Beans Bowles and Hank Cosby on sax and flute, to Eddie Willis, Robert White, or Joe Messina on guitar, to Joe Hunter on keyboards. The sound changed slightly each time someone new played. That so many talented musicians wanted to be in the band meant there was a healthy dose of competition to get the gig, something Gordy liked.

"Berry was a manipulator who loved stoking competitive fires," recalled Marvin Gaye.

Berry's recording sessions were generally loose and fit with the Funk Brothers unstructured style. The musicians were laid-back and not impressed by orders and schedules. Often they took extended drinking breaks at Cole's Funeral Home, next door to Hitsville. Once, when Gordy himself was producing a session, the rest of the band stood silently as Benny Benjamin sauntered in, eating ice cream, almost a half-hour late. Gordy turned to the band and asked, "Why does this guy do this to me?"

"Do what, man?" Benny asked.

"But I'm the president," said Gordy.

Benny stared at him for a moment. Most expected Benny to come up with one of his patented and outrageous excuses, from having just escaped a shooting to being delayed by crowds for a visiting circus. Instead he calmly asked, "The president of what?"

Gordy just shook his head and walked away until Benjamin was ready. Few others could have behaved this way without incurring Gordy's wrath.

By today's digital recording standards, the early Funk sessions were anarchic, with engineers jamming all the musicians and singers onto just two tracks. Everything was cut live. If anyone made a major mistake, the recording had to be restarted. But Gordy knew that getting a groove was more important than whether someone played a wrong chord or misplaced a rhythm. If a cut sounded good, it sometimes was released with technical mistakes.

Gordy was fortunate that he found some of the city's best musicians willing to play at odd hours, on short notice, and for little pay. When union scale was approximately forty-seven to sixty dollars per three-hour session, Gordy paid a musician as little as five dollars per side (eventually, when Motown boomed, they earned between $25,000 and $60,000 a year). They were not allowed to record as solo acts, and no matter how many hours they put in on a song, or how big a hit it became, they never got more than their flat fee. Although some moonlighted for other small Detroit labels, such as Golden World and Ric-Tic, Gordy strongly discouraged it, and if he heard any similarities to Motown's sound he went ballistic. He once fined the Funk Brothers one thousand dollars each for playing on Edwin Starr's 1965 Ric-Tic hit, "Agent Double-O-Soul."

Furthermore, no matter how significant their contributions to the songs they recorded and reworked, musicians did not get credits from Motown until the 1970s. Artists, producers, and the label's executives never referred to them in interviews. Their names were known only inside the company. The same happened with the studio band Motown later used in California, where leading musicians such as Carol Kaye were never acknowledged. "There is sometimes a tear," James Jamerson commented years later, shortly before his death, "because I see how I was treated and cheated." For talented players like Jamerson, the gripe wasn't only about money but about the lack of recognition. It was intolerable to have millions of people listen to your bass lines—his playing appeared on an estimated two hundred million records—and have nobody know who played them.

But early on, no one was complaining. Gordy's loose system also worked well for the background singers—the Rayber Voices and, later the Andantes—who had wide latitude to improvise.

A normal session started with written chord sheets. But Berry wanted the right feel, not strict adherence to sheet music. He would usually lock in the drumbeat and then hum a line for the musicians to start playing. They were encouraged to ad-lib extensively until he heard a sound he liked. And he was strict about keeping them commercial, not letting them stray too far from what fans might buy. He would constantly urge them to "stay in the pocket." Sometimes Gordy would lose the fight to keep them focused, especially when Benjamin arrived drunk and retakes consumed the day. Mickey Stevenson even resorted to propping an almost catatonic Benjamin against his drums on days when he was especially wasted.

Since the engineering was done on the antiquated two-track machine, Gordy wasn't happy with much of the studio sound. It forced him and the musicians to innovate. When they looked for a spot for a vocal booth (the studio was too small to house one), they cobbled one together in the hallway closet. There were no windows in the basement control room, so Gordy and his engineer couldn't see the singer, and they communicated through microphones. Yet the hallway turned out to be a good spot, and the vocal sounds recorded there were clean and crisp. A downstairs bathroom became the first echo chamber, although someone usually had to keep an eye on it to make sure no one flushed the toilet during a session. After some trial and error, the attic was converted into an expanded echo chamber, and it worked well except for the occasional car horn or sound of rain hitting the roof. Gordy set partitions around the band's different instruments so they did not bleed into one another. When he didn't like the barely audible feedback from the amps onto the guitars, he had the guitars fed directly into the control room to ensure they were clean on the final recording.

The musicians usually played virtually on top of the background singers. "Working in such close quarters may have been cramped, but it was conducive to a better rapport between the singers and the players," said the Supremes' Mary Wilson. "When the band got into a groove it inspired the singers, and vice versa."

Before electronic synthesizers were popular, Gordy was creative about sound effects. He tried everything from dragging chains along the wooden floors, to having people jump and stomp, to striking screwdrivers against Coke bottles, to shaking jars of dried peas. On the 1964 smash hit "Baby Love," critics liked the "hand clapping" on the backbeat. It was actually two-by-fours hooked together with strings, which someone jumped on to create a noise. "Ain't no way we gonna pay twelve people session fees to clap hands," said Funk Brothers leader Earl Van Dyke.

Gordy was usually at the mixing board, blending and remixing. "Mixing was so important to me that it seemed I spent half my life at the board." Smokey Robinson and others teased him that he was a "mix maniac," but Gordy countered that while the differences in many mixes were subtle, they could make or break a record. Gordy reworked the songs totally on instinct. From his Ford Motors work, he was fascinated with a way people were increasingly listening to popular music: on car radios. He experimented on mixing songs so they sounded great on those tinny players. Mike McClain, Motown's chief engineer, built a small radio that approximated the sound of those in cars. Everyone listened to early mixes on that radio. The sound that worked well—light, with a steady, even beat and a continuous-loop melody—also sounded good on small transistor radios, the popularity of which was expanding quickly in the early 1960s.

"Berry's instincts were nearly flawless," said the Temptations' Otis Williams. What is most startling is that Gordy was musically illiterate. Besides banging out a few chords on a piano, he could play no instrument or read music.

He was supremely confident that the basic sound he had created was the key to success, with the singers almost being secondary. When asked if his label was producing a sound and not songs, he told a Detroit reporter: "You probably haven't any voice. But there are probably three notes you can sing. I can take those three notes and give them an arrangement and some lyrics. That makes a song. And your song will sell."

There were also elements that Gordy later set as rules for many Motown songs—putting the lyrics in the present tense and having an easy-to-remember melody that created a sense of déjà vu when people heard it. He also utilized a new format for groups, with the lead singer working against the background singers rather than with the ensemble. There was constant shifting between sections of the song, sometimes with the background singers coming in behind the verse and other times the lead singer and group combining on the chorus. And the chorus usually had an exaggerated importance. Hand claps, heavy drums, and often-repeated choruses helped make the songs memorable. Most had several hooks, either in the lyrics, chorus, melody, rhythm sections, or background vocals. It was the similarity between the songs that gave the label a unique sound. Many later dubbed it the Motown sound. (It would take the mainstream media years to report on what music fans knew early on. In late 1967, *Time* did its first feature on

Gordy and said, in the stilted racial language of the era, that "the result is the 'Motown Sound'—basically the Negro rhythm-and-blues style that has captured a vast white audience in recent years.")

.   .   .

In the middle of trying to get Motown off the ground, Raynoma surprised Gordy one day as he was heading into the studio to produce a follow-up to "Money." Liles walked up behind him and in her high-pitched, cheery voice said, "Oh, Berry, we're getting married next week on Thursday." It had been almost one year since Kerry's birth, and Ray's parents had been pressing her to get Gordy's commitment.

Gordy nodded, only half listening, and mumbled, "Yeah, sure."

Each day after that, Liles kept reminding Gordy that their marriage was just around the corner. She gave him a day-by-day countdown. When Thursday arrived, Robert Bateman drove the couple and both sets of parents to Toledo, Ohio, some sixty miles from Detroit.

Gordy felt pressured and blamed himself for working so hard that he had not allowed himself to step back and decide whether marrying Ray was what he really wanted. He sat in the car, unusually quiet. When they were only thirty miles from the church, Gordy decided not to go through with it. Initially, he could not bring himself to say anything. But he wondered if he was a mouse or a man and reminded himself that he had to be true to himself. When they arrived at the city limits, Gordy whispered, "I'm not getting married."

It was as though he had blasted it over a loudspeaker. The car fell silent. He told the stunned group that getting married "doesn't feel right to me," and in a soft but determined voice he asked Bateman to turn the car around and return to Detroit. Bateman, not wanting to be caught in the middle, pretended not to hear Berry and just continued driving. But Berry asked again, this time making it more of a directive. Finally, Ray spoke up.

"Take us home," she said softly. "I wouldn't marry him."

Everyone in the car had an opinion. Voices cascaded over one another as Mother Gordy tried to change her son's mind, and Ray's father kept chiding his almost son-in-law. Finally, Gordy exploded, demanding that the car pull off the road so he could get out and return to Detroit on his own. This time it was Ray's turn to explode.

"Oh, no, motherfucker!" No one else spoke. "You're not getting out of here! This is your mess, and you're riding all the way back with it. There's no way you're getting out now."

This time, the car turned around and started the ninety-minute trip back to Detroit. No one spoke. When they dropped off Ray's parents, her mother leaned over to her and whispered, "Don't you dare give that nigger his ring back." Once back at Hitsville, the whole company came running out, holding champagne bottles above their heads and yelling, "Congratulations!" One look at Liles and Gordy and everyone stopped. Ray did not berate Gordy. Instead, she acted as though nothing unusual had happened. Although she appeared calm, it was a silent, cold war between them. That night, Gordy walked in behind her in the bathroom. She was bent over the sink brushing her teeth.

"Will you marry me?" he asked.

Robert Bateman again drove them to Toledo. They returned that same day to Hitsville, legally married, and went back to work as though nothing had changed. On their honeymoon night, Berry left to go out on his own, not returning until 11:00 the next morning. Raynoma confronted him, asking where he had been.

"What's your problem?" he asked. "I married you, didn't I?"

She again asked him where he had been.

"What difference does it make where I was? I have things to do. Look, I married you. There are things I have to do in the evenings that don't concern you. They don't require an explanation, and you have to trust me or . . . Regardless of where I am, I married you, and I intend to keep it that way."

CHAPTER 8

"Honesty and Raw Soul"

AS THE 1960S STARTED, THIRTY-ONE-YEAR-OLD BERRY GORDY WAS anxious. He wanted his company to distinguish itself from similar labels run on shoestring budgets from the basements of producers' houses. But nothing he heard sounded quite right.

In February, he gave his first interview to *The Detroit News*. Gordy was described as the owner of a recording studio "that he believes is the only one in Detroit devoted to popular music rather than singing commercials." The article introduced readers to "a young man identified as 'Smoky' Robinson, seated at a piano, crooning into a microphone, 'Babee-ee-ee. . . . ' " Gordy said, "We don't go for 'Dilly-dilly-gum-gum' type lyrics." Hundreds of aspiring artists crowded his studio monthly, he said, and instead of turning them away the entrepreneurial Gordy had even figured a way to make some money from those rejected—"They can take a coaching and music course for $100." Gordy boasted he was most proud of his song "Money (That's What I Want)," because "there is, after all, no more complete and meaningful message than that."

Then, only a few months later, his friend Smokey finally brought him the song he was looking for: "Way Over There." When Gordy heard the melody and lyrics, coupled with Smokey's passionate rendition, he was so excited that most coworkers thought he'd had a winning night at one of his regular poker games.

The "way over there" in Smokey's song referred to where his lover was, but to Gordy " 'way over there' was where my dreams were—for Motown, for happiness, for success." With its falsetto and hand clapping, it was strongly influenced by gospel.

For this first in-house national release, Loucye was in charge of distribution, and she promptly put together a list of all the Chess distributors as well as a master DJ list. The family and the company's few workers gathered around a long table and packed the disc-jockey copies as if on an assembly line. Gordy, confident of success, took out the company's first ad in the trade publication *Cash Box*. There was no advertising executive, so Gordy designed the ad himself, influenced by an old Western-movie ad he had recently seen. Starting with small print in a short line at the top and then spreading out wider in each subsequent row, with progressively larger type, the copy resembled a pyramid and made a powerful statement:

> From out of the Midwest comes a new label destined to take its place among the leaders of the industry; Tamla, prexied by one of the young, driving geniuses of the music business today, Berry Gordy, Jr; a man who has given you such great hits as "You've Got What It Takes"; "Money-(That's All That I Want)"; "I Love the Way You Love" & "All the Love I've Got" and who now brings you a record soon to be numbered among his greatest successes. "WAY OVER THERE" BY THE "BAD GIRL" MIRACLES, TAMLA NO. 54028.

In small print at the bottom, it read, "A Product of Motown Record Corporation." On the left of the ad there was a head shot of Gordy with the words "Mr. Hitsville" underneath.

When his sister Esther saw it, she asked if he thought it was too arrogant.

"Who's gonna know I wrote it?" Gordy replied in earnest.

Esther just smiled.

Gordy worked hard to get airtime from key disc jockeys, although he admittedly knew virtually nothing about promotion. In Cleveland and Cincinnati, DJs gave "Way Over There" airplay, and sales picked up. But Gordy fretted about the East Coast, where the song wasn't getting airtime.

"Back then, disc jockeys ruled the airwaves," recalled Otis Williams, "and could make or break just about anybody."

They didn't just spin records, they were major personalities within local black communities. Their shows not only made new stars; they also used their programs to preach, editorialize, and jive about hot-button local issues. The Magnificent Montague may have been the leading DJ of the era, operating out of Chicago and later Los Angeles. He developed a reputation for outrageous commentary. But he was also a record company's best friend. He would repeat a song if he liked it, sometimes running the same tune fifteen times. Tommy Smalls (Dr. Jive) ruled New York, but Hal Jackson also had a following because of his political and social activism. The rotund, high-pitched Joltin' Joe Howard was a Detroit legend, although "Frantic" Ernie Durham, renowned for his rapid-fire delivery, had carved out a large chunk of that market. Ken Bell, at KJLB, was another Detroit contender. In Baltimore, Maurice "Hot Rod" Hulbert was famous for wild rhymes and raps. Jocko Henderson in Philadelphia coined phrases that instantly became part of the local slang. Other top spinners included the gravel-voiced E. Rodney Jones in Chicago; John Bandy in Washington, D.C., who was dubbed "Lord Fauntleroy" for his affected British accent; and in Pittsburgh, Sir Walter Raleigh, who wore a monocle and relished doing his shows in a mock-Cockney dialect. There were also pioneering black women such as the Queen, Martha Jean, first in Memphis and then Detroit; Chattie Hattie in Charlotte; Mary Dee in Pittsburgh; and Dizzy Lizzy in Houston.

The DJs gathered every year at the National Association of Radio Announcers convention. When one discovered a new act, he or she would often call up the others, and soon the black radio circuit would buzz about the latest hot album. But they were also competitive, and each strove to make his or her own discoveries.

When someone told Gordy that DJ Georgie Woods, who was the kingpin in Philadelphia, was not playing "Way Over There," Gordy hurried to see him personally. Gordy fretted that he was not a member of the club—the large record label promoters who courted the DJs with gifts and cash—and that he did not know what to do or say.

At Philadelphia's WDAS, Gordy leaned against a wall of the small studio and watched as Woods, a large man with a booming bass voice, did his show. Gordy was uncharacteristically quiet, smiling occasionally when he thought Woods glanced at him. Finally, when the show was on a long break and the studio emptied out, Woods and Gordy were alone. Still, Woods merely shuffled papers and cleared his desk, ignoring Gordy. Finally, one of Woods's assistants came into the room. Without looking up, Woods gruffly asked her to get him a hot dog.

"Hot dog?" Gordy popped up. "I'll get it." And then he ran out of the studio. A few minutes later, he returned.

"Whatcha got there?" asked Woods, nodding at what Gordy had in his other hand.

"Oh, I got a really great record here, 'Way Over—' "

"Give it here." Woods roughly yanked the record from Gordy, put on his earphones, and started playing the record on a nearby turntable. A few seconds later, he pulled off the needle, still saying nothing. Gordy remembered, "My heart dropped."

Then, suddenly, the on-air light went on, and Woods slid his chair back toward the large boom microphone. His deep voice overrode the show's musical introduction. "Here is a brand-new record, a brand-new group, a brand-new smash. . . . 'Way Over There' by the Miracles. It's hot, folks!" One thousand records were ordered by Philadelphia stores within forty-eight hours.

Gordy repeated, with mixed success, such visits to DJs in most major cities. And as he traveled and listened incessantly to the song, he became convinced that, as good as it was, it would have been better if strings had been added to the background. Sales had peaked at sixty thousand copies, excellent for an unknown Detroit label but not good enough for Gordy. Finally, unable to any longer control himself, he hired some string musicians from the Chicago Symphony Orchestra to get the sound he wanted.

During the new recording session, when the Miracles heard the improved arrangement they became inspired, and their second version of the song was even stronger than the original. Gordy and his small crew went through the ordeal of pulling the original records from stores and independent distributors and swapping them with the new one. The DJs also switched to the latest version. "They loved it, too," recalled Gordy. "In fact, everybody loved it—that is, except the public. I had lost the magic. We never sold more than the original sixty thousand copies."

He realized the original recording had "an honesty and raw soul," while the second was only a contrived copy. The sound produced by his makeshift studio in his home suddenly seemed more appealing. Nevertheless, he had still managed to officially put Motown on the music scene by releasing a song nationally. And Gordy's contacts with black DJs turned out to be more important than just getting his songs airtime. Shortly after releasing the recut of "Way Over There," a white-owned company to which Gordy had distributed the record tried to take over the Miracles' contract. Gordy invited several prominent DJs to Detroit, where they called the company's owner and threatened to boycott his label's black releases unless he stopped trying to sign the Miracles. He relented. For the DJs, it was a moment of solidarity with a young black record-label owner and a vote of confidence in Gordy's future prospects.

"If it were not for the black disc jockeys, there would have been no Motown," said former Detroit DJ Ken Bell. "At first, we broke the records before the white stations did. . . . You can't even give it away if it's not played on the radio. And the black disc jockeys helped Motown get its sound across to the white stations. The black disc jockeys were very, very instrumental, and Berry knew this and treated us accordingly."

CHAPTER 9

"I Call It Music with Black Stars"

SUDDENLY, GORDY WAS HOT, AND WANNA-BE SINGERS AND YOUNG songwriters deluged him. Not all made their pitches through traditional auditions. Gordy had gone to see two of his acts, Marv Johnson and the Miracles, at a local DJ-sponsored record hop—where, in return for some airtime, artists donated their time at a nightclub. As he worked his way through the dense weekend club crowd, he heard a tiny voice behind him.

"Mr. Gordy. Mr. Gordy."

"Yeah," Gordy said, turning to see a small, light-skinned black teenager with a wide face and enormous doe eyes skipping toward him.

"Mr. Gordy," she said, panting and trying to catch her breath. "I've been trying to get you all night. I got a song."

Gordy rolled his eyes. He was not in the mood for a pitch.

If she saw his exasperation, she did not let on. "It's great," she continued, her lithe voice carrying over the din around them. "It's great, it's really good. Can I have an appointment with you?"

Gordy started walking faster, hoping he might get away from her. She stayed only a step behind.

"I have no time for a meeting," he said gruffly, hoping the tone would stop her.

"Oh, *please*, Mr. Gordy . . . ," she implored him.

He smiled. He liked her spunk. "All right," he thought, "if she wants me to hear her song, she can let me hear it right now."

"Can you sing it?" he asked as he ducked and angled through the crowd.

She did not hesitate. "Oh, yeah, really good." A gracious smile broke across her sweet face. "I can sing it good."

"Well then, sing it," he said, still looking ahead and walking quickly.

"Sing it?" She seemed puzzled.

"Yeah."

"Now?"

"Yeah, right now." ("That will teach her from running after somebody at the wrong time," Gordy thought.)

She jumped right into the song.

You know you took my heart, and you broke it apart.

She sounded nervous in her first lines, a slight tremble to her voice. Then she found her confidence.

"Over all the noise, confusion and everything," Gordy later recalled, "I loved that raspy soulful sound. I slowed. All of a sudden, I did have time."

"What's your name?" he asked her.

"Mary," she said softly. "Mary Wells."

"OK, Mary, meet me at the studio tomorrow."

"But how will I get in?" she asked.

"Don't worry. You'll get in."

The next day at Hitsville, she told Gordy she had written that song for Jackie Wilson. No, he told her, he thought she was the ideal person to sing her own song. He did not know that Wells had been singing gospel music from the age of three in a family of ministers and missionaries. She was so excited that she literally whooped and jumped around the office.

Mary Wells was lucky to have found not just a record label willing to gamble on unknown talent but a man who was working unusually hard to stand out from the slew of other small garage labels. Determined to keep things simple, he reduced the entire business to three basic functions: create, make, sell. It became Gordy's slogan. *Create* covered the writing, producing, and recording of a record. The *Make* phase, run by his sister Loucye, was the manufacturing and pressing of discs. That grew quickly to support inventories, deliveries to far-flung distributors, and billing. The final phase, *Sell,* was the most challenging. It involved getting airplay, marketing, and advertisements necessary for a record to stand out from the flood of new releases. Gordy was the company's only salesman, but he knew he would need help if he was to have a realistic chance of expanding.

Gordy's opportunity came unexpectedly. It was generally accepted in the record business that pop DJs, all white, would never play records by up-and-coming black artists. There was a white DJ, Tom Clay at WJBK, however, whom Gordy had met when he was managing Marv Johnson. When Gordy told Clay about his new company, Clay introduced him to Barney Ales. The twenty-six-year-old Ales was an aggressive local distributor, of the kind that were key to small record companies. While the largest record labels—such as RCA and Columbia—had their own nationwide networks, Motown and others had to sell to many independent distributors across the country. Those distributors, in turn, arranged local radio play and sold aggressively to retail stores. Beneath the distributors was another layer, so-called one stops. They were minidistributors that sold to thousands of retail outlets that wanted only a few copies of a record, such as a local drugstore that sold records on a rack in the rear of the store.

Ales was tall, somewhat heavyset, rough speaking, and gruff, and he did not seem to be someone with great people skills. But Clay assured Gordy that Ales was gifted. Up to then, Gordy had used a local Detroit distributor, B&H, to handle his recordings. B&H's specialty was R&B. Ales, on the other hand, sold everything, including pop. "Berry knew I had the best connections at the one stops," said Ales. "I could get all his records promoted at white stations, something Berry had tried, with pretty poor results." Gordy decided to take a chance and let Ales, the first white person to be associated with the new company, distribute both the Tamla and Motown labels.

In July 1960, Ales took on the Miracles' "Way Over There," as well as Mary Wells's "Bye Bye Baby," just released on Motown after a marathon twenty-two studio takes. Ales got good airplay for both throughout the state, but Gordy was disappointed that the sales didn't take off, especially for the Miracles, who he thought had a surefire hit.

Gordy thought it might be better for Ales to concentrate on only one of the records, so he moved the Motown line to a competitor. Suddenly, Gordy stopped hearing Wells's "Bye Bye Baby" on the radio. He called up the new distributor, who claimed he was trying hard to get airtime, but it was not easy since the market was saturated with new artists and established acts. The very next day, Ales got the Motown label back. In a couple of days, Mary Wells was again being played.

After he got to know Ales better, Gordy asked if he had had anything to do with the radio-play slowdown.

"Absolutely not," said Ales, arching his eyebrows and feigning surprise. "All I did was call the DJs to let them know if they wanted to do something for me, they might want to play my new Shirelles record on Scepter Records. And oh yeah, I did tell them that Mary Wells was no longer my record." Ales looked at Gordy and broke into a devilish grin. Gordy was impressed. He knew Ales should be more than just a distributor for the label, but he wasn't sure what to offer him.

Ales began hanging out at Hitsville. The two men got along well, trading industry war stories. But Ales was also a bit of a mystery and marvel all at once to Gordy, who listened for tips about how to break his artists into the lucrative end of pop music. Ales was also a poker player. They played for hours in a back room. It was there that Gordy again saw what a fierce competitor Ales was and decided he wanted him at Motown more than ever.

It was Ales who, during this budding friendship, convinced Gordy to join him on a most unlikely sporting event for the inner-city Gordy: pheasant hunting in a remote rural area of northern Michigan. In order to make Gordy more acceptable to local whites, Ales had told them that he was bringing a black doctor from Detroit. While pheasant hunting did not become Gordy's favorite pastime, the trip deepened their friendship. Ales did something that greatly impressed Gordy. Before leaving Detroit, he contacted every local DJ he knew along the almost two-hundred-mile route north. As he entered each station's coverage area, he flipped the car radio to their dial number. By prearrangement, they were all playing Motown songs. "He knew I had done it," says Ales. "I knew I had him."

Ales was out to impress Gordy because he wanted to be Motown's exclusive Detroit distributor. Shortly after their hunting trip, Ales's company suddenly put restrictions on the number of promotional records he could give away, as well as on the discounts he could give to buyers. Ales complained one day when sitting with Gordy.

"Why don't you come over and join me?" Gordy asked.

"Nah, we're too close," Ales said. "How can I take orders from you?"

Ales was not sure he wanted to gamble on a start-up company that could not offer long-term security. "I had a new house, a new car, a second kid, and I owned a piece of the distributor where I was working," recounted Ales. "I had little desire to switch."

Both men left it at that but agreed to think about it.

•   •   •

In autumn 1960, Smokey Robinson sought out Gordy for help in finishing lyrics he had written in less than thirty minutes. Gordy liked the song, "Shop Around." He was surprised when Robinson said he didn't feel the song was right for him and the Miracles and that he wanted someone else to sing it: Barrett Strong. Gordy and Smokey sat at the piano and reworked the lyrics and the chorus. At the end of their jamming session, Gordy suggested that Claudette, Smokey's girlfriend and fellow Miracle, sing it. Smokey agreed.

"Shop Around" was released, but it wasn't until he heard it on the radio that Gordy was disappointed. He thought it was too slow and flat and decided to recut it. Only slightly gun-shy as a result of his unsuccessful recut of "Way Over There," he telephoned Smokey at 3:00 A.M. and told him to rouse the group and musicians and come into the studio immediately. Smokey, half asleep, balked at first, but Gordy promised him that if he recut it the song would go to number one.

Smokey rounded up the bleary-eyed and short-tempered musicians. When the piano player didn't show, Gordy himself played. The session started at 4:00 A.M. and ended after dawn. This time, Gordy's instincts were right. He gave the song a faster rhythm. But the most important change was that Smokey now sang the lead. His light voice gave the song a yearning that Gordy had originally hoped Claudette might impart.

Gordy gave the record to Barney Ales, who orchestrated enthusiastic promotion by the national white distributors. Within a few months, "Shop Around" became Motown's first crossover hit, topping the R&B charts and peaking at number two on the pop charts. It also made the Miracles the first Motown group to appear on ABC's wildly popular *American Bandstand.* And Ales had, by moving "Shop Around" up the charts, created the machinery for Motown to repeat its success with future releases.

"[It] sent the company sailing into orbit," said Smokey. "We were flying high." It also did not surprise him, since he knew that this type of hit had been Gordy's goal: "Berry wanted to make crossover music. Crossover at that time meant that white people would buy your records."

Gordy later liked to brag that if one of his records sold a million, whites bought 70 percent. "I don't like to call it black music," Gordy once told the *Detroit News* music critic. "I call it music with black stars."

"Gordy milked it down so it was acceptable to whites," said Abraham Silver, who helped coach several early Motown vocalists. "That was his big trick."

At the Michigan State Fairgrounds, Gordy could not contain his enthusiasm as he jumped onstage to give Motown's first gold record to Smokey and the Miracles. They stood there crying and hugging one another. The normally tightfisted Gordy had been so excited with the success of "Shop Around" that he even surprised the group with a new Ford station wagon wrapped in green and red ribbons, their names emblazoned on the doors in fire-engine red.

"But I was still not satisfied," recalled Gordy. "I felt #1 and #2 were miles apart. I believed that if I had been able to put together a strong in-house Sales Department sooner, that record might have gone to #1."

Gordy wanted Ales more than ever to direct sales full-time. "Berry was a great charmer," said Ales. Ales talked to his wife about working for Motown. She was for it. Ales demanded $125 a week. At the time, the highest-paid Motown executive was Loucye Gordy at $35 weekly. Gordy agreed, but did not tell anyone else how much Ales was earning.

Motown was frenzied with the success of "Shop Around." It was a much more disorganized place than Ales expected. "Things were very different when I got there than what I had imagined," said Ales. "They actually had no idea what to do when they made a record. They would be happy with orders for one thousand when I knew I could sell ten thousand of the same record. I saw a lot of ways to boost their business right away."

Ales was a real pro by the standards of most Hitsville executives, and they enthusiastically welcomed the sharply dressed, fast-talking newcomer. Ales's personal friends, however, were not happy. "I've always been color-blind," Ales said. "I used to be in promotion in cement, so here were black guys, and I was used to it. Berry ran Motown with his black family just like a Jewish or Italian family. It was a great family. But I did take a *lot* of heat back in the early 1960s for working for a black guy. A lot of whites couldn't get that. I didn't care. It was their problem." Tom Noonan, another white executive who later joined the sales department, remembered, "When friends would see me, people would often ask what it was like to work for a black company, and I would say, 'The money is green.'" Al Abrams, an early public relations employee, remembered a white Detroit newspaperman asking him, "What's a nice Jewish boy like you doing working for a bunch of niggers?" Phil Jones, another later addition in the sales department, recalled a neighbor asking almost the same question: "How can you work for that nigger?"

Later, Ales discovered that whenever he traveled for Motown, local companies invariably booked him into hotels in black neighborhoods, assuming he had to be black. Once, in Detroit, Ales and his wife went with Gordy and Raynoma to an upscale restaurant.

"We don't serve colored people," the host told the foursome.

"That's all right," replied Gordy, without missing a beat. "I don't eat them." Ales roared with laughter, and the group refused to leave until they were served. Incidents like this allowed the two men to bond early on.

The only one at Motown who was not so pleased was Raynoma, who sensed from the start that Gordy and Ales's special connection meant, for the first time, that she was being left out. When Ray mentioned her concerns to Gordy, he abruptly cut her off. "Look, the guy is hired, and if you don't like it, you can kiss my ass."

Gordy was too preoccupied with expanding his business to worry about Raynoma's feelings. And as it turned out, his choice was ideal, because soon even Ray had to admit that "Barney Ales was phenomenal." But she was still slightly wary of the smooth-talking man: "I knew that a knife in the hand of Barney Ales would find its mark. And I started to watch my back."

CHAPTER 10

An Avalanche of Talent

FACING INCREASING DEMANDS FOR PROFESSIONAL AND BUSINESS advice from his growing roster of acts, Gordy created International Talent Management, Inc. (ITMI). For 10 percent of all of their earnings, it acted as personal management for the artists, getting them club and television bookings, providing career advice, handling personal finances, and even paying their taxes. Gordy's business-savvy sister Esther ran ITMI. And by managing his performers' careers, as well as being their record company, Gordy had created a musical version of the old Hollywood studio system, in which performers were signed, had their careers developed, and stayed contractually bound for many years. Few artists questioned whether their interests were best served by having their record label also act as their manager.

"A lot of acts were new," remembered the Marvelettes' lead singer, Gladys Horton. "They were young, and they were inexperienced. It was easy to take advantage of them." Motown's contracts, renewable only at the label's discretion, tied up the new artists for seven years.

"If I knew then what I know now," Martha Reeves told a reporter years later, "I'd have had my own lawyer and management firm."

"Money and fame weren't the issues to high school girls in the beginning," recalled the Supremes' Mary Wilson. "Motown was the club everyone wanted to join. It was just cool, you know? And if you are sixteen, cool is the meaning of life itself."

When Junior Walker was given a standard Motown contract to sign, he asked Gordy what exactly he was agreeing to.

"Can you read?" Gordy asked Walker.

"I can read some stuff, but not everything."

"Go ahead and sign," Gordy said. "We won't mess you around."

Independent managers and lawyers, however, would likely have objected to some of Motown's early practices that went unobjected to by the young acts. While Gordy allowed the artists to examine the label's books twice a year, no trade association—such as the Recording Industry Association of America, which was among other things responsible for certifying gold records—was allowed to see Motown's accounts. (Gordy did not want to pay the fees the association demanded for membership.) That policy didn't change until the late 1970s and explains why none of Motown's 1960s hits was ever officially certified as having gone gold. So when Gordy presented an artist with a "gold" record—as Smokey and the Miracles had received for "Shop Around"—it was literally just a disc spray-painted gold and framed. Marvin Gaye once took one of his gold records out of its frame, chipped off some paint, and discovered it was actually a Supremes record.

Also, whenever a producer/songwriter created a new song, it belonged to that producer. All the charges for the studio time, the musicians, the engineers, and the sound mixers were charged to the producer until the vocals were laid down. Once an artist sang the vocals, all the charges were then transferred to that artist's account. It did not matter if the artist did not want to record that song or even if it was never released, it was still a debt owed to Motown. And if two or more artists laid down lead vocals over a prerecorded instrument track—as happened frequently—the best vocal would get released, but the other acts would still be charged for the costs of the instrumental.

Gordy also cross-collateralized royalty accounts. If someone was signed to one label as a songwriter and another as a singer, as Smokey Robinson was, then costs used in preparing a recording could be charged against his songwriting royalties. Also, the royalties from a hit song could be used to offset outstanding debts on a recording from the same artist that had not earned any profit.

Motown paid all its artists, writers, and producers a weekly salary. However, the salary was only an advance against earnings. Some acts built substantial debts to Motown during fallow creative periods. While a manager might have objected vehemently to these practices—none of which was illegal, although some were not commonplace in the industry—no one raised any complaints, since it was Motown's own management company representing the artists as well.

In the case of Stevie Wonder, his mother willingly signed a Motown-prepared contract that allowed a company lawyer to act as his legal guardian, putting most of his money into a trust fund until he was twenty-one. And until that age, Wonder received only a $2.50 weekly allowance although he had earned hundreds of thousands in royalties. He had difficulty getting extra money when he wanted to buy musical instruments so he could practice at home or when he desired to buy his cash-strapped mother a house.

Beans Bowles, who helped manage the accounts held for those artists who were minors, later said, "The problem was that Berry kept those accounts going for too long. He didn't know when to stop treating people like kids. They wanted to be respected as adults."

Motown was organized as an S corporation, a legal structure that provided liability protection while passing all the profits directly to Gordy. He was extremely reluctant to share any company stock, although he eventually gave 2.5% each to his sister Esther and to Smokey Robinson.

But Gordy, even years later, strongly defended the company's contracts. He told *Playboy* that the many artists' complaints were "bull" and that Motown's contracts "were standard in the business. . . . Usually, when you sign an artist who's a nobody, whatever contract you give them is more than great. Six months later when they have a hit, the contract isn't good enough, at least according to the lawyers and manager who want to take over their careers."

Gordy gave the example of Elvis Presley, who had signed a management agreement with Colonel Tom Parker, giving away 50 percent of his earnings. "That was a lot," acknowledged Gordy, but, he speculated, "it may have been worth it to Elvis. . . . Maybe he made a reasonable deal." When pushed by *Playboy* about whether Motown was in a position to take advantage of young, inexperienced artists, Gordy said, "Absolutely, but so was every other company."

Gordy's arrangements were possible in part because he was fortunate to live in Detroit, a backwater music town. If Motown had been in the competitive environment of New York or Los Angeles, or even Nashville, a roster of lawyers and agents would likely have fought to represent every artist that walked through the doors. Also, in the other cities, aspiring artists had many labels to choose among. In Detroit, which at that time had the fourth-largest urban black population, there was no other record company to attract anyone with ambition and talent. Michigan law required only that a parent or legal guardian sign contracts for anyone under twenty-one. Many Motown artists were therefore accompanied to contract signings with only their parents, themselves often not high school graduates.

The music scene was so laid-back in Detroit that acts did not even send audition tapes. Rather, they just showed up at Hitsville and waited until someone either took notice or told them to get lost.

During the summer of 1960, as "Shop Around" was fast climbing the pop charts, Gordy walked through the tiny reception area and noticed Robert Bateman auditioning four teenage girls who were singing an a cappella version of the Drifters' "There Goes My Baby." They had come recommended to Bateman from a friend after they had won an amateur talent contest. Gordy noticed that one of the girls, skinny and with large eyes, seemed to burst with self-confidence and energy.

"Would you sing that again?" Gordy asked the lead singer.

"OK," she smiled. Then she leaned over to the other girls and whispered loudly, "That's Berry Gordy!"

When they finished, they stood waiting for Gordy's reaction. He smiled and nodded his head approvingly. They started giggling and patting one another in excitement.

"Are you going to sign us to a contract now?" the skinny one asked.

"What about school?" asked Gordy.

"We're all seniors," said the lead singer, though that was not exactly true.

"Come back and see me when you've graduated," Gordy told them. Although the girls were impatient, they had no choice. Still, they showed up almost daily at Hitsville, hanging out, making friends with producers and songwriters, and occasionally filling in as background singers for other artists. Those four girls—Diane Ross, Mary Wilson, Florence Ballard, and Betty McGlown—were from the Brewster projects, an enormous government-run housing complex of eight fourteen-story buildings built in the mid-1950s. For them, particularly the driven Flo Ballard, a record deal promised a way out.

Florence Ballard, sixteen, nicknamed "Blondie," was the eighth of thirteen children, with fair skin, auburn hair, and a curvaceous figure for her young age. She was the group's founder. Diane Ernestine Ross, fifteen, was the second of six children and had just moved into the projects in 1958. She had a boisterous personality and almost bouncy enthusiasm. The first thing most people noticed about her were her large, almost luminous eyes. Mary Wilson, also fifteen, the granddaughter of slaves, had only recently discovered that she had a talented voice when she sang in the school's glee club and then tried out for a talent show (where she met Flo Ballard, who beat her). Betty McGlown, seventeen, a tall, thin, dark-skinned girl, had been brought into the group by her boyfriend, Paul Williams, a member of the Primes.

The girls' families became fed up with their nonstop talk about music and almost daily rehearsals. "The fact that Berry Gordy did not sign us [at first]," recalled Mary Wilson, "only fueled our desire to be part of Motown."

To get experience, they played at local bars and sock hops. Only Betty McGlown began losing interest in pursuing this career. The other girls seemed more determined than ever. Mary Wilson slowly gained more confidence, Flo Ballard kept improving her voice, and Diane Ross had, in Mary Wilson's words, "become a real lady . . . [but] her stubbornness was almost childlike." Little things, at times, began to bother the other girls about Ross—for instance, they would all agree beforehand on how they would dress for a show in order to complement one another; then Ross sometimes showed up with a different outfit that made her stand out from the others. As they worked together, their act got better, but, Wilson noticed, "so did feelings of competitiveness, jealousy, and distrust." By the end of the summer, McGlown had quit, tired in part of trying to discipline Ross. And the girls feared their group might be finished before it even got going when Flo Ballard's mother called and told Ross and Wilson that Flo was also dropping out. A few weeks later, Ross and Wilson met Ballard, who had a faraway stare. After talking to her for hours, they learned what had happened: an acquaintance had raped her at knifepoint. She had been a virgin and was devastated by the brutality of the crime, coupled with the betrayal of trust.

"From this day on," recalled Mary Wilson, "I'd see Flo's basic personality undergo a metamorphosis, from being reticent and shy with a sassy front to being skeptical, cynical, and afraid of everyone and everything."

However, the girls eventually convinced Ballard to continue. And their persistence paid off when, in January 1961, they were finally signed to Motown. By then, Barbara Martin had replaced Betty McGlown.

"None of us thought about hiring legal counsel," remembered Mary Wilson. "Our parents trusted that Berry and Motown would do only what was best for us." The contract was vintage Motown, with the recording label acting as the booking agent, manager, accountant, and financial adviser. It paid the girls no advance, and only the company had the discretion to fire and hire new members. Motown was under no obligation to ever release any recording the group made. The royalty rate was so low that even if one of their records sold one million copies, each girl would earn only about five thousand dollars.

Signed as the Primettes—a sister group to the Primes, who later became three members of the Temptations—they needed, Gordy quickly decided, a better name. Flo Ballard was the one who coined the Supremes. (It won out over possibilities such as the Darleens, the Sweet Ps, the Melodees, the Royaltones, and the Jewelettes.) And soon the group had only three members once again, as Barbara Martin left when she became pregnant in October 1961. Nothing fazed the remaining girls, who brimmed with self-confidence. "Honey, we is terrific" was one of Ballard's favorite sayings.

They were the sweethearts of Hitsville. Wilson was popular with the men, Ballard had a sharp and sarcastic sense of humor, and Ross played an innocent waif who did her best to get others to do things for her. "Long before she was a star," said Gordy, "there was a drive in her that could not be denied. Nor could her appeal—which she used to full advantage."

As the girls were coming into Hitsville one day, they overheard Gordy ask the receptionist, "Where are the girls?"

Mary Wilson remembered what happened next: "Elbowing each other to beat a path to Berry's side, we cried, 'Here we are!' We were now Berry's shadows; wherever he went, we followed. Our mentor had finally taken us under his wing."

The other girls noticed more changes in Ross. She would at times tease her partners about their bodies or clothes or throw tantrums if she didn't get her way and then almost immediately laugh and pretend she had been joking. Wilson and Ballard did not think she was motivated by malice but rather just considered her insensitive. "At one time or another," recalled

Wilson, "each of us lost our patience with her, but compared to our main goal—the success of the Supremes—everything else was secondary." That easygoing attitude changed only later, when Ross, never one to walk away from anything she coveted, started to pursue some of her partners' boyfriends.

But the Supremes were just one group among literally dozens of artists who bombarded Gordy and Hitsville. Although most would never get a deal, enough talent passed through those doors to fuel what were to be Motown's boom years. Beyond artists who wanted a record deal, sometimes local musicians who were heavy drinkers or drug users stopped by and made contributions to lyrics or a musical arrangement in return for an immediate payment of a few hundred dollars, forgoing any contract or future royalty. While unorthodox, this practice helped Motown draw on just about every bit of talent in Detroit.

Even an event like the company's first-ever Christmas party, in 1960, was not free of the flood of new talent always looking for a chance to get Gordy's ear. He was exchanging jokes with Smokey Robinson and Mickey Stevenson when Gwen Gordy urged him to take a brief break.

"Berry, you've got to hear this guy," she urged him.

He looked exasperated and declined. But Gwen had the same stubborn streak as her brother. *No* did not stop her.

"But he's good, I'm tellin' you." She pointed determinedly at the window into the studio.

What Gordy saw when he looked in was a young man, slim and good-looking. He was sitting at the piano and stroking the keys as though in deep thought.

"That's Marvin Gaye," Gwen continued, not letting Gordy have a moment to back out. "He's been singing with Harvey and the Moonglows but wants to go solo."

"Why don't you put him on your label?" Gordy asked.

"He wants to be with you."

Gordy knew Gwen well enough to know she would not stop unless he at least met Gaye. He went in the studio and sat on the piano bench next to the twenty-one-year-old.

Gaye knew who Gordy was but acted cool and just kept playing soft jazz melodies without looking in his direction. His eyes on the keys, he said in a smooth voice, "Berry Gordy. How you doin', man?"

"Fine. I heard that you're a really good singer."

"I'm OK."

"Well, how about you doing something for me?"

"What do you want me to do?" Still, Marvin did not take his eyes off the piano keys as he kept playing lightly.

"I don't know," said Gordy. "Whatever you want."

Gaye did a jazzy version of "Mr. Sandman." Gordy listened and tried not to show how excited he was. He thought Gaye's voice was pure, honest, and soulful.

"Not bad. I like that. I really do."

"Thank you" was all Marvin Gaye said, his gaze still focused on the piano keys.

Gordy told him that he was special. He would, years later, say Gaye was "the truest artist I have ever known."

Gaye did not need to have Gordy say anything more. He was confident that "Berry [had] seen how big my talent was."

What Berry did not know then was that his sister Anna had become romantically entangled with the singer. Anna was a clever and respected thirty-seven-year-old businesswoman, running the record label bearing her own name, when she met Gaye. She was seventeen years his senior. "Gaye was probably the most desired man at Hitsville," recalled Raynoma Gordy. "He was lovable, romantic, charismatic, sensuous, and brilliantly talented. The girls . . . died over Marvin." Anna, who had previously been married to a saxophone player much older than she, was initially cool to the cocky Gaye, who wandered around with a group of giggling girls often trailing behind. They loved his unusual sense of style, which included a wide array of hats—berets, tam-o'-shanters, and large fedoras—all worn at rakish angles.

Gaye later said, "I was twenty and still a very lonely little boy." Anna cared for him, and he thought of her as an experienced teacher. "And I hope this doesn't sound too cold—that I knew just what I was doing. Marrying a queen might not make me king, but at least I'd have a shot at being prince."

Gaye's persistence paid off, as the couple soon started dating, and it was not long before they married.

•   •   •

A year before that marriage, in 1961, Berry's sister Gwen married another artist who was very important in Motown's early growth, Harvey Fuqua. Fuqua was tall, dark-skinned, and a sharp dresser, with his trademark silver silk suits and pointed snakeskin shoes. Women loved him. Fuqua had his own hit records as a founding member of the Moonglows, the premier vocal group at Chess Records during the 1950s (1958's "Ten Commandments of Love" was his biggest hit), and he was also a talented songwriter and producer. Fuqua had discovered Marvin Gaye (then spelling his name without the *e*) in Washington, D.C., and made Gaye a backup singer in the Moonglows. He became Gaye's mentor, similar to the relationship between Gordy and Smokey. Fuqua's eye for talent was so good that Chess Records employed him first as a scout, and then as an executive, while he continued to record albums. In 1960, Fuqua had joined Anna Records and soon was paying ten dollars weekly to rent a room from Esther Gordy Edwards and her husband, George. While working there he met Gwen. Although he established his own record label—Harvey and Tri-Phi—in 1961, he suffered from the cash-crunch and distribution problems that plagued many small labels. When Berry eventually asked Fuqua to join Motown as its promotion director, polishing the tour acts and dealing with radio stations and DJs, he gave up his own venture. Fuqua brought with him several remarkable performers he had discovered: besides Gaye there were the five men who made up the Spinners, who had already had a top-ten R&B hit; Junior Walker (who had thankfully changed his name from Autry DeWalt Jr.) and the All Stars; the five-foot-one Frederick "Shorty" Long (his big song would be 1964's "Devil with the Blue Dress," but his career ended tragically when he drowned in the Detroit River at the age of twenty-nine); and writer/producer/vocalist Johnny Bristol.

·   ·   ·

The Temptations had struggled for a few years with a couple of unknown, locally produced albums and a long list of appearances at Detroit's juke joints as their credits. Known then as Otis Williams and the Distants, the five-member group was led by Williams, a former teenage gang member who had found a straight path in music.

Williams provided smooth vocals in a group in which all the men had strong voices. He had flair and sported a processed pompadour that looked like patent leather. He had copied the hairstyle from Tony Curtis; swept back in front and on the sides, rolled up on top into cascading curls, and finished in the back with a sharp duck's ass, it was so large that even he admitted "you'd see it coming around the corner before you saw me." Unknown to Gordy, Williams was having a torrid affair with Mary Wells, Motown's new female star, so he wanted to be part of the new label for more reasons than his own career.

The Temptations might not have ended up at Motown if not for a bit of lucky timing and Gordy's good ear. Two years before signing with the label, the group was playing a hop at Saint Stephen's community center when Gordy walked in with Smokey and the Miracles. They were supposed to close the set that evening, but the crowd wouldn't let them take the stage because they kept screaming for more of the act that called themselves the Primes. After several encores, Otis Williams ran to the bathroom. There, Berry Gordy was at the adjoining urinal.

"I like what you guys do onstage," Gordy said, "and I like your record. If you ever leave where you are, come see me, because I'm starting my own label."

Williams felt "right there and then that I would take him up on his offer," even though he just merely thanked Gordy for the nice words.

Soon after that chance meeting, the Primes went through an upheaval. They left Johnnie Mae Matthews, their manager of two years, and also shook up their lineup; several members left. When Otis Williams called Gordy for an audition, he was still short two members. Those spots were filled only a week before they met with Mickey Stevenson.

Melvin Franklin possessed a deep, rich bass over which women swooned. Franklin, a fanatical Batman fan, liked his friends to call him the Black Batman, and almost everything he owned was inscribed with Batman logos. Paul Williams, an original member of the Primes, had, according to Gordy, "a heart-stopping baritone." Eddie Kendricks had an electrifying falsetto, and Elbridge "Al" Bryant was a strong tenor.

When they showed up for their audition, they had rechristened themselves the Elgins. After Stevenson heard them, he called Gordy to the makeshift rehearsal space in the basement, surrounded by boxes, lumber, and tools. Gordy offered them a contract on the spot. After they joined Motown, it was discovered that another group—which later joined

Motown—was already called the Elgins, so they brainstormed for a new name. The Temptations beat out also-rans including the Siberians and the El Domingos. Gordy later rechristened them the Pirates, but after a single under that name bombed he let them switch back to the Temptations.

At first, they just hung around Hitsville's offices. "We used to work in Motown's offices," recalled Franklin, "mopping the floors and taking out the trash. Everybody felt we were talented. We just wondered how long it would take."

The Temptations were more than just men with great voices. They also became known for striking showmanship, intricate stage choreography, and amazing wardrobes. Their stage act was athletic—Franklin had been a high school all-city basketball player, and Williams could turn flips in midair. And they indulged their fans with urbane harmonies and elaborate chore-ography executed with deadpan diligence. Eventually, under the guidance of Motown's Cholly Atkins, they developed the Temptations Walk—a simple slide of the feet and swing of the hips—that became their trademark, much as Jackie Wilson had done with the split or James Brown did singing with a microphone stand. Their first stage outfits—now on display at Motown's Historical Museum—were green sharkskin suits, ruffled white shirts, and heavy black boots. Their pants were so tight that they looked sprayed on. In 1964, when they were booked for nine days at the Brooklyn Fox Theatre to-gether with British singer Dusty Springfield and Marvin Gaye, among oth-ers, they sent the crowd wild in their bright purple suits offset with large white buttons, flowing white shirts, and white patent-leather shoes. "It was about style and elegance," recalled Otis Williams, "but also suggested ro-mance and, frankly, sex, something Paul [Williams] deliberately made part of our image."

"The Tempts epitomized tall, dark, and handsome," said Gordy. "Up on that stage were five stars, each of whom could have been a lead singer."

·   ·   ·

Not long after signing the Tempts, as they were called around Hitsville, Gordy was in his office having breakfast when Mickey Stevenson ran in, out of breath.

"BG, you got to come hear this little kid *now!*"

Gordy trusted Stevenson and knew somebody special must be in the studio. As they rushed downstairs, Stevenson told Gordy that Ronnie White, one of the Miracles, had brought a kid in for an audition. Gordy was surprised to find a young blind boy who was singing, playing the bongos, and blowing on a harmonica. He was a whirlwind of activity. Gordy did not think his voice was that good, but he found his playing, especially the harmonica, "infectious." The eleven-year-old was soon signed as Stephen Hardaway Judkins.

He had been born on May 13, 1950, as Steveland Morris, the third child of six in a low-income family in Saginaw, Michigan. His birth was premature by a month, and complications had set in from too much oxygen in his incubator. That caused a dislocated nerve in one eye and a cataract in the other, worsened by a condition called retrolental fibroplasia that resulted in a permanent loss of sight. He had no recollection of ever seeing anything, no memories of what people's faces looked like or what colors were.

His mother, deeply religious and superstitious, took him to a series of faith healers and seers, seeking a cure. It wasn't until he was seven that Stevie fully understood that he was blind and different from his siblings, although he still didn't quite understand what it meant. He just assumed that everyone had the same limitations. When he learned how his disability made him different, he became able to calm his mother's concern. "I know it used to worry my mother," he said, "and I know she prayed for me to have some sight someday. So finally I just told her that I was happy being blind, and I thought it was a gift from God. I think she felt better after that." And largely to compensate for his lack of sight, Stevie worked hard to make his hearing and memory acute.

After the family moved from Saginaw to Detroit, Stevie's mother at first kept him inside the new apartment, not only because she feared the strange new streets but also so he could learn the new furniture layout. It was there, bored, that he began pounding out rhythmically on pans and tabletops. His mother bought him a harmonica, and he soon was playing and singing his own ditties. His family noticed that he seemed to have natural musical talent—he was the only one in the family with any—and fortunately for him they encouraged it. His mother, a member of Detroit's Whitestone Baptist Church, had him join the choir, with his clear and distinctive voice.

After learning of Stevie's musical interests, the Detroit Lions Club, at an annual Christmas party for blind children, gave him a set of drums. Soon Stevie was pounding away, often to the consternation of neighbors and even his parents. When a neighbor moved and did not know what to do with her banged-up piano, she gave it to the ecstatic youngster. Another neighbor donated bongo drums, which were always with him on his apartment's front porch. And he was never without his portable radio, listening omnivorously to R&B and jazz artists. Even when his mother took him for a haircut, Stevie had the radio pressed against his ear, bopping slightly in the chair, making the cut a challenge. On his school bus—which he took to attend special classes for kids with sight disabilities—he remembered being the only one who listened to B. B. King. "I loved B. B. King," he recalled. He did not then know he was the only black kid on the bus.

Stevie had decided he wanted to become a minister. That ended when a local churchgoer saw him pounding the bongos on his front porch. She thought that playing such worldly music was a sin and reported him to the deacon. "They told me to leave," he recalled. "And that's how I became a sinner." So he spent more time practicing with his instruments and singing on the building steps, frequently with a friend his age, John Glover. In one of those wonderful bits of serendipity that helps propel a talented person onto the right career path, Glover's adult cousin was Ronnie White. One day in 1960, White stopped by to visit just at the moment Stevie was giving one of his impromptu front-porch sessions. White recognized his special talent and arranged Stevie's Hitsville audition.

With all its musical instruments, Motown was like a giant toy shop to Stevie. His fellow students, and even teachers, were discouraging him from music. "People at school told me I couldn't make it," he recalled, "that I would end up making potholders instead. But after I thought I was going to be a musician, I became very determined simply to prove those people wrong."

Other artists and musicians at Motown helped Stevie. Everybody was protective of the youngster, and they politely ignored the times he sometimes burst into a live recording session, unable to see the red light that warned everyone else to stay outside. As they got to know him better, they fell in love with his mischievous sense of humor and even learned to listen patiently as he talked incessantly in abstract terms. And they liked that he never used his blindness as an excuse but instead joked about it. Stevie would have someone read him a passage from a book until he memorized it. Then he would pretend to others that he was reading the book. Other times, he'd take a bicycle as if he was about to ride it around the neighborhood; or he'd have to be pulled from behind the driver's seat of someone's car as he threatened to drive away. And when not joking about his eyesight, he relentlessly mimicked everyone at Hitsville from Gordy on down.

Stevie wanted to use his real name—Steveland Morris—though most at Hitsville agreed he needed a stage name. Clarence Paul, his conductor, called him Little Stevie. One day in the studio, as Stevie seemed a whirlwind of energy, Gordy remarked to no one in particular, "Boy! That kid's a wonder." The name stuck.

•   •   •

Not every artist just strolled into Hitsville and pleaded to be signed. Sometimes, Gordy had to go after hot acts, and he did not always get them. Levi Stubbs, Lawrence Payton, Abdul "Duke" Fakir, and Renaldo "Obie" Benson had been around for nearly a decade by the time Hitsville was attracting attention. Having changed their name early in their career from the Four Aims to the Four Tops, they were seasoned performers. They had toured with Billy Eckstine and played Las Vegas, in addition to years of dates in the Borscht Belt and in small song-and-dance revues, racking up countless miles touring in a dilapidated station wagon.

Initially, critics had chided them as merely a genial soul barbershop quartet. But Gordy saw them as something much better. "Smooth, classy, and polished, they were big stuff," he said. "I wanted them bad." Gordy's early songwriting partner, Billy Davis, had briefly been a road manager for the Tops in the 1950s, and later wrote some songs for them. Davis had convinced Gordy the group could be much bigger than a mere lounge-touring act.

Gordy also admired the tight bonds among the four singers. He figured that if they were so loyal to one another—none had ever broken away for a solo career—they would be equally loyal to Motown.

Gordy invited them to his office. Levi Stubbs spoke for the band. "We'd like to sign with you, but we heard you won't let artists take the contracts away from the office."

"That's right," Gordy acknowledged matter-of-factly.

"Why not?" Stubbs asked.

"Because when I do, they don't come back." The group laughed. Gordy continued. "I would rather have your attorney come here to the office, take as much time as you need, and go over them. This way we'll be right here to answer questions and explain what we do that other companies don't."

Gordy had made that same offer to the Temptations when he gave them a contract after their audition. They had taken him up on it by bringing in a Detroit lawyer recommended by some friends. Fortunately for Gordy, their lawyer was better versed at divorces and workmen's-comp cases than entertainment law, and he told them the contract was "standard" and recommended they sign it. "What he didn't know," recalled Otis Williams, "and we didn't know would haunt us for years to come."

The Four Tops didn't know about the Tempts' experience, but they still felt uneasy about having a lawyer come to Motown's offices for a hurried review. Gordy tried to assuage their concerns by launching into his standard sales pitch about how Motown was dedicated not just to churning out hits but also to building star careers. The four artists listened carefully, and when Gordy finished they admitted they were impressed. But again they asked to take the contracts with them so their lawyer could review them at his leisure.

Gordy gave them the contracts, against his better judgment. They did not return.

CHAPTER 11

Hitting the Groove

ALTHOUGH THE FUTURE OF MOTOWN LAY WITH MUSIC LIKE SMOKEY Robinson's "Shop Around," the label paid many of its bills from 1960 to 1962 with less distinctive blues releases. Popular R&B singer Little Willie John's sister Mable—who had been Gordy's driver for a while—had moderate success with her 1960 and 1961 releases "Looking for a Man," and "Who Wouldn't Love a Man Like That." Singin' Sammy Ward had "Big Joe Moe" and other hits, sometimes pairing with the strong-voiced Sherri Taylor. And Amos Milburn, a hard-drinking, piano-playing bluesman, had "Return of the Blues Boss" in 1962. But by the end of 1962, few of the blues artists were still with Motown. They had done what Gordy had wanted—generated cash—but they did not fit with his plan for pursuing the most lucrative part of the business: pop. When she eventually left, Mable John told Raynoma, "Our directions are diverging. I'm R&B, Mr. Gordy's going pop."

The success of the Miracles' "Shop Around" spurred a burst of recording inside Motown. Gordy now employed fifty people. In a 1962 interview with the *Detroit Free Press*, Gordy said, "The talent here [Detroit] is terrific and was largely untapped when we came along." When he said that he was in the business of "popular music," the reporter asked him what that meant. "It is what the majority of what the people buy," said Gordy. That attitude allowed the word to spread quickly in black neighborhoods that if you had a decent voice or were talented in putting verses to music, Motown might be a place to make dreams happen. Local kids camped out on the front lawn or sometimes lined the sidewalk, trying to get someone's attention or even a glimpse of one of the stars.

Berry realized that it was impossible for him to produce all the new work coming his way, so he gladly accepted volunteers. When Smokey Robinson suggested ideas for working with Mary Wells, Gordy gave him a green light. Then in quick order came Clarence Paul, Mickey Stevenson's assistant, who wanted to work with Stevie Wonder; Stevenson hooked up with Gordy's brother George, who huddled with Marvin Gaye. Gordy personally, however, took time to develop hits for the Supremes and the Temptations.

Because some of those now wearing producers' hats had no experience, Gordy created a Motown department modeled after one he had learned about during his assembly-line days at Lincoln-Mercury. Dubbed "Quality Control," its purpose was to ensure that the Motown sound had an identifiable beat and the right tone. The idea was that all the producers first had to run their mixes past Quality Control, which then sent along the best ones to a weekly Friday-morning meeting, where Gordy and others picked upcoming releases. In Motown, although departments had impressive-sounding titles, often only a few people made up an entire division. Berry thought Quality Control needed only one good person but at first was thwarted in finding someone with a strong opinion and good ear—not a performer or producer who might make decisions based on jealousy or competitiveness.

He settled quite unexpectedly on Billie Jean Brown, whom he affectionately called "the kid." A journalism student at the local Cass Technical High School, she had spotted an employment notice to become Loucye Gordy's assistant, writing press releases and liner notes for nine dollars per week. When she was made the company's first librarian, she diligently organized the tapes, which had been in complete disarray. Her salary was boosted to twenty-two dollars per week. She had also helped Raynoma with Jobete's publishing duties and had caught Berry's attention by running him out of Loucye's office when she thought he was interfering with her bill-payment work—he liked that she was not impressed that he was the company's owner. His decision to pick her came one day when he happened to notice she was huddled in her office—a corner of the shipping room—listening to some 45s.

Gordy asked her which record she liked the best.

"You mean which one do I hate least, don't you?"

Before Gordy could answer, she went on in considerable detail about why she disliked each song. That was good enough for him. He put her in charge of Quality Control. "I could always be counted on to give my honest opinion," Brown recalled.

The department became a critical cog in Motown's production machinery and also a training ground for many musicians. (For instance, Richard Street, the former Distants' singer who eventually replaced the Tempts' Paul Williams, spent six years working there.) Recordings run through Quality Control were rated on a one-to-ten scale. On a normal Monday, there were about twenty recordings to review. Anything that scored under a five was rejected. Those above five made it to the Friday meeting, at which everyone stood up and sang the company song when Gordy entered. In order to generate camaraderie, Gordy had held a contest to devise the best song, something that expressed the pride in what everyone was doing. Not surprisingly, Smokey won:

> *Oh, we have a very swinging company,*
> *Working hard from day to day.*
> *Nowhere will you find more unity,*
> *Than at Hitsville, U.S.A.*

The other three choruses were just as corny, but apparently many of the label's workers believed the words.

•   •   •

It was at the Friday meetings that Brown's authority ended. "Of course," she said, "the final decision was always Mr. Gordy's. After all, it was his money."

Gordy controlled those meetings, attended by Brown, as well as some from promotion and a few department heads. "I did try to control almost everything," Gordy admitted to *Playboy* years later. "It was my ball game, my vision, my dream."

Careers were literally made or broken there, and as a result everyone wanted to attend. Even the producers who had not made Billie Jean's Quality Control cut wanted to be there to protest her decision. And Berry did not mind if some at the meeting were from the noncreative side—to

Gordy, they might provide reactions similar to those of typical record buyers. The votes of noncreative workers counted the same as that of any producer.

Berry set three ironclad rules for the meetings. First, no producer could vote on his own record; next, Gordy could overrule a majority vote; and finally, anyone who was more than five minutes late was locked out. The last rule was particularly important, since many of the artistic types who populated Motown's hallways paid little attention to punctuality. Usually, however, after a few lockouts they became much better at managing their time. The one exception was once, early on, when Smokey—the only performer allowed in—arrived just barely five minutes late. He literally banged on the door and begged to be let in. Gordy relented. "After all," Gordy later commented, "it was Smokey."

What made the Friday meetings so productive was that Gordy encouraged people to be honest and blunt. He promised there would be no reprisals for anything said, and it was a pledge he never went back on over the years. No one recalls anyone being punished because of something said at those meetings. And when people realized they were truly free to say whatever they thought, frank expression became not just a right but rather a duty. No one was free from criticism, and Gordy often led the attack.

"Berry Gordy is one of the most critical people in the world," said Smokey. "He built Motown by criticizing—to the point of pain—every song and every production. He was unmerciful. If he could punch a hole in your product, he would. If he couldn't, he knew it was bulletproof and had a chance at chart action."

One of the biggest gripes voiced by former workers and artists is that Gordy sometimes crossed the line from legitimate criticism to outright humiliation. Even high-ranking executives described instances in which they felt Gordy publicly stripped away their dignity. At one meeting he called the label's top executives "a dumb bunch of niggers." At another, with Diana Ross present, Gordy instructed one of Ross's assistants to fix a malfunctioning tape recorder on the other side of the room by crawling across the room on her knees. He did not want her to disrupt the meeting by walking around. Struggling halfway across on her knees, she finally burst into tears, got up, and ran out. Gordy just continued as though nothing unusual had happened.

While the words could sometimes become heated, those unique product-evaluation meetings were key to Motown's growth. The company's strength was that it was small and nimble, able to respond to changes in the marketplace, and not encumbered with a burdensome bureaucracy that stifled creativity. Instead, thinking "outside the box," a later corporate maxim, seemed natural to early Motown workers. And there was also a spirit based on their high-risk venture, a feeling that they had little to lose and much to gain.

"People had a lot more freedom then than I think outsiders ever realized," Lamont Dozier, one of the label's chief songwriters, recalled. "[Gordy] let you do what you wanted to do. You didn't have to get permission other than say, 'I want to go into the studio, and I want to cut this.' Nobody looked at what you were doing. When you sent it to him finished, either he liked it or he didn't like it."

Gordy had some sense that the label was making history, and he tape-recorded the product-evaluation gatherings. Eventually, Gordy openly taped many other meetings with his workers and artists. "He used to walk around with a frigging tape recorder," said sales executive Phil Jones. "He recorded everything. He taped every meeting." (Gordy evidently still has those tapes but has never released them.)

Gordy prided himself not only that Motown eschewed a cumbersome bureaucracy while encouraging creative thinking but also that there was no punishment for failing. A bad record or failure to make a hit or sign an act might be cause for disappointment but wasn't going to get anyone fired in the early days.

"I never wanted people to feel how I felt in school—dumb," recalled Gordy. "It was an atmosphere that made you feel no matter how high your goals, they were reachable, no matter who you were."

Gordy liked to talk about the company as an extended family, marked by unusual bonds of closeness as well as fierce competition. Friendships formed easily among people sharing the same interests and many of the same hopes and aspirations. Even when they were not working in the studio, musicians, producers, background players, and others came to Motown just to "hang around." The kitchen was a popular spot, where Miss Lilly, a heavyset, slow-talking, elderly woman, turned out comfort food, including spicy chili, hot dogs, fried chicken, and piles of creamy mashed potatoes. "Family" was anyone who was in the building at 1:00 P.M., which was lunchtime.

"It was a great place to hang out," recalled Otis Williams. "Everyone there was young and driven by the same dreams. You didn't have to explain yourself; we all had that passion about music and success. You wouldn't think twice about pitching in to help with whatever had to be done, whether it was singing backgrounds or mopping the floor. Joining Motown was more like being adopted by a big loving family than being hired by a company. This isn't just nostalgia talking, either. It really was a magical time."

Many others, including Mary Wilson, Martha Reeves, Marvin Gaye, and even less famous workers such as Earl Van Dyke, described the early days of the company as one happy family.

On any given day, a visitor to Hitsville might find Pops Gordy doing some repairs on the house, or Smokey Robinson cutting the grass. Everybody pitched in as if the business was his or her own. A music class was offered on Wednesdays in a small upstairs room to anyone who wanted to come. Taught by Raynoma, one of the few people at Hitsville with formal music training, it was evident early on that while many of the artists and songwriters were naturally gifted, they might not know what chord they were playing or writing.

Those who came aboard during this time often stayed with the company for decades. Fay Hale became head of the processing department, Frances Heard the tape librarian, and Ann Dozier, Lamont's wife, joined as Loucye's assistant. Gordy also got his first secretary, Rebecca Nichols. He grew to trust her, and she stayed with him for more than thirty years.

"[And] you could find a Gordy lurking in practically every department," said Gordy. "My own family was and is close," noted Smokey Robinson, "but I'd never seen anything like the Gordys—four sisters and four brothers who made it clear to their lovers and spouses and anyone else that their family came first. The Gordys took care of business, but mainly they took care of each other."

The nepotism evidently did not bother anyone. Even those who later clashed with Gordy give him his due for creating a special environment and empowering the artists.

"Berry inspired us then," recalled Otis Williams. "He knew what he was about, had a lot of confidence, and was full of piss and vinegar. He knew he was going to make it and made you believe you would, too. We couldn't know then that we'd just latched onto the tail of a comet, but that feeling was in the air."

The concept that the company was literally an extended family also created problems, however. It meant that Gordy acted as a domineering father
figure who occasionally treated his acts like wayward children. This pater-
nalism, which might have been comforting to many artists early in their
careers, seemed condescending as they grew older and gained more confidence. One of Gordy's favorite lines when someone complained was "I'll
take care of you." That was enough in the company's formative years to buy
some time, but it later fell on deaf ears as the artists realized the concept of
"family" did not extend to making the business a cooperative venture.

"To exploit is not necessarily bad," said Gordy. "To make use of someone's talent in a positive way benefits everyone. It was that 'exploitation' that
made many of them stars, big stars, and superstars. . . . Stardom affects people in many different ways, and some can make it through the vicious cycle.
Others get caught up in drugs, some go mad with power, some forget who
their friends are, some forget who they are."

But not only did friendships thrive and fall by the wayside; romances
among the small group also flourished and failed as well. In Motown's early
years, it seemed almost more like Peyton Place than a record company.

Smokey became the first to marry another artist, Claudette. All of
Gordy's sisters married within the business, Gwen to Harvey Fuqua, Anna
to Marvin Gaye, and Loucye to saxophonist Ron Wakefield. Gordy's niece
Iris married producer Johnny Bristol. Eventually, Mary Wells married Rayber singer Herman Griffin; the Marvelettes' Wanda Young married the
Miracles' Bobby Rogers; Georgeanna Dobbins, also of the Marvelettes,
married the Contours' Billy Gordon; and A&R director Mickey Stevenson
married singer Kim Weston.

More than marriages, however, affairs flourished, and it often seemed
one needed a scorecard to know who was with whom. "There were dozens
of little affairs between this singer and that producer," said Marvin Gaye.
"Show people tend to be sensualists. It's not our fault." The Supremes'
Mary Wilson was with Eddie Kendricks and then later with Duke Fakir of
the Four Tops; sixteen-year-old Gladys Horton of the Marvelettes paired
off with Hubert Johnson of the Contours. Otis Williams of the Temptations went with the Supremes' Flo Ballard. And Diana Ross had affairs,
besides her long one with Berry Gordy, with Smokey Robinson, Eddie
Kendricks, and Brian Holland. Even gossip of gay affairs, most of it incor-

rect, kept making the company rumor circuit, including whether a young fan, Tony Turner, who had become a hanger-on at Motown, had an affair with Eddie Kendricks. Gossipers liked to notice that many butch-looking girls waited just as eagerly outside the dressing rooms of the female Marvelettes or Vandellas as female groupies waited for the Temptations or Four Tops.

"Sometimes it seemed as if the company was just one big bed," recalled Tony Turner, who became a roadie for some of the Motown artists like Mary Wilson and the Temptations. (In 1994, Turner submitted a draft biography of Gordy to New York publishers. The *New York Post* reported that in one chapter he claimed that Gordy had had a ménage à trois in Paris with a Motown singer and a French woman and had pressured some Motown stars into having abortions. Gordy was furious, denied the charges, and filed a $250 million libel suit against Turner. The book has not been published.)

·   ·   ·

With the staff growing quickly, Gordy faced for the first time the prospect of letting someone outside his family handle Motown's finances. Up to now, that had been the responsibility of Esther's husband, George Edwards. But he had recently been elected to a fifth term in the state legislature, and Motown was finally too much for him to handle in his spare time. (Gordy had contributed to Edwards's original election to the legislature by persuading Jackie Wilson to record a campaign song—"By George, Let George Do It.")

Gordy fretted about bringing in an outsider. A Detroit attorney, Sue Weisenfeld, who had done some work for Motown, set up a meeting between Gordy and Harold Noveck, a tax attorney. Gordy told him, however, that he didn't need a tax attorney but rather someone to manage his finances.

"It just so happens," said Noveck, "my brother is a partner in an accounting firm."

Gordy didn't know if he should be looking for an accountant either, but he decided to interview several candidates, including Noveck's brother. He placed an ad in the *Detroit Free Press* and after a week had forty résumés. Then he skimmed the paper's financial section and developed ten questions—to which he didn't know the answers—which he wanted each applicant to respond to in writing.

Gordy knew nothing about accounting. He invariably tried to steer the discussion around to something with which he was familiar, especially sports and boxing. Inventing the name of some welterweight champion, he would see if the applicant admitted he had never heard of the person or if he tried to lie. If he said he recognized the fictitious name, he had failed Gordy's "bullshit test" and was off the list. With some of the others, Gordy brought up Charlie Parker and referred to him as the "greatest tenor-sax player in the world." Parker actually played alto. And still at other times, he might ask why a bird in the hand was better than two in the bush. "I wanted," Gordy recalled, "to make sure that they spoke a language that was common to me."

When he finally met Sidney Noveck, Berry discovered an entirely different type of person from the others he had interviewed. Instead of someone trying to please him by pretending he knew a little something about everything, Noveck said he'd rather not comment since he knew so little about the things about which Gordy was asking. Short, plain, unassuming, Noveck did not try to sell himself. He answered only six of Berry's ten queries on the questionnaire, the only applicant to fail to answer all of them. When Gordy asked him about the other four, Noveck replied in his flat voice, "I'm not sure. I'd like to check them out and get back to you."

"Oh, maybe you ought to take up accounting," Gordy said, trying to add some levity to the dull meeting.

"I did," Noveck replied, not getting the joke. "I don't want to give you answers that may not be correct."

"I understand." Gordy said good-bye to Noveck and thought he would never see him again. He then pored over the questionnaires of the other applicants and reviewed his interview notes. He settled on one and decided to offer him the job.

The following day, before Gordy made the call, Sidney Noveck telephoned.

"Mr. Gordy, I have the answers to those other questions."

"I wanted to say, 'No shit,'" Gordy later wrote, "but he was a sweet little man. So I just said, 'Okay, what are they?'"

"Question five applies to a tax case that was recently heard. The law had been changed. And on question eight I had to check the record to be absolutely correct." Noveck went on in substantial detail with his answers and reasoning. As he was talking, Gordy realized he was precisely the person he wanted running his personal and business finances. "One of the luckiest days in my life was when I met the Noveck brothers," he later said.

The Novecks were godsends to Gordy. Not only were they scrupulously honest, but they also made Gordy a more careful and responsible business-man. Raynoma Gordy dubbed them the "definitive 'no' men—any pro-posals for company improvements received an automatic 'negatory.' Berry thought they walked on water, and anybody looking at Berry's bank ac-counts would think so too." As a team—accountant and tax attorney—they worked hard to save Gordy even small amounts in his business, sums that totaled millions of dollars over the years. And they often stood their ground and fought with him over financial decisions they thought impru-dent or risky. Years later, during IRS audits, the Novecks' painstaking work always paid off—there were no extra assessments or findings against the company, a remarkable achievement for almost any corporation, especially one in the entertainment business.

Jay Lasker, who was president of Motown in the eighties, referred to the Novecks as "those Jews." Although he personally disliked them, Lasker be-lieved the Noveks were "the reason Motown Records survived." And he used to enjoy recounting a story in which Gordy had supposedly shared some cash payments for some records with another Motown executive. When Harold Noveck learned of it, he insisted Gordy pay taxes on the cash receipts, which he did. A few years later, the other executive had a falling out with Gordy and threatened to report him to the IRS. Gordy merely smiled and told him he had paid his taxes, so the threat was useless. "That's why I love Harold Noveck," Gordy told Lasker.

Finding the Novecks allowed Gordy to focus exclusively on music. But in the summer of 1961, Gordy was learning a new, hard lesson from the success of "Shop Around": "A big hit could put you out of business," he said, only somewhat sardonically.

In those days, independent distributors usually paid record companies for a current smash only if they knew they were going to get others coming down the pipeline. The distributors would otherwise keep the money from those companies unlucky enough to turn out only a one-hit wonder. Mo-town had no new hits coming along, and many distributors withheld pay-ments, which in turn caused Gordy to fall behind in payments to pressing plants and other suppliers. And although Motown had released twenty albums in its first full year, none was as big as Gordy had hoped. He was owed money on many of those records as well as on "Shop Around."

But just when Gordy became nervous about the company's finances—Loucye had come to him with a distressing report about how much money they owed—he found salvation at a Friday product-evaluation meeting. The song was a catchy little tune—"Please Mr. Postman"—by the Marvelettes, consisting of fifteen-year-old Gladys Horton, Wanda Young, Katherine Anderson, Georgeanna Dobbins, and Juanita Cowart. Gordy had seen them first at a talent show at Inkster High School, in a Detroit suburb. They were originally signed as the Marvels, but Gordy decided the Marvelettes was a catchier name. (When they auditioned for Motown, they humbly called themselves the Casingettes—"all agree they can't sing yet." Motown would have to give written excuses to get them out of school so they could appear on *American Bandstand*.)

A new production team—Brian Holland and Robert Bateman—calling themselves "Brianbert" was responsible for "Please Mr. Postman." Gordy was especially proud of Holland, who had "brilliant producing instincts," though this song was the first tangible evidence of his talent. Bateman, who along with Gordy was the best person at Motown in editing two-track tapes with a razor blade, left less than a year later, but Holland stayed and played a major role in Motown's success.

"Please Mr. Postman" became the company's second million-selling record and its first number-one pop hit. (It was actually the first number-one pop hit ever produced in Detroit.) It was, for a black-owned recording company, with black artists, a remarkable feat. Many inside the company mistakenly thought that the Marvelettes would be the label's next monster act, but the group never again matched the popularity of that song.

Motown was on its own. Success for a black singer during this time was sales of between one hundred thousand and three hundred thousand 45s. For a black artist that led at most to headliner status on the so-called Chitlin Circuit, a collection of ex-vaudeville houses in black neighborhoods. "I played the Chitlin Circuit with comics, dogs, and one-legged dancers," recalled Smokey Robinson. "It was bizarre and brutal, especially down South, where you couldn't get a hotel for the color of your skin and the accommodations weren't fit for a dog."

The black-music genre was filled with one-hit wonders, as many of the independent distributors emphasized the momentary hit single over the development of an artist. And while there certainly had been successful black artists—Nat King Cole, Johnny Mathis, Miles Davis, Thelonious Monk, Sam Cooke, and Ray Charles among them—their records had been released on the major white-owned labels, RCA, Columbia, Decca, and Atlantic. Other black-owned labels had tried hard to do what Motown was achieving, but none had flourished. Black Swan, the first, founded in 1921, lasted three years before closing shop. Texas's Duke-Peacock struggled with its blues roster until ABC eventually bought it. Chicago's Vee-Jay Records, which had a talented roster of solo artists, R&B groups, and good blues singers, might have accomplished what Motown did, were it not for the poor family management that ran it into bankruptcy in the 1960s.

Gordy's management, and the talent he had pulled together, both on the artists' side of the ledger as well as with workers from PR to sales, made the difference. And it was Barney Ales, running sales, whom Gordy credited with the tremendous commercial success of "Please Mr. Postman."

Gordy knew Ales's best attribute was that he "was an extremely tough negotiator." "I knew I was the best," Ales said, recalling the cockiness for which he was widely known. "I would challenge them to try and replace me. They couldn't. I knew that." Gordy decided to take advantage of Ales's talent to help break the logjam with distributors who were slow in paying. One day, shortly after the song had hit the top, Gordy called Ales into his office and chided him for selling to distributors that Loucye had alerted everyone were on hold for nonpayment. Ales didn't hesitate before letting Gordy have it.

"If we don't ship to those areas, that's gonna kill us. We'll lose chart positions. We'll lose momentum. We won't have hits, and we'll be in more trouble."

But Gordy knew that was wrong. The collection problem would continue if Ales only made his money based on how many units he sold. So Gordy told Ales about his new emphasis on bill collections and then surprised him by putting him in charge.

Barney was not happy. But soon he was calling the distributors he knew and explaining his predicament. As it turned out, Ales was much better at setting up an efficient collection system than Loucye had been. "I was very tight on distributors and what and when they paid," said Ales. "If you owed us one thousand dollars, we wanted the money. I'd really push them and cut the distributor off fast if they weren't paying. You had to know how much slack to cut them, and I would know if they were good or not for the money. I would pull the records and give them to a competitor." Before long, Gordy was ecstatic that money that had been delayed for months started flowing in. Ales did such a good job at collecting the money that when he soon asked Gordy for a raise, he got it without a fight.

·   ·   ·

The success of "Please Mr. Postman" seemed somehow to further loosen the mood around the company and led to a burst of new songwriting and recording. In the spring of 1962, the Miracles released "I'll Try Something New," one of Gordy's favorite Smokey compositions. That was followed by another successful release, "You've Really Got a Hold on Me." Gordy, who had become competitive with Smokey to be recognized as the label's hit songwriter, countered with "Do You Love Me?," a song that he not only produced but sang the vocals for the demo. Whether or not his coworkers were just schmoozing him, they almost convinced Gordy to release the song with him as the artist, but at the last moment he deferred. On the day of the final cut, he decided to use the Temptations, but they were nowhere to be found. (They had gone to a local Baptist church to watch some gospel singers, but no one looked there.) So instead, Gordy scoured the hallways and found the Contours, a local group of six young men. That he could so easily pick another group illustrates Gordy's unstated belief that the singer was to serve the song, not vice versa. It also meant that Motown producers could, for instance, freely use additional voices on the recordings of the Marvelettes in order to make them sound richer and fuller. No one told the Marvelettes until years later.

Raynoma and others had thought the Contours "looked like hoodlums" when they had first arrived at the company a year earlier. One of the Contours, Hubert Johnson, was Jackie Wilson's cousin. It was Wilson who had opened the door for them at Motown. But Gordy had been unimpressed when he listened to them in a lackluster audition. "Uh-huh. Thanks, guys. Come back in, oh, maybe in six months." They actually returned a half hour later. "We sang the same song the same way," recalled Joe Billingslea, "and got our contracts half an hour later."

They had not released a record since being signed. When Gordy informed them they could cut the song he had written, they started shouting and hugging him so hard that he gasped and had to tell them to stop. He had picked a good group. Billy Gordon's screaming and scratchy lead vocals, coupled with the soulful sound of the background singers, made "Do You Love Me?" Motown's biggest 1962 release. This led to a seven-year contract for the group known as much for their onstage gymnastics and tongue-in-cheek skits as for their wild singing.

Another performer who benefited from being at the right place at the right time was Martha Reeves, who had been part of a four-girl group called the Del-Fi's before working as Mickey Stevenson's secretary in the A&R department. Her break came one day when Mary Wells didn't show up for a recording session. Stevenson wanted someone behind the microphone while the studio musicians laid down their tracks. He picked Reeves, who he knew was an aspiring singer. She only had to stand there and do nothing, he told her. But when the music began, she started singing—a clear, powerful voice filled with emotion that made the studio workers stop and others nearby walk down the hallway to see who was belting out the lyrics.

"I had been patiently waiting for my big break in the recording studio," Reeves later recalled, "so instead of taking it lightly, I imagined that this song was mine and sang it as best I could."

"She sounds good on this song," Gordy said when he heard her singing. "Let's release it on her."

She brought in her ex–Del-Fi's colleagues, and Gordy signed two of them—Rosalind Ashford and Annette Sterling—along with her. He told them they had fifteen minutes to come up with a new name—he didn't want to run into any legal problems since they had performed as the Del-Fi's before coming to his label. They considered—and luckily rejected—the Pansies and the Tillies. Finally, Reeves, who had just seen singer Della Reese perform at a local Baptist church, combined *Della* with part of the name of the street she lived on, Van Dyke, to come up with the Vandellas.

The news from Hitsville was not just about those artists releasing debut songs. Mary Wells had become a star. Flaunting a diva attitude onstage and dressing in sparkling gowns and outlandish wigs ranging from black bouffants to bright blond ponytails, the teenager seemed to be the solo female star Motown knew it needed to become a major label. Smokey had given

Wells "The One Who Really Loves You," "Two Lovers," and "You Beat Me to the Punch."

And Marvin Gaye was just starting to make a name for himself. Even before he had a hit, he was brimming with self-confidence that bordered on cockiness. "I don't compare myself to Beethoven," he once told a journalist. "I must make that clear. I just think that I'm capable of all he was capable of. I think the only thing between me and Beethoven is time. Beethoven had it from the beginning. I'm acquiring it."

Some who knew Gaye believe his massive egocentricity masked great self-doubt—after years of major hits he still told a music reporter, "I don't feel I've accomplished anything. . . . I'm still quite insecure." That he never learned to read or write music did not help him.

For a while, Gaye thought his personality was best suited to being a great blues star—"I'm a blues singer and basically a blue person. Moody. Brooding." Then he changed his mind and told anyone who would listen that it was only a matter of time until he became a star crooner.

"My dream was to become Frank Sinatra," Gaye later recalled, though he also admired Dean Martin and Perry Como. "I loved his phrasing, especially when he was young and pure. He grew into a fabulous jazz singer, and I used to fantasize about having a lifestyle like his—carrying on in Hollywood and becoming a movie star. Every woman in America wanted to go to bed with Frank Sinatra. He was the king I longed to be. My greatest dream was to satisfy as many women as Sinatra."

With such a grand vision, he stubbornly resisted commercial tunes brought to him by Gordy and others. "I'm constantly at war with my company and my managers," he later told *Soul* magazine. "I want to sing songs that will make people say, 'What the hell is he singing that for?'" He pointed out that singers could successfully cross racial lines—Felix Cavaliere, the Italian lead singer of the Rascals, fantasized about being a black soul singer and had two releases that went to number one on the R&B chart. At Marvin's insistence, Motown released *The Soulful Moods of Marvin Gaye*, a compendium of mundane standards targeted more to a middle-class white audience than to the hip white and black teens who were flocking to the rest of the label's tunes. Motown thought it might be possible to market the twenty-year-old singer with the greasy, processed pompadour as the next Nat "King" Cole or Sam Cooke. It was on this album that he added an *e* to his surname. He needed to do more than that. It bombed. Chastened, Gaye spent his time as a studio musician for part of the year, even playing the drums on "Please Mr. Postman."

To some inside the company, Gaye, after his failed album, appeared to be the least likely hit maker. Then Mickey Stevenson and George Gordy joined Marvin to write a song to match Gaye's mood, "Stubborn Kind of Fellow." Jivey and upbeat, it was nothing like the crooner style Gaye sought. He was not happy with the song's R&B style, but he sang it well in a husky, strong voice. Martha Reeves, who was still working as Stevenson's secretary, helped on the background vocals with her ex–Del-Fi singers.

"You could hear the man screaming on that tune, you could tell he was hungry," said Dave Hamilton, who played guitar on the song. "If you listen to that song you'll say, 'Hey, man, he was trying to make it because he was on his last leg.'"

The song cracked the R&B top ten, and while it did not assure Gaye stardom, it meant he was not at the bottom of the roster as far as Motown producers were concerned. Gaye was frustrated when the song did not cross over to the white pop charts; still, he was happy he had a hit. Before the year was out, he released another similar-styled R&B song, "Hitch Hike," which he wrote with Mickey Stevenson and Clarence Paul. It also climbed the charts and got Gaye over the fear that "Stubborn Kind of Fellow" might be his only hit. Moreover, it showed that he was able to handle a grittier singing style than many had thought him capable of. It also helped many at Motown ignore Gaye's volatile moods and the days when he was difficult. Though he was now a star, Marvin Gaye seemed more relaxed to most who dealt with him. But internally he was still secretly holding to his belief that he was destined to be a great balladeer.

CHAPTER 12

Battle of the Stars

IN 1961, AS "SHOP AROUND" WAS CLIMBING THE CHARTS, THE Regal Theater—Chicago's premier music showplace—booked its shows for the following autumn. When Gordy realized that all but one were Motown acts, it seemed obvious that he should put together his own road tour. The previous year, Barney Ales had suggested a similar idea, but Gordy had not thought the time was right.

It was a Herculean task for a small company like Motown. Almost everyone worked in-house, from the artists and producers, background singers and musicians, road managers, and even chaperones for the youngest artists. (Stevie Wonder was Motown's only child star, and not only was he assigned a traveling tutor, but Gordy went even further, putting things like mealtimes, study, playtime, and bedtime on an exacting schedule.) For Gordy, the tour would promote the company, further boost the established artists, provide exposure for unknown acts, and, most important, raise some more cash. His plans for using touring to build an artist roster would become an industry norm by the late 1960s. He was, as in many other matters, just a few years ahead of the rest of the business.

It was Esther's responsibility to find a national promoter with the right contacts. It was not easy, since only four acts—the Miracles, Mary Wells, Marv Johnson, and the Marvelettes—could draw an audience. But Esther convinced the energetic Henry Wynne of Supersonic Attractions to take a chance by booking the entire roster. Wynne was black, and Esther told him that as two black companies they needed each other. She also promised him that if he did this tour, he would have an inside track to grow with Motown. Esther also established a system that ensured little tour money ended up in the performers' pockets. The money was controlled by ITMI. The artists were given ten dollars weekly to buy necessities. All other earnings were sent back to Motown, where they were kept in accounts for them.

On a bitterly cold October morning in 1962, the forty-five members of what was now the Motortown Revue gathered outside Hitsville. Most of them had never been out of Michigan. A decrepit-looking bus—with MOTOR CITY TOUR painted on its sides—idled halfway down the block, and a convoy of five cars was double-parked along the narrow street. For the artists, stagehands, and chaperones, the bus and the cars would be their homes for the next few months. Many were nervous about leaving family for the first time. In the chilly weather, they bundled together, rubbing and blowing on their hands in losing efforts to stay warm. Some held paper bags with lunches packed by their parents, who had come to bid them farewell.

Gordy was not there. He had been in the studio all night, putting in fourteen hours on a frantic remix of the Supremes' next single, "Let Me Go the Right Way," which he had written and produced. It was to be released in two weeks, while the Revue was on the road, and he was determined it would be a breakthrough for the no-hit group.

Smokey Robinson rushed in and interrupted, "You're a madman! What mix is it now, one hundred?"

Gordy didn't even glance up. "No, one hundred and one," he said.

"They're loading the bus. Don't you want to say good-bye?"

Unshaven and with his clothes rumpled and coffee-stained, he stumbled outside to the frigid air without a jacket or sweater. There, standing in small groups were the artists he had so aggressively nurtured over the past two years: the Miracles, the Supremes, Marv Johnson, Marvin Gaye, Mary Wells, the Marvelettes, Martha and the Vandellas, and Singin' Sammy Ward. Choker Campbell, the tour's bandleader, was smoking a cigarette; Bill Murray, the energetic MC known professionally as Winehead Willie, was entertaining the Supremes with war stories about his earlier tours. Beans Bowles had been selected as tour manager, but he was also doubling as a musician. He had his own assistant, Eddie McFarland, who was moving up and down on his toes to stay warm. Esther was giving a final lecture to the tour's three chaperones: Diane Ross's mother, Ernestine Ross, Bernice Morrison, and Ardena Johnston.

Although no one, of course, knew it that morning, their three-month, ninety-four-performance schedule was so rigorous that they would sleep only three nights in motels. The rest of the time they slept on the bus. Because they did not have rooms to change in, the girls invented a crash course for getting ready for shows, and they often wore wigs since they seldom had a chance to wash and set their hair. It started a trend among Motown's female artists, so much so that eventually when the Supremes became international stars, they traveled with a small caravan of wigs—Diana Ross, in particular, became known for enormous ones that dwarfed her.

Gordy, always image conscious, warned the men not to harass the women and girls—his biggest concern was that the girls might get pregnant. "He gave us this little speech," recalled Contours singer Joe Billingslea, "that we were representing Motown."

Esther urged them to be on their best behavior. That brought a snicker from Marvin Gaye, which was met by a stern look from Esther. Engines started up. Gordy wished everyone good luck. In a matter of minutes, they had crowded into the bus and the cars and set off toward the freeway.

The tour was to begin with an engagement at the Boston Arena in November. After that they went to Washington, D.C., and then continued south for a series of one-nighters before ending with a ten-day run at New York's Apollo.

The pace was brutal, and the bus was not the most luxurious mode of travel. "It was very cramped," recalled Otis Williams, "and there was no such thing as personal space, so you developed another kind of camaraderie." The younger artists relied on the more experienced musicians in their twenties or thirties for guidance about how to best cope with life on the road.

Although the chaperones tried hard to maintain some control, especially watching the young women, it was difficult. Many of the girls were still in their teens—the Marvelettes were all eighteen, as were Diane Ross and Mary Wilson; Flo Ballard was nineteen. Even the oldest girls, Martha Reeves and the Vandellas, were only twenty and twenty-one.

"The chaperones on the Motortown Revue tours tried to keep us out of trouble," said Williams, "but love still found a way." Beans Bowles had always warned the young male artists, "Don't mess with any of Berry's sisters." They didn't. But since Gordy's sisters weren't on the bus, that meant there were no rules for most of the men. Flo Ballard and Otis Williams were typical. They often sat together, a jacket thrown over their laps so no one could see them holding hands, a flirtation that became an affair by the end of the tour. (It didn't last long. Williams soon fell hard for Patti LaBelle, then of the Blue Belles. They eventually broke up when Williams wanted LaBelle to give up singing and move with him to California.)

Smokey and Claudette would have added to the list of the tour's couples in love except that Smokey missed a couple of dates because of a bad case of the flu. Soon after Smokey returned, Claudette had to go home, ill with troubles from a tough pregnancy that ended in a miscarriage, the first of six. (She eventually had a child through an experimental procedure that utilized an artificially constructed brace for her weak cervix.)

The musicians often furtively passed around small flasks of whiskey on the bus or smoked joints and blew the smoke out the window. Even keeping the young artists in the front of the bus, dubbed "Broadway," and the musicians in the rear, derisively called "Harlem," did not always work well.

· · ·

Some of those on the bus remembered that Gordy had seemed preoccupied during the send-off. They shrugged it off since they knew he was obsessed with recutting the Supremes' song. But what few knew was that his marriage to Raynoma was fast falling apart and taking an emotional toll on both of them. Gordy was incapable of being monogamous. When young, Gordy had tried hard to impress women. He had almost invariably failed and developed, according to those who knew him, a lack of self-esteem about attracting the opposite sex. Now he relished the attention he received as Motown's owner.

At first, Raynoma rationalized his all-night absences by convincing herself that he needed to be out with artists and producers at clubs. Her only rule was that Gordy be home by 6:00 in the morning, and he usually made it with minutes to spare.

His first serious affair while still married to Ray was with a beautiful young Detroit native, Margaret Norton. Norton, at only seventeen, was, even by Ray's judgment, "one of the prettiest girls ever to step foot in

Hitsville." Norton pretended to be the girlfriend of singer Barrett Strong so she could lounge at the office until Gordy finished. Ray found out about the affair only after Strong's sister finally told her.

She confronted Norton and heard more than she wanted to. Norton boasted that on the night Gordy and Raynoma married, Gordy had left their house after the wedding to have sex with her. Gordy adamantly denied everything when Ray challenged him. While she continued working at Hitsville, Raynoma was in a fog that only deepened as Norton began calling and taunting her with intimate details of her sexual exploits with Gordy. At some Detroit department stores, salesclerks thought Margaret Norton was actually Gordy's wife.

It wasn't long before Ray retaliated by having her own affair with Sonny Sanders, an original member of the Rayber Voices. Each night, she rushed home by 5:30 A.M. just before Gordy returned from his own trysts with Norton. They were barely civil to each other, but Gordy was clueless about Ray's affair.

One night, after an argument with Norton, Gordy left a party and returned to the small Lawton Street apartment to which he and Ray had recently moved from their top-floor pad at Hitsville. He arrived at 1:00 A.M. Gordy was surprised that Ray was not there. He waited for her, drifting in and out of a light sleep. By 5:00 A.M. he was panicked, thinking something terrible had befallen her. Then finally, at 5:30, a car pulled up to their apartment, and Ray hopped out. As the car drove off, Berry recognized its driver, Sonny Sanders.

Gordy confronted her, but she said she had been at an all-night movie theater with Sanders and her own nephew, Dale. Then, during the coming weeks, Gordy heard office gossip that Ray was having her own affair with someone in New York, a place where Motown business regularly took her. Again, he questioned her. This time she refused to answer. Plopping down on the bed, dressed only in his underwear and an old T-shirt, Gordy finally admitted his affair with Norton. His confession sparked Ray to tell all about her fling.

Upon hearing the truth, Gordy's face contorted in anger, and without warning he charged Raynoma, dragging her roughly from the bed. He lifted her off the floor and hurled her several feet. She smashed into a dresser. Perfume bottles and glass jars flew off the top and shattered.

"A dead and sickening silence filled the room," remembered Ray. "He stood in the middle of it, breathing heavily. In seconds, he was dressed and gone for good." Raynoma stopped going to Hitsville.

Gordy's closest friends knew that his personal life was in disarray. To avoid dealing with his emotions, he threw himself into work. The fourteen-hour overnight crash on the Supremes' song had not been that unusual for several months.

Gordy and Ray finally got a mail-order Mexican divorce. A Motown lawyer, Sue Weisenfeld, handled the details. Ray, however, was still harassed by Margaret Norton. She fell into a depression, took large doses of tranquilizers, and kept two pistols nearby. She began to worry that Gordy might hurt her. Desperate to find a new mate, she dated a series of men, each progressively worse than the last.

Only a few months after their split, however, Gordy began holding out hope to Ray that the two might reunite. That greatly buoyed her, and she even returned to work at Motown. But the calm was shattered by another call from Norton, telling Ray that she was pregnant with Gordy's child. Ray had had enough. She went looking for Norton and tracked her to the Westside Bowling Alley, where she was hanging out with Gordy and some Motown artists. Ray did not acknowledge anyone, but staring straight ahead she determinedly strode almost on top of the startled Norton. Her long overcoat hid the .25-caliber pistol she shoved into Norton's side.

"Listen, bitch," Ray said, smiling. She kept her voice to a whisper so no one but Norton could hear her. "What are you doing here with my husband?" She pushed the gun deeper. "OK. I want you to get up slowly and walk outside with me. I'm sick of you. I'm sick of your phone calls. So get up now, bitch, and walk out. Make one whimper and I'm going to blow you away."

The others at the bowling alley could not see the gun, but Raynoma's fury was evident, and they knew something was wrong when Norton meekly walked outside with her. They had just reached a rear alley when Smokey Robinson crept up quietly behind Ray and grabbed her while yelling at Norton to run. Norton dashed down the alley as Ray kicked and screamed. When Ray stopped shouting, Smokey released her. By then, a small group had gathered. Berry—who had missed the confrontation inside—muscled his way through the crowd. He saw Ray standing with her shoulders slumped, the gun still dangling from her hand. "His face searched mine," she remembered, "and he saw in it everything that had happened between us, the victory and devastation." Ray simply turned around and left. No one in the stunned group said a word.

That evening, Ray parked her car in front of Norton's house. She rocked ever so slightly back and forth in the seat. She had decided to kill Norton and then take her own life. When Norton, however, did not return by the early morning, Ray drove away. She had decided instead to leave Detroit.

She moved to New York, where Berry agreed to let her open the first satellite office for Jobete. The hope was that away from Gordy and the painful memories of Detroit, the emotionally fragile Raynoma might be able to use her musical expertise to find new talent for Motown. At first, she left her two sons in Detroit, but they joined her the following year.

Ray was barely out of town when Gordy started dating Jeana Jackson, a striking friend who lived in Connecticut. Although their relationship was brief, it was long enough to produce a sixth child, a girl named Sherry. After breaking up with Jackson, Gordy returned to Margaret Norton. Their relationship was volatile, involving nights of drinking and abusive verbal fights, but they were unable to break apart. "I couldn't get her out of my system," Gordy said.

·   ·   ·

The Motortown Revue offered Gordy a good excuse to get his mind off his personal problems. He decided to surprise his artists with a visit. The Revue had been performing to sold-out audiences at Washington, D.C.'s Howard Theatre when he simply stepped onto the bus one day. Some of the men were in the back playing poker, something that many Motowners enjoyed in all-night games at Hitsville. Gordy joined them, and everyone watched as one after another dropped out of the increasingly high stakes. Finally, only Gordy and Choker Campbell were left. Gordy, as was his habit when he concentrated intensely, chewed his tongue. He finally quit when he was six thousand dollars in the hole. While he may not have been happy, it enhanced his reputation among the younger artists who were impressed not only that he had so much money to lose but also that he was such a risk taker.

Gordy then turned to business. He was pleased to discover that the artists had grown more competitive with one another since leaving Hitsville. Most of them besieged him with requests to be moved farther back in the show's lineup, since the later spots were the prime ones. Addressing them as a group, Gordy said he'd let that night's audience decide—whoever left the stage with so much applause and shouting that the noise drowned out the introduction of the next performer would get promoted. From that point on, Mary Wilson said, "when you hit the stage, you really had to go for blood."

That night, Gordy watched from the side of the stage. The Supremes opened the show. The boisterous crowd quickly took away what little confidence they had. Gordy thought they looked petrified, and while they did not impress the audience he was certain that one hit would change their personality. Martha Reeves and the Vandellas followed. They had no hit either, but they had attitude, with Reeves strutting sexily around the stage and working up the crowd. The Contours were next, and Gordy thought they were "fearless" as they jumped around the stage, gyrating wildly to the music. Marvin Gaye, whom Gordy labeled a "showstopper," followed their high-energy act. When he finished "Stubborn Kind of Fellow," the screaming from women was so loud that Gordy could barely hear the announcement for the next group, the Marvelettes. "Marvin will be moving up," Gordy thought to himself.

But Gladys Horton, the Marvelettes' lead singer, had barely sung the opening words from their raging hit "Please Mr. Postman" when the audience went crazy. "I knew there would be no moving Marvin now," thought Gordy.

After the Marvelettes, Motown's leading diva, Mary Wells, took the stage. She started jiving with the audience, bantering before launching into her standards. Gordy was impressed with how polished and experienced she was onstage.

The Miracles were the final act. Smokey had recovered and had rejoined the tour. They were the group with the most touring experience, and their stage act was slick. "He [Smokey] just stood there and made love to the women," Gordy recalled. "He could do that better than anybody. He fell to his knees and lay on the floor, singing up a storm. . . . Smokey was king."

After the show, young women mobbed Smokey. Gordy had seen that type of sexual fever before when he had worked with Jackie Wilson, but this was the first time he had witnessed it for one of his artists, someone he helped create. To Gordy, it was another indication that Motown was starting to work, that it was producing acts that had star status, even groupies.

Although Gordy decided not to change the lineup, he liked the competition he had fostered. "Berry loved having people at each other's throats," said sales executive Tom Noonan. "It gave him better control. He loved friction. He liked it that way."

At times, Gordy became fanatical about encouraging competition, ridiculing songs or performances he thought were inadequate, and overpraising his producers and songwriters who came up with hits. The atmosphere encouraged suspicions that some writers tried to steal songs or that credit wasn't assigned correctly, but those accusations seem endemic to recording companies and were not any more prevalent at Motown than at other labels.

As might be expected, the competition exacerbated personal rivalries. On the Revue, Diane Ross and the Marvelettes' Gladys Horton took strong dislikes to each other. They traded insults over each other's costumes, and Ross irritated Horton by sending her handwritten messages, threatening to "kick her behind." One night, after a concert, Horton walked through the parking lot. She was leading a young blind boy named Lee across the street. Unknown to Horton, Ross was sitting behind the steering wheel of the station wagon the artists shared. She flipped on the ignition and floored the gas pedal, racing the car, with its headlights off, toward Horton. Then Ross slammed on the brakes, and the car screeched to a stop a few inches short of a terrified Horton. Horton left the boy standing in the middle of the street as she screamed and ran around to the side of the car. Ross rolled down the window just enough to put her hand out and flip Horton the finger before she sped away.

When Gordy heard of the incident, he demanded Ross apologize to Horton. But the feud was set for the rest of the tour. Ross sulked that it was Horton who had originally picked on her, but few listened. It eventually became a common theme for her.

"Over the years," recalled Mary Wilson, "Diane's spats with Mary Wells, Gladys, Dee Dee Sharp, Brenda Holloway, and especially Martha Reeves were company knowledge. If you ever asked Diane why she got into fights, she'd say, 'They're picking on me.' But that wasn't always the case."

And as the tour continued, Diane wasn't the only one having fights. People grew more tense. Riding for days in the creaky bus, cramming occasionally into rundown motels, and fighting for space in the dressing rooms led to frayed nerves and short tempers. Stevie Wonder, the youngest on the tour, kept playing his harmonica or telling jokes so late into the night that he stopped only when someone threatened to "beat your ass." Not everyone got along. At one point, the Temptations and Contours got into a fistfight over some women and a bottle of wine. But despite these flare-ups, the tour chaotically made its show dates.

·   ·   ·

Before the tour had left Detroit, Gordy had warned everybody that there could be some uncomfortable moments in the South. They anticipated them at gas stations, restaurants, and even some motels. Gordy and his planners, however, were naive about the extent of the problems there. Nineteen sixty-two saw a marked increase in civil-rights protests, sit-ins, and demonstrations. Northern activists—Freedom Riders—had made their way south, sometimes on buses similar to the one used by the Motortown Revue, starting just a year before the Motown artists arrived. The bus's Michigan license plates did not help.

Segregation was still legal in many southern states. Often the artists were ordered to the rear of a restaurant to get food, and when they refused it almost led to fistfights. Once the bus had to take off hurriedly when a restaurant owner went to get his pistol. In Miami Beach, fifteen police cruisers and dogs followed the artists from their hotel to the theater. In South Carolina, white people jumped out of a pool when some of the Motown artists went for a swim. In Elvis Presley's hometown of Memphis, the audience was segregated into separate areas, requiring the artists to perform each song twice.

Otis Williams remembered a series of confrontations that surprised the mostly northern artists. Some of the women were turned away from a Mississippi rest room by an elderly shotgun-wielding man who yelled, "Don't you niggers step one foot off that bus, or I'll blow your asses to kingdom come!" In South Carolina, the Revue performed at a club where there was a rope strung down the middle to divide black and white patrons. "What the fuck is the rope for?" Williams had demanded but knew the answer before he heard it. "There were far too many scenes like that to recount," he said.

In Birmingham, someone fired shots at the bus. No one was hurt, but it thoroughly shook the artists. "Me in my little Motown star bubble," recalled Mary Wells, "all of a sudden everything kind of crashes."

News of the gunshots caught Gordy by surprise when he learned of it back in Detroit. It was, as Gordy later recalled, the first time he had confronted overt racism since he had been six years old and heard the word *nigger*. The attack brought back a flood of disturbing memories, including when he was twenty-six and had been frightened by the 1955 lynching of fourteen-year-old Emmett Till, who had been killed when racists thought he had been disrespectful to a white woman. Gordy had never faced racism as a Detroit adult, and he was almost completely apolitical and not involved in the incipient civil-rights movement under the leadership of the Reverend Dr. Martin Luther King Jr. But social issues aside, Gordy was very concerned with the personal safety of his performers. His first reaction was to cancel the rest of the tour. But Esther, after conferring with the chaperones, convinced him not to.

Three weeks later, more bad news arrived in the middle of the night when Gordy was awakened by a telephone call informing him that Beans Bowles and Eddie McFarland had had a car wreck on the way to Tampa. The entire group had partied the night before, celebrating a successful run of shows in the Carolinas. McFarland had fallen asleep at the wheel of his station wagon and crashed into a large truck. Beans Bowles had been in the backseat playing his flute. In the collision, the flute punched through his armpit and stuck out of the back of his neck. Both his legs were broken. McFarland suffered serious head injuries. Both men were in critical condition.

The following morning, Gordy, Esther, and McFarland's mother left on the first flight out of Detroit. At the hospital, they discovered that Bowles had stabilized, but McFarland was still critical. Gordy's faith in southern whites was temporarily restored when the state policeman who found the wreck turned in the twelve thousand dollars in cash for gate receipts that Bowles had had in the car. (Later, a local reporter told Beans that he had been lucky to come across "the only honest cop in five hundred miles.")

Gordy had Esther join the tour and take responsibility for all the details— including paying any motel bills and collecting receipts—that had been managed by Bowles and McFarland. Three nights later, Esther reached Gordy just before that show began and told him that McFarland had died.

The night before the funeral, the company held a wake at the Detroit recording studio. Everyone not on tour was there, including McFarland's parents, to pay tribute to the young, happy-go-lucky McFarland. The place was subdued. But when Barney Ales came in, he was laughing. Ales always seemed to have jokes for any occasion, mostly ones about Jews, blacks, Poles, and women. "Now he had some dead jokes to tell," recalled Raynoma, who had come in from New York. She watched, enraged, as Ales whispered to Gordy, and the two stood on the side of the room, laughing. Finally, Raynoma walked up to them and hissed through clenched teeth that their behavior was totally inappropriate. Although they fell silent for a moment, they picked up again after she left. Raynoma recalled it was "like two naughty boys after being scolded by an old schoolmarm. The kinship between Berry and Barney had deepened, and I felt distrustful. 'Just watch him, that's all,' I told Berry. Barney, in turn, was watching me."

After McFarland's death, the only Motortown Revue date that Gordy was interested in was the mid-December appearance at New York's Apollo Theatre. Most of the artists found New York, particularly Harlem, initially intimidating. "Harlem was the most crowded ghetto of my worst nightmare," remembered Martha Reeves. She and her colleagues watched nervously as New Yorkers checked them and the bus out, without so much as a smile. "We heard comments like 'Detroit niggers' and 'singing motherfuckers,'" Reeves recalled. When the groups arrived at the Apollo, the man at the stage door was equally unfriendly. "Who are you motherfuckers? What y'all want?"

Adding to their anxiety, they knew the New York audience had a reputation as the country's toughest, ready to shout down acts they didn't like. However, McFarland's death had given most of the artists an attitude that made the shows seem less important and therefore less nerve-racking. The Motown acts sailed through a packed schedule of forty-two shows in ten days and nights. New Yorkers loved them. And it was such a successful engagement that Gordy actually recorded the final show and released it as an album, *Recorded Live at the Apollo, Vol. 1.*

Billboard's review of Motown's engagement confirmed to Gordy that the company had made it: "The Tamla-Motown rock and roll show opened New York's Apollo Theater last week and in its first few days appeared to be on its way to cracking box-office records. . . . This is not the first show ever sponsored by a label, but it is one of the most successful."

While everyone was ecstatic over the Apollo run, the live recording was far from studio quality, and many of the acts sounded quite amateurish compared to the polish they would have in a few years. The Supremes got weak applause after a screechy rendition of "Let Me Go the Right Way." Marvin Gaye stumbled through "What Kind of Fool Am I?" Mary Wells interrupted her song to talk about her "boo-boos." The Contours sounded like an R&B act trying too hard to impress the audience. Stevie Wonder was almost funny as he tried mimicking adult singers. And the band was flat, described by one critic as "wedding hall mediocrity."

·   ·   ·

The competition that Gordy liked fostering on the Motortown Revue was a mere warm-up to what he orchestrated after the acts returned to Detroit. By Christmas of 1962, Gordy had negotiated a deal to buy the city's renowned five-story Greystone Ballroom for $125,000. As a kid, he knew it as the music palace that allowed blacks in only on Monday nights. Now, just a couple of years into his own label, he owned it. The company's large holiday party was held there, and Gordy awarded a Motown Spirit Award to the person he thought most exemplified the label's spirit: Smokey Robinson. (The person who was a close second on Gordy's list, the Tempts' Melvin Franklin, received it the following year.)

It was at that Christmas party where there were the first real signs of success for the artists. The Marvelettes, still riding high from their number-one hit, "Please Mr. Postman," walked in with star attitudes. "They were wearing big, fancy hats and with an attitude that let you know they were in the money now," recalled Otis Williams. "I envied them—I'm sure everyone else did, too—but it wasn't a bitter thing. You just wanted the chance to prove you were as good, and that competitive atmosphere Berry encouraged was like a spur, driving you."

The Marvelettes were not the only ones who looked sharp. Many of the men wore mohair suits, which were then the rage, while the women were decked out in custom-made jewelry and flashy dresses. As Mary Wilson later recalled, even if they weren't making much money, "almost every cent we did make went on our backs."

The Greystone was a perfect setting for Motown's Christmas party, but Gordy had grander ideas for it. There, he refined his concept for a battle of the stars, in which the artists competed with one another for audience favor. Usually, he would match just two acts against each other: Martha and the Vandellas against the Marvelettes; the Temptations against the Contours; or the Supremes against the Velvelettes, five talented women who never found a breakthrough hit. Everything seemed to be going along great until one night when Gordy matched Little Stevie Wonder against the older, polished Marvin Gaye. Gaye had a dedicated following, especially among women who found him sexy. Gaye played that appeal to the hilt. Stevie Wonder, on the other hand, had only one hit, "Fingertips (Part 2)." It resulted from a live recording at Chicago's Regal Theater when Wonder had stayed onstage for what he thought was an encore and broke unexpectedly into song with the band. (Mary Wells was about to take the stage thinking Wonder was done with his set.) "Fingertips" sounded like a revival meeting. It was a jumpy, impromptu two-minute-and-forty-nine-second performance that consisted of Wonder's screeching harmonica play and his repetitive scream-ing of "Yeah, yeah, yeah." In the middle of the song, one musician can be heard on the live recording yelling, "What key? What key?" One critic re-marked that it "was little more than recorded hysteria." But somehow the mistake gave the recording a raw energy and edge that the public loved, and it shot up the charts to become a number-one pop single, the second in Mo-town's history. It sold more than one million copies and stayed number one for fifteen weeks. (Gordy was listed as a producer on that hit, although Clarence Paul, who cowrote the song with Wonder, later admitted that Gordy had not even been there when the song was recorded.)

The "Fingertips" album went number one the same week that the sin-gle topped the charts. This was a rare feat that only established stars such as Frank Sinatra and Tony Bennett had achieved. The double success of "Fingertips" gave Motown a dramatic boost inside the music industry, eliminating any lingering doubts about the label's staying power and influ-ence.

Despite the tremendous success of Wonder's hit, Gaye and many other artists on the label derided it as a fluke. Coming off his own moderately successful "Pride and Joy"—his first crossover hit—Gaye considered the Greystone battle with Wonder a nuisance he had to tolerate in order to sat-isfy Gordy's peculiar promotion concept. Also, Gaye was slighted that Gordy had matched him against the young, blind singer. Although Gaye really liked Wonder, he told his friend Beans Bowles that he couldn't understand why Gordy was "puttin' that little blind sucker on before me." (In 1969, Gaye got into a prominent public fight with another blind singer, José Feliciano, who had criticized Gaye's soulful rendition of the national anthem at the World Series in Detroit. Gaye called Feliciano a "fink" and told *Soul* magazine, "People get their arms busted, their legs broken, and other things for saying less than [what Feliciano said].")

Wonder began his act singing and blowing feverishly on his harmonica on the jivey "Workout Stevie, Workout." Gordy had helped Wonder develop a stage presence inspired by Ray Charles, and it worked well. Like other blind performers, Stevie exhibited so-called blindisms as part of his act. He had rhythmic movements of the body and head, swayed and rocked, and often rubbed his eyes as he performed. His most distinctive move was to throw his head back and move it from side to side. He was dressed in a glitter-trimmed suit, his oversized harmonica had been polished to a gleaming shine, and his name was emblazoned across his drum set in sparkles. By the end of the song, the crowd was dancing and going wild.

Gaye countered with one of his hottest numbers, "Hitch Hike," dancing and sliding effortlessly around the stage. The crowd loved it, too, and would not stop stomping and shouting. At the end of the first round, Gordy thought Gaye held a slight advantage.

For his second song, Stevie did a bluesy "I Call It Pretty Music but the Old Folks Call It the Blues," and then he went right into his smash, "Fingertips." The crowd gave its biggest and noisiest reception yet. It was hard for anyone in the audience to miss that Stevie Wonder was having the time of his life.

Gaye was now eager to make people quickly forget about Wonder. But as he skipped onstage and started his hit, "Stubborn Kind of Fellow," there were a few boos. Then the cackles and boos grew in number and volume. Gaye seemed confused but kept singing.

"Marvin," someone in the audience shouted, "you should be shame o' yourself takin' advantage of that little blind kid." Some other voices shouted similar sentiments. Gaye ignored them and continued with his song, determined to win over the audience. When he finished, the smattering of applause was drowned out by boos and hissing. His jaw was clenched, and his face hid his embarrassment as Gaye signaled the band to start the next planned song, "Pride and Joy." But before he could start, Gordy ran onstage and yanked the microphone out of Gaye's hands.

"Thank you very much," Gordy announced. "The show's over." He motioned for someone to start playing records. Gaye scampered offstage, and Gordy followed. He found Gaye backstage, sitting by himself, his head buried in his hands. Gordy put his hand on Gaye's shoulder. Neither man said a word.

"There was nothing to say," Gordy later recalled. "Though I still felt competition bred champions, I could see that it also had a downside. And in this particular case of putting a grown man against a little blind boy I had blundered badly."

That was the last battle of the stars at the Greystone.

CHAPTER 13

"How Many Think It's a Hit?"

By the beginning of 1963, Motown had outgrown Hitsville, and Gordy had bought some neighboring houses. "Hitsville is the only high-rise that went sideways," joked Barney Ales. Jobete Publishing was at 2644 West Grand. At 2650 West Grand, next door to Hitsville, were offices for Gordy and Esther. Over the next three years, another five houses were added, one each for finance, management, artist development, administration, and sales. West Grand Boulevard provided an odd assortment of neighbors for a record company, including the Ethical Hair Shop, Your Fair Lady Boutique and Wig Room, Phelps Funeral Parlor, and the Sykes Hernia Control Service.

But Gordy didn't mind the street's mix. Each of his buildings had a distinct flavor. He liked strolling through them, stopping by each department and chatting with his workers. It gave him a sense of how much his business had grown.

The main one, Hitsville, still housed the recording studio and was where the artists and producers usually gathered. A typical day might find Smokey Robinson rehearsing dance steps in one room, Mary Wells in another toying with lyrics, while Brian Holland experimented with new songs on a piano, or Robert Bateman tried new chords on another piano on the far side of the house.

Across the street, Gwen and Anna Gordy and Mickey Stevenson ran Artist Development, an idea Gordy had initially resisted as unnecessary. It included a concept modeled after the movie-studio charm schools of the thirties and forties. It almost seemed archaic in an era in which most musical acts embraced nonconformity. The Gordy sisters were fashion mavens, however, and had applied their interest to makeovers for new artists. Years earlier, Gwen had been a student at the local Maxine Powell Model, Host, and Hostess Agency. It was Detroit's first black modeling and finishing school. They now hired Powell, an accomplished actress and model, to work with the artists.

"When I went into Motown," Powell recalled, "you couldn't sell them to a record hop. Some were rude, some were crude, and some hadn't been anywhere. They weren't the best singers in the world, but they all wanted the same thing, and they worked hard." Her daily two-hour classes were mandatory.

"Young ladies always . . ." was her stock opening line. She covered everything from applying makeup and observing proper table manners to correct public and private deportment. She encouraged the girls to wear hats and gloves when walking around Motown—and a few actually did. She had them walk with books on their heads to learn good posture and kept an eye out for any flaw; she even taught them how best to get in and out of a car "as a lady should." An entire class was dedicated to showing the girls how to take a seat—approach the chair at an angle, touch the seat with the inside leg, put one foot forward, slide in gracefully, then cross the ankles, put your feet flat on the floor, and make sure that your rear is precisely three inches from the back of the chair. Some rules were absolute: no closing your eyes when singing; no frowning; no finger snapping; and no spreading your legs or sticking out your buttocks.

The Supremes were her star pupils and spent six months with her in a small building adjacent to Hitsville's main headquarters. Beanpoles such as Diane Ross and Mary Wilson, not happy with their bodies in the days before rail-thin figures were cool, found new curves in padded bras and hip pads. "Mrs. Powell's efforts paid some interesting dividends," recalled Mary Wilson. "Not only did we have a lot more self-confidence, but other people began treating us differently." Nothing was overlooked. They were taught how to jump on top of a piano during a concert while still looking ladylike, and even how to shake hands—"The firmness of the grip is very important," recalled Diane Ross. Ross was the only artist that Gordy sent for five months of additional grooming to the John Roberts Powers School for Social Grace in downtown Detroit. It was early evidence that he had special plans for Ross.

When Powell said, "We're training them for Buckingham Palace and the White House," she didn't know how right she was.

The label's female acts were not the only ones who received Powell's polishing classes, as she also worked with the men. Only Marvin Gaye initially refused the charm school, but eventually he became so enamored of Powell that he made her the godmother of one of his sons.

"They taught you how to walk," recalled Melvin Franklin. "They taught you about makeup. They taught you about personal hygiene. They taught us what questions to answer with the press and what not to answer. . . . I became very programmed. You represented Motown very well. People used to say, 'There's a record industry, and then there's Motown.' We were inside of our own capsule, our own world. It was very secure there."

The Four Tops were seasoned before signing with Motown in 1964. But the Motown publicity department's "Fact Sheet" made them sound as though they were unpolished novices before Artist Development got its hands on them: "They were taught how to move onstage, how to dress, walk, and talk to reporters."

Though there was hyperbole surrounding it, Artist Development was not a department taken lightly inside Motown. Once, Gordy signed a big singer with an even bigger voice, Oda Barr from Las Vegas. When Artist Development got her, it put the 240-pound Barr on a strict diet. After someone went into her hotel room one day to get her and discovered her eagerly eating her way through a box of Hershey bars, Gordy simply canceled her contract.

While Powell helped Artist Development, the talented Harvey Fuqua ran promotion from a small office next to the Gordy sisters. His staff worked in small cubicles on the second floor. Fuqua was responsible for convincing a friend, Cholly Atkins, half of the renowned dance team Coles and Atkins, to join Motown. Atkins, who had done choreography for Gladys Knight and the Pips, the Cleftones, the Cadillacs, and Fuqua's own Moonglows, among many other successful acts, was in his early fifties when he came to Motown. He taught the artists everything from how to dramatically make a stage entrance to how to execute complex dance routines that dazzled audiences. And he appreciated that while the dance moves were important, the music was key and had to be highlighted. "I would get a set of the lyrics and get the story line of what they [the performers] were singing about," Atkins said. "I made sure that we did things that corresponded with musical tracks along with the lyrics." Motown's artists loved Atkins. "Paring us with Cholly was a match made in heaven," recalled the Tempts' Otis Williams.

Fuqua also hired Maurice King as the label's musical director and conductor, and King oversaw the onstage productions, made arrangements for the bands, and taught harmonies to the artists. King had been the Flame Show Bar's bandleader before joining Motown. An exacting taskmaster who also pitched in as a vocal coach for many of the singers, he strove for perfection in the songs, the dance routines, and even the stage dialogue he developed for each act.

· · ·

Each department met once a week. The A&R department met on Mondays. On Tuesdays, Esther convened her ITMI meetings. The purpose of ITMI was not only to manage and plan an artist's career but also to work with booking agents. By this time, another Gordy family member, Berry's cousin Evelyn Turk-Johnson, had joined Esther. Soon Esther's son, Robert, was on board. And Gordy's sister Loucye had taken control of Jobete after Raynoma and Gordy split.

Thursdays were reserved for marketing. There, Barney Ales and his salesmen—Phil Jones, Al Klein, Irv Biegel, Mel DaKroob, and later Tom Noonan—mapped out strategies for breaking recordings onto the charts.

Fridays were still reserved for the product-evaluation meetings. But as Motown grew, the weekly get-togethers to pick which recordings to release became more contentious. There was often standing room only. There was more at stake with each decision, and the most successful producers sometimes had such inflated egos that they were no longer content with a simple no from Gordy.

Barney Ales described a typical Friday meeting. Mickey Stevenson, Billie Jean Brown, and Smokey Robinson were there early. The next wave was the legal administrator, Ralph Seltzer, and his assistant, Bette Ocha; then Esther Gordy, followed by writers and producers Hank Cosby, Clarence Paul, Harvey Fuqua, Freddie Gorman (later a member of the Originals, Motown's first-string male background vocalists), songwriter Ivy Hunter, and the songwriting team of Brian and Eddie Holland and Lamont Dozier. Just as Gordy was about to close the doors, the final stragglers arrived, including Phil Jones from sales and Loucye Gordy and Fay Hale from manufacturing.

The Holland brothers and Dozier—known simply inside Motown as HDH—had just had a hit in March 1963 with "Come and Get These Memories" by Martha and the Vandellas. They looked especially confident.

Ralph Seltzer, who had a law degree, was responsible for approving all the creative budgets. He sat next to Mickey Stevenson, who looked at him almost with a sneer. He resented that noncreative people had any control over his product, and he did not hide his disdain.

Norman Whitfield, tall and lanky and full of freckles, was one of the newest producers at the table. Gordy would later tell *Billboard* editor and Motown aficionado Adam White that "Norman was probably the most underrated producer we had. . . . [He] worked his way up from the bottom." Before he was hired at Motown, Whitfield used to hang around the studios. Sometimes Gordy considered him a pest and had ordered him out of the control room, but eventually Whitfield's persistence paid off. Gordy gave him a shot in the Quality Control department at fifteen dollars per week. He became a jack-of-all-trades, being Mickey Stevenson's assistant, cleaning the studio, and arranging auditions for new talent. Whitfield, a Harlem native who ended up in Detroit after his father's car broke down there en route home from a family funeral in California, wanted to produce. By 1963, even though he had no formal musical training, he had his chance. He was confident—as Otis Williams said, "cocky as hell, even before he had a whole lot to be cocky about"—that his talent would quickly make him one of Motown's most innovative producers. He was often more willing than his counterparts to take chances on the recordings he produced. Some who worked with him considered him rough, but others said that he knew precisely what he wanted and actually enjoyed his tough in-studio image. He had already collaborated with Stevenson and Marvin Gaye on "Pride and Joy" but was not yet at his prime. Whitfield was to become the one major songwriter and producer who seldom shared production credits.

Gordy broke the silence as the door to the meeting room was closed, telling the group that there were a lot of songs to go through and that "garbage" would be eliminated quickly. Ales and everybody else knew that by *garbage* Gordy meant anything that wouldn't reach the top forty. That hard standard was one of the reasons Motown's assembly-line process for choosing songs focused so relentlessly on commercial hits at the cost of any other type of music.

Gordy glanced at the stack of discs waiting to be played. He and Brown had decided early on that it was not possible to judge the best quality of a song from a tape. Therefore, Motown had its own disc-cutting operation in the basement of one of the West Grand buildings, and all the songs that went to Quality Control, and then to the Friday meetings, were transferred to discs.

Gordy turned in his seat so he faced Smokey and asked if he had anything good in the works for Mary Wells. Smokey was working on "My Guy," and although it wasn't ready yet he told Gordy that it would be a definite number-one hit when he finished it. The other producers laughed, and some waved their hands as if to dismiss Smokey's braggadocio. They all seemed to be speaking over one another.

"Number one?!"

"I'll bet."

"How much do you want to lose?"

Smokey quickly backpedaled.

If it ever got released, Gordy deadpanned, "My Guy" probably wouldn't even make the charts. (When it was eventually released in 1964, "My Guy" was a monster hit, capturing the number-one spot faster than any other Motown release to that date.) Ales thought that the way Gordy handled Smokey was a warning to the others not to overhype their work.

The first finished record played that morning was an HDH song, "Can I Get a Witness," sung by Marvin Gaye. It had a gospel up-tempo beat, and Gaye's voice complemented the passionate lyrics.

Gordy began the typical voting procedure by asking how many thought it was *not* a hit.

Four hands went up.

"How many think it's a hit?"

Seven hands shot up.

Gordy turned to those who had voted for it and asked why they liked it. Some liked that it sounded different from other songs on the market.

Mickey Stevenson, ever quick with a sardonic comment, liked it because "the lyrics don't make no sense." Phil Jones said he knew it was good because he had taken it home the night before and his kids had danced to it. "White kids!" as if the pale-faced Jones needed to remind anyone. Ivy Hunter felt it was a hit just because "it is."

Gordy asked the group to pick their favorite between a current pop hit on the charts—Peter, Paul and Mary's "Blowin' in the Wind"—and "Can I Get a Witness." Most complained it was like comparing apples and oranges—Gaye's was a dance tune and the other a slow folk song. But Gordy kept pushing them to select one, and finally all selected Gaye's song.

Ales knew what was coming next. Gordy asked, "Now, if you were hungry and had only one dollar, would you buy this record or a hot dog?"

Whenever he asked this, the group always picked the hot dog. But Ales knew that Gordy was secretly judging how long it took them to make up their minds. Here it took long enough to let Gordy feel the song had definite hit potential. It was approved.

The next song was another HDH production, "(Love Is Like a) Heat Wave," by Martha and the Vandellas. From the first chords, Ales and others started tapping their feet and moving in their chairs to the catchy beat. "Sometimes you just knew it was good right away," recalled Ales. Gordy, as was his trademark, showed no emotion and tried not to telegraph to the others how he felt before they voted.

This time everyone thought it was a hit. There was nothing more to say except for Gordy's slightly excited announcement, "This has to go out as soon as possible!" Then he took a breath to calm himself. "Next record?"

For several hours, the same process was followed. Sometimes they argued the merits of one song as opposed to another, but by the end of those Friday sessions the core of Motown had at least agreed on what next wave of recordings the company was betting its future success.

The night after that meeting, Gordy felt so strongly about "Heat Wave" that he did something unusual. He took the recording with him and stopped by the Greystone Ballroom and played it during the label's weekly record hop. Normally, whenever a new song was played, the dance audience took a little time to warm up to it. Gordy was prepared to play "Heat Wave" about four times to see whether the audience would take to it. "But the minute the needle touched the first few bars," he later wrote, "the wood on the dance floor was nowhere to be found." It was the hit that finally made Martha and the Vandellas into an "overnight sensation."

HDH were on a roll. That summer they hit again with "Mickey's Monkey," recorded by the Miracles. And in the fall, they were the first to write a hit for the "no-hit" Supremes—they broke into the top thirty with "When the Lovelight Starts Shining Through His Eyes." That came just in time to save Diane Ross from being so demoralized that she considered giving up on her career. Otis Williams of the Tempts, the second slowest Motown group to have a major hit, had noticed Ross's mood and had frequently exhorted her, "You can't give up!" "Eventually talent wins out," Smokey Robinson told her. "Problem is you never know when."

"The idea of failure was tough on all of us," recalled Williams, who remembers crying with his own band members when they learned they had their first hit. Not surprisingly, after the Supremes' first chart breaker, Ross was almost floating around Motown's hallways. "There was no way to articulate that feeling," said Williams. "Nothing ever beat that first time."

What few initially knew was that Diane was also beaming because after a brief affair with Smokey Robinson she had set her sights on Brian Holland. While she continued flirting with Gordy, she soon started pursuing Holland. Holland's wife, Sharon, became suspicious. She showed up at the studio once, loudly telling anyone within earshot, "I know Diane Ross is messing with my husband, and if I catch her I'm going to kick her butt." One night at the 20 Grand she made good on her threat. She confronted the Supremes as they were about to take the stage and started shouting obscenities at Ross and threatening to beat her up. The other Supremes actually had to hold back Ross, who was willing to get into the fight despite her smaller size. Pushing her away, they spoke to her about the danger she was creating for all of them. Soon afterward, Ross ended her flirtation with Holland but almost immediately began dating a white record promoter in Baltimore, Eddie Bisco.

The end of Ross's interest in Holland did not, however, affect the Supremes' relationship with HDH. That continued to flourish and was similar to Smokey's relationship with Mary Wells. Whoever wrote the first hit for an artist kept creating for them unless someone came along with something better, and even then, as Gordy laid down for everyone to know, "it had to be a lot better."

•   •   •

The assembly-line approach to producing songs was working well by the fall of 1963. When a song proved successful, the songwriters often cannibalized it, taking sections and reshuffling them for a follow-up hit with a similar sound.

Motown's copyright attorney, George Schiffer, helped the label strike a European distribution deal with recording-industry giant EMI. Some of the Tamla artists and songs were already hits in Europe, convincing Gordy that his sound cut across cultural and language barriers.

Gordy was feeling pretty confident about Motown's progress. Not every day, however, was problem free. It was a November Friday and the product-evaluation meeting had just ended. Barney Ales called Gordy on the phone and sounded serious.

"Berry, we got a little problem," Ales said. "Marvin [Gaye] just left here screaming about his record not being pushed. And you know we work our asses off promoting the hell out of his stuff." Gordy, who had generally been pleased that Gaye had married his sister Anna, also worried that the marriage might make Gaye feel he had more power to argue for what he wanted.

Before Gordy could answer, he heard someone enter his office. He looked up to see a distraught Gaye. "They're fucking with me, BG," said Gaye.

Gordy told Ales that Gaye was in his office and hung up.

"I was down in the sales department, BG," Gaye continued without waiting for any response from Gordy, "and they're bullshittin', man. They were supposed to get my record more airplay, but all they're pushing is Martha and the Vandellas' 'Quicksand' and the Miracles' 'Mickey's Monkey.' 'Can I Get a Witness' [Marvin's current song] is just barely breaking into the top thirty, and it's been out over two months."

Gordy knew that Gaye was excitable, so he deliberately waited a moment before answering and then tried to sound as calm as possible.

"Marvin, I've told you, you can't be running into the sales department screaming at those guys. It's just not wise on your part. You're the artist. I want them to like you—not hate you. I told you before, you got a problem, come to me." Gordy then reminded Gaye about all the sales department was doing for him.

Gaye was unimpressed. "I don't like the way they talk to me. They told me they didn't have time. They fronted me off."

Gordy decided to deal with Gaye's unhappy mood by scheduling a meeting for later that day with him, Phil Jones from sales, and Gaye's mentor, Harvey Fuqua. Gaye seemed satisfied and left.

It was not long after that, while Gordy was reading some mail, that somebody screamed that President Kennedy had been shot. Immediately, Gordy huddled with others around one of the office's radios. JFK was popular among Detroit's blacks. "I believed him to be a great president," Gordy later recalled, in a sentiment that was not atypical of his friends, family, and coworkers. There was little chatter as the news went quickly from a report of critical wounds to the death announcement shortly after 2:00 P.M. No one spoke. Eyes were cast to the floor, some cried, and others felt almost woozy, as if somehow the tragedy had unsteadied them. Family and friends began calling, partly to pass along the news but also to talk to someone, to share the anguish that was quickly enveloping the nation. (Gordy later paid a private tribute to the fallen president by naming his next child—a son born in March 1964 from his liaison with Margaret Norton—Kennedy William Gordy. The middle name is Smokey Robinson's real first name.)

Then Gaye called and asked Gordy if the meeting was still on or whether it was canceled because of the assassination. Gordy was in a fog but managed to grunt a yes.

The atmosphere at the meeting was tense and somber. It wasn't long, however, before Gaye and Phil Jones were arguing loudly over whether the problem was a lack of zeal from the sales department or the quality of the song itself. Jones was blunt, telling Gaye that the song did not have the right ingredients to make number one, and the only reason it had stayed on the charts as long as it had was the sales department's strenuous efforts.

"Bullshit," Gaye said, shaking his head. Gaye said that his song was number one on the R&B chart, but only number twenty-two on the pop chart, pointing out that black artists like him, who sold more records in black stores, were at a disadvantage when it came to the pop chart since the people who compiled it tended to call only the large white record stores. Jones, who was white, as was Ales, was trying hard to get the three main charts—*Cash Box, Billboard,* and *Record World*—to change their tabulation procedures. Gordy, Jones, and Fuqua spent the better part of an hour explaining this to Gaye. Finally, to everyone's relief, Gaye seemed to understand that the sales department was trying its hardest to make his record move as high as possible up the charts.

As the meeting ended, Gordy looked at Gaye and said: "So once again, Marvin, I'm asking you. Don't run into the sales department cussing them out. Be a good boy, OK?"

The word *boy* caused Gaye's face to flush with anger. "See!" he screamed. "See, BG! That's a whole bunch of bullshit. You think I'm a boy just like the white man." There had long been a simmering tension between Gordy and Gaye. Gaye had told others he thought Gordy "had a short man's complex. . . . But even in the beginning I knew we were destined to clash." Gaye also complained that Gordy ran Motown like "a loving Gestapo" and that he resented Gordy's power.

No one else said a word. Gordy stood up and stared at Gaye, who just stared back.

"Give me my money, motherfucker," said Gaye, reiterating another complaint he had with the sales department about what he thought was a discrepancy in his latest royalty statement.

Gordy ignored this. "*Boy* is not a bad word," Gordy said softly. "My father calls me *boy*. I call my sons *boy*. It is not what a person says, it's what they mean. If they mean something bad by it, then it's bad. If they don't, then it's not."

Gaye lost it. He stated pounding the desk with the palm of his hand. "See, that's how you do it," he yelled at a fevered pitch. "You con everybody, BG. Talking to you, man, you try to switch shit around and stuff."

This time Gordy didn't say anything, but anyone who knew him well could see from the glint of his eyes and the slight wrinkling of his forehead that he was furious. Suddenly, he swept his arm across the desk, forcing everything on it to fly across the room.

"What the fuck you talking about, man?" Gordy exploded as he moved toward Gaye. He walked in front of him, literally only inches from Gaye's face. "Don't you realize that the president was killed today? Don't you understand that I stayed here just for a meeting with you to solve a problem because I care about how you feel? How about how I feel?"

Gaye tried to shove past him, but Gordy would have none of it, throwing a shoulder into him. Again, Gaye tried pushing Gordy away, but this time Gordy shoved him and knocked him back, pinning him on the desk, one arm pressing into Gaye's chest and the other at his neck. Before any of the other stunned executives could pull Gordy off, he let go. Gaye stood up, clearly shaken. "I never saw Marvin so rattled," said Jones. Gordy stormed out without saying a word.

That night he was so upset by what happened that he even called Raynoma in New York to talk about the incident. "You won't believe it," he told her. "Marvin Gaye and I had a fistfight today."

Gaye told Gordy a few days later that he understood what had happened and that it was forgotten and that they should move on. Gordy, by that time, was long over his anger and more than willing to embrace Gaye and keep the company on track. Things were too good to let an argument, even a fistfight between the owner and one of his rising stars, disrupt Motown's harmony.

CHAPTER 14

The Defector

BY 1964, MOTOWN WAS GENERATING SO MANY HITS—FORTY-TWO of sixty records produced that year broke into the charts—that it had become the third most successful singles label in America. The Four Tops, who had left Gordy's office two years earlier with a contract they never signed, had returned for a meager four-hundred-dollar advance. They admitted to Gordy that while they did not like the original contract, they had been more concerned that a small black-owned label would not survive in the cutthroat business. Those fears had evaporated. And their confidence in the label was not misplaced. Gordy asked HDH to develop a song for them that would break them out of their supper-club style. Their first Motown effort—"Baby, I Need Your Loving"—was an instant hit and greatly expanded the group's appeal.

Gordy, of course, was delighted that the Four Tops were now under contract, but they were not the act that had his attention as the year started. That was instead diva Mary Wells. She had been Motown's biggest hit maker ever since "Bye Bye Baby," a song she had written when she was only fifteen. Then Smokey Robinson's boast about "My Guy" turned out to be right when the song shot to the top of the pop chart in May 1964. Jackie Wilson had romanced her, and she had joined the Beatles on tour in the United Kingdom. But Gordy knew that the record business, especially pop, needed the next song quickly, so no sooner had "My Guy" been released than he was badgering Smokey, "What's next?" "I'm working on it" was

Smokey's regular refrain. He was trying to develop something different, while Gordy kept urging him to stay with a similar sound because that was what Wells's fans expected. (Smokey did write, later that year, "My Girl," reversing the gender of the Wells hit, and it also went to number one, this time for the Temptations.)

As Gordy applied more pressure on Smokey, he was surprised to learn that Wells was not returning calls from anyone at Motown. Although Wells could sometimes be difficult, Gordy thought he had always had a good working relationship with her.

"What's going on?" Gordy asked Mickey Stevenson, who knew more company gossip than anyone else. "I think this Herman Griffin cat [Wells's husband] is putting a lot of shit in her head," Stevenson told him. "BG, I think you need to check her out." Gordy could not believe that no one had told him of any problems. Stevenson said that no one had wanted to bother Gordy.

When Gordy finally reached Wells on the phone, he noticed a different tone in her voice. He asked to meet with her, but she said it could only be at her house. Gordy thought that somewhat strange but agreed.

She kept him waiting a half hour before making a grand entrance into her living room. "Have a seat" was all she said, waving her hand at an ornate settee in the middle of the room. Then she suddenly left, returning a few minutes later. Gordy tried to be cool, asking her simply what was happening.

"Oh, I don't know," the twenty-one-year-old singer said, tossing her head back and sighing as though the weight of the world was on her shoulders. "I'm just here trying to do some things." She seemed tense.

Wells had a quick answer for all his questions, but none was satisfying. She had not been to the studio, she claimed, because she wasn't well, and when he inquired what was wrong, "Nothing much" was all she mustered. When he asked if she had a problem she wanted to discuss, she did not say a word but looked away.

The more Gordy pried, the more she withdrew. "Mr. Gordy, I think you should talk to my lawyer," she suddenly blurted out.

Gordy was caught off guard.

"Well, I have a lawyer from New York," she continued. "I think you should talk to him. His name is Lewis Harris, and he'll be over to the office tomorrow."

Gordy knew it wasn't good news. He stood up and stiffly told her he would be happy to meet her lawyer. "I lied," he later admitted.

The next morning, Gordy ran late and arrived at the office just minutes before Harris was due. Waiting for him was a letter from another New York attorney, this one about Raynoma. It informed him that the Mexican divorce they had gotten two years earlier was invalid, and they were still married. Just as he was digesting that bit of bad news, his secretary, Rebecca Nichols, buzzed and announced Lewis Harris.

Harris was blunt. He told Gordy that now that Wells was no longer a minor, she was disavowing all her Motown contracts. When asked why, Harris simply stated it was because she could do better with other companies.

Gordy tried convincing him that a good recording deal involved more than money. He gave Harris a tour of Motown, showed him the studio, the writers' and producers' room, the management operation, the promotion and sales department, and finally Artist Development.

Harris was impressed. "Mr. Gordy, I have never seen a company that does this much for any artist." He assured Gordy he was returning to tell Wells to keep her contracts in place. Harris called Gordy the next day to say that Wells had fired him. He then gave Gordy a piece of parting advice.

"Mr. Gordy, you'd be better off spending half of the time doing what you do for the artists and the other half telling them what you're doing. Believe me, they'll never understand if you don't."

Wells's next choice for a lawyer, Detroit native Herbert Eiges, was not so easily sold by Gordy. A legal battle between Gordy and Wells was soon under way.

•   •   •

From New York came more bad news. Barney Ales told Gordy the New York police had broken up a record-bootlegging operation—an industry headache—and all the fraudulent copies were Motown hits. But the worst part was that the bootlegging chief was none other than Raynoma, who was supposed to be running the New York Jobete office.

Gordy at first thought Ales was joking, albeit in bad taste. He knew that Ales and Ray had never gotten along well. But Ales was dead serious. It turned out that the break in the case had come when Raynoma had an accomplice sell five thousand copies of Mary Wells's "My Guy" from the trunk of her silver Lincoln Continental. One of the clerks at the store where the bootleg records were sold called Detroit and was transferred to Ales. It did not take Ales very long to figure out the Lincoln belonged to Raynoma.

Later that same day, Raynoma called Gordy from jail. She needed money fast. He thought back to their many conversations during the last year in which she had pleaded for a larger budget. Jobete's New York office, she claimed, cost more than anyone in Detroit realized. Gordy had always rebuffed her, telling her that getting the extra money to run New York was her problem, and that if she couldn't find it she should close the office. She had obviously resorted to some fairly extreme ways of coming up with extra cash.

She pleaded with him to bail her out. He refused.

Ray managed to make bail that night, through the lawyer for her boyfriend, who had been arrested with her. The next morning, Barney Ales was at the New York office waiting for her when she showed up. Ales had already padlocked the door. He looked at her with a mixture of disappointment and disdain.

"What the hell is this?" asked Ray indignantly.

"We're closing the New York office. I'll wait while you remove your personal belongings."

Gordy was infuriated. He summoned Raynoma to Detroit, where Ales and the Noveck brothers gave her forty-eight hours to decide whether she wanted to face a criminal prosecution or to sign a general release from Motown and all its entities. She also had to formally agree to dissolve her marriage to Gordy. As part of the settlement, Ray would receive a onetime payment of $10,000, $1,382 a month in alimony for ten years, and an additional $150 a month for child support for Kerry until he reached eighteen. She agreed. (The relationship between Raynoma and Berry remained turbulent—when she remarried, Gordy loaned her and her new husband money to start their own recording label, and later she would sometimes work for Motown when her business stagnated. When she published her mostly negative 1990 memoir, *Berry, Me, and Motown,* Gordy was briefly outraged but again forgave her.)

The legal fight Gordy had with Mary Wells was resolved as well—with her leaving Motown. Twentieth Century–Fox's record division, which signed her for a $500,000 advance, agreed to pay Motown a percentage of her royalties for three years. But Mary Wells could not settle down. Over the next two decades, she moved among five companies, producing more than twenty albums, but none recaptured the star status she had had with Motown. She never had a release chart higher than number thirty-four. "Actually, the underlying message of Wells's departure turned out all right for us at Motown," recalled sales executive Tom Noonan, "because when she left and had no hits, it told all the other artists that if you were disloyal and left the label, you'd go nowhere." Widespread—and unfounded—rumors that Gordy had used his considerable power with black DJs to squelch Wells's post-Motown releases also added to the label's appearance of invulnerability. (Many fans and critics noticed that the chain-smoking Wells's voice seemed progressively weaker over the years. In 1992, she succumbed to throat cancer.)

Gordy had thought no one would ever leave Motown. Before Wells had made her move, Smokey Robinson had received an unsolicited offer from Scepter Records' president, Florence Greenberg, to leave Motown for a reputed one-million-dollar advance. "How could she think I would [leave]?" he asked Gordy. "What did she think of me?" Gordy had interpreted Smokey's decision as strong evidence that everyone else at the label, especially top stars like Wells, was happy and not going anywhere. So not only was he unnerved that the label had lost its top female star, but also he felt one was needed to give Motown legitimacy inside the industry. Despite a number of hits from the rest of the label during 1964, Wells's departure caused general distress throughout the company.

Smokey, who had had a lock on writing hits for Wells, had lost a working partner and would now have to compete with the label's other writers for any new singer. It would take time, Gordy told others, to find a new star, develop the right material, and then promote and break her in the business.

Martha Reeves noticed that Gordy "was a little changed" after Wells's departure. He redid all of the artists' contracts—adding two more years to their original terms—and had everyone re-sign.

While the fight with Wells was still going on, Barney Ales made a prescient comment to *Billboard*. He noted that the situation with Wells was not that unusual, since artists with top records are usually flooded with enticing offers from competitors, but he said he would like to alert the industry to a little-known Motown group that he predicted "will have the next No. 1 record in the U.S.": the Supremes.

The break for the long-suffering group, whose highest-ranking song had peaked at number twenty-three, finally came in June 1964. The Friday product-evaluation meeting had ended, and Mickey Stevenson and Smokey Robinson stayed behind to argue with Gordy over selections that had been turned down. Stevenson was particularly upset over the reaction to a song that he had written for Kim Weston, a relatively new, sultry singer. (Johnny Thorton, a cousin of Brian and Eddie Holland, had discovered her.) As the three bantered, Esther Gordy came in and announced that Dick Clark's office had just called.

"They want Brenda Holloway on the *Caravan of Stars,*" Esther said excitedly. Holloway, who had been signed to the label a year earlier, was having a lackluster career. (The next year, however, the Beatles selected her to open for them on their North American tour.)

The *Caravan of Stars,* like Clark's other show, *American Bandstand,* was one of a handful of television shows that could transform midlist performers into stars. Instead of working in a studio setting like *American Bandstand, Caravan of Stars* took hot acts on the road to perform in front of eager audiences. Gordy thought of it as the "ultimate record hop."

Clark loved Holloway's "Every Little Bit Hurts," a waltz-tempo tune that Hal Davis and Marc Gordon had produced out of a small satellite office in Los Angeles that Motown had opened the previous year. Everyone knew Gordy did not like waltzes, so when the song had been played at one of the Friday meetings most expected Gordy to veto it. But he saw it as a blues-styled ballad and said it would be a smash—and it was.

Gordy saw Clark's interest in Holloway as an opening for the Supremes. He suggested that Esther might be able to get the Supremes on the *Caravan of Stars* along with Holloway. Esther was ahead of her brother and had already asked the show's producers. But the Supremes simply weren't big enough. She had also tried squeezing other Motown acts into the show but was turned down.

"They only want Brenda," she told Gordy.

Gordy shook his head furiously. He told Esther that "Where Did Our Love Go" could be a major hit, but that without Dick Clark it wasn't going to reach a white audience. Esther said it was impossible—Clark's production team was already complaining about being over budget. "Budget!" Gordy screamed. "To hell with budget. I'll pay them if I have to. If we can get them on his show, he's got to play their record."

Esther agreed to try again.

Shortly after Esther left, Ales was on the phone and wanted to set up a meeting over something personal. Smokey and Stevenson left. Ales was gushing. "Smash, smash!" he shouted into the phone. "Fantastic. Everything is great. Chicago came in for another five thousand on Brenda. The Tempts' 'I'll Be in Trouble'—fifty-one with a bullet [meaning the record's sales were rising fast]. 'Where Did Our Love Go' is getting some action, too. And your record, 'Try It Baby,' on Marvin is cooking. We're hot, man."

Gordy knew Ales too well not to realize that he was being set up for another pay-raise request. He tried to be cool, asking Ales why he needed to meet.

"Oh, nothing," Ales said as nonchalantly as he could. "Just get together, go over some stuff, bring you up-to-date on what's happening."

"Isn't that what you're doing now?" asked Gordy.

"Oh yeah, but we need to look into each other's eyes, you know, face to face."

As Gordy agreed to a meeting the following Monday, Esther reappeared at his office door. "It's done," she announced, beaming. Dick Clark had agreed to put the Supremes on *Caravan of Stars.*

Before Gordy could relax and relish the good news, he had the anxiety of preparing for his meeting with Ales, the only person who Gordy felt got the best of him in negotiations. He was determined not to let it happen again.

Instead of waiting for Ales to show up at his office, he instead popped into Ales's office early Monday morning. Gordy slipped quietly into a chair in front of Ales's desk. Ales seemed initially flustered but after a few minutes of small talk got to his reason for seeing Gordy.

"Oh well, I've been wondering just how important you thought I was around here."

Gordy did not answer.

"Selling is the lifeblood of any organization," Ales continued, "but you're always talking about how our creative people are what makes Motown so different. Don't you think I deserve a bonus?"

Gordy had expected something similar but feigned surprise and sat straight up. He reminded Ales that the previous month he had given him a bonus for the entire department.

"I gave that all to the men. They're the best in the business, and I have to keep 'em happy." Ales flashed a big grin.

Gordy hesitated.

"I got a better idea," Ales continued without giving Gordy time to respond. "Forget the bonus. How about two percent of gross?"

Now Gordy was dumbfounded. He could not believe that Ales wanted to make money whether or not Motown turned a profit.

"All I can say is that other companies give gross participation to their top people," Ales hammered away. "Gee whiz, Berry, two percent of everything that comes in is not the worst thing in the world."

Gordy slumped in the chair. Ales had beaten him again. He paid Ales the bonus he wanted that same day.

CHAPTER 15

The Ghost Tour

WHAT GORDY DID NOT KNOW ABOUT ESTHER'S DEAL WITH DICK Clark's producers was that she had taken his offer to subsidize the Supremes' touring costs literally. Clark had agreed to book the group on the condition that he paid them only six hundred dollars weekly, with Motown responsible for all other costs. Gordy didn't like it but figured the money would be well spent if it meant getting a breakthrough for his long-suffering group. Ross's mother agreed to be the group's chaperone, for no pay.

The *Caravan of Stars* tour was set for thirty-six performances nationwide. The Supremes were at the bottom of a seventeen-act bill. At first, Ross, Wilson, and Ballard got polite applause, while audiences went crazy for the Shirelles or Gene Pitney. But as the tour progressed, the recently released "Where Did Our Love Go" started climbing the charts. In each successive city, word spread about the hot song. Clark started moving the Supremes up the list of acts and had to reprint the posters several times as the group's growing popularity outstripped his ability to predict where they should fit on the bill. By the time the tour ended in August, the song was on the way to number one, and the Supremes had crossed over and had become stars after eleven previous failures. (That success prompted Gordy to immediately have the girls sign a new and longer contract.)

Dick Clark was pleased with the group's success, but he was also happy to be rid of them. They had kept many of the other acts awake by practicing late at night on the bus, and Diane Ross had too many fights with other artists. Once, Ross had a spat with Brenda Holloway, who she thought had taken her can of hair spray. Another fight was with the Crystals' Delores Brooks, whom Diane accused of stealing a pair of her shoes. Their shouting got them both temporarily kicked off the bus. Another time, she jumped on the back of Mary Wilson, pulling her hair and punching her. Other women complained that Ross hogged the single mirror in the small dressing rooms they all used. "Diane always had a temper," said Mary Wilson, "and while some people might have seen her actions as the result of conniving, her behavior was actually more like that of a spoiled brat. Once she made up her mind about something, there was no reasoning with her. . . . Diane would fight with anyone, and often she would take a minor issue and keep on it until you reacted."

While the Supremes were still on tour, Gordy began badgering all the writers, especially Holland-Dozier-Holland, to develop a new song for them. This time it was easier, as it was clear that the group did well with an up-tempo pop beat that fit easily into formula songs with catchy words.

But the girls were not as concerned about their next hit as they were with finding out how much money they had made. Mary Wilson always spoke for the group on finances, and she went excitedly into Esther's office to find out how much each of them would soon be receiving.

"There is no money," Esther told her matter-of-factly. "Motown managed to get you on the Dick Clark tour only because he wanted Brenda Holloway. I told him to take you, too, and he agreed."

Wilson was stunned. "But Mrs. Edwards, we've been on the road for three months, and most of the shows were sellouts. Surely there must be some money coming to us."

"You were only paid six hundred dollars a week. Deduct from that the price of room and board and food for yourselves and Mrs. Ross, and that leaves nothing." Then she added, "It probably cost the company, but you needed the exposure."

Ross and Ballard were shocked when Wilson reported back to them. All they had to do was look out the window of Hitsville to see that they were among the few not enjoying the growing wealth filtering into the company. There, parked all over West Grand Boulevard, was a small fleet of new Cadillacs. When the singers, songwriters, and producers got their first big check, many simply went to the local dealer and endorsed it directly over.

They all made sure they had different colors and options. One day, Mickey Stevenson drove up in a new light-gray car, and a little later Berry arrived with his new one in the same color. Someone would clearly have to swap. A few days later, Stevenson was in a sedate black Cadillac.

The Supremes were now anxious to release their next song, "Baby Love." But just prior to the release, Gordy insisted it "didn't have enough life, and the opening wasn't catchy enough." The girls were taken back to the studio. The tempo was speeded up and the distinctive "Ooo-ooo-ooo" was added at the beginning. The Supremes thought it was childish to repeat just a few words through an entire song. But when it was released in September, it went to number one in a month. By November, it was also number one in Britain, the first time a Motown release had achieved that.

The Supremes' remarkable success was matched by many other Motown acts during the summer and early fall of 1964. Martha and the Vandellas' smash, "Dancing in the Street," was Gordy's personal favorite, and he later noted, "My goal to hook people in the first twenty seconds was never accomplished better." Reeves's vocal performance on that song is considered by most critics to be her best ever. Produced by Mickey Stevenson, and with Marvin Gaye joining the Vandellas as backup, the song's driving dance rhythm dominated the charts through the fall.

The hits seemed to come so easily that Gordy began to think the label was invincible. But he kept getting reminders that he still had business lessons to learn. Shortly after the Supremes had topped the British charts, Gordy received a call from an assistant to Brian Epstein, the Beatles' manager. Epstein had visited Hitsville a few months earlier and told Gordy how he and the Beatles loved the Motown sound. Now the Beatles wanted to record three Motown songs: "Please Mr. Postman," "You've Really Got a Hold on Me," and "Money (That's What I Want)" for their next album. Because they were the Beatles, Epstein offered Gordy one and a half cents per record sold for each song, instead of the industry standard two cents. Gordy, however, felt the Beatles needed his songs more than he needed them. He said he'd be happy to have the Beatles record Motown songs, but he wanted a two-cent royalty. The following day, Gordy again got a call from Epstein's assistant, and once again the same offer was made. This time, Gordy was told, he had until noon in Detroit—thirty minutes away—to wire his answer.

Gordy still wanted to refuse but decided to run it past others. In ten minutes, he had gathered his brother Robert, sister Loucye, Smokey Robinson, Billie Jean Brown, Barney Ales, and Ralph Seltzer. Brown and Seltzer thought Gordy should hold out. Robert warned him that he was being stubborn and could lose a lot of money if the Beatles did not record the songs. Ales was adamant that Gordy should accept the offer and reminded him that the royalty discount "is done all the time." He estimated the Beatles could sell up to ten million copies, meaning $150,000 for Motown. And Loucye echoed the same sentiment—"special rates aren't that unusual," she told him, "especially if they do more than a couple of songs."

Gordy listened but concluded, "Brian Epstein would never not use a great song just to save a half cent. No way. I'm holding out."

And Gordy did hold out until two minutes to twelve. Then, getting nervous the Beatles might drop his songs, he wired them accepting the lower rate. Everybody congratulated him. Then, two hours later, Gordy was stunned to learn that Capitol Records, the Beatles' label, already had the records in stock at their distributors. All three Motown songs were on the album. Epstein's last-minute gamble to save some money had worked. And Gordy had learned, as he later wrote, "never out negotiate yourself."

Another lesson Gordy learned at this time came shortly after the release of the Supremes' third single, "Come See About Me," from their *Where Did Our Love Go* album. On that album, Gordy had directed Ross to sing many of the leads, moving Mary Wilson and Flo Ballard further back, much to their disappointment. On some of the songs, Ross even stopped singing the backgrounds, leaving them to her partners. "Besides being upstaged," said Mary Wilson, "Flo and I also felt that the records suffered."

However, the newest single was moving up the charts, and everybody at Motown expected it also would hit number one. Gordy was in San Francisco for a record-distribution convention when he got a call from the owner of one of the city's largest record stores; he asked for the Supremes to make a quick stop at his store to sign some autographs. Gordy did not want to hurt his feelings, so he thanked him for the idea but averred that the group's schedule was too crammed and it would be almost impossible. The next day, Gordy woke up to radio ads promoting the Supremes' supposed appearance at the store. Furious, he called the owner and chewed him out, reminding him that he hadn't promised the group would be there.

"Yeah, but you didn't say they wouldn't."

"What I said was I didn't think so."

"I know, but you said you'd think about it, and you never called back. I've got five thousand fans out here waiting, and if the Supremes don't show up there's gonna be a riot."

Gordy, as he often did when challenged, became stubborn and defensive. He told the store owner it was his problem, and the Supremes would not show up.

"Well then," said the store owner, "I'm definitely gonna sue you. And the girls."

Gordy knew it was his fault for not having been definite the day before. He slammed the phone down. And he then went and got the girls and took them to the store. He translated that lesson into something he called "the three Ds, but not four": be direct, decisive, and deliberate but not dumb.

•   •   •

Toward the end of 1964, Gordy decided to have the popular Motortown Revue star in what would become an annual holiday show at Detroit's downtown Fox Theatre. It began that year on Christmas Day and ended with a New Year's Eve performance. He scheduled four shows daily, and tickets sold quickly. Gordy followed his long-standing rule that it did not matter how many hits an artist had, placement in the lineup depended solely on how crazy they drove the audience. It became a lesson the Supremes would not forget.

When the shows began, the Supremes were hot and were placed third from the prestigious closing spot. Only Marvin Gaye and the Miracles followed them (Smokey's closing song, "Mickey's Monkey," invariably brought the house down). Two days after the show opened, the Supremes flew to New York to appear on *The Ed Sullivan Show*, a live program on Sunday nights that was the most watched in the country. The Supremes performed "Come See About Me," their third straight number-one hit, but when they returned to Detroit they had lost their spot to Stevie Wonder, who had become increasingly popular with local audiences.

The Supremes weren't the only ones disgruntled. A few nights later at the theater, Smokey asked to see Berry alone. Once they had grabbed a private room, Smokey bitterly—and unusually for him—complained that

Ross was stealing his act. One of his trademark moves in "Mickey's Monkey" was to get almost prone on the stage, whispering the lyrics, and then slowly raise his body as his voice grew stronger, urging the band, "A little bit louder now, a little bit louder now." Ross had adopted a move where she fell to her knees during her act while singing, "A little bit softer now." The crowd loved it. Some other Motown artists weren't surprised. "She'll outrehearse you," said Marvin Gaye, "outdress you, and outperform you, so you best stay out of her way."

"It's ridiculous," Smokey complained to Gordy. "She's doing my whole bit. You gotta stop her!"

"Smoke," Gordy said, "the Supremes lost their spot, and Diana's just trying to get it back."

"And mine, too!"

Gordy laughed. "But Smokey, you're the star," he assured him. "You'll just have to come up with something else. There's no way I'm gonna stop her."

When Gordy turned away his closest friend, he knew that what he had been feeling about Ross was more than just fondness for one of his singers. "I guess I loved her before I even knew it."

Actually, many in Motown had recognized how enamored Gordy was of Ross. No one knew, however, that Ross was the inspiration for a song he had written, "Try It Baby." Gordy had had Marvin Gaye record the song, with the Temptations doing the background vocals. The song—which repeats the refrain "You'll see that nobody loves you but me"—is one of the best indicators of how infatuated Gordy was with her.

Ross, usually brimming with confidence, had acted coy and shy with Gordy. But her friends knew she had targeted him early on. Even before the group had a breakout hit, Ross confided to Mary Wilson, "I'm going to get him." And when Flo Ballard toured briefly with the Marvelettes because one of them was pregnant, Ross took advantage of her spare time at Motown by insinuating herself as Gordy's unofficial assistant. "Many people around Hitsville thought the job was a joke," recalled Mary Wilson. "At the time, I didn't understand why she would want him; he wasn't sexy. But he had power, and as I would soon see, that is perhaps the strongest aphrodisiac in the world."

As 1964 drew to a close, Ross and Gordy seemed to be everywhere together. Not surprisingly, the black press prominently covered them, including *Jet* and *Ebony*, the black magazines with the largest circulation. The white magazines such as *Time* and *Look* soon followed. But behind the scenes, problems were brewing. "The higher we ascended," said Mary Wilson, "the more Diane wanted for herself." Since she was dating Gordy, there was little the girls could do about it.

Gordy had come to believe that while original hits were important to the Supremes, the girls were ideal for performing standards and Broadway songs. That would give them entrée to the country's top nightclubs. Even if a group had a number-one hit, it was not as important as getting booked into New York's Copacabana. Once an artist played the Copa, which regularly featured Frank Sinatra, Sammy Davis Jr., and Tony Bennett, other clubs followed. The problem for Gordy was that the Copa was not interested in new acts.

Gordy, of course, knew there was a risk in having his groups do standards from composers such as Rodgers and Hart, Irving Berlin, and the Gershwins, since that was not the music Motown's listeners wanted. Even Motown's slogan, "The Voice of Young America," was meant to appeal to buyers in their teens and twenties.

Still, every time the Supremes did a TV show, Gordy tried to interest the producers in the idea, but they always turned it down. They only wanted the group's hit song of the moment. Finally, after much prodding from Gordy, the show *Hullabaloo* agreed to let the Supremes perform "You're Nobody 'til Somebody Loves You" for a show that was scheduled to tape a few months later. The timing was perfect. The television taping would follow the company's first-ever international Motortown Revue, opening in London and then proceeding to Germany, France, and Holland. That Revue would give the Supremes time to practice, since Gordy had inserted the song into their road show.

Besides the Supremes, the first U.K. Revue included the Miracles, Martha and the Vandellas, and Stevie Wonder. As Motown's success had grown, so had the entourage for the Revue. Everyone wanted to go to Europe. When the Revue left the United States, there were more chaperones, road managers, and assistants than ever—even Gordy's three oldest children, as well as his mother and father.

The Motown sound was extremely popular in London, and large crowds swarmed around the artists wherever they went. It was also the first time many of them, including the Supremes, ever saw themselves described as "Negresses," by the British press. But they quickly learned that no offense was intended. When the girls saw their picture in a newspaper, the lighting was wrong and they looked washed-out. Many at Motown mistakenly believed it was because the British photographers had so little experience in shooting black personalities. After that, they mockingly called their tour "the ghost tour."

The Brits were fascinated not only with their music but with personal details—what type of men they fancied or how they traveled with fifteen large suitcases and a shipping container of huge wig boxes. Other Motown acts who had not had big hits in England were virtually ignored and jealous of the attention given to the girls.

"We were exotic darlings," recalled Mary Wilson, "sexy and cute, and all the more interesting because we were black and hailed from what the foreign press liked to portray as a rat-infested ghetto. . . . Just a few months before we were eating crummy road food in an old bus; today we were flying first-class, drinking champagne, and eating caviar" (all charged to the girls' expense accounts, of course).

They toured for three weeks across England in a stretch limousine, accompanied by wardrobe assistants and hairstylists, and took constant breaks for shopping and pedicures and manicures. The other Revue acts toured in rented buses. Meanwhile, the Supremes and Gordy even spent a week at the lavish hundred-room country estate of Lord and Lady Londonderry.

"I found myself living in scenes that I'd only seen in movies," recalled Mary Wilson. Not long after, the girls proudly told one another they had made it as BLAPs, Black American Princesses. (Later, when Wilson had a torrid affair with a married Tom Jones, she spent a small fortune jetting around the world to join him for a night or two—and she followed that with a succession of affairs with well-known men, from Steve McQueen to Flip Wilson to *Hill Street Blues* star Mike Warren. "I love money," she told a reporter once. "I really love money.")

At Pinewood Studios, Gordy and his parents met the Beatles, who told a thrilled Gordy how much Motown had influenced their own music—in particular, they mentioned Smokey Robinson's writing, James Jamerson's bass playing, and Benny Benjamin's drums. The Beatles did not meet the

Supremes until a later visit in New York, but when they did it was a let-down. "We expected soulful, hip girls," recalled George Harrison. "We couldn't believe that three black girls from Detroit could be so square!" The girls were decked out in flashy dresses, jewelry, chinchilla and red-fox jack-ets and were surprised to find the Beatles' room filled with the pungent odor of marijuana. John Lennon sat in a corner just staring straight ahead at nothing in particular. Attempts at British humor seemed to go right over the girls' heads.

No matter, the Beatles' enthusiastic and public endorsement of Mo-town propelled the label's popularity. The *New Musical Express* ran a cover story with a banner headline, THE BEATLES' FAVORITE ARTISTS ARE COMING TO BRITAIN, and named the Supremes the number-three musical act in the world. John Lennon added to the frenzy by telling another interviewer that Marvin Gaye's "Can I Get a Witness?" was one of his favorite songs. The hugely popular British female star Dusty Springfield was also a key Motown enthusiast, and she hosted a television special, *Dusty Springfield Presents: The Sound of Motown.* Although Springfield had wanted Martha and the Vandel-las to be the featured performers, Gordy insisted it had to be the Supremes— "My face was broken, along with my heart," recalled Reeves. (Springfield's choice of Reeves may have had something to do with a crush she had on the Motown singer. Rumors had started after someone learned that Springfield had spent one night in Reeves's room. In her autobiography, Reeves only wrote, "I was amazed at just how others regarded our friendship, but I couldn't have cared less what anyone thought.")

By the time the Revue reached its second British city, Manchester, Gordy decided it was time to start rehearsing "You're Nobody 'til Somebody Loves You." In a five-hundred-seat theater, the crowd's enthusiasm sharply sub-sided when the group sang the song. Gordy was not concerned but contin-ued to take notes during the show about ways to improve Gil Askey's arrangement and their performance. But the moment he went backstage after the first show, he sensed that Ross was seething.

"Can I see you alone?" she hissed.

Outside the dressing room, alone with Gordy, Ross exploded. "I don't know what you are trying to do, but I'm not gonna let you ruin my career," she shouted. "They hate the song, and so do I! I'm not doing it anymore." Her large brown eyes widened as her anger grew.

It was the first time she had ever refused to perform a song he wanted her to do. He pleaded with her, reminding her that millions would see her on television and that the song could open the door to a new phase of her career.

"I don't care," she snapped. "I'm not doing it. I'm not ruining my career for you or nobody."

Again, he urged her to see the possibilities for her entire career.

She stared icily at him. "I'm not singing the song anymore," she repeated, enunciating the words as if he had somehow not heard her before. "I'm just not gonna do it."

Gordy had had it. "I'll tell you what. Just make up your mind who you want to satisfy. It's either me or them. It's your decision." He turned before she could say anything else and walked away. As he returned to his seat, he was nervous, as he realized the virtual ultimatum he had given her could force her to leave the label.

When the Supremes finally took the stage, Gordy tensed. As each song ended, he waited to hear the opening chords of "You're Nobody," but it didn't come. Near the completion of their set, when he had given up hope, he bolted upright in his seat as they began it.

After their set, he rushed to their dressing room and excitedly ran up to Ross. He told her how happy he was that she had performed the song.

"What song?" she asked nonchalantly, rummaging through her makeup drawer and not even glancing up at him. "I still don't like it, but . . . ," she glanced up at him, "I did it for you." Then she stood up and walked away.

After Manchester, the Supremes performed "You're Nobody 'til Somebody Loves You" at every show. They got into a groove and developed more confidence with each performance, and audiences started responding far more enthusiastically.

For Gordy, the tour was as much about his feelings for Diane as it was about his acts and business.

"Each time I thought about Manchester," he later admitted, "I realized how much Diana meant to me. I was madly in love. I think she knew it."

If Gordy had any doubts, they were put to rest when the tour ended in Paris at the Olympia Music Hall. Many celebrities were in the audience, from Marlene Dietrich to Sarah Vaughan. After the last show, Gordy and Ross were walking along a small side street in silence. Ross broke it.

"Black, why don't we stay a couple of days after the others leave?" she inquired, her voice soft. (They used "Black" as a nickname for each other.)

Gordy's heart pounded. He was ecstatic at the thought of spending time alone in Paris with Ross. Although they had been together a lot over several months, their relationship was not yet sexual. But he wanted to show her how cool he was, so as nonchalantly as he could muster he said, "Sounds great, Black."

For the next two days before the rest of the group flew home, Gordy tried to mask his nerves. He fretted that either she might change her mind or some emergency might force her to leave early. "Those two days seemed like two years," he said. When he finally saw off his parents, children, and the rest of the Motowners at the hotel, he was so excited that he found it hard to concentrate on even saying good-bye.

That April evening, alone in Paris, the two took a stroll and then headed back to Ross's opulent suite. Gordy opened the curtains wide so they could look out on the city as night fell, and they ordered champagne. They repeatedly toasted each other, almost giddy with happiness, and soon both felt tipsy. He would later describe her smile that night as "the most peaceful, joyous, beautiful smile I could have imagined."

He stared at her, besotted by the serene look on her face. She was beautiful. Her eyes were closed, as she rested her head back. They slowly kissed, and Gordy ripped off his clothes as he tried to undress her at the same time. He rolled on top of her. Years later, in his autobiography, he recalled in one of his frankest admissions, "Everything stopped working. The more I tried the less able I became. I never felt more panicked, more embarrassed, more useless. I rolled over, plopping my face down into the pillows with thoughts of smothering myself."

"I think it would be better if we just stayed friends," she said, trying to make him feel better but only adding to his anguish. She reached over with her two small arms and hugged him tightly. He got up without speaking and left for his own room.

They spent the next day as friends and enjoyed an easygoing afternoon. Neither mentioned the previous night. They rented a speedboat and later played in the water. That night, they visited several clubs. As they drank at one, she slid next to him and, in a whisper, serenaded him. Back at the hotel, again they went to her room. This time, their love affair began in earnest.

Gordy and Ross were determined that their affair would not reduce the focus on her career. It could only help to have captured the record label's owner, but Ross wasn't the only one in the group carrying on an affair with someone inside the company. Mary Wilson had moved in with Abdul "Duke" Fakir.

When they returned to the States, it was back to work for both the Supremes and Gordy. *Hullabaloo* aired, and Gordy's instincts were right—people loved the Supremes singing "You're Nobody 'til Somebody Loves You." After that show, every television program asked them to sing at least one standard. The girls did their first television commercials—for Coca-Cola—with the lyrics written by HDH. They also recorded their hits in German and Italian, learning the words phonetically.

"Stop! In the Name of Love" became their fourth consecutive number-one song. It was followed quickly by another number-one hit, "Back in My Arms Again." And, along with television specials, they finally made the cover of *Time*. They became the first pop group to play New York's Philharmonic Hall at Lincoln Center, opened Houston's Astrodome, and were the stars of Florida's Orange Bowl parade. The girls now received a weekly allowance of five hundred dollars each, and anytime they needed money, whether to buy a car or move to a new apartment, Motown gave it to them. (Their clothes and travel expenses, as always, were simply charged to their royalty accounts.) They had limousines when they wanted them, champagne, thousand-dollar dresses, and a large entourage. Gordy gave each a fur coat at Christmas. And they never saw a tax return. They never received a royalty statement.

"Money was no longer an object," recalled Mary Wilson, "and we never asked the price of anything." Their buying was so lavish that Detroit's Saks Fifth Avenue frequently closed to the public just so the girls, accompanied by a few personal shoppers, could wander the aisles without being bothered by adoring fans. Sometimes they flew to New York just to shop.

By the summer of 1965, General Artists Corporation, the club-booking agency that represented Motown, finally got the break Gordy wanted: the

Copa's owner, Jules Podell, agreed to book the girls. It was the club's first booking of a black group in the sixties and one of the youngest ever. As a result, the Copa was in the driver's seat when it came to negotiations. Not only did Gordy have to pay for many things that would have ordinarily been the club's responsibility, but he also had to sign a three-year agreement he dubbed "a slave contract." It guaranteed that the Supremes would appear for two- or three-week runs at least once a year. There would be two shows a night, seven days a week. The first year they would receive $3,000 a week, the second year $10,000 weekly, and the third year $15,000. All of the options were at Podell's sole discretion. But Gordy was willing to do the deal despite the restrictive terms and poor pay.

Although Motown bore most of the shows' production costs, Gordy cut no corners. It was the most expensive show he had ever undertaken, and he personally oversaw every detail. Gordy considered his losses as an investment to building stars. The Artist Development department worked full-time on the choreography, costumes, staging, and musical arrangements. Publicity, ITMI, and Barney Ales and his sales staff all ensured that the press, top DJs, record distributors, and other industry bigwigs were there. Gordy copied the style of many Broadway producers who first tried their acts out of town before bringing the polished version to New York. He picked the Rip-Tide Club in Wildwood, New Jersey. The Supremes rehearsed during the days and performed at nights. The Motown staff that accompanied them held daily meetings critiquing every detail of the show. The Copa opening was set for July 29, 1965, and Gordy told everyone it was "the biggest opening of our lives."

Cholly Atkins and Maurice King worked closely with the group. Atkins gave the girls their stylized hand gestures and their distinctive sideways looking-over-the-shoulder stance. Gordy would not permit the slightest change unless he approved. As the opening neared, musical director Gil Askey and arranger Johnnie Allen joined the troupe. Ross, however, often refused to do what Atkins and King asked of her. If they insisted, she ran to Gordy. According to Mary Wilson, "Diane was making noises that she wanted to be set apart from us. She and Berry never hesitated to hold that over the head of anyone who crossed her." It was during this rehearsal that a European magazine carried the news of her name change to Diana, and the other girls felt "this was just one more step away from us, one more way of setting herself apart."

Shortly before the group moved to New York City for opening night, Gordy received a call that his sister Loucye was seriously ill in a Detroit hospital. His parents were insistent he return home. It was not until he arrived that he learned she had had a cerebral hemorrhage and needed surgery to relieve a buildup of cranial pressure. Loucye, still cognizant of everything happening around her, personally asked Gordy to make medical decisions for her. But Gordy had not been there when she was taken ill, nor had he been involved with the discussions between the doctors and her family. When he told the family that he wanted a second opinion about the surgery, they balked. It was too late to start getting other opinions, and besides, Loucye's doctor, who had already arranged for a specialist to perform the surgery, would be insulted.

Berry still wanted a second opinion. So Loucye's doctor arranged for another specialist to examine her. At the last minute, however, the specialist was called away on an emergency. Gordy was torn over what to do: cancel the surgery while he arranged for another doctor or trust Loucye's physician and go ahead with the surgery as planned. To postpone it now, the doctor told Gordy, would pose a much more serious threat to Loucye. Gordy finally gave his permission.

Sitting in the waiting room, the family said little. They seemed lost in their own thoughts and prayers. Gordy kept thinking about how much Loucye had sacrificed for him over the years—taking him into her home, working so hard at Motown when it was nothing but a family start-up. She had been there through the difficult years, and Gordy badly wanted her to be able to see the successes that were now coming faster than even he could have imagined.

After several hours, the doctor came in. "The patient died," he simply said. Then he turned and walked away. Gordy was stunned. He sat alone for a long time, damning himself for not going with his instincts and postponing the surgery. Family and friends tried consoling him. Many told him not to worry, that he did the best he could. He decided that night he had to make Loucye's death count for something, and he promised himself that he would never again let anyone talk him out of what he felt was right.

When he returned home from the hospital, completely exhausted, he discovered that his ex-wife Raynoma, who had been in Detroit, had forced her way past his Spanish housekeeper and gone on a rampage, ripping up pictures of Gordy with other women. He was too wiped out even to get angry.

At Loucye's funeral, Marvin Gaye sang "His Eye Is on the Sparrow." It was one of his most inspired moments, a heart-wrenching performance in which he cried throughout the song. "We were all racing around the track as fast as our legs would carry us," recalled Gaye. "The only thing that made us stop and consider our own mortality was Loucye's death. That was a cold and ugly shock."

Loucye's funeral was held the same day the Supremes opened at the Copa. After the burial, most of the Gordy family boarded a plane for New York. They had agreed that that night's performance, and later an album, would be dedicated to Loucye.

Just before the show, the gravel-voiced, cigar-smoking Podell added a few extra rows of makeshift chairs to create new ringside seats for arriving bigwigs, pushing many of Gordy's guests and staff farther back. Although Ales and Gordy were frustrated that some of their invited DJs, reporters, and record distributors were not at the front, they realized the one person with whom they could not argue was Podell himself. What they could not tell from Podell's flat expression was that he was very impressed that a black pop group with which he was barely familiar had packed his club for an off-season engagement. He had learned earlier in the day the surprising news the group had sold out their entire run.

When the show began, with a downward swing of Gil Askey's arms, Gordy found a place at the very rear of the club. He wanted to be able to observe the staging, lighting, how the girls moved, and the audience's reactions. He had convinced himself and half of the staff that if the Supremes flopped, it would set the label back ten years.

"And now, ladies and gentlemen," the announcer's deep voice intoned over the buzz of the crowd, "Jules Podell proudly presents the Supremes." The girls seemed to glide onto the stage, snapping their fingers, decked out in long sequined gowns. The opening number was the 1960 show tune "Put on a Happy Face," which Askey had done to a jazz arrangement. "Diana was cooking," Gordy recalled.

Gordy anxiously glanced over at Podell's table. Sammy Davis Jr., columnist Earl Wilson, and Ed Sullivan were with him. Motown spent thousands that night on drinks and small gifts for many of the attending celebrities.

(The girls, of course, did not know that all costs for promotional items were charged to them.)

With a succession of hits and standards, the Supremes brought down the house. Gordy had been right: opening at the Copa meant that similar venues suddenly clamored for them—Las Vegas's Flamingo Hotel, for instance, booked the girls, sight unseen, one year in advance. Gordy had again accomplished something ahead of his time: crossover acts that could play the premier show-club circuit. The only sour note was that after opening night Gordy decided that Ross should take over Ballard's one lead song, "People," from *Funny Girl.* When Ballard learned of it, she stormed along New York City streets, causing taxis to slam their brakes to avoid hitting her as she loudly kept repeating, "Flo's not taking this shit! My voice is hoarse, but it ain't so hoarse they should take that song away from me!" After that, Ballard became more defensive, disagreeing with almost everything Gordy said. "From that moment on," remembered Mary Wilson, "Flo regarded what was in fact the highest achievement of our career as a disaster. She was sad and moody, and I could see the three of us being torn apart."

Wilson did not think it could get any worse, but she was wrong. "Diane was obsessed not with being *a* star, but *the* star."

Ross told Atkins she did not like her placement onstage during the group's performance of "The Girl from Ipanema." When he refused to move her, she informed Gordy and then made the move on her own.

CHAPTER 16

Dueling Songwriters

By 1965, as Motown accumulated more hits on the charts and its stars were recognized almost everywhere, Gordy was called "star-maker" or sometimes "magic man." He received the Small Businessman of the Year Award from Detroit's mayor. The company, which had $4.5 million in sales in 1963, had grown to $10 million the following year, and reached $15 million by 1965. There were now more than 100 employees and 175 artists.

During the label's first five years, Smokey Robinson had been king, not only as the Miracles' lead performer but also as a songwriter, creating successful songs for himself, the Temptations, and Mary Wells, among others. Smokey was unique in Motown because of his close friendship with Gordy—he was the only artist Gordy encouraged to write songs for himself and others. As for other artists, "Berry was very clear," recalled the Tempts' Otis Williams, "artists performed, writers wrote, and producers produced. It was that simple. . . . In his paternal, sometimes condescending way, he let it be known that he wasn't interested in having an artist who wrote and produced."

By 1965, Smokey's dominance had been seriously challenged by the Holland-Dozier-Holland team, all of whom were in their twenties. With driving, simple melodies, they always created an easy-to-remember hook. Each side had its own fans inside Motown. After HDH gave Marvin Gaye another hit with "How Sweet It Is (to Be Loved by You)," Smokey answered with "My Girl" for the Temptations, their first to reach number one and the first time that the lanky David Ruffin, sporting his trademark thick, black-rimmed glasses and a sharkskin suit, sang the lead for the group. HDH countered with "Nowhere to Run" for Martha and the Vandellas, and no sooner had that started climbing the charts than Smokey wrote one of his best ever, "Ooo Baby Baby," for his own Miracles.

Although there were plenty of other songwriters and producers at Motown—in 1965 even Gordy coproduced "Shotgun" as the first commercial success for Junior Walker and the All Stars—Smokey and HDH were by far the most successful. But by 1965 HDH began pulling away, benefiting from one of Gordy's rules that if two records were both equally strong at the Friday meetings, the recording nod went to the producers who had the last hit. HDH's success fed upon itself. Their "I Hear a Symphony" went number one for the Supremes, and even when it came to new groups, they produced hits such as "This Old Heart of Mine (Is Weak for You)" for the Isley Brothers, Shorty Long's "Function at the Junction," and the Elgins' "Heaven Must Have Sent You."

Over the next couple of years, HDH produced an amazing twenty-eight songs in the top twenty, of which twelve went to number one. They not only turned out successive hits for the Supremes but gave the Four Tops five number ones, "I Can't Help Myself (Sugar Pie, Honey Bunch)," "It's the Same Old Song," "Reach Out I'll Be There," "Standing in the Shadows of Love," and "Bernadette." The last was a critically acclaimed song that Levi Stubbs, the Tops' deep-voiced lead singer, sang so well that Gordy later commented that Stubbs "made Bernadette live—I wanted to meet her." Berry liked that HDH worked fast. For instance, in July 1965 Columbia Records—where the Four Tops had been prior to Motown—decided to rerelease the group's 1961 "Ain't That Love." Gordy got wind of it and assigned HDH to develop a rival song. The songwriters got their instructions from Gordy in the morning, wrote a new song—"It's the Same Old Song"— by noon, and rehearsed with the band and then laid down the vocal tracks by the end of the day. Motown rushed out "It's the Same Old Song" three days later, and it entered the charts on the same day as CBS's release. The CBS song stalled at number ninety-three after a week, whereas HDH's new song remained a hit for weeks, peaking at number five.

Smokey, of course, had the disadvantage of often being on the road performing with the Miracles, an arduous activity that sapped much of his energy. Still, he managed to send in songs as he traveled, often collaborating with one of the other Miracles—Ronnie White, Pete Moore, Bobby Rogers, or even longtime friend Marv Tarplin, the group's guitar player. Not only did they write and produce songs for themselves during this time—"Going to a Go-Go," "I Second That Emotion," "More Love," and "The Tracks of My Tears," a song Gordy considered a "masterpiece" and many music critics consider their best—they also created hits for Marvin Gaye with "I'll Be Doggone" and "Ain't That Peculiar," as well as for the Marvelettes with "Don't Mess with Bill."

As successful as 1965 was, Gordy remained concerned about Stevie Wonder. He had not even come close to the top of the charts since "Fingertips (Part 2)," two years earlier. Motown had made one of its few miscues in not promptly following up with new hits for him, and they allowed him to stagnate with second-rate material. His second album, *The Jazz Soul of Little Stevie*, had not done well, and a single, "Work Out, Stevie, Work Out," had reached only number thirty-three on the charts. His two 1964 singles, "Castles in the Sand" and "Hey, Harmonica Man," had reached fifty-two and twenty-nine respectively. His 1965 "High Heel Sneakers" did not do any better.

Gordy was anxious to develop a new song for Wonder because he feared his voice might change. (He was fifteen in 1965.) But when Wonder got back into the studio, Gordy and others discovered they were already too late—his voice had already changed. But their concerns that it might stop his budding career were misplaced. Gone was the high pitch that many thought prevented him from tackling songs with real depth, and it was replaced with a more powerful and steadier voice that resonated with feeling. The voice change had also unexpectedly boosted Wonder's confidence, and he began tapping into one of his unexplored talents, songwriting. By late 1965 he was ready with a new song he had cowritten, "Uptight (Everything's Alright)." It revitalized his career—reaching number three on the singles chart—and reintroduced him to the public as an adult performer. It marked the start of a multiyear run for Wonder. With the same prolific cowriters and producers, Sylvia Moy and Hank Cosby, another song, "Shoo-Be-Doo-Be-Doo-Da-Day" was also a hit. Even Stevie's mother, Lula Hardaway, got a songwriting credit for "I Was Made to Love Her"—a song that hit number two but was unable to dislodge the Doors' "Light My Fire."

In early December 1965, Smokey wrote "Get Ready" for the Temptations. It rose immediately to number one on the R&B chart but climbed no higher than number twenty-nine on the all-important and more lucrative pop chart. "It wasn't a bad song," recalled Otis Williams, "but I thought it lacked an edge." Norman Whitfield saw that as a weakness. Since HDH had its hands full, Whitfield was relentless in pursuing other artists at Motown. He could write and produce soft, smooth ballads, but his real talent lay in more intricate and powerful arrangements. Whitfield was intense, not overly friendly, but clearly gifted. Gordy and others admired his willingness to redo a song over and over until it was perfect for release, as well as his ability to take a song that hadn't turned into a hit for one artist and produce it again for other artists until he found one that could make it move up the charts.

Though Smokey Robinson had had the Tempts exclusively, at the Friday meeting just after "Get Ready" had stagnated for them, the group listened to Whitfield's new production for the group, "Ain't Too Proud to Beg." Reactions to the new song were mixed. Finally, Gordy weighed in: "I love the feel—it's street. But it doesn't have enough meat. I gotta hear more story."

The following Friday, Whitfield returned with an improved version. It was narrowly rejected. He was greatly disappointed as the group went along with Gordy's feeling that the song was not quite ready.

The third week, Whitfield brought in a reworked track on which lead singer David Ruffin had to push his voice hard to record in a higher key. During the recording session, Ruffin had to stop to catch his breath, and by the time he finished he was drenched in sweat. The group knew they had something different and thought it would be a major hit. Gordy agreed. When he heard the reworked tune, Ruffin's voice "came jumping off that record begging like I'd never heard before."

Whitfield had taken the Temptations away from Smokey. He worked with Eddie Holland on the group's three biggest hits for 1966; besides "Ain't Too Proud to Beg," the group had "Beauty Is Only Skin Deep" and "(I Know) I'm Losing You." The songs were all different but kept intact the Temptations' distinctive character. And his songs also emphasized all five of the group's members as distinct singers instead of featuring just one lead singer backed up by a homogenized chorus. Even the Tempts, who had liked Smokey, were pleased with the change.

•   •   •

Motown continued to be a magnet for new talent. It was around this time that a young couple from New York arrived. Nick Ashford, a former jazz dancer, and Valerie Simpson, a gospel singer and pianist, joined the growing songwriting staff at Jobete. One day, Harvey Fuqua was looking for material for his protégé Marvin Gaye to sing with Tammi Terrell. The beautiful, twenty-three-year-old Terrell (née Tammy Montgomery) had finished an unsuccessful stint as a background singer in James Brown's revue, where she had a reputation as a promiscuous heavy drinker. Terrell was the third female vocalist that Fuqua put together with Gaye, following Mary Wells and Kim Weston.

Ashford and Simpson mentioned to Fuqua they had some demos. Like many other songwriters, they wanted to produce as well as write. Although Motown had grown substantially since its early days when everyone was encouraged to tackle almost any project, Gordy, to his credit, still ensured that, if you had some talent, you could ask for more responsibilities until you finally got in over your head. With a green light from Fuqua, Ashford and Simpson began producing, using his lyrics and her melodies. When they brought their first collaborative effort with Gaye and Terrell, "Ain't Nothing Like the Real Thing," into a Friday meeting, there was virtually no debate. Everyone liked it and voted it a hit, and it was. When their second production for the duo, "You're All I Need to Get By," was presented a few months later, Gordy liked it so much he didn't even bother to take a vote, and no one at the meeting complained. For both those hit songs, the newcomers Ashford and Simpson had beat out competing versions from the veteran team of Harvey Fuqua and Johnny Bristol.

A white songwriter from Chicago, Ron Miller, had gotten his foot in the door with Motown one night when he had delivered pizza to Mickey Stevenson's hotel room, discovered who he was, and began barraging him with songs he had written. The opinionated Miller's unique talent was in writing songs that sounded like a combination of show tunes and blues. Since they resembled old standards, Gordy did not want to put them on Jobete, which everyone now knew was a Motown company. Instead, he concocted a new name while flipping through the Detroit telephone book:

Stein and Van Stock. "It sounded old line," Berry recalled, "classy, and Jewish."

Gordy's favorite Miller composition was "For Once in My Life," a song most people don't even think of as a Motown tune, although it was recorded in an up-tempo, hip version by Stevie Wonder in 1968. It became an instant standard and was covered by Andy Williams, Perry Como, Tony Bennett, and Frank Sinatra. When it was released, *Billboard* did a review and called it an old classic from Stein and Van Stock Publishing, precisely what Gordy had hoped for.

By 1966, Motown had almost two hundred acts under contract. Although many of them are well known in music history, some still seem unlikely candidates for the label. They included sixties comic Soupy Sales, Paul Petersen of *The Donna Reed Show,* character actor Scatman Crothers, Irene Ryan (Granny on *The Beverly Hillbillies*), Jack Soo (who later played Detective Yemana on *Barney Miller*), and later a number of mainstream black actors: Leslie Uggams, Barbara McNair, and Diahann Carroll. Gordy would even expand the company's reach, over the next couple of years, into white garage-rock bands with its Rare Earth label.

Although the heart and soul of Motown was still in Detroit, there were now small satellite offices in New York and Los Angeles. Gordy, however, paid little attention to what happened there. Every major decision had to come from Detroit. Sometimes he wasn't even initially aware of who was running his other offices.

On July 4, 1966, as he walked out of Hitsville, Gordy's ex-wife Thelma drove up. Berry IV and Terry were in the backseat, and they yelled in unison, "Hi, Daddy!" As he turned to see them, Gordy also could not miss, as he described it, "the grinning white man in the front seat with Thelma."

"Berry," Thelma yelled out, "this is Shelly Berger. He runs your California office."

"Oh, Mr. Gordy," Berger said, his head halfway out the car window, the grin seemingly frozen on his face, "this is great!" He stuck his arm out to shake Gordy's hand. Gordy shook it reluctantly. "Why don't you come with us to the company picnic?" Berger continued. "We could play some ball. Y'know, L.A. versus Detroit?"

"Nice to meet you," Gordy replied flatly, glanced at Thelma, waved at the children, and then walked away.

Shelly Berger had actually been hired by Motown's Ralph Seltzer to find television and film tie-ins for Motown's artists and music. Word spread quickly of Gordy's cold greeting of Berger, and at the picnic people shunned him. But after the picnic, Gordy asked others about Berger's work in Los Angeles and learned the ex-actor with a cutting sense of humor was creative and talented. The following week in Detroit, a Berger-arranged Dick Clark show—*Where the Action Is*—was set to use many Motown acts for a heavily promoted television special. Slowly convinced that Berger was the right person to run the Los Angeles office, Gordy met with him before Berger returned to Los Angeles. Gordy finally worked around to the question that had been gnawing at him: How had Berger met Thelma?

"I didn't really," Berger said, somewhat surprised at the question. "I was just a new guy in town, and Rebecca [Nichols] asked Mrs. Gordy if she would give me a ride back to my hotel. Royal treatment, I thought. Who knew that by riding with that nice lady and those little kids my whole future would be hanging by a thread?"

He broke into one of his trademark smiles that had initially irritated Gordy. Gordy relaxed, and later the two, who became close friends, often joked about the dangers of relying on first impressions.

Berger's arrival in Motown's Los Angeles office came when the label was having a rare slowdown—the last two Supremes releases had failed to maintain their string of number-one hits. That prompted Gordy to issue a very short memo: "We will release nothing less than Top Ten product on any artist. And because the Supremes world-wide acceptance is greater than other artists, on them we will release only #1 records."

"Is he kidding?" Shelly Berger said, laughing out loud when he saw that memo. "What does he think this is? The Ford Motor Company? 'We will only manufacture red cars!'"

That memo was more a sign of Gordy's frustration than a realistic directive. But somehow it seemed to spur the writers, especially HDH. A succession of hits soon followed, including "You Can't Hurry Love," "You Keep Me Hanging On," "Love Is Here and Now You're Gone," and "The Happening."

Gordy relaxed again. "We dangerous," he said one day when passing Brian Holland in the hallway.

Gordy's line could have had a double meaning for anyone who knew what was happening at Motown. It wasn't just about writing and producing songs; as success settled in, the place had been infected by Gordy's love of gambling. What had changed from his early days was that he now had enough money to lose and not have it pinch his lifestyle. "He was a reckless gambler," Ralph Seltzer said. "On any given day, he could lose fifty to one hundred thousand dollars—on a whim."

Those who worked with him saw that Gordy was almost obsessive about gambling on anything. "Berry's such a hardcore bettor," recalled Marvin Gaye, "that if you were in his office and it was raining, he'd pick out two raindrops that hit the window at the same time. He'd take one, you'd take the other, and he'd bet you ten bucks that his raindrop would slide down and hit the bottom of the window before yours." Some are convinced that Gordy's persistent efforts to open up his artists to a Las Vegas venue was so that he could be near the gaming tables.

The high-stakes poker games that started in the mid-1960s were big for their time. Even Gordy, who had a high tolerance for large losses, would later remember the card games from this time as "killer-poker." When royalty checks arrived, a group of regular players, including Harvey Fuqua, Mickey Stevenson, Johnny Bristol, Eddie and Brian Holland, and Ron Miller joined Gordy at one of their homes, all of which had been recently purchased. Literally thousands of dollars rode on each game. These were hard-core gamblers who loved the game. Occasionally, a less serious player joined the regulars. For instance, Smokey Robinson always wanted to play, but he lost so much money quickly that Gordy banned him in order to protect him. Still, Smokey showed up, often begging to get into the games. Since the others knew he had a lot of money, they were eager, despite Gordy's ban, to have him play. One night, Gordy gave Smokey another chance. He soon tried to bluff his way through a five-thousand-dollar pot and lost; and when he had a winning hand, he was so easily read by the others that they all dropped out quickly, leaving him almost nothing to claim. After that performance, Gordy made the ban permanent.

Gordy took his gambling seriously. Once, he played blackjack with the Supremes' Mary Wilson and lost four thousand dollars to her. At the end of the night, she forgave the debt, telling him "it was only a game." He beamed and thanked her. A few days later, they played again, and this time Wilson lost $6,200. At the end, she was startled when Gordy asked for the money.

"But Berry, the other day I let you go—"

"That was *you*, Mary," Gordy interrupted. "It's a lesson you have to learn."

CHAPTER 17

"More a Family Than a Business"

MOTOWN WOULD NEVER HAVE A MORE SUCCESSFUL YEAR THAN 1966—75 percent of all its releases hit the charts in an industry in which companies averaged only 10 percent. By this time, critics and fans knew that the music coming out of Motown was much more than a collection of clever pop tunes; it was often astonishingly innovative. Not only was the music different from anything that had preceded it, but success had imbued many of the artists and songwriters with a confidence that meant they were now turning out some of their very best work.

Adam White, who later ran *Billboard* magazine in Europe before becoming a senior executive at Universal Music Group, was a typical nineteen-year-old Motown fan in 1966. He still vividly recalls, for instance, the afternoon he was in a car crossing the Seven Bridge near Gloucester when he first heard the Four Tops' "Reach Out, I'll Be There" on the radio. He was so excited by the song that he insisted the driver pull over so he could listen in quiet. "I couldn't believe this extraordinary music was coming out of that car radio speaker," remembered White. "It's a moment I can never forget. That's the power Motown music had then. It was simply the most dynamic, vibrant music I had ever heard." By 1966, millions of record buyers were showing they agreed. (Although Motown's stars were known worldwide, the man who had made it possible was still not widely recognized. When Gordy appeared on the TV quiz show *To Tell the Truth* that same year, not one of the four panelists guessed his correct identity.) The recording studio seemed to be running nonstop. The studio band was often called in on short notice. And the autumn brought the most hectic touring schedule yet for many of the artists. If a group was on tour when one of their records broke onto the charts, Gordy would fly them back to Detroit, whisk them to the studio, and quickly record a follow-up.

The busiest were the Supremes. Ross, Wilson, and Ballard not only worked hard but were also entranced by their indulgent lifestyle. They now had so many designer fashions that they traveled with dozens of suitcases. And they continued to think they were the recipients of the company's largesse.

One night in London, Mary Wilson pulled Gordy aside. The girls seldom had a chance to socialize, and they wanted to.

"Flo and me," she told Gordy, "we like to have fun at night. Don't make us go to bed just because you're jealous of Diana meeting somebody else."

Gordy was defensive, mumbling that what she said was one of the dumbest things he had ever heard.

"She's the one who needs to save her voice and get sleep, not us," Wilson continued, pretending she had not heard Gordy's dismissal. "She leads. All we do is 'doobee-doobee-doo.' "

Gordy did not say anything.

"If you're jealous of her," Wilson continued, unfazed, "that's your problem, but don't make us suffer."

Gordy was flustered. He shook his head. "Mary, you'd say anything to get out at night."

She merely smiled. She could not imagine that he thought she did not know about his affair with Ross.

"Let me think about it," he said as he walked away.

When Gordy returned to Ross's room and told her about Wilson, she was amused, more at the idea that Gordy might be jealous than at anything else. Ross told him she had no desire to go out. He was flattered that she was willing to listen to him. But Ross's moods affected Gordy. Most in the company noticed when he was out of sorts with her or responding to her upswings, as well as her fits of anger and bouts of sadness.

As for Ross, while she was egocentric and focused almost exclusively on her career, she made an effort to do special things for Gordy. Twice she threw him surprise birthday parties. Those, in turn, prompted him to surprise her. Once, when the Supremes were performing in San Juan, Puerto Rico, Gordy began thinking what he could do to thrill her. It was not hard to work out. For months, Ross had been talking incessantly about how she missed her nine-year-old brother, Chico. Often, when she spotted a similar-aged youngster, she told Gordy he reminded her of Chico. Gordy enlisted some discreet employees into pulling off his surprise. Then, luring Ross to the tropical lobby of their San Juan hotel, Gordy could hardly contain himself—only two sofas away the real Chico had taken a seat and had his back to the couple.

Ross glanced over his way and stared for a moment. "Here I go again," she said. "See that kid right there? Boy, I'm telling you, he really looks just like Chico."

Gordy shrugged, trying to appear uninterested.

"I just don't know anymore," she said, almost as much to herself as to Gordy, "but I swear the back of his head is identical to Chico's."

"Whose head?" Gordy deadpanned.

"That boy," she said as she jabbed her finger toward the real Chico. "That boy right there."

Gordy looked over, still feigning boredom.

She shook her head as if to make sure she was really awake. Ross walked around to look at the boy's face. Gordy held back a few steps. Chico, who had been told not to recognize her, played it cool.

"Chico?" she asked.

Finally he couldn't hold back and cracked a big smile. "Yeah, it's me!"

Ross screamed, jumped up and down, grabbed Chico, and almost suffocated him she hugged him so hard. Then she started crying hysterically. Gordy had tears in his eyes. She glanced over at him with a look that told him how much it meant to her.

•　　　•　　　•

Many artists grumbled among themselves how unfair it was that Gordy would do almost anything for Ross. Their affair was discussed regularly inside Hitsville. Some wondered whether they received less promotion for their own records and tours because of Gordy's interest in Ross and the Supremes. The one artist, however, who stayed out of office gossip, possibly because he was married to one of Gordy's sisters, was Marvin Gaye. To Gordy's delight, he seemed interested only in advancing his own career.

After the Supremes' smash performance at the Copa, club bookings for many artists had flooded into Motown. Martha and the Vandellas had a great run at the Copa, as did the Temptations. Stevie Wonder played to standing-room-only crowds at Miami's Eden Roc, while the Four Tops filled every seat at the popular Latin Casino.

Marvin Gaye, whose sexy, sultry lyrics and stage antics had earned him a wide following, was more popular than ever, especially with millions of women. Gordy had directed his writers to develop songs that Gaye could sing directly to women: "Pride and Joy," "You're a Wonderful One," "How Sweet It Is (to Be Loved by You)," or "Little Darlin' I Need You." Gaye claimed that the secret of his success was that he always pretended he was singing to his wife, Anna. It was a shrewd thing to say. In truth, Gaye, who had been an avid marijuana smoker since his teens, loved to party and could not keep his hands off women. "I've got this problem, Smoke," he once told Robinson. "I can just look at the pussy and come." Gaye seldom said no to women and then became angry at himself for failing to do so—an anger that often gave way to sadistic sexual rituals. It wasn't long before Gaye discovered that Anna was also having affairs. The two often had outrageous fights at Detroit's best nightclubs.

Beyond relishing his sexual image, Gaye had his own ideas of precisely what his act should be and how it should further his career—he was less open to advice from Esther and the staff at ITMI than were other Motown acts.

At one point, early in the nightclub-booking frenzy, Gaye was signed to play a week at Bimbo's 365 Club in San Francisco. "Marvin was in heaven," recalled Gordy. "This was his dream."

Gordy cautioned Gaye not to get carried away with his audience. Gaye agreed. Then Gordy offered to help prepare him for the stint, but Gaye politely refused. He had a secret plan, he told Gordy, and preferred to work it out on his own. Gaye did closed rehearsals with Harvey Fuqua, Maurice King, and Cholly Atkins.

Opening night at Bimbo's was standing room only. Gordy settled into his seat with no idea of what he would see. The audience went insane when Gaye appeared. The stage was black as the band struck up a Broadway-tune intro. Then a single small spotlight found Gaye, who was dressed in tuxedo and top hat and holding a thin black cane. Women started shrieking. He stood there for a moment. The crowd settled a bit. The band built to a crescendo and then suddenly stopped playing. That is when Gaye started snapping his fingers and singing slowly, "Me . . . and my shadow . . . strolling down the avenue."

Gordy could not believe what he was hearing. He hoped he was merely having a bad dream. But by the end of the first verse, Gordy had a sinking feeling. As Gaye started making sharp turns, tipping his hat, flipping his cane, and tapping it on the floor, all Gordy could think was that this was one bad impersonation of Fred Astaire. Where was "Pride and Joy" or "Wonderful One"?

Gaye's second number was "Blue Moon." Each song was another slow standard, and each dampened the audience's enthusiasm. Soon, it was only applauding politely. When Gaye announced that he had put together his hits in a medley, the crowd again came to life. But it lasted fewer than five minutes.

Gordy's surprise now gave way to anger. It worsened when Gaye finished the medley and sighed, "Now that that's over, let's get into some real music." And he started singing "The Shadow of Your Smile."

Gordy turned to a colleague, shock on his face. "What the fuck?" he asked. When the show finished, Gordy rushed backstage. Fuqua, King, and Atkins knocked into one another trying to hide from him.

Then suddenly Gaye sauntered around the corner. He flashed a big, satisfied smile. He was so excited that he waved away the man who was trying to towel some perspiration off his upper lip and asked Gordy what he thought.

"Marvin, what the hell were you doing out there?"

"You didn't like it?"

Gordy looked at Gaye, who was standing there like a child waiting to be praised. Gordy knew how hurt he would be if he heard the brutal truth at that moment, so instead he said the show was all right, but that Gaye might think of singing more of his hits.

Gaye seemed confused. His yes-men had been telling him only how wonderful the radical changes were. No one in the dressing room said a word. Although he was still seething, Gordy tried something conciliatory.

"I must admit, though, you really did look phenomenal in that top hat and cane. Where did you learn those steps?"

"Cholly put me through hell. Did you like 'em?"

"I think BG's got a point," seconded Fuqua, who was standing in the rear of the dressing room, far out of the line of fire. "We should probably change the show for the weekend and do more hits."

"You think so?" Gaye asked, crushed.

They all chimed in yes. The show was changed. But Gordy never let any of them forget what they had done and how they had failed both the artist and Motown by not having the courage to speak their minds.

The Bimbo's show was not the only time Gaye would surprise Gordy and others with his peculiar ideas for his career. He flirted briefly with the idea of being an actor or professional comedian. Once he telephoned Gordy in the middle of the night, excitedly gushing to the groggy Gordy how he had just come up with an incredible idea for a new career: boxing. "I'm a frustrated athlete," he told a Detroit reporter. Another time his obsession was football. That mania had gone so far that he actually tried out for the Detroit Lions at an open-call practice camp. In preparation, he had worked out with weights, going from 170 to 195 pounds, and learned football terms. Smokey Robinson reported that at the tryout, Gaye "got his ass kicked." Gaye was still devastated, however, when the team diplomatically told him he was too old. He moped around the Motown offices. Then he pulled Smokey aside to tell him that he had abandoned football to focus again on boxing. "Why don't you just stick to singing?" Smokey asked him. After a few weeks, Gaye started to emerge from his funk. Flashes of his good sense of humor showed again: "BG," he told Gordy one day, "I guess I roar better than I rush."

Gaye had had a strict religious family upbringing, in which movies and dancing were forbidden. But Gaye had seen his father, a prominent Pentecostal preacher, wearing his mother's clothes and knew that five of his uncles were gay. At school, when teased by others about his father's flamboyant and effeminate ways, Gaye backed away from confrontation. His almost nonstop women chasing, as well as flirting with tough, male-dominated sports, might well have been his own attempt to distance himself from the father who had physically and emotionally abused him as a youngster. And he was always searching in vain for a woman to measure against his mother, whom he considered pure and perfect. When his relationships turned sour, as they inevitably did, they often became physically abusive.

But Gaye showed little of his troubled soul to his Motown colleagues.

Instead, he often hid his darker side with humor, usually drawn-out jokes, frequently told with mock-British accents. But Gaye was not the artist that most Motowners would have immediately thought of as the company's biggest joker. That title belonged to Stevie Wonder, who loved unpredictable practical jokes. Often he poked fun at his disability. Typical of his stunts was the time when he stopped Gordy, who was heading to the studio.

"I like that suit, Mr. Gordy," Wonder said. "And that's a great tie. Green, isn't it? Where'd you get it?"

Gordy knew that Wonder would occasionally get someone to give him the details so he could pretend he was actually seeing it himself. Gordy, who was wearing a tie, decided to fool him.

"I'm not wearing a tie. I took it off just before I came into the studio."

"Well, if you are wearing a tie, can I have it?"

Gordy smiled at his persistence. "Okay, Stevie, who told you?"

"What? Am I blind!?"

His mother, Lula, had taught his five brothers and sisters to deal with him as though he were a regular kid, without any problem. That family atmosphere had given the youngster a level of confidence over his disability that was rare. And Gordy had helped as well when he hired a private tutor, Ted Hull, to tour with Wonder. Hull, also legally blind, was a strong, positive influence.

There was even one aspect of Wonder's blindness that Gordy and some of the other men envied. Whenever he was introduced to someone, he would reach out and feel the person's face and sometimes their shoulders so he could always identify them again with that sense of touch. When he met an attractive girl, Wonder's hands frequently found their way by "accident" to the girl's breasts. Feigning embarrassment, he would quickly apologize for his "mistake" and then smile in the direction of Gordy or any other men, as if to say, "Eat your hearts out!"

Wonder's love for high jinks matched perfectly with that of Raynoma's mischievous son, Cliff. Although only a youngster during those early years at Hitsville, he got away with things because he was the boss's adopted son, and he often hung out with Wonder, who encouraged his pranks.

·　　·　　·

As Motown's success grew, coupled with its reputation for an easygoing atmosphere, performers from other labels wanted to move to it. Gladys

Knight, along with her Pips—a backup trio consisting of Gladys's brother Merald, nicknamed "Bubba," and cousins Edward Patten and William "Red" Guest—had excellent reputations and solid careers before Gordy saw them at the Apollo in 1966. In 1952, Knight had won a two-thousand-dollar first prize on the Ted Mack Amateur Hour for her rendition of "Too Young." She had been only seven. Now, Gordy courted the twenty-two-year-old Knight. Although she was worried that her group would be overshadowed by Motown's already established acts, Knight eventually was persuaded to sign with the hottest black-owned label in recording history.

"Despite all the success," recalled Otis Williams, "Motown still remained more a family than a business." When the artists did not have shows, rehearsals, or studio recordings, they could often be found lounging on the front lawn on West Grand Boulevard, cracking jokes and horsing around. Locals rode by in their cars, honking their horns and waving at Detroit's hottest stars. Some fans even made pilgrimages to Motown just to see the stars and the place that generated the music they loved.

Others, aspiring artists hoping to be discovered, also inundated Motown, hoping someone might spot them. Among so many wanna-be artists, it helped to have a recommendation from someone Gordy knew and respected. For instance, Hal Davis, who worked in Motown's California office and was known there as "Mr. Motown," told Gordy once that he was sending a girl over for an audition. Since Davis had discovered Brenda Holloway, Gordy was obviously not about to ignore him. The woman Davis sent was Chris Clark, an avid Motown fan, and the audition meant everything to her.

Clark sat nervously in the waiting room. Motown's receptionist, Juana Royster, noticing how much Clark was fidgeting, felt sorry for her and told her to just go upstairs to Gordy's office. "Don't worry," she told the worried singer. "Mr. Gordy is a very nice man. Just be yourself."

Gordy was on the phone when he looked up to see a tall, young, white woman, with long straight blond hair, appearing to be more of a hippie than a singer. He motioned her to have a seat and put on her demo record. While he did not like her songs, he thought her voice was promising. He asked if she would perform something live for him right then. Gordy knew that a demo could be misleading and make a singer sound much better than she really was. When Clark asked if he had a piano, he told her he'd rather hear what she sounded like without any musical accompaniment.

Clark hesitated for only a moment before she started belting out a soulful rendition of Etta James's "All I Could Do Was Cry." It was probably also a clever choice since Gordy had cowritten the song.

"Where'd you get so much soul?" he asked after she finished.

"I spent years traveling on the road with jazz musicians, and I picked up a *lot* of things. Not the least of which was soul."

Gordy liked her. Her voice was good, he had discovered that she could write songs, and her razor-sharp wit was appealing. When he said he'd sign her, she was giddy. As she ran down the stairs, Royster stopped her.

"So, how'd it go?"

"Oh, I was nervous at first, just sitting there waiting, with that big black ape staring at me."

Royster was shocked, and it showed on her face.

"Oh, no, no," Clark interjected. "I mean that ceramic ape sitting on his desk."

Royster was relieved. "Oh, that one."

But Clark couldn't let it be: "Oh, I definitely wasn't talkin' 'bout that *other* one."

They both laughed, and so did the rest of Motown as the story spread quickly.

Chris Clark was one of the first white artists Gordy signed. The soft-spoken platinum blonde also became the first white woman with whom he had a serious love affair. (Marvin Gaye once labeled Gordy "the horniest man in Detroit, . . . [who] married blacks but fooled around with whites." Many in Motown would have disagreed and said that Gaye was actually the horniest man in Detroit.)

Clark and Gordy wrote songs together, and she helped him on creative projects. At times, Gordy was brazen enough to take Clark along on a Supremes tour, positioning his hotel room between Clark's and Diana Ross's. After Clark finished her first album, Gordy enthusiastically ordered the sales department to make it a hit. But the boss's desire was not enough. Phil Jones found Clark's songs impossible to sell and thought she wouldn't even have a record deal if she hadn't had an affair with the boss. "I called a lot of radio guys and sent it everywhere," said Jones, "because Berry was pushing me so much. I asked them what they thought of it. They all thought it was shit. 'It sucks,' they told me."

CHAPTER 18

Color-blind

MOTOWN HAD NEVER HAD A COLOR PROBLEM. EVEN EARLY PRESS coverage noted that. The *Detroit News*, for instance, in a 1965 profile reported, "A Negro, Berry Gordy draws no color in choosing aides, employees, or artists. His vice-president for sales, Barney Ales, is white, as are Irv Biegel, single sales director; Ralph Seltzer, administration director; Edward Pollack, financial controller; Bernard Yeszin, art director, and Michael McLean, engineering chief."

Gordy's mother had an interesting way of showing her friends how blacks and whites integrated seamlessly. When she brought girlfriends for a company tour, she always stopped at the white sales department. "Please tell my friends who you are and what you do here," she would ask Phil Jones.

He stood up and announced, "My name is Phil Jones, and I sell LPs, the big records with the small holes," and then sat again. Then Irv Biegel would stand. "I'm Irv Biegel, and I sell 45s, the small record with the big holes." Gordy's mother would run through the entire department. She would then thank them, and as she walked out with her friends she would say softly, "And my son owns it all."

When asked once by a black Detroit-based reporter why he hired whites, Gordy was blunt: "First of all, I make the money, it's my money. I do what I want with it. But black people have shown a lack of understanding of what I'm doing as a general market businessman. They say, 'Why do you hire this white man, or why this or why that?' Because this white man can do what I've hired him for better than I can do it."

"He [Gordy] was preaching success in 1963," wrote author and music historian Nelson George in his study of Motown, *Where Did Our Love Go?*, "not black success."

But that did not mean that Gordy was not acutely aware of the difficulty of selling black artists to white distributors and record buyers in the company's early days. He had never forgotten the powerful lesson when his brother's record, "Everyone Was There," had died quickly after the public realized a black artist was behind the white-sounding song. And he was concerned that white southern record store owners might not always be anxious to stock records of new black artists. That is precisely why Gordy had released some of his early albums without showing the artists' faces. The Marvelettes' *Please Mr. Postman* album had only a line drawing of a mailbox on the cover; *Bye Bye Baby* by Mary Wells showed only a love letter. An Isley Brothers album had two white lovers on the cover, and the Miracles' *Doin' Mickey's Monkey* sported only a cartoon of an ape. Once the artists became more popular, that changed, although even then Gordy took few chances— for instance, after the Temptations had already had a hit single, their next album, *Meet the Temptations*, still had photographed the group so darkly against a dark background that they were almost in silhouette.

One of the few times Gordy raised the race issue was after a sales meeting at which he had been the only black person. Gordy pulled Ales and Jones to the side and asked why the whole department was white.

"You just now noticed?" asked Ales.

Gordy smiled. "I guess I never saw black and white, I only saw record sales."

Of course, Gordy knew the sales force was all white.

"When I put this team together, you know, there were no black salesmen who could sell to our distributors," Ales said.

"Have you tried to find any?" Gordy asked.

"Well, no, but we don't need anyone else right now," Ales admitted frankly.

"Well, I think you should. If black promotion men can get white stations to play a record, why can't black salesmen get white distributors to buy them as well?"

Gordy was referring to Motown's promotion team, responsible for getting airtime on black and white radio stations. Everyone on the promotion team was black, from the first member, Harvey Fuqua, to Sonny Woods, an old Gordy friend who had briefly sung with the Midnighters, and Weldon McDougall III, who promoted records on tour with the artists. Later, Gordy added veterans such as Cincinnati's leading DJs, Jack Gibson and Larry Maxwell, both of whom had natural talent for creative promotion.

Ales was surprised at this discussion. "He had never asked me anything about anyone at the company based on race," he recalled. Even Gordy later admitted he felt "a little strange" in bringing it up.

"Getting radio play is one thing," Ales said, nonplussed, "but selling records is another. The distributors are going to give you a lot more resistance than any DJ. It would really be tough—especially in the South."

"That may be," said Gordy, "but I think we're so strong now we can change things. It's time."

"He's right," Phil Jones interjected. "I think we can."

"Then let's get it on," Ales told Jones.

Ales soon discovered the real source of Gordy's agitation, and it was not quite a sudden burst of consciousness. At a recent record convention in Quebec, a picture had been taken of the Motown sales staff and independent distributors. *Billboard* ran the picture. "There were too many white faces," said Ales, laughing at the memory of it. "Berry took some heat for that, so he decided we needed to add at least one black face in the sales department. But he would never admit he gave in to any pressure. That wouldn't be Berry."

Ales and Jones found Miller London, a short, thin salesman with a great smile. No sooner had London arrived for his first meeting with a major distributor in the South than Phil Jones got a hysterical call.

"Phil," the distributor yelled, "you sent a nigger down here to sell white pop accounts? Are you fuckin' nuts?"

"How much money do you make a year off Motown?" Jones asked coolly.

"Oh, I don't know," the distributor said, calming a bit. "Quite a bit I guess."

"Well, if you want to keep making that 'quite a bit,' you better get used to looking in that nigger's face."

Miller London had been sitting anxiously outside the distributor's office. Suddenly, the distributor rushed out with a big smile. "Miller, nice to see you," he drawled in a most facetious way. "Come on in, my friend."

"Miller was in," Gordy noted. "But it took about a year of insults, threats, and narrow escapes before he could breathe easily."

Soon, other talented black salesmen, including Eddie Gilreath, Chuck Young, Ralph Thompson, and Skip Miller, joined London. They benefited from the smooth operation that Ales had established. Since Motown was so hot, Ales could afford to bully the distributors. He would sometimes scream at them over the phone, threatening to withhold the next major release unless one of his current favorites received more airtime. And he showed no sentimentality by switching regional distributors if one was lagging on payments. In a hard-nosed environment in which some companies relied on substantial payola or physical enforcers to get airtime or payment, Ales's brusque, take-no-prisoners style was ideal. When a white Detroit DJ had once asked for some "big black bucks" to help him move to a new house, the label sent the Holland brothers and Lamont Dozier to do the moving for him. The embarrassed DJ kept playing Motown records and did not again ask for any money. Ales got away with such behavior only because Motown's music was so hot that the distributors had to stock it, and popular demand meant DJs had to air it.

On the same day that London was hired, Tom Noonan, a fifteen-year veteran with *Billboard,* joined the company as a senior sales executive. He soon discovered another side of the slick Barney Ales. Two days after he arrived, Ales told Noonan to pack his bags, because the members of the sales force and their spouses were leaving for a six-day conference in Puerto Rico. When they arrived, Ales did not like the hotel, so he made them all pack up and move to another. "Barney really likes to go first class all the way," recalled Noonan. "Then every day, we would hang out on the beach and drink heavy. We all used to drink a lot back then. And drink at night. And then start again the next morning."

After a couple of days, Noonan asked Ales about the sales meetings. "Don't worry," Ales told him. "Finally, we get to the last day," recalled Noonan, "and Barney says, 'Let's get the staff together for a meeting.' And we meet for an hour or so, just like a staff meeting in Detroit."

On the plane back to Detroit, Ales instructed Noonan, as the junior member of the team, to "do a report for Gordy about our week and just fill out the days."

"At first, I didn't know what the hell to do," said Noonan, "so I went ahead and did a very detailed memo about what we supposedly did that trip, filling in all the days with things I thought we should have probably talked about. It was about ten pages long. Well, when Gordy got it, he went crazy for it in a good way. He kept referring to it at meetings for weeks by saying, 'Now that was a great concept that was discussed on day three about . . . ' It became known around the office as 'that goddamn memo' because Barney and the others would keep asking me, 'What the hell else did you put into that goddamn memo?' Because they didn't know what was in it, they didn't know what to expect when Berry raised it, and it drove them nuts, because I hadn't kept a copy."

Ales still arranged other "working" weeks for the sales group in other beach resorts, but never asked Noonan to write another memo.

CHAPTER 19

Skipping the Revolution

THE LACK OF RACIAL TENSION INSIDE MOTOWN DURING THE turbulent mid-1960s was remarkable. Outside the West Grand Boulevard headquarters, the country was in considerable strife. There was, of course, the swelling civil-rights movement led by Martin Luther King Jr. And the growing antiwar movement against the U.S. military role in Vietnam was starting to polarize large groups of Americans, many of whom were incensed that black Americans suffered disproportionate casualties on the front lines.

Gordy had no interest in politics or history. He did not read newspapers or books and had little sense of social destiny or moral responsibility stemming from his remarkable success. He had, as he wrote years later in his autobiography, an almost benign view of how his music fit into the volatile times: "In all the camps there seemed to be one constant—Motown music. They were all listening to it. Black and white. Militant and nonviolent. Antiwar demonstrators and the pro-war establishment."

The 1965 race riots in Watts were something that Gordy watched from afar. He remained an observer as the nonviolence of the civil-rights movement was increasingly challenged by a more strident creed of black power. Some of his artists, such as Marvin Gaye, were frustrated that the company avoided any social message in such troubling times. "I felt myself exploding," said Gaye. "Why didn't our music have anything to do with this? Wasn't music supposed to express feelings? No, according to BG, music's supposed to sell. That's his trip."

Two years later, it was almost impossible for Gordy to avoid what was happening, as the summer of rage arrived dramatically in Detroit. The city had its worst race riot in half a century, with National Guardsmen, tanks, and helicopters ordered to enforce a strict curfew. Hitsville was in the middle of one of the most devastated neighborhoods, but the rioters, undoubtedly out of respect for the country's largest black-owned record company, left Gordy's buildings unscathed. After seven days of rioting, there were 43 dead, 5,000 homeless, and 3,800 arrested. More than 1,200 homes and businesses had been destroyed.

In his autobiography, Gordy does not discuss the conditions that caused the riots or the devastation that resulted, but rather softly reminisces about how enterprising Motown workers handled the crisis. Gordy had ordered the offices closed, but people came to work anyway. He later proudly recalled how, amid bursts of gunfire, "nervous producers scurried between buildings, protecting master tapes."

"We continued business as usual," Gordy wrote.

Gordy's memory is selective. Trouble of every kind beset the label. The Motortown Revue was in Detroit on national tour when the riots started. Martha Reeves was in the middle of singing "Dancing in the Street" when the message came that she had to stop, and the audience was told to go home. Gordy canceled the rest of their Detroit shows and sent the tour to New Jersey. When rioting flared again there, they fled south to the relative calm of Myrtle Beach, South Carolina.

And Gordy never revealed that during the riots, one Motown artist and self-proclaimed black Muslim nationalist, Abdullah, attacked A&R executive Ralph Seltzer in his own office. Abdullah had called Seltzer a "blue-eyed devil," jumped on the desk, and grabbed Seltzer by the throat, sticking a letter opener to his neck before other workers yanked him off. (Gordy forgave Abdullah, who the following year released the single "I Cumma Zimba Zio.")

Shortly after the Seltzer attack, a rumor spread among Detroit's black DJs that Gordy had said, "If a black disc jockey never played another one of my records, I wouldn't give a damn." Although the quote was often repeated and attributed to him, it is not at all certain Gordy ever uttered it. What is interesting, however, is that the city's black DJs were willing to believe it. They had in the past complained about being cut out of key events hosted by Motown. For instance, for a Motown-sponsored Joe Louis trib-

ute in Detroit, black DJs heavily promoted the event. As columnist Jim In-
gram wrote in the *Michigan Chronicle,* "But when it came time to dole out press
passes or time to call up radio newsmen for press conferences, the white
boys got the calls while many Black newsmen who wanted interviews with
Black personalities such as Sonny Liston and Sugar Ray, had to listen to
them on stations owned by whites. Has Motown been completely taken over
by whites as many have reported?" The DJs briefly boycotted most Motown
acts, except for Stevie Wonder, whom everyone seemed to like.

Gordy never confronted the DJs but waited until their anger subsided,
and his records were soon back on the air. The avoidance of conflict and
controversy was something he tried instilling in his singers through Artist
Development. Although thousands of fans, for instance, sent letters to Motown asking for the Supremes to wear their hair natural, the label thought it
might give the girls a radical edge that could scare away white fans. Mary
Wilson recalled that she and others were taught how to conduct media interviews about only the most innocuous subjects, such as "our music, our
gowns, whom we had met recently, what our homes were like, and so on."
When the Supremes toured England in 1968 and were inundated by British journalists with questions about the Vietnam War and the black-power
movement, they didn't know what to say and were roundly castigated for
having sold out as superficial girls concerned only about glamour in an age
that demanded relevance. Still, such criticism did not hurt them commer-
cially. Nearly half of all the soul records sold in Britain in 1968 were Motown releases.

When Gordy decided it was time for the Supremes to get a more serious
veneer, he had them endorse Hubert Humphrey in the 1968 election, but
the press treated it mostly as a joke—it was in fact arranged by Gordy almost entirely to get publicity for Diana Ross. Motown's artists were not involved in the era's hot-button issues. As Contour singer Joe Billingslea
noted, they seemed almost frozen by their ambition to fulfill the American
dream as they saw it—a great home, nice car, and super clothes—at a time
when racial strife and the Vietnam War made their ambition "not cool."
While blacks were being sent in disproportionate numbers to fight in Vietnam, Motown artists played to packed halls of mostly white college kids
who had somehow gotten draft deferments.

Even artists like Marvin Gaye, who was interested in politics, found few
reasons to get involved. "It's hard for my brother to understand," he told a

reporter in 1969, "but I can't be militant because there's nothing to motivate it, no spark to ignite the fire. I've lived a beautiful life, had my loved ones and health, and been successful. I can afford the luxury of waiting for real equality. But many of my people can't." Smokey Robinson, responding once to questions about why Motown artists did not use their music to send social messages, said, "People come to be entertained, not to hear a lecture."

Few people outside of Motown and Gordy's own family knew how little politics and the upheavals under way interested Gordy. But they could see that he was, at the very least, insensitive to what was happening. As black protests increased on the streets, Gordy entertained lavishly at his Detroit mansion and worked instead on getting his sumptuous home photographed by the *Detroit Free Press.* His mother, wife, and sisters regaled reporters with descriptions of their evening wear for society events. Gordy boasted that golf had become the company sport.

Still, in his role as a successful and prominent black entrepreneur, he was inundated with requests for contributions, benefit shows, and personal or corporate endorsements. Gordy believed that the NAACP had been the main reason for black progress to date, and he was disappointed to discover that many black activists now castigated the venerable civil-rights organization for having done too little. He was also surprised when young members of the black-pride movement chastised Motown for sounding too white. And he was mystified that some activists insisted that "Dancing in the Street" was really a metaphorical theme song for black revolution. While Gordy certainly did not agree with many of the ideologies that asked for help, he also remembered his own family's advice that he should make some contribution to the progressive black social movement, even if he helped only the most moderate voices. He certainly did not want to embrace any overt black militancy, lest he scare away Motown's huge white audience.

Gordy eventually formed a new label, Black Forum, to be a spoken-word line of albums featuring speeches by prominent black social and political leaders. Black Forum released an eclectic group of records, including speeches and lectures by Dr. Martin Luther King Jr., Stokely Carmichael, Elaine Brown, Ossie Davis, Wallace Terry, and Leroi Jones (Imamu Amiri Baraka). "It was an attempt to get blacker than we really were," recalled Phil Jones. The Black Forum records sold so poorly that Gordy did not even release one featuring Langston Hughes and Margaret Danner.

Before he let the label lapse after eight albums, however, Gordy had released two important collections of King's speeches, *Great March to Freedom* and *Great March to Washington*. Gordy was personally moved by King's message, especially his underlying belief that no good could come from hatred or violence. Jesse Jackson, one of King's aides, visited Motown often.

"I saw Motown," Gordy said, "much like the world Dr. King was fighting for—with people of different races and religions, working together harmoniously for a common goal." Yet when it came time years later to campaign for a national holiday for the slain civil-rights leader, Gordy was virtually silent; Stevie Wonder, however, became a major lobbyist to Congress on behalf of the holiday.

There were clearly attributes of King to which Gordy could not relate. During an early meeting in Detroit, King said he wanted to donate any royalties from an upcoming album to the Southern Christian Leadership Conference (SCLC). Gordy suggested that since it was his artistry that would be responsible for selling the record, maybe only half should go to the SCLC and the other half personally to King and his family. "Absolutely not," King told him. "There is enough confusion out there right now, as it is. I cannot allow the perception of personal gain, right or wrong, to confuse the message of the cause."

To Gordy, that type of selflessness not only was completely alien but meant King must be "a great man."

Gordy was also mostly oblivious to the difficulties his own artists endured when they toured in the mid-1960s. "Racially motivated violence was unpredictable," recalled Otis Williams, "and could erupt anywhere, at any time." In Kentucky, the valet for the Four Tops was attacked by a group of white racists and had his head cracked open. On one tour, the Temptations and the Four Tops took turns guarding the stage with baseball bats and guns after some local whites had threatened to disrupt the shows. Another time, a car of whites circled some of the Temptations after a show. "You niggers, you motherfuckers," the white kids yelled, "don't you ever come back here again." Word of these confrontations spread quickly around the label, but evidently no one at Motown thought to hire extra security to travel with the acts when they played in potentially hostile settings.

However, Gordy could no longer ignore the black-white schism when Martin Luther King was assassinated in April 1968. It was one of the few

A young Berry Gordy in front of Motown's first million-selling record, "Shop Around," by the Miracles.

Hitsville, Motown's original headquarters, at 2648 West Grand Boulevard in Detroit. Gordy and his family lived on the second floor and the rest of the house was converted into offices and a tiny recording studio.

(Courtesy of Peter Benjaminson)

At the Roostertail nightclub, Gordy (far left) is joined by his sister Esther Edwards (behind him) and his father (two seats behind her). Mary Wilson and Flo Ballard of the Supremes are at the far right table, while Diana Ross sits, as is her custom, at Gordy's table (across from him).

(Courtesy of Peter Benjaminson)

That same night at the Roostertail, during a performance by the Four Tops, Marvin Gaye (third from left), the Supremes, and the visiting Everly Brothers take the stage for an impromptu finale. Motown's early acts were accustomed to performing together on tours, sometimes in mock competitions orchestrated by Gordy.

At a 1967 Detroit dinner honoring Motown, most of the label's vice presidents gather with Gordy. From left: Smokey Robinson, the Miracles' lead singer; Esther, Gordy's sister and most trusted confidante; the sales wiz Barney Ales; Gordy; and Brian Holland, part of the label's most successful songwriting trio.

The scene of many outrageous parties, this sprawling turn-of-the-century, Italianate-style mansion boasted a marble-covered ballroom, billiard and screening rooms, a gym, an English pub, a two-lane bowling alley, and a manicured Greek garden. The main hall was dominated by a large oil painting of Gordy dressed as Napoleon Bonaparte.

By the late 1960s, the Motown sound was internationally popular. The Four Tops (from left to right: Renaldo Benson, Levi Stubbs, Abdul "Duke" Fakir, and Lawrence Payton) in London while on their first U.K. tour.

The Supremes—the British tabloids' favorite gossip subjects—arrive in England, with Gordy toting a camera like any other first-time tourist.

Part of the reason for Motown's British popularity was the strong endorsement of the Beatles. Here, the group is with Berry's three children and his father.

Motown had an unmatched roster of stars. Among them was Marvin Gaye (above), who dreamed of becoming a crooner similar to Frank Sinatra. He was the label's sex symbol, with an enormous female following.

Little Stevie Wonder (right) was discovered by Gordy when he was only eleven.

The incredibly talented David Ruffin (left) was the distinctive lead tenor for the Temptations—although his desire to stand out as the group's star would lead to fights and his ultimate ouster.

At a 1969 party in Los Angeles, Gordy introduced the Jackson 5, a group he had signed only one year earlier. Here, Marvin Gaye chats with *American Bandstand*'s Dick Clark. Marlon Jackson is between them.

By 1970, the Jacksons had already sold eight million copies of their albums. From left to right: Tito, Marlon, Michael, Jackie, and Jermaine.

The person who brought the group to Gordy's attention was Suzanne de Passe, who went from a New York disco club booker to one of Motown's most important executives. Here she is with Tom Noonan, one of the sales department executives.

(Courtesy of Tom Noonan)

Gordy was color-blind when it came to hiring workers. Motown's sales department ended up mostly white. Above, several Motown executives, including Barney Ales (seated, far right), finish a dinner meeting with the label's New York distributors.

(Courtesy of Tom Noonan)

Gordy gathers with Ales (to his left) and more Motown distributors from New York and Washington, D.C. Mike Lushka, the executive who later testified about a complex scheme for hiding royalties from artists and songwriters, is second from right.

Gordy was apolitical and tried to keep his company and artists away from the 1960s social upheaval. Marvin Gaye was one exception, getting involved, much to Gordy's displeasure, with a broad range of political issues. Here he meets with the U.S. ambassador to Ghana, Shirley Temple Black, and U.N. secretary-general Kurt Waldheim to discuss an African literacy campaign.

Another Motown exception to Gordy's edict was Ewart Abner, the label's president for several years in the 1970s. Shown here with Stevie Wonder, Abner was militantly Afrocentric. Many senior white executives who helped build Motown considered him an unrepentant racist, and during his tenure many of them were fired or quit.

(Courtesy of Tom Noonan)

The performer who meant the most to Gordy was not the one who sold the most records, but the one he fell in love with, Diana Ross. At a Motown barbecue, Ross rests for a few minutes with her infant daughter, Rhonda. Few knew that Rhonda was Gordy's child.

(AP/Wide World Photos)

Most other performers at Motown disliked Ross. They considered her too ambitious and imperious. However, Michael Jackson was utterly enamored with her, and told many colleagues that he wanted to model his career after hers. Here, a presurgery Jackson poses with Ross.

Gordy became fascinated with Hollywood, and Diana Ross was his vehicle into filmmaking. Ross's movie debut portraying Billie Holiday in *Lady Sings the Blues* won her rave reviews, a Golden Globe, and an Oscar nomination for best actress. At Cannes, where her film was shown, Ross waves to throngs of photographers and fans.

After a mediocre performance in the follow-up film *Mahogany*, Ross's career and Gordy's film-making ventures were mortally wounded by the miscast flop *The Wiz*, a film rendition of the smash Broadway musical. Critics savaged her work. Nipsey Russell (left), as the Tinman, and Michael Jackson (right), as the Scarecrow, did not help the film's cool reception.

Diana Ross arrives at the 1976 Detroit funeral of Flo Ballard, one of the original Supremes, and the one considered by many to have the most talent. Ballard, who had been forced out of the group several years earlier after long battles with Ross, had fallen on hard times before dying at thirty-two. At the funeral, thousands of early Supremes fans gathered. Ross was surrounded by four burly bodyguards, and the crowd hissed and booed her arrival. She seemed nervous, and let out a loud sob, stumbling so that her bodyguards almost had to carry her by the arms to her pew.

No relationship at Motown lasted longer than the friendship between Smokey Robinson and Gordy. Smokey was only a teenager when he first met Gordy, and he and his group, the Miracles, were one of the first signed by the new label. When Smokey's great career stalled in the 1970s, and he temporarily lost his way in the sex and dope binges that ruined many Motown performers, Gordy personally intervened, the only time he did so. They remain close friends.

Few performers at Motown had more tortured lives than Marvin Gaye, but he managed to produce successful albums despite his addictions. Given to quixotic quests, at different times Gaye flirted with becoming a professional boxer, an actor, and a football player. He was crushed when he failed to land a position after trying out for the Detroit Lions.

Gaye married Gordy's older sister Anna but divorced her after fourteen turbulent years. He met his second wife, Janis Hunter (left), in 1973, when she was a sixteen-year-old high school sophomore. David Ritz, Gaye's biographer, said that she became an "obsession [that] would possess him totally. . . . The woman would inspire, engage, and preoccupy him in a manner bordering on madness."

(AP/Wide World Photos)

On April Fool's Day, 1984, the day before Marvin's forty-fifth birthday, he was shot to death by his father, a prominent Washington, D.C., Pentecostal preacher. A Los Angeles police detective leads Gaye's father, in handcuffs, into the police department's central headquarters to book him for his son's murder.

(AP/Wide World Photos)

At Forest Lawn Memorial Park, stars, friends, and family gathered to bid Gaye a final farewell. Gordy comforts his sister Anna, who was Gaye's first wife.

In the late 1970s and early 1980s, there were far fewer hit acts at Motown. Lionel Richie and his group, the Commodores, were one of Motown's few bright spots. The group had sixteen chart hits, and when Richie left for a solo career in 1982, he became the only performer to ever have nine number-one hits in nine consecutive years. Both he and Stevie Wonder received awards at the 1982 American Music Awards.

The self-described "funk-punk king" Rick James (here with Motown sales executive Tom Noonan) represented another new aspect of Motown in its later years. James developed an outrageous touring act that included onstage dope smoking and X-rated lyrics.

By the late 1980s, Motown was a shadow of its former glory. When Diana Ross joined the label's most successful songwriting trio—Lamont Dozier (left) and Brian and Eddie Holland—as they were inducted into the Rock and Roll Hall of Fame, none of them were still with the label.

Gordy sold Motown to a group of private investors for $61 million in 1988. That same year he took his trophy when he was welcomed to the Rock and Roll Hall of Fame. As Gordy wrote in his autobiography, "From eight hundred dollars to sixty-one million. I had done it. I had won the poker hand."

times he was moved to act. King was not even a year older than Gordy, and although the two had little personal contact over the years, Gordy considered him a distant friend.

"I couldn't contain my anger," Gordy recalled. "I wanted to fight. But who? I knew I couldn't make it a personal fight—I had to be part of some organized response."

Gordy sought advice from the three men inside Motown who were most outspoken about social issues. Ewart Abner, who had a strong sense of black pride, had been hired by Gordy to work as the director of ITMI. Abner, who was very knowledgeable about black music, had been a partner in his own markedly successful recording venture, Vee-Jay. It had failed largely through intense fighting between its black and white executives over the company's direction. Junius Griffin was an ex-journalist who had served as an assistant to King for two years before Gordy hired him away as director of publicity. He was passionate about the civil-rights movement. And the third was George Schiffer, a white, Jewish liberal who had been with Gordy from the very beginning, handling copyright and legal questions. As a result of talking to them, Gordy agreed to Coretta Scott King and Harry Belafonte's request that he put on a benefit concert of Motown artists to launch King's dream for a Poor Peoples' March on Washington.

Griffin and Abner accompanied Gordy to Atlanta, together with Stevie Wonder, the Supremes, Gladys Knight and the Pips, and the Temptations. After the concert, Gordy and the artists briefly joined in the march as it started out for Washington. That there were other famous black personalities there, from Sammy Davis Jr. to Sidney Poitier, made Gordy feel less conspicuous about putting himself at the forefront of any controversy. But after that event, Gordy returned to Detroit and focused exclusively on running Motown. His brief engagement had not set off in him any latent desire for social activism.

Two months later, when Robert Kennedy was assassinated in Los Angeles, Gordy thought it was "crazy" and that the "bad guys were killing off our dreams one by one." But this time he did not leave Detroit and stayed focused just on work. In his autobiography, Gordy finished his discussion of the King and Kennedy assassinations with this mundane transition: "Against this backdrop of craziness and uncertainty, Motown continued to create and grow."

• • •

Many who worked with Gordy believe that his ability to stay focused on his work was one quality that allowed him to be so successful. He was not given to flights of fancy, running off on some Don Quixote–inspired chase of idealistic goals, and could not easily be persuaded by the many competing interests in the black community to divert his energy to their problems.

In the wake of RFK's murder, while the country mourned the loss and pondered what the killing meant for the 1968 presidential elections, Gordy concentrated on dealing with the growing pains resulting from Motown's fast success. Except for arranging the Supremes' press conference to endorse Hubert Humphrey, he stayed out of politics during that critical election. And while some at Motown cringed when, the following year, President Nixon's eldest daughter, Tricia, invited the Temptations to the White House and told them that along with the Turtles they were her favorite group, Gordy was ecstatic and bragged about the Nixons to all who would listen. "What is BG's fucking problem?" mumbled a distressed Marvin Gaye as he wandered through the sales department after listening to Gordy wax on about how excited he was over Nixon's endorsement. "Fucking Nixon don't know shit about music." Many in the sales department weren't quite sure if the egocentric Gaye would have felt the same if he had been invited to the White House. Political allegiances seemed to shift quickly at Motown depending on business.

CHAPTER 20

Cracks in the Wall

TO ANY OUTSIDER, MOTOWN IN THE LATE 1960S APPEARED TO BE a model success story. Its artists were producing steady hits and were famous worldwide. The company itself again needed to expand. By 1967, it had outgrown West Grand Boulevard and relocated its administrative offices to a ten-story high-rise, the Donovan Building, in downtown Detroit. The worn marble floor hinted at the building's earlier grandeur, but by the time Motown took over it was decaying and depressing, with drab green walls. Its creaking wrought-iron elevator cage, operated by an elderly and frail black woman, belonged to another era. In its new home, Motown no longer afforded the easy accessibility to the local black community that had been its trademark. And while Gordy was generally pleased about the move, he noted, "along with that growth came problems—more bills, more conflicts, more taxes, more egos."

The artists also noticed a difference. "Hitsville ended in the late sixties," said Otis Williams, "when part of the daily operations were moved from West Grand Boulevard to a regular, cold, ugly office building on Woodward near the Fisher Freeway, and the recording began taking place in other studios. It was also then that Berry installed a more conventional corporate upper-management staff made up of people whose business was business, not music."

By moving to the sterile Donovan setting, the company had not only shifted geographically but also altered its laid-back personality. The new operation struck many as too sophisticated, remote, and impersonal. Motown had lost its family atmosphere. Part of the problem was that there was no place at the Donovan Building for the artists to hang out. While Raynoma—who had returned to the label—lobbied hard for a hospitality center where the artists and producers could lounge, the Noveck brothers, Berry's trusted accounting team, greeted her idea with "uncomprehending stares." Also, Gordy's increasing concern with personal security meant the building itself was not as easily accessible to the artists as Hitsville had been.

"Berry was always a nut on security," recounted Tom Noonan. "Even at West Grand we always had white bodyguards. Berry used to buy three to five extra seats at a public event, and one bodyguard would always sit away, watching over him. He always seemed concerned about the threat of kidnapping, especially about one of his kids. But at Woodward Avenue, it got much more visible. There were two girls to check security and a camera, and you'd have to hold up your pass and check in, and you couldn't even get on the elevator unless the woman checked your pass. It might seem all very ordinary today, but back in the sixties it was really something. And when people used to come and visit me, they would always ask, 'What do you have here, Fort Knox?'" (One of Gordy's former security guards, Benny Medina, is today one of the most powerful Hollywood managers, representing stars from singer Jennifer Lopez to actor Will Smith.)

The atmosphere at Woodward was also different because the money crunchers brought in by Gordy concentrated on profits, forgetting sometimes about the talent. As a result, the first department to get the ax was Artist Development, which had been responsible for creating the unique Motown look for its artists. "They didn't, or couldn't," said Otis Williams, "see how Artist Development gave a performer greater confidence and polish or made an act look different or sound better."

Raynoma, who had returned to Detroit in 1967, heard her former friends complain bitterly. "Berry had isolated himself from the people who had helped him build the company," she said, "creating a houseful of discontent." It wasn't long before she had an opportunity to see the disarray firsthand as Gordy surprised almost everyone by rehiring her.

But not all of the problems were caused by the Woodward move and the hiring of traditional corporate managers. The growing pains also resulted from too much success, too fast. It had been only a decade since Gordy had borrowed eight hundred dollars from his family and thrown up a sign in front of a house. Now he had a company that was raking in money and influencing pop culture. Many who had hitched their wagons to Motown early on—not just artists but also producers, writers, studio musicians, and sales staff—had gone from being poor kids to having great wealth, often combined with intoxicating fame. Nineteen sixty-seven was another enormous year for Motown, as it sold more than thirty million singles. The company was also starting to sell hit albums, an even more lucrative end of the business. The new wealth showed when Gordy hosted Motown's first national sales meeting in 1967. It was a lavish three-day affair. Thirty-five record distributors were flown to Detroit, with their spouses, then whisked around town by chauffeurs, treated to a Vegas-style gambling night, champagne river cruises, and a black-tie finale at the city's most prestigious nightclub.

As the money flowed in, alcohol and drug problems became more prevalent. The Contours, for example, who seemed set for stardom with early recordings marked by great energy, folded in 1968 as a second-string version of the Four Tops. A series of crippling personnel changes, many prompted by drug abuse, had left the group shattered; Hubert Johnson, one of the group's founders, would later kill himself. Martha Reeves's cocaine use led to a series of breakdowns and hospitalizations. When Raynoma visited Reeves once in a locked psychiatric chamber, she found her in a strait-jacket, swaying slowly back and forth. "Ray, don't let these doctors come back in," Reeves whispered. "They're trying to kill me." Elaine Jesmer, author of *Number One with a Bullet,* a racy 1974 novel based on Motown, also visited Reeves. She did not help the singer's condition when she warned, "I heard what happened to you, and all of this was *not* an accident. Watch yourself." After Reeves was finally released from the hospital, her brother, Thomas, drove her to see Gordy. They met alone in Gordy's office. "Go away and get well," he urged her. He leaned over and cut off the plastic hospital band still on her wrist. "Go on, go take care of yourself." Reeves kept asking about her career and when she should call him. He never answered.

"Unlike the old days," Reeves wrote in her autobiography, *Dancing in the Street,* "the company was no longer there for me. I never saw another royalty check from Motown after that day. The man who was once my hero had turned his back on me." (Four years after her meeting with Gordy, Reeves found salvation by becoming a born-again Christian—"I was released from Satan's grip, and from that day forward everything changed." Still, her rebirth did not prevent her from filing a lawsuit against Motown trying to gain the right to her group's name and back royalties. The case was finally settled in 1991, returning to her the still-valuable name.)

The Temptations illustrated the difficulties the label confronted even with its most successful acts. "Money changes everything," said Otis Williams. When they were poor, Williams recounted, they dreamed of being wealthy. What they did not anticipate was that the flow of money removed restraints on buying anything they wanted, including women, booze, and drugs. "Getting high was just the thing to do," recalled Williams, "and for too many it was the beginning of the end." Nothing seemed to shake the desire to party. For instance, the group was excited when it had the chance to meet a childhood idol, Frankie Lyman, backstage at a show at the Apollo. But they all noticed the sunken face and deep-set eyes, by-products of heavy drug use. A few months later, Lyman was dead of a heroin overdose. The Tempts thought it was a terrible waste, but it never made them reconsider their own excesses. All five were lavish spenders, buying extravagant clothes, cars, and homes. They had personal entourages, consisting mostly of small-time hustlers and hangers-on who liked to be where the action was and helped suck the singers dry of cash.

Each of the five had different problems. Paul Williams, who had never drank in his life, started drinking and was often visibly inebriated at rehearsals and performances. Soon, he was drinking two to three bottles of Courvoisier daily, and as a result of one particularly embarrassing performance—complete with slurred speech and missed lyrics—at Las Vegas's Flamingo Hotel in 1969, he got the group blacklisted there for several years.

Years earlier, Al Bryant had not only developed a chronic drinking problem, but one night after finishing a set he had smashed a beer bottle into Paul Williams's face, barely missing his eyes and leaving a long scar. The group had voted Bryant out in 1964, but fans didn't mind because it was at this time that David Ruffin, a powerful tenor with a charismatic stage presence, had come on board. (The last time the Tempts saw Bryant, he was standing outside their dressing room at a Detroit show at the end of 1968. His hair was long and unruly, his skin was ashen, and he had deep, dark circles under his eyes. A decade later, he died in a trailer park in Florida of cirrhosis.)

Ruffin was incredibly good, and his throaty rasp was immediately distinctive from the rest of the group's voices. It did not take very long before most people thought Ruffin, who had learned to sing in gospel groups like the Dixie Nightingales and the Soulsters, was the best of the Tempts. Gordy called him a "natural star, electrifying—you knew it the minute he walked into a room." Otis Williams said he "was a fantastic singer and performer, and no one, from that time until today [1988], does what he did— he was an original."

Ruffin had a brother, Jimmy, who had signed with Motown in 1961 but would manage just one top-ten hit in thirteen years. As far as David was concerned, he was the only one with talent in his family. He was not in the least humble, boasting that he gained most of his professional inspiration from his actor idol, Richard Burton. As the Tempts became more successful and their fans singled him out, he acted as though he alone *was* the group. While touring in Puerto Rico, he suggested a name change to "David Ruffin and the Temptations." He refused to travel with his four partners in the groups' two cars but instead used his own mink-lined limousine, with his name scrawled across the side in a wild graffiti-style paint. Ruffin, though married, began dating Tammi Terrell, and they had a tumultuous relationship. "They fought," said Motown insider Tony Turner, "they made up, they drank, they slept around." Ruffin was often physically abusive, and his fellow group members knew something was amiss. Other Motowners saw Terrell with occasional black eyes, swollen lips, and deep bruises.

"None of us knew what to do to help," recalled Otis Williams. And all of the Tempts felt terrible when, in 1970, Terrell died at twenty-seven. A year earlier, she had been diagnosed with a brain tumor, but some friends thought that she was physically debilitated from neurological damage caused by Ruffin's often savage beatings. In one live performance with Gaye, Terrell literally collapsed in Gaye's arms and had to be taken offstage. (It so shook Gaye that it was four years before he toured again.) Gordy, never one to miss a sale, however, had Valerie Simpson do a remarkably good imitation of Terrell on a 1969 duet album with Marvin Gaye. The public never knew that Terrell was so sick that she was unable to record the album. It only became public when Gaye disclosed it years later, calling it "another moneymaking scheme on BG's part."

Tensions flared between the formerly close friends in the Tempts as they felt things slip out of their control. After one show, Paul Williams sharply told Eddie Kendricks that he missed a dance step onstage.

"Fuck you," Kendricks snapped.

"Well, fuck you, too!" yelled Williams.

In the next moment, Kendricks drew a knife and slammed Williams against a wall. Kendricks had been stabbed as a teenager in a gang fight and had a long abdominal scar. "I'm not going to be stabbed anymore," he screamed. "I'll be the one doing the stabbing."

Otis Williams broke up the fight before anyone was injured. But word of the incident spread quickly around Motown. Then the next episode took place when the Tempts were touring in Bermuda. This time, Kendricks and Ruffin had such a roughhouse fight in their hotel—smashing furniture and breaking windows—that the Bermuda government banned the group.

Gordy soon concluded that Bryant's drinking problem had been replaced with Ruffin's difficult attitude, and it threatened the group's unity. The Tempts had built their success on a stage act where the five men did tight, precise, synchronized steps that made them seem like a single fluid body. All five were considered equal leads. Now, Ruffin's desire to stand out led to increased bickering. Kendricks and Otis Williams, the two members who seemed to be holding up best under the pressures of success, began to secretly scout for replacements for Ruffin. "The feeling that David was going to be leaving," recalled Otis Williams, "one way or the other, was undeniable."

Ruffin was also abusing alcohol and drugs. He had started with marijuana and liquor and graduated to cocaine and sedatives as his career zoomed along. He rarely went onstage without first downing half a large tumbler of gin and soda. Then he would snort copious amounts of coke after the show was over and finally take pills in the early-morning hours so he could get to sleep.

During the middle of a ten-day stint at a Cleveland supper club, Ruffin sent a message through his driver that he would not make one evening's performance. He had decided it was more important to watch his new girlfriend, one of Dean Martin's daughters, open her own show in New Jersey.

The other Tempts were furious. "Ruffin's got to go," Otis Williams somberly announced. As far as the public was concerned, Ruffin had the flu. Motown did not want the serious backstage problems to leak out.

The situation came to a head at a Friday recording session in Detroit. The Tempts were behind schedule in releasing a new single. Gordy asked Norman Whitfield when the new tune would be ready.

"I got the tracks and the tunes, but not all the Tempts," Whitfield replied. "Everybody showed up but David. This is crazy, and it happens all the time." Whitfield seemed as though he was getting something off his mind that had been bothering him for some time. "I'm tired of it, and the guys are fed up." He did not tell Gordy, of course, that as a result of his own gambling he had often been late to the group's recording sessions, much to their anger.

Gordy called Shelly Berger, Motown's Los Angeles director, to accompany the Tempts on their next tour and to report back what was happening. Berger called Gordy after a few days to say the group was desperate to get rid of Ruffin. Gordy urged caution, telling Berger to warn the group not to act too hastily.

"I did," he told Gordy, "but they all voted. Unanimous."

Ruffin was out. And in almost no time the Tempts hired Dennis Edwards, an ex-Contour. He had a strong, gritty voice, with excellent gospel credentials, and was a solid replacement. Some critics, however, thought he had a natural tendency to sing against the rest of the group, thereby eliminating its characteristic shading.

But the problem was not in integrating Edwards into the Tempts, it was that Ruffin refused to accept his dismissal. His ouster shocked him. Otis Williams said Ruffin saw himself as so important "that the four of us would put up with anything." Ruffin kept defiantly showing up at shows, sitting in the audience, and sometimes actually tried jumping onstage. There were problems removing him since most of the fans still loved him and wanted him back in the group. Once they saw him, they would scream and stomp for him to stay. The Tempts hired extra security to keep him away.

Gordy finally appeased Ruffin with a solo career. That stopped him from trying to be part of the Tempts. Ruffin's first record, "My Whole World Ended (the Moment You Left Me)," was an instant hit. But when his career faltered after that, he sued Motown to break his contract, charging it was "one sided . . . appropriate only for a relationship between a guardian and a child or mental incompetent." Ruffin contended that his contract kept him "in economic peonage." A court ruled for Motown.

Ruffin's departure was not the last major change for the Tempts. The group had many more over the years, so many in fact that only die-hard fans can remember the names and tenures of all the replacements. As for original members, Eddie Kendricks, who had mixed feelings about letting Ruffin go, left in 1971 for a solo career. A simmering and often nasty feud between Kendricks and Otis Williams caused the split. Kendrick's departure left the group without his beautiful falsetto voice.

Paul Williams left that same year because of deteriorating health from his abusive drinking. He failed at running a celebrity boutique in the inner city and soon owed the government more than eighty thousand dollars in taxes. He killed himself with a single gunshot to the head in August 1973 at the age of thirty-four. He did it in his car, only a few blocks from Hitsville. At his funeral, more than 2,500 people—including fans, other artists, and politicians—crammed into and around the small Baptist church for the service. The other Tempts were the pallbearers, and David Ruffin sang one of Williams's favorite songs, "The Impossible Dream," before collapsing from grief.

Within days of Williams's death, there were rumors that fanned conspiracy theories—revolving around the Mafia, other Tempts, and Berry Gordy—alleging that he was murdered. Some said he was found with only his underwear on and that his clothes were never recovered. Eddie Kendricks, who was petrified by Williams's death, told everyone that his former colleague had used his right hand to shoot himself in the left side of his head. Some said the shot was not fired from close range but a few feet away by a mystery killer. David Ruffin worsened the fragile situation by telling Kendricks, "Them people will never leave you the fuck alone. They'll find a way to get you."

However, not a single rumor was ever confirmed. There is no credible evidence of foul play. The autopsy report rebuts the speculation, and, when coupled with his disintegrating personal life and deepening depression, there is little doubt Williams committed suicide. Most close to him have finally accepted that his death was self-inflicted: "Paul was an unhappy man," recalled Otis Williams. "He spoke of suicide to me and to several others." Still, though, a few Motown stars continue to fan more sinister ideas, as in Mary Wilson's 1990 *Supreme Faith:* "Paul's death was ruled a suicide, but in many minds there will always be questions as to the real cause."

The only original members who stuck with the group for their entire careers were Melvin Franklin and Otis Williams. One night, when the group had been in the middle of their worst problems, both men had taken a stroll and, amid tears and prayers, promised each other they would never quit.

• • •

While the Temptations were problematic, the group they had brought into Motown—the Supremes—was having its own difficulties. The emphasis on Diana Ross as a lead singer had created great tension with Mary Wilson and Flo Ballard. Ross's voice was high, sweet, and light. She had a habit of singing through her nose, with her shoulders hunched. As she later dropped the nasal tone, her voice took on a brassier sound. Mary Wilson had a good voice, combined with the most outgoing personality of the three and probably the most sex appeal, something she flaunted onstage. Most industry observers, however, thought that Flo Ballard, the group's founder and its original lead, had the best voice. Even the competitive Wilson acknowledged that Ballard had the strongest voice: "We were all good, but almost everyone who heard us agreed that Flo was the best."

Ballard's voice had character, was strong, and had a distinctive sound. "She was one of the best singers I ever heard," recalled Otis Williams. "All three of the Supremes had it, but even from the earliest days, whenever Flo took her part . . . she brought the house down. Her voice had a real depth of feeling and a strong, churchy sound. When Flo opened her mouth to sing, you sat up in your chair."

In comparison, Diana Ross was not impressive. African-American historian Gerald Early, in his social study of Motown, concluded that "among Motown's singers, only Diana Ross had a truly 'pop' voice, that is, an absolutely depthless, completely synthetic voice." Many critics chided her for not conveying any emotion. Lamont Dozier, who supervised the Supremes' background vocals, used to move the microphone farther away from Ballard, lest her strong tenor overpower Ross's lead.

But to Ross's credit, she also underwent the greatest transformation once the girls were onstage. Her nervous habits, like biting nails, disappeared, and she seemed natural and flowing, with a personality that was memorable.

"There was never any question in my mind as to who the lead singer was," Gordy later told *Playboy.* Some insiders believe Gordy chose Ross as the lead since she had the "whitest-sounding" voice of the girls. Her innocuous and less identifiable sound was more commercial since it easily crossed over to the large white pop audience Gordy so coveted.

Gordy was admittedly biased because of his affair with Ross—he always seemed ready to accept her version of events whenever problems arose between the Supremes and other artists. For instance, in 1966, when the Supremes and the Temptations appeared together on *The Ed Sullivan Show,* the groups had decided to perform a medley with each singing the other's hits. During rehearsals, David Ruffin's versions of the Supremes' songs were electric. Otis Williams recalled, "It's not slighting Diane to say that he blew her away." Ross began whining that the key was too low for her. When Maurice King did not take her moaning seriously, she complained to Gordy, who ordered King to push up the medley's entire key. It was then ideal for Ross and barely within Ruffin's range. (After the show, the Tempts were hurt to learn that Gordy sent the Supremes lavish gifts but had not even thanked them.)

Female artists at Motown felt that once Gordy selected Ross to become the Supremes' lead, their own careers suffered. Gordy admitted as much to *Billboard*'s Adam White years later: "I think that more resentment came as I fell more and more in love with Diana and was on the road with the Supremes. Or as I started to spend more and more time with them . . . I saw them [the Supremes] as leaders, . . . number one. Number two, I was falling more and more in love with Diana, and, of course, she inspired me to the hilt. And I'm sure that was resented by some of the other artists."

Among those who felt overlooked were Martha Reeves, the Marvelettes, Gladys Knight, and Brenda Holloway. Some, like Reeves, had already had their own run-ins with Ross, watching furiously as Ross had copied the Vandellas' costumes and stolen onstage "ad-libs" and her cooing and oohing style from other Motown singers. When Reeves tried confronting Ross after one performance, Ross merely called Gordy, who settled the dispute in her favor. It did not help morale that Gordy and Ross sometimes attended the shows of other singers, usually sitting in the front row. After, Gordy would present a laundry list of criticisms as Ross stood by smugly. To Reeves and many others, Gordy's protection of Ross made them feel second-rate.

Not surprisingly, Ross also got Gordy's ear when it came to dissension within the Supremes. From what Ross told him, Gordy believed the problem was that Mary Wilson wanted to be the lead and was jealous of Ross since she did not have a unique voice. As for Flo Ballard, Gordy viewed her as moody and not motivated enough to be a top pop star.

In London, while they were recording a BBC show, Gordy pulled Wilson and Ballard aside and castigated them for not supporting Ross and making her feel isolated.

They would hear none of it. "We're the ones being isolated," shot back Wilson. "She gets out there onstage and acts like we're not even there."

"Yeah," seconded Ballard. "She ain't nothing but a show-off."

Gordy tried telling them that Ross had always been a show-off, and that that was one of the reasons she was a successful performer. And he reminded them that they were part of the world's most successful female group and that Ross did not earn a penny more than they, nor did she ever ask to. Again, he asked them to reduce the tensions and to support her onstage. They agreed to try.

Back in Detroit, to Gordy's chagrin, the reports continued to be dismal about the Supremes. Road managers and chaperones said nothing had changed. And a new problem developed: Ballard had started drinking. It riled Gordy, who had a fairly simple saying about drugs and drink: "It's easier to stay out than to get out."

None of the three Supremes was a heavy drinker at first. But once the group became popular, as Mary Wilson recalled, "no occasion would be complete without the best liquor and the finest champagne." Ross and Wilson seemed to handle their drinking, but Ballard's tolerance was low. After a single glass, she often seemed unsteady. Her drinking increased as things became more strained within the group and she became increasingly angry. When they toured, Ross had her own dressing room, while the other two shared a room. Ross directed a growing entourage to run personal errands while Ballard and Wilson had to plead with Gordy for anyone to help them. "Whatever Diane wanted," recalled Wilson, "Diane got. In Flo's mind this was unfair, and her resentment began to consume her."

Once, before appearing on *The Ed Sullivan show*, Wilson spoke to Ballard and warned her to control her visible anger when Gordy or Ross said something that she didn't like.

"Well, what am I supposed to do?" Ballard asked.

"Just do what I do," said Wilson. "Nothin'. Don't say nothin' back."

"Fuck that! I'm not kissing Diana Ross's ass, or Berry's either. I'm fightin' both of them, and I'll win."

"You won't win, Flo. No one ever wins."

After that show, when one of Ballard's earrings fell off, Diana Ross stepped on it and crushed it. Most thought it an accident. But Ballard thought it was deliberate, and she attacked Ross in the dressing room, pulling off her wig and earrings before two of Gordy's bodyguards yanked her away.

Others at Motown knew things were spiraling out of control. Most had their own opinions about the causes. Smokey Robinson was convinced not only that Ballard suffered from jealousy but that her boyfriend, Tommy Chapman, Gordy's former chauffeur, had "pushed her off track, persuading her that there was more money to be made outside Motown."

At first, Ballard was not drinking before her shows. But soon, Ross and Wilson noticed she was. She started showing up late for press conferences, rehearsals, and travel departures. When Mary Wilson warned her to shape up and stop drinking, Ballard lashed back, "Honey, I am not working myself to death to make Diana Ross a star!"

Ballard's defiance was a serious problem. She began gaining weight and had trouble fitting into some costumes. Gordy didn't help. He often chided her for being too heavy, and she would respond sarcastically that she wasn't heavy, Diana was too thin. "I stopped a whole company of men on Fifty-seventh Street," she told him. "I didn't hear nobody calling for Diana."

One night, in front of other performers and fans, Gordy ran into Ballard at the 20 Grand in Detroit. He said loudly, "I agree with Diane. You have to do something about your weight. You are much too fat."

"I don't give a damn what you think!" she snapped. Then she shocked everyone by throwing a drink into Gordy's face and storming from the club. "I was shocked," recalled her good friend, and onetime lover, Otis Williams. "She'd always been so dedicated. . . . We figured it was only a matter of time. Berry wasn't going to stand for too much more of that."

Tensions in the group had been exacerbated toward the end of 1966 as journalists bombarded them with questions about whether they intended to change their name to Diana Ross and the Supremes. Mary Wilson and Flo Ballard denied it. No one from Motown ever told them such a change was contemplated. Meanwhile, it was Motown's own publicity department that was leaking word about a possible name change. "Over time we learned that the name would indeed be changed," recalled Mary Wilson, "and, when it seemed certain, Flo went over the edge."

Ross and Wilson were forced to perform as a duo when Ballard was so drunk that she actually missed two shows. Gordy sent Marlene Barrow, one of the Andantes, to take Ballard's spot when she did not show up for another performance. He was pleasantly surprised that the audience did not seem to mind. Soon, Cindy Birdsong, formerly of Patti LaBelle and the Blue Belles, was hired as a standby. Ross had met Birdsong during the Supremes' early touring days and liked her. Birdsong had a strong voice, resembled Ballard physically, and learned the routines easily.

At a United Negro College Fund benefit at the Hollywood Bowl, Ballard was again drunk and was stumbling backstage and slurring her words. Gordy ordered Birdsong to replace her. Because the audience was a fair distance from the stage, most fans did not even notice the substitution. However, when the group appeared on *The Tonight Show* shortly thereafter, Johnny Carson asked about the breakup rumors and why Birdsong had stood in for Ballard. Ross sidestepped the real problems and instead gave a prepared answer, telling Carson the situation was similar to a Broadway play, where there are stand-ins for the stars. "The show must go on. Except for me. They can't stand in for me. But Florence and Mary, we have two young ladies that will stand in their place."

Motown's executives huddled over what to do. Diana Ross complained that Ballard was making the group look bad. Mary Wilson's attempts to hide liquor from Ballard did little to stop her. It all came to a head in Memphis, where Ballard was so drunk and surly that Ross called Gordy. He did not commit Ballard to a rehab center. Instead, he instructed Joe Schaffner, the group's road manager and husband of one of the Marvelettes, to put her on the next plane to Detroit. On the way to the airport, Ballard just sobbed.

The Temptations' Melvin Franklin sent Mary Wilson a telegram imploring her to stand by Ballard and leave the group in protest—"Stick by Florence. It may happen to you. Think about it."

When the members of the group returned to Detroit in mid-April 1967, they gathered at Gordy's house. He told the girls, who had arrived with their mothers, that he felt he had no choice but to let Ballard go. Ballard's mother, Lurlee, spoke up: "But Mary still wants Flo in the group."

Everybody looked at Wilson. She later said that at that moment she realized that Ballard was "waiting for me to rescue her, waiting for me to tell Diane and Berry how they'd mistreated Flo, and how wrong they were." Instead, she was silent for a moment and then summoned her courage. "Mrs. Ballard," she somberly said, "Flo no longer wants to be in the Supremes. Yes, I want her with us, but she no longer wants us." She remembered, "In those few seconds, I saw nine years of work and love and happiness fade away."

Ballard was quiet. She seemed detached from everything swirling around her. But her mother was nearly hysterical. In Gordy's house, no one said a word as Ballard and her mother left, walking past Cindy Birdsong, who was sitting in the living room waiting for the meeting to finish. The Ballards drove off in their Cadillac. When Mary Wilson looked at Ross, she thought Ross was "almost giddy" and trying hard to contain her excitement. Shortly after the breakup, Diana told *Ebony* that the many stories of disagreements among her and Ballard and Wilson had been "all lies." She said it had been Ballard's "decision and that she wanted to go home and have babies and stay with her husband." Years later, in her autobiography, *Secrets of a Sparrow*, Ross was slightly more forthcoming: "At the beginning of 1967, by mutual consent, Florence left the group. Although we were very sad that things hadn't worked out with Florence, we also breathed a sigh of relief. We were tired of having to cope with her moods and trying to take care of her."

"Florence did herself in," admitted Smokey Robinson.

At the time, no reason was publicly given for her departure. Gordy never wanted to disclose any drinking or drug problems about his artists, even those who left the label. As Cindy Birdsong replaced Flo Ballard, the group's name officially became Diana Ross and the Supremes. It appeared for the first time on a Las Vegas marquee, the same week as the Newark race riots began. Just before that, there had been a final show at the Copa. Cindy Birdsong was not quite ready to take over, and Ballard hoped it might give her a chance to rejoin the group. But again, she was tipsy from liquor and had ballooned in weight so that she barely fit into her dress. Gordy ordered her out of the dressing room and for the final time sent her packing to Detroit. Gordy decided that Cindy Birdsong became a permanent member at that moment, whether she was ready or not.

Most everyone felt that Gordy was prepping Ross for a solo career, but the amount of time and money he spent on her now became an even more divisive issue for those artists who had been simmering over the attention the group had received. Gladys Knight, Martha Reeves, Brenda Holloway, the Marvelettes, and Valerie Simpson started openly complaining. Others gave up hope of getting any substantive Motown promotion for their own projects—for instance, the fiery Kim Weston left in 1967. Even some producers got fed up—Harvey Fuqua left his wife, Gwen Gordy, and the company. Clarence Paul was gone by 1968, angry over Gordy's priorities and that the money flowing in did not seem to trickle down much past the Gordys and a few top executives.

In 1967, when Kim Weston left, her husband, Mickey Stevenson, caught Gordy off guard with the news that he was also leaving. He had received a lucrative offer from MGM, the same label to which Weston was going. (Stevenson later confided to Raynoma that it wasn't only the better offer; he was angry that Gordy had failed to promote his wife's career, and he was tired of Berry's steadfast refusal to share any profits.) Gordy offered Stevenson a raise but would not give him any equity in the company. MGM, on the other hand, offered him equity if he could make their Venture Records subsidiary a presence in the R&B market.

Stevenson had a special talent in matching up writers, producers, and artists, and not only did he personally contribute to the songs, but he also was a keen motivator. Gordy considered Stevenson "one of the greatest creative forces during our formative years" and knew he would be hard to replace. Gordy wanted someone with stature who was known and respected by the artists. He was also determined to keep A&R under a black director. Gordy chose Eddie Holland.

Not long after Stevenson's departure, the director of Quality Control, Billie Jean Brown, took a leave of absence. Gordy replaced her with Brian Holland. As Gordy later noted, "Both moves further increased the power of HDH. Both were moves I would come to regret."

But before any problems between Gordy and HDH surfaced, the appointment of the Hollands to such key positions engendered considerable animosity among other producers. Since HDH already had a stranglehold on the Supremes and the Four Tops, other producers were frustrated that the Hollands now exercised control over which records were released. Many complained openly that they felt the Hollands' power locked others out of the system.

Gordy did not appear bothered by any of this. In the years since he had lost his first big star, Mary Wells, he had grudgingly accepted that some successful artists and producers would occasionally leave. Also, he had come to understand that many artists complained they were being shortchanged on promotion and attention, especially if their songs weren't all hits. It was their problem, he told colleagues, not one caused by his attention on proven hit makers like the Supremes.

•   •   •

Shortly after the name change for the Supremes, Shelly Berger used his Hollywood contacts to book an appearance for the revamped trio on an episode of the television series *Tarzan.* Although a B-quality series with only a moderate viewership, Gordy acted as though the girls had been asked to host their own show. "Because this was their first dramatic acting opportunity," he said, "I was frantic to make it work." The episode was shot in Mexico, with James Earl Jones costarring with Diana Ross and Mary Wilson and Cindy Birdsong relegated to bit roles as nuns. Gordy flew to the location to oversee the production. At one point, he worked with Jones and Ross on a song he thought might work for the show. When the director saw the trio, he exploded and sharply ordered an embarrassed Gordy off the set. Humiliated in front of Ross, Gordy ordered Mike Roshkind, his chief of public relations—often called by insiders "Berry's henchman"—to "find the person who owns the show." Soon, Gordy was on the phone with Sy Weintraub, the series owner, who was in his Los Angeles office. Weintraub was polite to Gordy but refused to get involved in any dispute, claiming he never got in the middle of creative issues. Gordy slowly came to the view that he was wrong in trying to insert the song without first asking the director for his opinion. So Gordy decided to make peace, and when he approached the director the following morning he was ready to be humble. But before he said anything, the director turned to him and was as friendly as possible. He said he had thought about Gordy's idea for the singing duet and decided it was ideal for the show. Gordy later found out that Weintraub had in fact called the director and ordered him to cooperate with Gordy. Not only did that episode return the highest-ever ratings for *Tarzan,* but it also taught Gordy a quick lesson about Hollywood—who you knew might just be as important, if not more so, than the quality of your ideas.

CHAPTER 21

"A Mafia Product from Start to Finish"

NEAR THE END OF 1967, WHILE THE SUPREMES WERE MAKING ONE OF their frequent *Ed Sullivan Show* appearances, Cindy Birdsong introduced Gordy to a friend of hers, Suzanne Celeste de Passe, a Harlem native and Manhattan Community College dropout. De Passe was then a part-time talent coordinator for the Cheetah, a popular New York disco. Gordy was attracted to the brash, pretty nineteen-year-old who showed infectious enthusiasm for the Supremes. Before long, de Passe, with her long, flowing hair and hip clothes, was a regular when the Supremes rehearsed. She walked around, jotting notes and making suggestions to Gordy. A few months after they met, when the Supremes were in Miami, de Passe was there again. She pulled Gordy aside and surprised him with her forthrightness.

"Mr. Gordy, I love your company," she said, "but I don't think it's being run right."

He was taken aback.

"They're not taking care of business, and I just thought you should know."

She told him how difficult she had found it recently to book some Motown artists for the Cheetah. No one at Motown had returned her calls, and she told Gordy bluntly that she found the company's behavior not only bad for business but "just plain rude."

When Gordy asked if she thought she could run the company, she did not hesitate: "I'd love to try." Her entire work experience at the time, besides her part-time work for the disco, included three days as a salesclerk at Bloomingdale's, one month in the city's garment district, and a part-time job as an equestrian trainer.

Gordy liked her so much that he decided she should work at Motown, even though he had no idea what role she could play. Two weeks later, he flew her to Detroit. She arrived expecting to find a plush suite of offices, but when the car pulled up to the original Hitsville building she was struck by how small it was. "I couldn't believe *this* was Motown."

Gordy put her on the payroll as his creative assistant and asked her to return to New York to wait until he figured out how to use her. "If Motown had been organized," she said, "they wouldn't have needed to hire me." Meanwhile, others questioned why she was even hired. Gordy simply told most who asked that he did not know but that his intuition was that she would be great.

When she finally moved to Detroit, Gordy met with her and set some ground rules. Criticism, he told her, was something he sought, and she should never fear giving her honest opinion. She took him at his word, and as a result her first day was almost her last. Esther Gordy was then running the art department and was showing her brother some new album-cover designs. He was not enthusiastic about any of them, but Esther was adamant that they were ideal. Gordy brought in de Passe for a second opinion. She walked in without knowing anything about Esther's power at Motown or that Gordy was setting her up to parrot his own reservations. De Passe focused on Gordy's admonition to be forthright. She studied the covers for a few minutes and finally pointed toward one for the Temptations.

"Outdated. Nobody's got processed hair anymore. They're into naturals for some time now. These must be old photos. And the Four Tops cover looks very stiff. Levi looks like he's smelling something." She leaned over the desk and grabbed one of the covers. "Smokey," she said, waving a Miracles cover, "my favorite artist. Where did they get these clothes?"

She continued tearing apart each of the designs. Esther stood fuming on the side. Gordy was amused. Finally, de Passe finished and said, "Basically, Mr. Gordy, I guess you could say they don't really work for me."

While Gordy knew de Passe had only done what he instructed her to do, he also knew she was in big trouble with Esther. He gave her a weak smile. Esther was silent. Gordy asked de Passe to wait in his office.

When she left, brother and sister stood a few feet apart, neither making eye contact. Finally Gordy asked Esther in a joking way, "So, what did you think of the new girl?"

"Either she goes or I go," the normally easygoing Esther said as she stormed out. Gordy disliked confrontations, but he despised ultimatums. He knew he could not, obviously, let Esther leave, but he also did not want to fire de Passe for doing what he had encouraged her to do. For a few days, while Esther refused to talk to him, he ignored the problem. Finally, he went to her and explained what had happened, trying to remove any blame from de Passe. Esther, having had some time to cool off, pleasantly surprised her brother by agreeing that he could not fire de Passe for only having spoken honestly. And in the coming weeks, Esther checked on de Passe's comments about the albums' designs with others, eventually deciding that the art department needed fresh ideas. She hired a new director.

From the start, Suzanne de Passe was a force to reckon with. "She could sell you the Brooklyn Bridge," recalled Jay Lasker, later Motown's president. Raynoma Gordy said, "She was a young woman of fierce ambition who'd step on whatever toes or incur whatever resentful feelings necessary to climb the next rungs. What was more, she tolerated Berry with twenty-four-hour-a-day dedication." Once, Raynoma was at a meeting when Gordy suddenly turned to de Passe, who often battled a weight problem, and said: "Suzanne, get up and show 'em how fat you are. Get up and pretend you're an ape— be a gorilla for everybody."

To Raynoma, it was typical Gordy, "pushing people beyond the limits of abuse." Some ignored Gordy's insults and incitements, others were humiliated, and still others got angry. But in this case de Passe just started hopping around the room, scratching under her arms like an ape, and whooping loudly.

"Suzanne had passed the test," recalled Raynoma. "I was mortified and embarrassed for her. But it was highly revealing. She didn't give a damn what she had to do; she'd do whatever it would take to make it."

"I spent the first five years at Motown constantly being frustrated," de Passe later said. "I wanted to be told by Berry that I was doing OK, and he just doesn't give that kind of approval. I kept trying because I couldn't believe that I couldn't do the job."

De Passe was determined to make a mark and, as a result, moved up faster into the executive levels than any other woman hired by Gordy. Some at the time, including Diana Ross, speculated that Gordy and de Passe were lovers. When a beautiful woman makes it in almost any industry, rumors that she is sleeping with her boss are prevalent and were much more so thirty years ago when female executives were rarer. "I would never have had to work this hard if I was Berry Gordy's old lady," she told *Essence* in 1981. De Passe believes that the sexism rife in Motown gave her a "great advantage" because she had "the benefit of being underestimated all my life."

Based on many interviews, there appears to have been no affair between Gordy and de Passe. Instead, he admired her because she was sharp, learned the business quickly, had strong opinions she was not afraid to give, and reminded him of his sisters, who had been indispensable over the years. Even those who grew to dislike her acknowledged de Passe's complete confidence and competence, attributes that seemed innate rather than gained through experience. She also was willing to do any job assigned to her, from holding the hands of artists having personal crises to going out on tour with the acts to writing television scripts for Motown specials to overseeing the promotional launch for new acts to helping producers finish recording sessions. Gordy also liked that she placed her commitment to work above her personal life. She had the dedication he wanted.

Within the first two weeks she worked for Gordy, de Passe told him she eventually wanted to be Motown's president. "I think I'd seen too many career-girl movies at the time," she said, laughing at the memory of that brashness fourteen years later, when she was president of Motown Industries.

·   ·   ·

In the dispute with Esther, Gordy was relieved he did not have to renege on his hiring of de Passe. No matter what his critics said of him, no one ever charged Gordy with failing to live up to a commitment. Around this time, for example, Diana Ross came to him bitterly complaining about the lowball contract she was still locked into at the Copacabana. (The Supremes earned $15,000 a week there, but they could fetch $50,000 for a single night elsewhere.) Even though Motown was forgoing money every time the Supremes played there, Gordy said there was no option since it was the deal to which he had agreed. Eventually, when the original pact expired, Gordy did not re-sign with Podell, despite a much-sweetened offer, because the Waldorf-Astoria offered an even better deal.

The cigar-chomping, tough-talking Podell had a reputation for having Mob contacts that ensured the Copa, among other things, had no labor problems. When Gordy did not renew, some Motown executives were nervous that Podell might call upon his purported Mob buddies to create trouble for Motown. Gordy was not fazed, and he turned out to be right—Podell never caused any problems.

However, that episode is one of many cited by numerous industry observers who contend that Motown itself, by this time, had developed its own Mob connections that protected the label. The conventional wisdom, oft repeated but never proved, is that Gordy had gambled too heavily and fallen into debt, and Mob-backed loan sharks bailed him out at the cost of getting their hands into Motown. A trip Gordy took to the Caribbean around this time became the subject of rumors about him being kidnapped by mobsters looking to get paid for gambling debts or him being held at gunpoint until he agreed to give up part of Motown's ownership to the Mafia. The fact that Motown had many white executives, including a key one, Barney Ales, who was of Sicilian ancestry, fueled the rumors. Ales thought the gossip was ridiculous.

The tales appeared publicly for the first time in the *Rock,* a now defunct 1960s tabloid trade magazine. In an article titled "The Motown Mob," by Pete Cain, incredibly strong accusations were levied against Gordy and the company. "If you're holding a Motown album pressed since 1966, you're looking at a Mafia product from start to finish," Cain reported. "The story of the Motown takeover is an entirely typical example of the Mafia mode of operation."

Rock set forth a grand conspiracy theory. It charged that when Motown started in 1959, the only reason local record jobbers paid the company the money it earned on sales was because the Mob, which supposedly controlled those jobbers, allowed it, so that it could eventually pull off a coup and control the label. A major problem with this theory is that no one, including Gordy, could have known that Motown was going to be any different from dozens of small, independent labels that started and folded after a few flops. Somehow the Mob supposedly was prescient only when it came to Motown. *Rock* gave credit to Gordy for the label's success from 1959 to

1965, "while the Mafia watched and waited." Gordy's fatal mistake, according to *Rock,* was when in 1966 he started bringing some of his acts to Puerto Rico and other Caribbean gigs. Gordy "dropped up to $75,000 a night gambling in Mafia-controlled casinos in Puerto Rico." The article claimed that Mike Roshkind, the white public-relations executive, had fired long-time Motown employees and "oftentimes Berry Gordy did not even know they had been let go." It also said that when Motown colleagues investigated Roshkind's background, they could not "trace or verify" any of his credentials. The *Detroit Free Press* once wrote, "If there is a 'Jewish mafia' within the well integrated company, as some outsiders claim, it is personified by Michael Roshkind."

Actually, there is little mystery about Roshkind. At fifteen, he was the youngest graduate in the history of Northwestern University. Roshkind served in the navy in World War II, was awarded the Navy Cross, and had an easily verifiable résumé from stints at ABC News, the Weintraub Advertising Agency, the public-relations outfit A. A. Schecter Associates, and Irving L. Strauss, another PR firm. Roshkind had even been a broadcast consultant to Adlai Stevenson in his 1956 presidential bid and to John Kennedy and Lyndon Johnson in later campaigns. He probably held the distinction of being the only Motown employee to make Richard Nixon's enemy list. Actually, Roshkind had never heard of Motown before an attorney friend called the forty-five-year-old public-relations whiz and asked him if he wanted to visit Detroit to take the label on as a client. "I was absolutely dumb about the record business," said Roshkind. He asked the attorney, "What is a Motown?" When Roshkind initially saw the ramshackle office on West Grand, he almost left. But when he met Gordy, they hit it off, and soon Roshkind had the account and visited Detroit regularly. After a year, Gordy convinced Roshkind to enter the company as a vice president.

The worst thing that could be uncovered about Roshkind is that he had a tendency toward arrogance, and many at Motown did not like him. "Roshkind had an unbelievable ego," says fellow vice president Phil Jones, reflecting a typical comment. "And was an incredible asshole."

Other evidence cited in *Rock* for the Motown-Mafia theory was that Gordy was "once beaten and left unconscious, supposedly by a squad of Mafia toughs. . . . Gordy won't discuss the beating or its purpose." And the paper listed other "facts": when Gordy attended his parents' fiftieth wedding anniversary, "he was accompanied by eight 'body guards'"; on the third floor of Motown's headquarters, "Motown's Mafia management, afraid that employees will carry information to Gordy or the police, have established a 'security department'—that department taps phones, photographs everyone entering and leaving the building, and sometimes follows visitors for miles when they leave"; "Gordy may have received a $1 million loan from the Teamster's Union pension fund"; and, in its most outrageous guilt-by-tenuous-association charge, the paper alleged that Gordy was "closely associated" with Mob bosses Joe Zerelli, William Tocco, Joseph Barberra Jr., and Anthony Corrado. It also listed Barney Ales's original Sicilian name, spelled incorrectly, and said that Phil Jones had previously worked for William Buffalino, "a Teamster attorney and president of the Teamsters local which is involved in juke boxes and vending machines."

All of these allegations, according to *Rock*, had been uncovered by the FBI and the Detroit police in unspecified probes. No source was ever provided for that claim. The article instead stated, "The police and the FBI are powerless to bring any indictments against the Mafia or Gordy without willing witnesses. So far, plenty of former employees have given information off the record, but no one is willing to risk his life by testifying in court."

Gordy was disturbed to see such unproved and reckless charges in print, although he initially joked about them. "We did that all the time," he recalled. "I'd go up to a person and say things like, 'Well, I'm not in the Mafia, and if you say that again, you'll find yourself in the bottom of the ocean with cement shoes on.' We'd say anything. We had fun." Gordy used to enjoy telling acquaintances that Motown had as many hit rumors as it did hit records.

Barney Ales, who had been in the cement business before moving to music, says he would sometimes "lean over like a tough guy, and say in my best mobster impersonation, 'Don't ask too many questions about us, 'cause the last guy who did is swimming with the fishes.' We'd think it was hysterical when someone would believe that bull and get nervous." Ales even occasionally boasted of the label's "heavy connections," especially when trying to get airplay. While he enjoyed regaling friends with those stories, many in the industry thought his implied threats were real. It wasn't long before Gordy and his colleagues realized that this was not how to best deal with the rumors.

Gordy next considered suing, he said, but his lawyers convinced him that as a public figure he was unlikely to prevail. He then decided to merely ignore the stories. "I have never been approached by anyone that I would consider Mafia in any way," Gordy told a reporter for *The Times* of London, "and I know a lot of people in and out of the record business. We have a policy of ignoring rumors."

Although he did not want to take time away from his core business, he admitted years later that ignoring the gossip was probably also a mistake, since it let the rumors proliferate unchallenged. "When misinformation hits the street, it's gossip," he told a reporter in 1994. "If it's not challenged, which we never did in the early days, it goes on as fact. Someone else picks it up, and the first thing you know, people are telling you that's what happened."

Despite the smoke, there is no credible evidence that the Mafia infiltrated Motown or that Gordy gave any underworld interests secret ownership in his company. Mobsters tend to be equal-opportunity exploiters, and their goal is to rake off as much money as possible while letting a company run itself into the ground. That never happened with the management that ran Motown. And while Gordy was at times a heavy gambler, he also earned enough money from Motown that he had the spare cash to lose at the tables.

Other Motown workers who had serious gambling problems and sometimes ran afoul of money enforcers helped fuel the rumors. Raynoma Gordy recounted when the songwriter Ron Miller ran into her office in 1968 claiming that if he didn't come up with five thousand dollars he owed on gambling losses, "the Mob is going to break my legs." "Gambling almost came with the Motown badge," said Raynoma. Still, this does not provide evidence that the Mob ran the company.

But these rumors were to dog Gordy and Motown forever. Sometimes they were repeated in books, such as Randy Taraborrelli's *Call Her Miss Ross,* in which he reprinted often-told stories: Gordy was swindled by card sharks in Puerto Rico, who then used the debt to get a piece of Motown; Gordy's Detroit house was attacked and vandalized as a Mob warning; Gordy himself had his legs broken by Mafia debt enforcers; and a bodyguard was shot and killed at a private gathering at Gordy's Beverly Hills mansion. Problems confirming those stories, such as no police reports in Puerto Rico or Los

Angeles, no hospital admission records, and no eyewitnesses, have not stopped people from repeating them over the years. Another book that pushed the Mob-controls-Motown rumors was the novel *Number One with a Bullet*, written by former Motown employee (and brief Marvin Gaye girl-friend) Elaine Jesmer.

The rumors were so widespread in Detroit that the FBI eventually called Gordy into their local office. Two agents chatted with Gordy for a while, asked for his autograph, and bid him a cheerful good-bye. Trying later to find some silver lining in the oft-repeated stories, Gordy smiled and said, "The one good thing about it was sometimes it was a little easier to collect our money."

CHAPTER 22

"Don't You Trust Us?"

AT THE END OF 1967, GORDY GAVE HIS HOUSE ON OUTER DRIVE TO his sister Anna and her husband, Marvin Gaye. He bought a plush Italian Renaissance–style mansion on Boston Boulevard. Gordy approached the move much as he did a new recording session—he worked around the clock.

Originally built in the 1920s by an auto magnate at a cost of more than one million pre-Depression dollars, the imposing three-story stone and slate building looked more like a museum than a private home. Gordy loved showing off the marble-floored ballroom, the billiard and screening rooms, the sprawling gym, the English pub, the two-lane bowling alley, and the manicured Greek garden. The house was filled with gold frescoes, Waterford and Lalique chandeliers, multicolored stained-glass windows, gilded ceilings, intricately tiled floors, and furniture that looked like it belonged in a royal court. The fifty-foot-long main room was dominated by a giant oil painting of Gordy dressed as Napoleon Bonaparte, done by a local Detroit artist. (Flo Ballard used to refer to him constantly as "little Napoleon.") Gordy used the mansion to host Detroit's annual Sterling Ball, the city's prestigious black high-society event. And it became the site of outrageous Motown parties over the years. Gordy used his influence with city hall to have the police cordon off several city blocks and provide extra security for special events.

When he finished moving into his new home, he emerged to face personal problems unlike any he had confronted before.

The first involved the Temptations. In January 1968, the group had been scheduled to tour Japan. But because of tensions over the USS *Pueblo*, a naval intelligence ship that had been captured by North Korea, the group wanted to cancel. But Motown's executives urged them to go. When the Tempts refused to budge, Gordy got involved. He tried browbeating Otis Williams, and when that didn't work he tried seducing him with possible perks: "You know those Oriental women," Gordy told Williams, "they love black guys. You guys will be able to get all the action you want."

Williams stood his ground, and finally Gordy backed off. But the canceled tour cost Motown substantial income, and Gordy was so furious that he never forgave the group.

Gordy soon faced a much more crippling problem than a recalcitrant group. HDH, his top songwriting crew, was unhappy. It was not entirely a surprise. HDH's recent songs, even for the Supremes, had been weaker on the charts. Gordy had heard rumors that HDH was so disgruntled that they were threatening to stop writing or producing anything. By February 1968, for a new Supremes album, Gordy had to resort to a song cut a year earlier and passed over at the time, "Forever Came Today." It peaked at number twenty-eight, the worst performance for a Supremes release since they had broken into the charts. Problems with HDH affected far more than just the output of hit songs. The Holland brothers held key posts: Brian directed Quality Control and Eddie ran A&R.

Gordy continued to hope this might be only a temporary malaise, even though several of his colleagues passed along rumors that the trio might secretly be negotiating with Capitol Records. Gordy could not believe it since they had lucrative, longterm writing and producing contracts. They had earned millions from their Motown hits and stood to earn millions more in future royalties. And although they had occasional complaints, they seemed loyal. Both Holland brothers had worked with Gordy before there was a Hitsville. They went too far back, he thought, for there to be a permanent split. Gordy finally decided he should seek out Brian Holland and find out what was wrong. Although Eddie traditionally negotiated for the trio, Gordy had a better rapport with Brian.

Gordy found Brian in one of the piano rooms. He could tell immediately that Brian was uncomfortable. "I hope you understand and have no hard feelings," Brian said, looking sheepish. "But that's my brother and you know how it is. . . ."

The situation suddenly started to make sense to Gordy.

"Eddie was much more money-minded," recalled Gordy later. Smokey Robinson also considered Eddie the likely source of any problems. Over the years, Eddie had frequently asked for bonus incentives. Gordy agreed to them, knowing how critical HDH was to Motown's success. Gordy had also agreed to several adjustments to the original contract but had recently drawn the line when Eddie requested a large, unsecured, interest-free loan. Now Gordy realized that his rejection of Eddie's loan was probably why the group was so upset.

Frustrated over the impasse, Eddie Holland didn't feel like writing, and he had convinced his two partners not to do any work. Gordy had no idea of what HDH's real value was to Motown, but following his own instincts and the advice of attorneys he decided to act preemptively to stop them from leaving. He sued HDH for four million dollars for breaching their contract by not producing any songs. He hoped the suit might snap them to their senses. While others at Motown rallied around Gordy, the lawsuit turned out to be a major mistake. It ended any wavering among the Hollands and Dozier. All three were now convinced they needed to break free of Motown. It was the most devastating defection Gordy had ever faced.

"See, this is what I was talking about," Gordy told Diana Ross one night, as the two of them relaxed over a bottle of wine at his house. "Remember when I wouldn't let you talk me into breaking the slave agreement we had at the Copa?" She nodded, gently stroking his neck, trying her best to be supportive. "Well, we had agreed to those terms. We had to live by it. It was the honorable thing to do. But everyone is looking only at dollars now, and they'll sell their honor for the right price." He slammed his fist against the small glass table next to the sofa. It smashed into a dozen pieces.

"Don't worry, baby," Ross said softly. "They aren't the only songwriters in town."

Gordy wished it was that simple. "As much as everyone wanted to help me, I knew the company's very survival was at stake. It was all on my shoulders. If what I did worked, I'd be a hero; if it didn't a bum."

While his lawyers pursued the lawsuit, Gordy shook up Motown in case HDH did not return. First, he had to fill Eddie and Brian's executive positions. A&R, retitled the "Creative Division," was placed under Ralph Seltzer's control. Barney Ales had originally brought Seltzer, a lawyer with thick black-rimmed glasses, into Motown for his administrative talents. His abrasive style irritated many longtime employees as he streamlined the bureaucracy. Now, most were puzzled as to why Gordy assigned him such an important creative role. Raynoma understood: "Berry considered good articulation, organizational skills, and a large vocabulary signs of intelligence. His opinion . . . was that a good administrator could administrate anything." Seltzer was a company man whose loyalty was to the bottom line. While that endeared him to Gordy, it did little to win favor with producers, artists, and songwriters. And Seltzer did not help by running his department largely from behind closed doors. His first directive was that instead of the company just recouping 100 percent of its recording costs by charging artists' accounts, it would make a profit on each session by also charging the producers 25 percent of the total costs. The producers were furious. But Seltzer, who did not care what people thought of him, ignored the complaints. Since Motown was now earning money from its recording sessions, Gordy did not bother to check any further on what the new rules did to company morale.

"Once Berry brought in Ralph Seltzer," said Ivy Hunter, a songwriter, "the family atmosphere was finally destroyed." When Hunter eventually expressed his frustration over Seltzer at a company meeting, the other executives remained quiet, and Hunter was punished by seeing all his projects sidelined. Others privately complained that new creative arrangements, such as having the producers meet separately, overlapped with the duties of Quality Control. And the meetings were becoming backlogged by delayed releases. They sometimes lasted five hours and still failed to get to all the recordings that were submitted.

To Gordy, however, every complaint was secondary to what he considered the key problem he confronted in the HDH departure: the lack of hit songs, especially for the Supremes. It was important not just to replace HDH but to find new songwriters quickly, to answer the growing chorus of complaints from artists such as Stevie Wonder, Marvin Gaye, and the Temptations, who were now clamoring to write and produce their own songs.

For some performers, the loss of HDH ended their best days at Motown. The Four Tops had depended on the songwriting trio. "Without them, we couldn't get a hit," recalled Lawrence Payton. After struggling with new songwriters to no avail, the Four Tops left Motown a few years later.

Gordy quickly cobbled together a new songwriting team. Deke Richards, who played guitar on many Motown albums, helped Gordy make the selections. They included Frank Wilson, a young writer and producer from the West Coast, and R. Dean Taylor, an artist and songwriter who Gordy thought was particularly clever with lyrics. Pam Sawyer, a British writer signed to Jobete, also helped with lyrics. And to ensure the young group had solid direction, Gordy appointed Hank Cosby, from the old A&R department, to oversee everything.

Gordy dubbed the new team "the Clan," signifying a group of friends bound together by a single purpose. Their mandate, Gordy told them, was to create a number-one hit for the Supremes. This time, Gordy wanted to keep individual egos in check, so he emphasized the collective effort by joining the team himself. He gathered everyone at a suite in Detroit's venerable Pontchartrain Hotel and announced they would stay there, working around the clock until they came up with the right song. On the second day of too little sleep and too much coffee, the group seemed nowhere nearer their goal than when they first checked in. To loosen the atmosphere, Gordy sat at the piano and started banging out some HDH-type chords. It was as though those chords flipped a switch for the others, and suddenly people were throwing out lyrics to Gordy's playing. Most were mediocre, but Gordy continued, hoping he might hear something good in the jumble of suggestions. Finally, Pam Sawyer said something that grabbed his attention: "What about a baby born out of wedlock?" she asked. "Love child."

Some thought it was the wrong concept for the Supremes, since the group was often heralded as America's sweethearts. But Gordy disagreed. During the rest of the jam session, the group took that idea and turned it into a positive story in which a girl, herself born out of wedlock, tells her new boyfriend that she won't go to bed with him since she doesn't want to be responsible for bringing another love child into the world.

From the Pontchartrain, the group went directly to the studio and recorded the song with Diana Ross—with Cindy Birdsong and Mary Wilson out of town, Gordy rushed two unknown backup singers into the session. When the song was released, it not only hit number one faster than anyone expected but outsold every previous Supremes record to date. More important for Gordy, everyone who heard "Love Child" thought it was another HDH classic. He was ecstatic.

Shortly after "Love Child" was released, Gordy was able to turn his attention to three television specials Motown had agreed to make with Ed Friendly and George Schlatter, the producers of the enormously successful *Rowan and Martin's Laugh-In.* The first production, titled *TCB—Taking Care of Business,* starred Diana Ross and the Temptations and aired in December 1968 on NBC. The show, much to the aggravation of Mary Wilson and the Temptations' Paul Williams, was a showcase for Diana Ross. The Tempts, who had not performed with Ross in quite a while, thought it was ridiculous that everyone in the production, including Suzanne de Passe, had to refer to her deferentially as Miss Ross. (Gordy had himself started the Miss Ross name when one day he had instructed a newspaper reporter in Las Vegas to "call her Miss Ross"—the other Supremes were always called by their first names.)

"What's with all of this 'Miss Ross' bullshit?" asked Melvin Franklin. "And how come I can't get no one to call me 'Mr. Franklin'?" The Tempts had known Ross since she was a child and were not about to start deferring to her. Paul Williams complained to one of the producers, "If it wasn't for me, *Miss Ross* would still be in the Detroit ghetto, and now I can't even have a conversation with her unless I clear it with half a dozen people."

One musical number, the "Afro Vogue," was performed on a set that consisted of hundreds of photos of Ross. The tensions backstage ran high. Ross barely spoke to any of the Tempts between the sets. When she said at one point that she needed some brandy for her throat, a Motown employee hurried to buy some. Unable to find a liquor store, she found a small bottle at a discount drugstore. When Ross took a sip on the set, she spat it out. "Who went back to the Detroit projects to get this?" she screamed. The public, of course, had no idea of the difficulties, and the final show seemed a polished and friendly event. The ratings were solid, and the show's soundtrack album went to number one.

It should have been enough to make Gordy temporarily forget his problems with HDH, but in the middle of this new work he had received a troubling call from Harold Noveck. Noveck, as was his style, was a person of few words.

"You're being countersued by HDH for twenty-two million."

His lawyers had told him to expect a countersuit, but somehow he had blocked the possibility from his mind. Now he was both surprised and angry.

"They're suing me?" he screamed. "For what?"

"For everything," was the droll reply.

"Like what?"

"Like everything. I'll have the complaint over to you tomorrow."

HDH filed a forty-page countersuit, claiming Gordy had shortchanged the trio on royalties, reneged on a promise to give Brian Holland a million-dollar stake in Motown, and took advantage of their youthful inexperience by duping them into signing substandard contracts. The trio, using three prominent Detroit law firms and one from New York, asked the court to put Motown into receivership because the damages sought were more than the company was worth. The group's countersuit stated that the three of them had "never read their contracts and if they had read them, they could not have understood their legal wording." Motown attorneys, they charged, had "told them the contracts were only written documents—only a matter of fun." And they charged that when the original contracts expired in 1967, Gordy reneged on verbal promises he had made to them. Eddie Holland described Gordy's business practices as "malice, fraud, and oppression." He also griped that Motown had blacklisted the trio inside the industry and had tried harassing them with private investigators. Gordy belittled all the charges as "bullshit."

This was the first of what would be three rounds in the longest-running music-related litigation in the U.S. court system. Gordy and the writers settled out of court in 1972, with Gordy largely prevailing since he kept the rights to the songs, and HDH acknowledged the validity of their original contracts. HDH split $799,000, and most of that went to overdue federal taxes. Sixteen years later, Eddie Holland again sued Gordy, repeating many of the 1967 lawsuit's allegations and adding some new charges. The suit was dismissed in 1996. But meanwhile, a trio of 1992 lawsuits charged that Gordy had defrauded HDH of royalties and also alleged that some of their songwriting contracts had been forged. That case began tortuously working its way through the courts and, as of 2002, is with its third judge. In the years since the suits were filed, HDH have tried and failed to build their own empire with two labels, Invictus and Hot Wax.

As Gordy later said, he didn't have to read the complaint because the press was filled with banner headlines and many details about the rift. And the bulk of the coverage was that a celebrated, prizewinning team of song-writers was suing Motown for fraud, deceit, and conspiracy. The press often portrayed HDH, as well as many of the other artists at Motown, as prisoners trapped inside Gordy's plantationlike company.

Gordy was furious and thought that HDH had contrived charges to counter his own suit. He was also understandably concerned that many people would believe them.

Gordy insisted that he should go directly to the press and make his case, but his lawyers, as well as Motown's press department, persuaded him it would only make matters worse and degenerate into a media feeding frenzy over a he said/they said battle. Smokey Robinson, instead, issued a prepared statement:

> Motown was started on the idea of whatever money a person has coming—give it to them. Whether it's a penny or a million dollars—if they've earned it—pay them. "Honesty is our policy." So it gets me angry to hear people who have been a part of our love and family feeling—telling people that Motown has not paid them every penny they had coming.
>
> Each year Motown pays out millions of dollars to its creative people who keep coming up with the product. . . . This makes it hard for me to understand how guys like the three well-known writers and producers, who to my knowledge, never had jobs before being made popular at Motown, could ever leave. They were paid millions in royalties and had key positions in the organization. What more could a young man ask for?

Gordy insisted to anyone who would listen that his original contracts were modeled on ones from United Artists and were therefore on par with standard deals in the industry. (They, in reality, were among the most oner-ous in the business, putting almost all the burden on the artist and little on the company.) He also contended that any royalty due an artist was paid promptly and that all costs charged to them were "authorized and correct." Gordy invariably ignored the fact that his contracts made his artists respon-sible for some costs that record companies themselves might otherwise pick up, including studio recording time, the musicians, the charm-school teach-ers, the chaperones, all touring costs, and even the costumes and makeup for live shows. Gordy prided himself on giving cash advances to acts that needed it, but of course they were guaranteed by future royalties and also came with a profitable interest rate.

Otis Williams recalled how the Motown system seemed so simple for the artists: "Motown hadn't given us the power to draw on the Temptations account, but there never was a problem getting money if you needed it. If I saw a television I wanted to buy, I'd call up and there'd be a check waiting when I got to Hitsville. Every now and then, somebody might tell you your account was running a little low, or something along those lines, but money was coming in, so we probably didn't think about it as much as we should have."

While most of the artists understood they would have to repay those advances, few understood how much interest was attached to the money that Motown gave them.

For instance, in 1969, Martha Reeves decided to find out how Motown was managing her money. "Here I was," she remembered, "performing at big-name establishments and having racked up several million dollars for the company selling our recordings." She went to Gordy and asked for a precise accounting of her finances for the seven years she had been signed to Motown. "Although I was an international star," recalled Reeves, "I was shocked to find that I was far from rich." (She eventually filed an unsuccessful lawsuit against Gordy and Motown, alleging they had underpaid her, and Motown countercharged that Reeves actually owed the label $200,000.)

And a key element was that Gordy owned the copyrights to all the songs. "You could write songs at Motown," said Marvin Gaye, "but you'd never own any of your copyrights. . . . You'd get paid as an employee—paid very little—but no one except Berry kept any ownership of the songs. We were all helping Berry build his catalog."

Writers and producers such as Clarence Paul also complained that "just about everyone got ripped off at Motown." Paul charged that Motown's contracts were far behind the industry in granting fair terms to performers and writers and that the company paid "substandard" royalty rates and that "tunes were stolen all the time, and often credit wasn't properly assigned."

To Gordy, the problem that developed was a result not of any failure to carefully explain all the terms of the advances but rather of the inability of many of the artists to live within their means. "When you're a star," he contended, "or just living like one, you tend to forget about those advances through the year that let you live that way. But at royalty time when you see the money you already spent reflected in the size of the check, it's understandably disappointing. But no one's been cheated."

Moreover, Motown's contracts included the powerful clause that allowed an artist's debts from one album to be paid off by royalties earned from another—in this way, one hit could pay for several flops, ensuring that the company almost never had a loser so long as it was able to turn out one hit for an act.

Further, since ITMI managed all the artists, there was an apparent conflict of interest of which few artists were aware. It is not clear, for instance, if in its management role Motown diligently explained the downside of taking large cash advances. Also, Motown's management banked the money for its acts and even paid their taxes, with many of the artists never seeing their own tax returns.

Instead of worrying, some artists viewed all the related connections as an advantage. Melvin Franklin, for example, recalled that all of Motown's services made him and other artists feel that "we were inside of our own capsule, our own world. It was very secure there." Gladys Knight told a Detroit reporter about all the roles the label played and concluded, "You just don't get this anywhere else. And everything that artists at Motown were getting free, we were paying for before." Of course, artists like Knight didn't know they were paying for all these "free" services, as the charges weren't always clearly identified.

Motown's reluctance to fully disclose some expenses charged to the artists' accounts raised suspicions. For instance, Otis Williams remembered that, whenever the group toured, "Motown handled all the financial arrangements and made the deals. All we had to do was show up and sing." Motown had little incentive to negotiate better deals on the expenses since ultimately the artist was responsible.

"I remember being told that all the money due us would be kept safely in an escrow account until the tour ended," said Williams. "Then Motown would settle each act's account and write a check for the balance. Or so they said. In fact, we never saw a single penny from any of those early tours, nor did we see any kind of written statement breaking down where the money went. Since we rarely stayed in a hotel and weren't eating in the finest restaurants, it's hard to imagine what Motown's 'costs' were. Something about it didn't hang right."

Even when artists were no longer kids and were earning not a few thousand dollars a year but millions, Motown often treated them paternalistically. "The tack Berry took with his artists when it came to money," recalled Otis Williams, "was an extension of his attitude toward them in general: he believed that he knew what was best for us." No one ever spoke to the artists about forming corporations, tax planning, or investing for retirement or future health costs. (For years, there was no health insurance at Motown.)

The problems were not limited to the artists who had signed early in Motown's history, when everyone, including company executives, had the excuse that they were still learning the business. In 1976, when Motown signed a funky white singer, Teena Marie, she had no lawyer. When she asked if she could take the contract home, a label executive chided her, "Don't you trust us?" She signed and was assigned as a manager the common-law wife of one of Gordy's brothers. Journalist Fredric Dannen later reported that while two of her albums earned about two million dollars for Motown, she received only about one hundred dollars a week for six and a half years. Teena Marie's eventual lawsuit against Motown was a landmark case in which a California court ruled that in order for a record company to return an artist, it had to guarantee a minimum of six thousand dollars a year.

The failure to provide full disclosure and the incestuous financial arrangements led to situations in which charges like those leveled by HDH could ring true, especially because they illuminated the conflicts of interest inherent in many of the relationships.

Gordy was correct that audits of Motown's books and records invariably showed that artists had not been cheated, but that is only by the terms of their contracts, and those agreements were all heavily tilted in favor of Motown. To music-industry observers, it is not surprising that young black artists received contracts in the 1960s that were onerous. Gordy, though a black owner of a successful record company, did not evidently feel any obligation to be a trailblazer by giving his black artists contracts that would break the long-standing tradition that had made them second-class citizens. He may not have done any worse by his performers than other labels would have, but he and Motown certainly did not do any better either.

It was not until the late 1960s, when many of the artists had become superstars, that they began learning how shabby their contracts were. "Maybe ignorance was bliss," said Otis Williams, "because it wasn't until many of us learned through a wider circle of acquaintances in all areas of the business that our contracts with Motown were substantially below industry standards."

CHAPTER 23

Suitcases of Cash

NUMEROUS MOTOWN ARTISTS EVENTUALLY CHALLENGED THEIR CON-
tracts, many over years of aggressive litigation. The bulk of those legal files
are crammed into multiple steel cabinets in the basement of the Wayne
County Court in downtown Detroit. Some lawsuits over royalty disputes
that arose in the 1960s are still pending as of early 2002. Many were settled by Motown, and prerequisites to all the settlements are no disclosure
about the terms and no discussion by the parties about the details. However,
in instances in which settlement figures have leaked, they have tended to be
sums that Motown considered little more than nuisance amounts, often less
than the costs of litigation.

Is it possible that Motown never cheated its employees, despite the many
claims? Were the contracts drawn so tightly in Motown's favor and the lavish lifestyle and touring expenses by the artists so great that, when the artists
received the small royalties left over, they immediately assumed their money
had been stolen?

Another explanation was offered in 1998 about what might have happened at Motown years earlier. Michael Lushka presented an insider's view
in several depositions in the seemingly endless litigation of HDH against
Gordy and Motown. Lushka had gone to work at Motown in 1969 and was
at the company until 1982. He started out as a regional sales manager and
then in 1971 was appointed the national sales manager. In 1979, he was
promoted to be the executive vice president of marketing and sales.

When Jay Lasker became president of Motown in 1980, he discovered that Lushka "was basically running the company." In Lushka's different roles, he was responsible for receiving Motown's orders from independent wholesale distributors and merchandisers (such as all rack jobbers and one stops), as well as for distributing free or promotional copies of records. What Lushka contended under oath is startling, and most of it is presented here for the first time in print.

In the music business, record distributors—the equivalent of whole-salers in a traditional industry—buy their discs directly from the record label that manufactures the product. Independent labels like Motown sell to different distributors across the country. For every album bought at a wholesale price by a distributor, the artists and songwriters receive a royalty. Any returns are charged back to the artist and songwriter. However, one loophole is that if the record company has manufactured too many discs by overestimating the public's demand, it will usually sell its excess supply to distributors at distress prices. Those records are then sold in turn to bargain-basement retailers. On the distressed sales—called cutouts in the industry—no royalties are paid. And to ensure that the distributors cannot resell cutouts as first-quality recordings, record companies typically punch a small hole near the center of the disc to indicate that that copy is a distressed product.

According to Lushka, cutouts were the key to how Motown cheated artists and songwriters of their royalties. Lushka alleged that Motown had secret arrangements with major distributors whereby it would sell them first-quality records but falsely enter them in the company's books as cutouts. The distributor paid for those records in cash, at a price higher than what they would have paid for distressed records but lower than what they would have paid for first-quality discs. Motown could accept a lower price on each record sold this way since it would not have to pay royalties to the artists or songwriters. Also, the cash received above the cutout price never appeared on the corporation's books, but Lushka says it became a slush fund used as payola to buy radio time for Motown's records.

If true, Lushka's claims explain how Motown's books always supported its version of the facts in the many artists' and songwriters' lawsuits. Those lawsuits had to rely on the company's books to verify the accuracy of royalty statements. The books would show that every royalty on every full-priced record that was sold was in fact paid correctly. What the lawyers for the artists and songwriters could never know was that the large amounts of cutout sales might have been part of a deliberate scheme to defraud them.

Lushka, in different depositions given over several years, provided not just vague accusations but hundreds of pages of details. The principals he has accused of wrongdoing—Berry Gordy, Barney Ales, Michael Roshkind, and the Noveck brothers—have all adamantly denied the charges. The independent distributors named by Lushka also vigorously deny the roles he attributes to them. No criminal charges have been filed over any of these issues.

"From about 1969 to February, 1981," testified Lushka,

in the regular course of Motown's business and my employment, [and] at the prior instructions/directions and with the consent/knowledge of my superiors (including Mssrs. Gordy, Abner, Ales, Roshkind and Lasker) and with the knowledge of Harold Noveck, a *secret* ostensible record promotion "cash fund" was established and regularly replenished. . . . These cash funds were ostensibly to be used to carry *secret* promotional expenses, including *secretly* inducing record airplay at radio stations throughout the USA. These sums ranged annually from about $100,000 to $500,000. [emphasis in original]

Lushka speculated that some of the money set aside for the fund never found its way to payola but rather ended up in the pockets of his superiors. (In 1973, Motown denied using payola in written testimony to the Senate copyrights subcommittee. A two-year investigation of payola in the recording industry resulted in 1975 in nineteen indictments against several record labels, but no one at Motown was indicted. In the 1980s, Motown's president, Lasker, thought payola was so endemic in the industry it should be legalized.)

Starting in 1974, Lushka alleges, he "went, on behalf of Motown, to various distributors and picked up suitcases of cash," at least two to three times a year. (He preferred briefcases to suitcases, he testified.) He also got shopping bags stuffed with cash. The first cash pickup, he says, was from Harry Opostolaris at Alpha Distributing in New York. On a second trip, he stopped in Philadelphia and gave Ernie Santone, of Abkco Distributors, an empty briefcase. Shortly after, Santone returned the briefcase filled with cash. Stan Lewis, of Stan's Records in Shreveport, Louisiana, and Bill Emerson, of Big State Distributing in Dallas, and Jack Lewerke at Hitsville in California, all gave him cases of cash, he asserted.

When Lushka returned to Motown after each trip—of which he estimated he made ten—"I gave it [the cash] to the people I reported to." That meant Ewart Abner or Barney Ales. (In a 1988 deposition, he said he had also once given cash to his Motown mentor, Michael Roshkind, but at a deposition three years later he could not recall doing that.)

If everything that Lushka testified to actually happened, did Gordy know?

"Yes, I would think he would have to know," Lushka said in one deposition. "He knew everything that was going on. . . . I believe he knew it. We had a lot of product going out as 'no charge' to pay back the monies that was given from distributors. . . . I was informed by Mr. Ales and Mr. Abner that Berry Gordy had full knowledge of what I was doing and what they were doing with the money." Lushka was held in such high esteem that he expected to be named Motown's president before Lasker was picked in 1980. (Ales says that Lushka was a coke addict who "wouldn't know the truth if it hit him in the face; he's a complete liar and fabricator." Abner is deceased, and Gordy refused repeated interview requests.)

To disguise the fraud, Lushka said that Motown falsified its sales orders and invoices. The reason he knew that is that as the label's general manager and vice president of sales, he personally wrote up the false sales orders and invoices, listing all good-quality merchandise as cutouts. "However, I was repeatedly directed, instructed or admonished," he testified, "*not to* keep complete or any records or accounts of material aspects of these cash no-charge record transactions" (emphasis in original).

The record-promotion slush fund was also financed by phantom increases in his salary, he claimed. He said that from 1973 to 1981, his salary was doubled on the books from $125,000 to $250,000. However, Lushka claimed that he never received the increase and that that money was instead diverted to the secret fund. "They [his immediate superiors] further agreed," Lushka said, "and did reimburse and repay me for the income tax costs of the 'slush fund' in the form of annual bonuses." At Harold Noveck's and Roshkind's instructions, "I made *oral reports* to the uses and applications of these slush fund monies." Noveck and other superiors repeatedly told him not to keep any written records, Lushka alleged.

The inflated salary was confirmed years later by Lasker in conversations with *Billboard's* Adam White. Lasker understood that the extra money was for payola.

Lushka also gave specific examples of how the kickback system worked in elaborate schemes to defraud artists of the money due them. In one case, a company called Deerfield specialized in cutouts and distressed merchandise. Deerfield bought a lot of distressed material but was losing money on it, so Motown made up for it by shipping them good records at distressed prices. Lushka wrote up the order, which was valued as $1.5 million in distressed records. However, a majority of the records shipped, according to Lushka, were first quality. And even then, Deerfield did not pay the entire $1.5 million, but rather half by check and the other half by barter that included hotel rooms, airline reservations, and other travel items that could be used by Motown. None of that barter value was recorded as a sale on Motown's books, said Lushka. Then, Deerfield returned a bundle of the records through "our distribution network . . . as clean merchandise." The price at which Deerfield had bought the goods—the distressed price—was substantially below the wholesale cost. (They had paid between twenty-five and fifty cents per record and received a refund of $2.54 to $3.00 on each.) Those returns reduced the performers' eventual royalties.

What had all the complex transactions accomplished, if Lushka is right? Deerfield had paid only a fraction of the real price for a large order of first-quality records. Motown had gotten some money for the records that were all sold off the books but also had received $750,000 of travel barter for only a portion of its real value. Motown then charged those travel arrangements to touring accounts at their fair-market value. And the artists themselves lost even more as their royalties were reduced by the returns from Deerfield. Jay Lasker later said that Motown's deal with Deerfield "smelled fishy to me from the first day I heard about it."

In addition to the sale of first-quality records as cutouts, Lushka also alleged in his sworn statements that Motown's manufacturing plants shipped good records "out the back door quite a bit." A former employee said that when money was tight at Motown, salary checks would occasionally be for less than the amount due; employees who were shortchanged would be allowed to pick up free records from a manufacturing plant and in turn sell them to local record stores, pocketing any cash they earned.

Among several examples Lushka gave was the Tapetronics plant in Detroit. "We had a new release coming out," said Lushka. "We had a two-week buy time before the release would hit the street. My distributor, Jim Schwartz, called me up [and] told me that he had just purchased 1,500 of this new release on 8-track and cassette. And I said, 'Can't be, but our release date is two weeks.'"

According to Lushka, Schwartz sent him overnight a box of the tapes, which was marked as having shipped from Tapetronics to the Schwartz Brothers in Washington, D.C. (Schwartz says he does not recall this.) When Lushka took the matter to Jay Lasker, "he informed me to forget about it." None of the units, said Lushka, was ever reflected on a Motown sales order nor counted as Motown income. Motown had three other plants besides Tapetronics.

Although all the people fingered by Lushka have adamantly denied his charges, HDH used his sworn statements as the basis for more lawsuits—this time alleging fraud—against Gordy and Motown. Lushka's credibility has been strenuously attacked. He was a cocaine addict. He was forced out of Motown in 1982 for unspecified reasons. And Lushka had filed his own unsuccessful lawsuit against Gordy after leaving. He had also, after Motown, worked as a consultant for Eddie Holland.

However, Lushka did support his charges with detailed examples and numerous names. He also pointed out that some of those he named—such as Motown Industries' chief operating officer, Michael Roshkind—had faced criminal charges for similar practices and had pleaded guilty to income-tax evasion (*U.S. v. Michael Roshkind*, USDC, C.D. Cal CR78-223-RMT). He named others at Motown who he said knew the truth and the details, including Miller London and Fay Hale. Neither of them made a statement on Motown's activities. Lushka also named Joe Isgro as somebody who knew what was really happening. The thirty-year-old Isgro had nine years of regional experience with record distributors before he landed in Los Angeles in 1977 as Motown's national director of pop promotion. He was there only a year but at a time when Lushka was a ranking executive. Isgro is someone who might have been enamored with the system Lushka described. Not only did Isgro have extensive Mob connections, but he was later indicted for felony racketeering and bribery stemming from his music-industry work. In a subsequent case, Isgro pled guilty to extortion. But as with many things circling around Lushka's testimony, the brief link to Isgro is tantalizing but leads nowhere. Isgro, in jail and facing possibly new charges, refused through his attorney to talk about Lushka and Motown. In the end, no ex-employee at the label was able or willing to confirm Lushka's story.

It is not possible to push Lushka for more facts and supporting evidence. He died of an apparent drug overdose in 1995 at the age of fifty-nine. "Lushka ruined himself," recalled his colleague Phil Jones. "He had too much too young and couldn't handle it. He got heavy into cocaine, and it consumed him. He was getting free records to people to pay for his dope." Lushka borrowed heavily from friends to support his habit. Once, he begged Jones and Gordon Prince, another colleague, for four hundred dollars to buy glasses for his daughter. It ended up being spent on coke. Finally, deep in debt, he lost his home in Encino, lost two Mercedeses, and ended up in a roach-infested motel room with a soiled mattress and a flickering black-and-white television.

Jones said he does not have personal knowledge to prove or disprove the most serious accusations that Lushka testified to in his depositions. But he said, "Berry had lost some control after he went to Los Angeles, but it got worse after a few years. When Berry left, the streets started running gold. Up to 1974, it was clean. But that is really when Berry lost control. After 1974, there was a lot of stealing. They were sticking up distributors. Abner got one hundred thousand dollars put into a special bank account. One distributor provided coke to those who wanted that. And if Abner and others got anything from Lushka, they would never have shared it with Berry."

The secrets of Motown, to the extent they existed and somebody might have been willing to talk about them, might have gone to the grave with Lushka.

CHAPTER 24

"We Would Survive"

THE ORIGINAL LAWSUIT WITH HDH DRAGGED ON FOR FOUR YEARS. When it was settled on January 3, 1972, for an undisclosed amount, both sides were still angry, having spent hundreds of thousands on legal fees. Gordy blamed Eddie Holland for having made the lawsuit into a "personal vendetta," and the Hollands and Dozier thought Gordy was vindictive because they had the courage to leave. "Gordy took the attitude it was one of his old boxing matches," one Motown insider familiar with the suits said, "and he would outlast HDH. He had more money, so as far as he was concerned there was no way he could lose."

HDH's litigious departure had left a pall over Motown. The trio had been the star makers at Motown since 1965. Even Gordy's successful effort to produce an HDH soundalike hit for the Supremes—"Love Child"—did little to stem the fear, since most artists felt he had made that extraordinary effort for the Supremes because of his love for Diana Ross. Those groups that had benefited from HDH's talent were worried that they might hit a long dry patch as Gordy frenetically looked for new producers and songwriters.

But as with any loss, the HDH departure also presented opportunities for others. The greatest beneficiary was Norman Whitfield. He soon became Motown's leading songwriter and producer. He almost single-handedly kept Motown on top immediately after HDH left.

Whitfield was serious and cocky. At one producers' meeting, when

Johnny Bristol accused Motown of playing favorites by giving so many good acts to Whitfield, the normally subdued Whitfield shot back: "Hey, man, the company ain't giving me shit. I just happen to be the best. So sit down and shut the fuck up." Not only was he brimming with confidence, but he seldom took a simple no as a final answer. For instance, in 1967 Whitfield had cowritten and produced "I Heard It Through the Grapevine" and originally had Marvin Gaye record it. But at the Friday decision meeting, although a majority there had voted for the song, Gordy had used his veto power to choose another song for Gaye, "Your Unchanging Love." Whitfield knew that he had a major hit, and he protested strenuously. He also later kept badgering Gordy to allow him to produce the song for another artist. Gordy finally relented. Whitfield produced an entirely different-sounding version—up-tempo and gospel—for Gladys Knight and the Pips, giving them their first number-one hit. That single sold more than one million copies. Within a year, Whitfield nudged Gordy to release the song again—this time as he initially intended, with Marvin Gaye.

Gordy thought it was too late. "It would be crazy to release the same song on Marvin so soon after it had gone to number one on Gladys and the Pips."

"Yeah, I know," Whitfield said, expecting Gordy's answer. "But they are two totally different arrangements."

"So what?" Gordy snapped. "They're still the same song. Forget it, Norman."

Other producers might have taken Gordy's second rejection as the last one. But Whitfield ignored it and continued to press for Gaye to release his own version. Once, he buttonholed Gordy as he entered Hitsville.

"Mr. Gordy," Whitfield said in his most solicitous tone, "I know you told me not to bug you about this song no more."

"Yes, I did."

"But sir, you always told us that name-value songs help albums sell better."

"Yeah," Gordy answered, trying to walk a little faster to get away from Whitfield.

"Well, 'I Heard It Through the Grapevine' has name value now. So can I put it on Marvin's album?"

"What did Billie Jean say?" Gordy asked, referring to the head of Quality

Control, who had returned to Motown after her leave of absence (she would leave Motown permanently in 1979 to go to law school and start a new career).

"She said it's too late," Whitfield admitted candidly. "The songs have already been picked and sequenced in the album."

Gordy liked his honesty. He also grudgingly respected his persistence. "All right, Norman, you got it. I'll have Billie Jean change the lineup and stick 'Grapevine' in."

The normally poker-faced Whitfield flashed an enormous smile.

Gaye's new album proved that Whitfield's original instincts were right. DJs around the country played that track so much that Motown was forced to release it as a single. Almost a year to the day after Gladys Knight had reached the top of the charts, Marvin Gaye hit number one with his rendition. It was Gaye's first number one, and it stayed there for seven weeks—selling almost four times as many records as Gladys Knight and surpassing any other Motown record to date. (Everyone at Motown was ecstatic with the success of Gaye's hit except Gaye himself: "My success didn't seem real," said the troubled singer. "I didn't deserve it.")

Not long after Gordy had given the green light for the release of Gaye's "I Heard It Through the Grapevine," Whitfield was again outside Hitsville waiting for Gordy to arrive. This time, he had a different acetate in his hand.

"Mr. Gordy, you've got to hear this new record I just cut on the Tempts. It's great. I can't wait for the meeting, you've got to hear this now." Gordy knew the song had to be special for Whitfield to show such excitement. Gordy took him into his office and put on the demo. It was "Cloud Nine," an upbeat tune with tough talk about life for inner-city blacks and a song with instrumentation—heavy electric guitars—that was a radical departure from standard Motown fare. Coming on the heels of a similar-sounding hit, "Dance to the Music" for Sly and the Family Stone, it appealed to Gordy but he feared it could be misinterpreted as encouraging drug use ("I'm doing fine up here on Cloud Nine . . . a million miles from reality . . . riding high"). But Whitfield argued with Gordy, trying to convince him that it was not about drugs and would do nothing to tarnish Motown's clean image. When it finally came time to vote on "Cloud Nine" at the Friday meeting, the majority voted to release it, and this time Gordy did not veto it. It was a wise move. Not only was the song a smash, but the following spring it brought Gordy his first ever Grammy (for Best R&B Performance by a Duo or Group, Vocal or Instrumental), and its success allowed Gordy to ignore that critics said "Cloud Nine" marked the start of the Tempts' "psychedelic phase."

Whitfield, of course, benefited from Motown's rule that the producer who gave an artist their last hit had the inside track at producing their next song. Within a year of HDH's departure, Whitfield was monopolizing the Temptations, Gladys Knight, Edwin Starr, and much of Marvin Gaye's work.

By the end of 1968, Motown had five of the top ten on the *Billboard* list:

> #1: Marvin Gaye, "I Heard It Through the Grapevine"
>
> #2: Stevie Wonder, "For Once in My Life" (It had sat in a can for a year because Gordy hadn't liked it, until Billie Jean Brown had insisted it be released.)
>
> #3: Diana Ross and the Supremes, "Love Child"
>
> #7: Diana Ross and the Supremes and the Temptations, "I'm Gonna Make You Love Me"
>
> #10: The Temptations, "Cloud Nine"

Motown held the top three spots for a month, a first in the record business. Years later, Gordy summarized his own feelings as the year closed: "The not-quite-grown-up kid who had once depended on lucky rolls of the dice and who had watched and studied the numbers guys on the streets computing the odds in their heads, had 50 percent of the ten top-selling records in the country. Impossible! And, we'd done it without HDH. The verdict was in: We would survive."

CHAPTER 25

A Born Star

THE FALL OF 1968 MARKED A PERIOD OF TREMENDOUS PERSONAL change for Gordy and the company. He bought his first house in southern California that autumn. At the time, he did not plan to relocate Motown's operations to California. But before long, he was enamored with Hollywood.

"He was a successful record-company executive in a town where the entertainment business is the only industry that matters," recalled Barney Ales. "And he loved it when he went out there. The weather was great, the parties were top-notch, and there were always a string of girls, one prettier than the next, who wanted to meet Berry. How could he not love it?"

Gordy, who increasingly disliked the bitter Detroit winters, had actually been talking for several years about setting up a major Motown satellite office someplace warmer, probably Florida. His feelings about Detroit had certainly changed since his sister Esther had told *Ebony* in 1966, "People try to get us to move away, to take on New York or Hollywood. . . . But Berry is crazy about this town. Whenever he has to leave, he always complains [and] counts the days until he can get back."

Barney Ales thought that it was such a sure bet that Gordy was ready to relocate that he actually bought a house in Florida. But it was clear that Gordy was looking only west when he telephoned Dick Scott, his personal assistant, on the Thursday before Labor Day in 1968. Gordy asked Scott to find a new school for some of his children—fourteen-year-old Hazel, twelve-year-olds Berry IV and Terry—by Tuesday; to Scott's shock, he wanted them enrolled for the new year in Los Angeles.

Gordy did not try to persuade anyone to follow him. He was too preoccupied getting himself and his family settled. For a month, the Gordys and his growing staff stayed at the Beverly Comstock Hotel. Warren Cowan, a friend and a partner in the public-relations firm Rogers and Cowan, enlisted the help of his well-connected wife, actress Barbara Rush, to help. By October, the Gordys were in their new house, high in the Hollywood Hills, the former home of comedian Tommy Smothers. The architecturally striking, modern wood-and-glass house was quite a change from Detroit. Invisible from the street, the house was at the end of a long driveway protected by large iron gates; near the house was a veritable exotic wonderland of lily ponds, flowers, and palm trees. Not far down the street, Gordy rented a house for Diana Ross. He wanted her nearby.

When Smokey Robinson visited Gordy at his new home, Gordy informed his friend that the move west was permanent.

"I thought you'd be going back and forth," Robinson said, somewhat surprised.

"That was the original plan," said Gordy. "But, Smoke, I'm telling you, this is the place. I love the weather, I love the L.A. attitude, and, as far as business goes, it's all happening here." It was a heady time for Gordy, but Robinson was unimpressed.

"I think it's a mistake, Berry."

"Why?"

"Detroit's your home and your heart. It all happened for you in Detroit. I can't see you leaving."

"I can't see me staying."

It wasn't long before Motown was running its operations from a steel-gray skyscraper at 6255 Sunset Boulevard, where Gordy ensconced himself in a penthouse suite.

·   ·   ·

"When Motown left Detroit, there was a great void," said Larry Payton of the Four Tops. Duke Fakir thought so, too. "It was dismal."

"Motown in Detroit had all but ceased to exist," recalled Otis Williams. "It was only a matter of time until we joined him [Gordy]. . . . It seemed that moving to L.A. prompted many changes in different guys' behaviors and for some reason an increase in drug use."

The company did not officially close its Detroit operations until 1975, but it was clear long before then that the future was in Los Angeles. But there was no official announcement about the company's relocation. Some artists, such as Martha Reeves, found out about the move only after they kept calling the Detroit offices asking to talk to Gordy: "Finally a receptionist who took my call said, 'Don't you know the company has moved to Los Angeles?' No, I didn't know. They hadn't even had the courtesy to tell me."

Some, like the Four Tops, who had been without any hits since HDH had left, refused to move west. So did the Funk Brothers' leader, Earl Van Dyke. Others moved only because they thought it was good for their careers: "As much as I hated to leave my hometown," recalled Mary Wilson, "my mind was made up. We were stars, and I was going where the other stars lived." The move west, however, affected some of the artists immediately. In 1969, Gladys Horton, the lead singer of the Marvelettes, decided to stay in Detroit and raise her family, so she left the group. Her replacement, Anne Bogan, while having a decent voice, could not match Horton's distinctive sound. And when Wanda Young, who became the group's leader, refused to move to Los Angeles, the group was essentially finished, ostracized from the new center of power.

"[Gordy's] head was in Hollywood," said Marvin Gaye, "and we were all supposed to follow after him like little puppy dogs." Gaye waited five years before moving out, one of the final Motowners to leave Detroit.

Raynoma Gordy, with her new husband, Ed Singleton, made a pitch to Gordy at the beginning of 1969 that she thought might revive Motown in Detroit. She noticed that the city was suffering from the race riots, the exodus of businesses from the downtown district, and the fading fortunes of the Big Three automakers. But she hoped that Motown's commitment to stay might start an urban revival. Gordy, however, was not receptive. "Who the fuck are you to tell me anything? Look, motherfucker, kiss my ass!" (At a company meeting in Las Vegas the following year, Raynoma actually complained about the abrasive A&R director, Ralph Seltzer, in front of most Motown executives—not long after that Raynoma again left Motown, but Seltzer was still in place.)

Aside from artists, many of those who made up the core of Motown's staff soon discovered that the move to California meant unemployment. Within a couple of years, between two hundred and three hundred Detroit employees were out of work, with most given no chance to transfer. "I don't know if Motown needed Detroit as much as Detroit needed Motown," said Chris McNair, an art director who worked there for four years before being dismissed.

Esther Gordy stayed in Detroit to oversee the company's diminished operations. Esther was the one person Gordy truly trusted, and her husband, George Edwards, was a Detroit political powerhouse. They were the ideal people to maintain Motown's presence in the Motor City.

But Gordy was oblivious to any of the personal problems and the difficulties in Detroit because he was focused only on using his new environment to introduce a new act. A year earlier, he was in an elevator at Motown in Detroit when Suzanne de Passe had urged him to hear a talented group of kids, all from one family. De Passe had first heard about the group from Bobby Taylor and the Vancouvers, one of Motown's few multiracial groups, consisting of six men, four white and two black (the group's guitarist, Tommy Chong, later became half of the comedy team Cheech and Chong). They had appeared on the same bill as the kids.

"I hate kids' groups," Gordy had impatiently told her at the time. "Minors, chaperones, the courts, tutors. . . ." He shook his head at the thought of all the aggravation.

De Passe corrected him. "Oh, no you don't. Not if they're great."

The kids who de Passe wanted Gordy to audition were five boys from Gary, Indiana, the Jacksons: nine-year-old Michael (born the year that Smokey Robinson and the Miracles cut "Got a Job"), eleven-year-old Marlon, thirteen-year-old Jermaine, fourteen-year-old Toriano Adaryll (Tito), and seventeen-year-old Sigmund Esco (Jackie).

Joe Jackson had raised his children with a strong hand and the strictest discipline. He was the eldest of five children, in a household where his own father had had an ironclad rule that no one could socialize with outsiders lest they fall prey to Satan. Joe was deputized by his father to ensure that all his siblings never ventured anywhere but to school and then home and that they never took part in any banned activities such as jump rope, games, dancing, or listening to music. When Joe was fifteen, his parents divorced.

He lived first with his father and then was shuttled off to his mother. Over the next dozen years, Joe's parents married other people, then divorced them, then remarried, and then divorced each other again before remarrying other people. That unsettled home life, coupled with his mother's open and extensive extramarital affairs, created in Joe a deep rage about what he considered lack of discipline or failure to adhere strictly to regulations.

Joe married a local Gary girl when he was eighteen, but they divorced in less than a year. Two years later, he married Katherine Scruse, a young woman of mixed race who had a limp from her childhood bout with polio. They had ten children over the next dozen years. (One, Brandon, died from respiratory failure a day after his birth.) To support such a large family, Joe maintained two blue-collar jobs, and Katherine worked part-time as a Sears cashier.

As had his father, Joe forbade his children from even talking to other neighborhood kids. He banished the outside world from their home. The Jacksons had only two bedrooms, one for Joe and his wife and the other for the boys—Rebbie and La Toya, then the only two girls, slept in an alcove off the living room. All the children were subject to beatings for the slightest infractions. Joe used everything from belts to wire hangers, rulers, and even razor straps. Sometimes, the children bore the results to school— bruises or a crusty, bloodied nose. On occasion, some of the boys were knocked unconscious. Joe even put boxing gloves on them and encouraged them to fight one another.

Once, four-year-old Michael went into the bathroom, only to discover his six-year-old sister, La Toya, lying on the tile floor, crying and bloodied, after being beaten by her father because of a poor report card. Michael, terrified that if he said anything he might himself be subjected to a beating, just stepped over his sister, washed his hands at the sink, and then returned silently to the dinner table. (According to La Toya, there was also sexual abuse—Joe has always adamantly denied that, just as he has denied the physical abuse. Gordy, years later, when told about the maltreatment, didn't believe it. "I don't know what happened at home before he [Michael] got to Motown." Then he added, "But he had a childhood at Motown.")

Joe was also merciless with his taunts, calling the boys sissies for not fighting back when he hit them, chiding Jermaine when he developed a stammer in the second grade, and making them feel that, whatever they did, they were worthless. He also enjoyed terrifying them. Sometimes, he burst out of a closet wielding a kitchen knife and wearing a grotesque latex mask—the louder they screamed, the more uncontrollable his laughter. When he arrived home each day, there was a palpable fear among the children about whether he was in a mood or not.

Although Katherine tried weakly to protect her children, she feared Joe and was herself occasionally his victim. She found solace in being a Jehovah's Witness, a religion to which she had converted in 1963. She raised her children in the same faith, with its strict tenets, including bans on smoking, swearing, gambling, fishing, hunting, having premarital sex, and engaging in homosexuality. No celebrations of birthdays or holidays were allowed. Part of the children's obligation was to "witness" at stranger's houses by going door to door to spread the faith. (After Michael became famous, he disguised himself by wearing a rubber fat suit to try to fool the neighbors.)

Joe's one outside interest was a banal R&B band in which he played guitar. It did local gigs for twenty dollars per night. Joe decided to make musicians out of his children. He formed the Jackson 4 with the oldest boys. When three-year-old Michael showed some talent, the group became the Jackson 5. In less than a year, Michael had replaced Jermaine as the group's lead singer. Joe rehearsed the boys three to four hours daily. Sometimes he woke them in the middle of the night for a practice session because he couldn't sleep. When they started playing publicly—at schools and in local contests—the awards began piling up. Joe wasn't satisfied. He sensed his kids had commercial potential, so his demands increased. The postschool workouts were so arduous that sometimes the children collapsed from exhaustion. He used a whip to ensure that no one strayed off note or failed to remember a dance step. Joe was especially hard on Michael, chastising him publicly as dumb, ugly, and awkward. Years later, Michael told a friend how he had learned to hate his father and that he felt they had been trained and raised as circus animals.

But Joe's tortuous workouts paid off. When Michael was only seven, the Jackson 5 won a citywide amateur contest. Joe next packed the children into the family's VW bus and drove to Chicago, where they played at a string of nondescript dives.

Yet within a year, the Jackson 5 had enough experience to open for Gladys Knight and the Pips. She thought they were so good that she had several Motown executives come to one of the shows, but they were not impressed. So the group instead had to go on the Chitlin Circuit, which literally took them across the country. That summer, they won an amateur-night competition at New York's Apollo Theatre. It wasn't long before they were opening for many acts there. The following year, 1968, they released a single, "Big Boy," on a Gary label, Steeltown Records. Later that year, the group opened for Bobby Taylor and the Vancouvers, the act that at last got Motown's executives interested in the Jacksons.

•   •   •

A few days after Suzanne de Passe had spoken to Gordy, he and some other executives gathered in a room on the eighth floor of his Woodward Avenue office building in Detroit. The Jacksons had driven from Gary in their VW bus. Gordy had his assistant, Dick Scott, bring in a new piece of equipment the company had just bought—a video camera—to record the audition. Gordy was barely seated when the group tore into the Temptations' "Ain't Too Proud to Beg." He instantly liked them. They were a surprisingly polished act for a group of kids. Gordy, normally ready to end an audition after one song, sat entranced as the group went on to "I Wish It Would Rain" and "Tobacco Road" before ending with little Michael Jackson dancing across the floor as he sang James Brown's "I Got the Feelin'."

Gordy was especially won over by Michael, who always kept his eyes directly on him. "This little kid had an incredible knowingness about him," Gordy recalled, "that really made me take notice. He sang his songs with such feeling, inspiration and pain—like he had experienced everything he was singing about."

"Michael was a strange and lovely child," recalled Smokey Robinson. "I always saw him as an old soul in the body of a boy. He was driven, determined, intense."

"Somehow, even at that first meeting," Gordy later said, "he let me know of his hunger to learn, and how willing he was to work as hard as necessary to be great, to go to the top. He let me know he believed I was the person who could get him there."

When the Jacksons had finished, they stayed in a tight circle, waiting for Gordy to say something. There was applause from the other executives there and then silence as Gordy thought carefully about what to say. He walked over to them and tried, as he often did, not to show how he felt.

"Obviously, you've done a lot of hard work, and it shows," Gordy said.

"The only thing that can stop you from success now is you. Keep your humility and discipline, continue to work hard, and we'll do the rest."

There was visible excitement among the Jacksons. Then Jermaine spoke up: "Uh, Mr. Gordy, does that mean you're gonna sign us?"

"Yes. Yes, it does."

The Jacksons broke into yells and cheers, jumping up and down and grabbing one another ecstatically. Later, when Ralph Seltzer presented the Jacksons with a standard Motown contract, Joe never even considered having an attorney check the details. Seltzer, in vintage Motown style, did not, of course, mention that they might want someone to review the contract for them. Not long after the Jacksons signed to Motown, Bobby Taylor ran into Gordy in the hallway. He bragged to Gordy how excited he was to have played a role in finding the Jackson 5.

"Taylor, let me tell you something," Gordy told him. "As soon as they get rich, they're gonna forget who you are."

•   •   •

Good as they were, it was almost a year before Gordy thought the Jacksons met his exacting standards. He finally brought them to southern California and put them up close to Motown's headquarters in the nearby seedy Hollywood Motel, a hangout for prostitutes renting rooms for one-hour tricks. But the Jacksons did not mind. The setting for their Motown debut was a three-story Tudor-style mansion that Gordy had recently bought and christened Gordy Manor. The Jackson 5 performed some songs by the Olympic-size pool, wowing a crowd of industry executives that Gordy had invited.

A few days after that event, Ralph Seltzer got a call from a New York lawyer who had the distressing news that the Jacksons supposedly had a manager. Gordy was shocked and furious since Joe Jackson had assured Motown there were no contractual restraints. Gordy was even more upset when he finally got a call from Richard Arons, who said he was actually Joe Jackson's partner. It took Gordy and his lawyers several months—and a sizable payment to Arons—before the Jacksons belonged solely to Motown.

Working with the Jacksons reminded Gordy of the early days at Hitsville. He especially liked that the youngsters were willing to take direction. He had firm ideas about what was best for them. Michael reminded Gordy of Frankie Lyman—that was the feeling he wanted for the Jacksons. As he had with "Love Child" and the Supremes, Gordy assembled another team of songwriters—this time dubbed "the Corporation"—to develop a hit for the new group.

The Corporation quickly came up with "I Want You Back," a song they all agreed would be a perfect launch. Gordy had Diana Ross host an exclusive party for three hundred industry executives at Hollywood's Daisy Club. Their first album was titled *Diana Ross Presents the Jackson 5.* Ross later was criticized for having taken credit for discovering the group, but it was actually Gordy and Motown's publicity department that thought that spin would be good for the Jacksons. They developed a story that Gary mayor Richard Hatcher had introduced the band to Ross. Michael perpetuated the lie by saying, when asked by the press at the Daisy Club how Motown found him, "I thought I would never be discovered, that is until Ms. Ross came along to save my career."

At that party, Michael, age ten, had been told by Gordy to say he was only eight. Motown's public-relations team had decided it would make him look like even more of a prodigy. Michael went along, as did the rest of the Jacksons. Five days later, the Jackson 5 opened for Diana Ross and the Supremes at the Los Angeles Forum. Less than two months after that show, "I Want You Back" was released as a single. By the end of the year, following the group's first television appearances, the song was climbing the charts. Ed Sullivan took notice and booked the group for his show.

Gordy sent Suzanne de Passe and the West Coast creative director of talent, Deke Richards, with the Jacksons to New York for the live show. He always worried that a live performance left no room for error. Gordy preferred recording the band and the background vocals and then mixing them for the show, so that only the lead singer was singing live. But the Jacksons' appearance would be different, with them all singing live, and as a result riskier.

Because of the three-hour time difference between New York and Los Angeles, Gordy did not see the show when it aired live. But he was relieved when de Passe called him to report it was "great . . . a smash!"

Later that evening, he settled in front of his television to watch the West Coast feed of the show. He loved the look de Passe had created for the group: bell-bottoms, hats over their Afros, fringed suede vests, and tiny platform boots. But once they started performing, Gordy's heart sank—the tempo was off, and he thought they sounded flat. When de Passe called again, Gordy was steaming.

"Well, how did you like it, boss?" she asked.

"That tempo! How did you let them do the tempo like that?"

"The tempo—what are you talking about?"

"It was too slow, too slow."

"Oh," de Passe said and then waited a moment before answering, as though she was scrambling to come up with an explanation. "Well, that was Deke. He's a producer on the record, that's what he was here for, wasn't it?"

Gordy went on the attack, telling her that she was in charge, she knew the record inside and out, and anything that went wrong was her fault. "Why didn't Deke take the fucking record," Gordy screamed, "play it and get the tempo off it and count the band from that? I mean, it wouldn't have taken a genius to figure something out like that."

De Passe started crying.

But the next day, Gordy's explosion was forgotten in a flurry of media coverage celebrating the music industry's new darlings. The phenomenal coverage surprised even the hard-to-please Gordy. No one else had seemed to notice the tempo change, and Gordy never mentioned it again.

•   •   •

Many outsiders were surprised that a group so young could be so poised and polished. The key to the group, as Gordy had realized early on, was Michael. Michael believed his talent was God given, and he never doubted that he could do whatever he wanted to onstage. His music school had been the basement of the Apollo, when the Jacksons had opened there for many acts. When he was five and six, he had studied James Brown's Apollo performances for hours, reveling in his wild, untamed moves. He had crouched in the theater's basement passageways, watching intently as other acts performed. He mimicked the dance steps, the dips, the bumps, and the outstretched arms. Stage workers saw him moving and dancing for hours. And when he was in Motown's Los Angeles studio, he did the same thing. Michael studied the producers and engineers, determined to learn as much as he could. "I was like a hawk preying in the night," Michael later recalled.

Shy and withdrawn and so soft-spoken that often people had to strain to hear him, he felt at home only when performing. "I was raised onstage," he told one journalist. "And I am more comfortable out there than I am right now. When it comes time to go off, I don't want to. I feel like there are angels on all corners, protecting me. I could sleep onstage."

.   •   )

"I Want You Back" hit number one on January 31, 1970. Just a few months earlier, Gordy had moved eleven-year-old Michael in with Diana Ross, in the hope that she would pass along advice and guidance to him. Twenty-five-year-old Ross, however, was so consumed with her own career that she had little time to be a surrogate mother. Still, in a couple of months, she infused in an impressionable Jackson a confidence that he would be a major star, and he came to idolize her and her lavish lifestyle. Certainly, he had seen nothing like it in his austere upbringing. In the short time Jackson lived with her, Ross taught him that his public image had to be protected at all costs. By the time "I Want You Back" hit number one, Gordy finally leased a house in Los Angeles—twice the size of their Indiana home—for the entire family, and Michael rejoined his siblings and parents.

Gordy, meanwhile, was working the Corporation—now the most important team in Motown's stable of 103 songwriters—to find a follow-up hit. "One record's not going to do it," Gordy told them. "The second record's as important as the first, maybe even more so."

Shelly Berger, who already managed Diana Ross and the Supremes and also the Temptations, now took on the Jacksons. Berger was always clever at marketing—in 1965 and 1966 he had arranged for the Supremes, who had a large white following, and the Temptations, who had a large black audience, to tour together so each group could greatly broaden its appeal. Now, Gordy did not want the Jacksons to alienate their enormous white following by coming across as too black. Motown versed them—as they had other artists a few years earlier—to avoid sensitive political or social questions. "Listen, Diana Ross didn't become a star by being black," Gordy told a publicist he had hired to work with the Jacksons. "As far as I am concerned, the Jackson Five aren't black either. So let's have none of that black stuff."

Gordy preferred the Jacksons dull, not controversial. However, Gordy and the public-relations department, try as they might, could not control Joe Jackson. They often cringed when he gave impromptu press interviews. In 1971, after MGM signed their answer to the Jacksons—a five-member family band called the Osmonds, they recorded a song, "One Bad Apple," that sold one million copies and went number one. Joe Jackson believed a false rumor that Gordy had had a chance earlier to record that same song with the Jacksons but had rejected it. "He handed those white boys a song we should have recorded," Joe Jackson fumed to a reporter. "To me, that's fuckin' unbelievable. And Mormons, too. They don't even let blacks in their religion! Every time I hear those white boys imitating my sons, I cringe."

But one area in which the Jacksons made little initial headway was on the concert front. Shelly Berger was fielding offers from medium-sized clubs for two thousand dollars per night. But he feared that if he booked them, the promoters would be harder pressed to accept future increases. Berger had an outlandish idea for marketing the group for live venues, but it depended largely on how many consecutive hits they could turn out. Gordy predicted to him that the group would have five in a row. That was enough for Berger, who then sent out telegrams to major promoters and arenas, offering the Jackson 5 for a stunning price of twenty-five thousand dollars per night. He wanted to show the Jacksons that Motown, in its management role, would turn down offers that other managers, who lived solely on commissions, might accept. It was Berger's way of demonstrating that Motown had the singers' best interests first.

Meanwhile, Suzanne de Passe—now president of Motown Productions—was responsible for completing a makeover for the Jackson 5. Hollywood stylists and fashion designers redid their hairstyles and stage costumes. While Motown's charm school did not exist in Los Angeles, Gordy hired some local social arbiters to give the boys some lessons.

The Corporation did what Gordy asked and kept coming up with the right songs. On February 24, 1970, Motown released "ABC." The song-writers had flip-flopped several times before signing off on whether the song should be "1-2-3" or "ABC." Katherine Jackson, the children's mother, overlooked lines like "Shake it, shake it, baby." Record sales and the flood of money had apparently persuaded all the Jacksons that their religious be-liefs took second place.

By April, "ABC" was number one, knocking the Beatles' "Let It Be" out of the top spot. It sold more than two million copies, a giant jump from "I Want You Back," which had sold six hundred thousand. At this point, Berger was rejecting five thousand dollars per night for the Jacksons. The third song was "The Love You Save"—Gordy rushed it to the studio even though the songwriters thought it was unfinished—and it shot to number one by June, selling just fewer than two million records. Again, they knocked the Beatles from the top and earned the distinction of being the first group to have their first three Motown releases go to number one on the pop charts.

The booking offers had now gone to twenty thousand dollars per night, but Berger still said no. Not long after their third number one, Berger ran into Gordy's office with the news that the Los Angeles Forum had booked the Jacksons at twenty-five thousand dollars per night, plus a percentage of the gate. Gordy wanted to tell the group personally. He called them together.

"Guess what?" he announced, barely able to contain his grin. "You guys are doing the Forum!" Then he told them how much they would be paid.

"That's wonderful," Michael said softly. "On whose show?"

"Yours."

"Yeah," Michael continued, "but who's the star?"

"You all are. You're the stars."

Michael, Jermaine, Jackie, Tito, and Marlon looked at Gordy and one another in disbelief.

"Once they comprehended they were stars," Gordy later recalled, "they *were* stars."

The Jackson 5 sold out the Forum, with a record 18,675 people cramming into the theater to see pop's hottest new act. They received not only great reviews but also tremendous word of mouth. Booking requests poured in. But Gordy was still not satisfied. As always, he was concerned with the next record and had decided that, after three up-tempo hits, the group needed to show diversity with a ballad. This time, the Corporation received help from two additional songwriters. Hal Davis and newcomer Willie Hutch came up with "I'll Be There." When it hit number one—where it stayed for five weeks—the Jacksons had again made pop history. This time they knocked Neil Diamond's "Cracklin' Rosie" off the top, and it became Motown's biggest record, selling more than 3.1 million copies. Their first four Motown releases had gone to the top of the charts in less than a year. Their fifth release, "Never Can Say Goodbye," snapped their own streak when it peaked at number two.

And for the first time in Motown's history, the label had a group that appealed to a young enough audience—preteens—that it could extensively market merchandise, from buttons to posters to clothes to toys. A quarterly magazine, *TCB*, focused just on the Jacksons. Motown even successfully released a single called "Jackson 5 Rapping," on which there was no music but only the five Jacksons talking innocuously about themselves. The cleverly titled *Jackson 5ive* Saturday cartoon series was based on the group and featured their music. While the Supremes had had a Coca-Cola endorsement and also Schafer Bakeries' "Supreme Bread"—white bread with packaging that featured the likenesses of the girls—they had never reached the success the Jacksons had acquired in virtually no time. "We're going to make a mint," an ecstatic Gordy told a Motown colleague. "We're gonna make a fuckin' mint on these kids."

Michael had become the leader of the group—much to his father's disdain, since Joe thought all the boys should get equal billing. But Michael was the scene-stealer in almost every show and the one performer that fans screamed for the most. His uncanny stage presence had many critics comparing his dancing to that of Sammy Davis Jr. when he was a child star. But Michael's talent really put him into his own league. Producers who worked with him were always amazed that the child playing hide-and-seek would suddenly transform behind a microphone and put emotion and heartache into adult lyrics.

Toward the end of 1970, the Jacksons were scheduled for three shows in Texas as part of a national tour that was packing stadiums and concert halls. Since Motown had only whites managing the tour, the Southern Christian Leadership Conference threatened to picket the shows. When Gordy heard the complaint, he reacted as those who knew him best would have predicted. The group had all the success it needed without the Texas dates, and Gordy canceled the shows. "The Jackson Five are bigger than any race issue," he said. "No one can tell me how to run these boys' careers. Black or white, I make the decisions. This is *my* group."

The five young boys with the quiet and shy ways and hard-work ethic had gone from obscurity in Gary, Indiana, to being household names, living in the glitter of Hollywood. Their phenomenal success certainly did not silence the critics, some of whom still predicted the group would have a short life. "But what longevity can you expect from the Jackson Five?" asked the

Detroit News's Bill Gray in 1972. "The lead singer is 12 and probably headed for a voice change. Their appeal is very young (pre-teen) and their music is bubblegum."

The Jacksons marked the end of an era for Gordy and Motown. "They would be the last stars I would develop with the same intensity and emotional investment as I had with the earlier Motown artists," Gordy later wrote in his autobiography. "They would be the last big stars to come rolling off my assembly line."

CHAPTER 26

Winds of Change

As the Jacksons soared, Diana Ross and the Supremes were breaking up. Ross had decided to fulfill her long-held desire to go solo; she had felt for years that her two partners were not essential to her success. The tension and backbiting between Ross and Mary Wilson had become public, with the press frequently reporting on petty incidents between them. Still, while their split might have been inevitable, the breakup was casting a pall over Motown.

Ross kept telling the press that she was "sad" at leaving because "no one understands how close we are, the three of us, even the four of us, considering when Florence Ballard was with us. I'll always be a part of them spiritually."

Ross, Wilson, and Cindy Birdsong released their last single, "Someday We'll Be Together," a song Harvey Fuqua and Jackey Beavers had written years earlier. It became their twelfth and last number-one hit. Their final concert was January 14, 1970, at Las Vegas's Frontier Hotel. As the girls waited to go onstage, Mary Wilson recalled, "Diane and I just glanced at each other in silence. There were no 'good-bye's' or 'good luck's,' not even a hug. We could have done those things, but we both knew it would be a farce."

Ross remembered that night a little differently, not surprisingly, as all revolving around her: "A quiet sadness filled me as I realized that I was leaving, not only because I wanted to but also because I had to. They had hurt me very badly, beyond repair. We weren't a group anymore."

The audience was packed with celebrities, and critics agreed that the group gave one of its best performances. There were many standing-ovation encores, and even the girls seemed teary at the postperformance party.

Gordy promised to find the two remaining Supremes a great replacement for Ross. Publicity director Mike Roshkind told the press that the Supremes' breakup was like a two-for-one stock split and that Motown would actually benefit. The label launched a massive search and decided on Jean Terrell, the sister of heavyweight boxer Ernie Terrell. Most were skeptical. No one outside of Motown knew that after Terrell had been publicly introduced, Gordy flip-flopped and tried to replace her at the last moment. When Mary Wilson threatened to quit if he did that, he gruffly told her, "All right, then I wash my hands of the group." Even though Gordy appointed Shelly Berger as the group's manager and gave them the respected Frank Wilson as producer and Gil Askey as musical conductor, it seemed unlikely they could be successful without Diana Ross.

The new Supremes did manage two top-ten hits, "Up the Ladder to the Roof" and "Stoned Love," but the group would change singers five more times before disbanding permanently seven years later. Jean Terrell sued Gordy and Motown, demanding back royalties. Mary Wilson left for a solo career in 1980, wondering if the label "had actively conspired to kill the Supremes." She later also unsuccessfully sued Motown, trying to regain the use of the name *The Supremes,* claiming the label had stolen it from her—"Morally, it should have been ours. . . . When we signed our contracts, we didn't fully understand the clause stating that Motown owned the name."

While the new Supremes struggled, Diana Ross prepared for her solo debut on May 7, 1970, also at the Frontier Hotel.

Gordy had managed to raise her nightly Vegas concert fee to one hundred thousand dollars, a remarkable sum at the time. And he told *Ebony,* in an article published shortly before her show, that "Diane's success is almost built-in. She's not really taking a big chance because people are buying her like mad. Vegas is buying her, Miami is buying her, the Waldorf in New York. She's a super-star and everybody is trying to buy her; like the stock market, she's up now because everything she's done has been a total success."

But before Ross's Vegas debut, Gordy had butterflies for the first time in years. He was too nervous to even gamble, so instead he paced nervously around his suite. Mike Roshkind joined him. The jarring ring of the telephone broke their thoughts. Roshkind took the call, and after grunting a few times put it down glumly.

"Terrible news," he said softly, almost as though, if he said it quietly enough, Gordy might not notice.

Gordy did not want to hear any bad news but asked what had happened.

"No reservations," Roshkind announced flatly, still not looking at Gordy. "Only about five hours to go to show time." Roshkind shook his head as if in disbelief.

Gordy hoped that Roshkind was playing a bad joke. But it was real. The call had been from the Frontier's management. About thirty tickets had been sold for the hotel's six-hundred-seat headliner room.

Gordy knew that if Ross learned what was happening, it would destroy her self-confidence. He came up with a unique plan: to tear twenty-dollar bills in half and give them to people on the street, promising if they attended Ross's show, they would get the other half.

Before they left the hotel, Roshkind called the Frontier's booking office and told them not to worry, that historically Ross got a big last-minute audience. Assured that the hotel was not about to cancel the show, Gordy grabbed a thick wad of cash that he kept handy for his gambling, and he and Roshkind hit the Vegas strip. They stopped cabdrivers, meandering tourists, and local workers. They gave out hundreds of torn twenties, promising all who took the money a reserved seat as well as the rest of the money.

A crowd formed outside the showroom early that evening. Gordy and Roshkind were ecstatic when they saw the long line. They then tried to match the serial numbers on the torn twenties. It did not take very long to realize it was impossible. They couldn't match one. The crowd was restless. Gordy was getting nervous that he could lose his audience.

Roshkind suggested Gordy use his gambling line of credit to come up with the cash. Gordy rushed to the cashier's cage and ordered ten thousand dollars in twenties. Then Roshkind and Gordy walked along the line, collected the torn money, and replaced it with crisp, new twenties. Before the doors opened, the crowd had been paid and was in a festive mood. (Gordy, not one to lose money, later had two junior assistants at Motown spend nearly a week matching the serial numbers on the torn twenties and taping the bills together.)

The show was filled with small miscues, from lighting that was off its mark, the wrong tempo on some songs, and a broken zipper on one of Ross's quick-change gowns. After it was over, in her dressing room, Ross glowered at Gordy.

"That was a horrible show," she seethed. "People paid to come see me and didn't get their money's worth!"

Gordy tried assuring her the show was great, but she would not hear of it until she saw the favorable reviews the next day. After that, the audiences at the Frontier continued to build during her two-week engagement.

Ross had a nationwide concert tour after Vegas, and Gordy knew that Ross, now on her own, demanded increasing help. She already had a road manager, Roger Campbell, and an assistant for him, as well as her own personal assistant, Liz Moran. But she wanted someone else to put out fires as they arose—a man or woman Friday—and preferred it was someone she knew. Gordy surprisingly chose his ex-wife Raynoma, who had last left Motown after her scathing public attack on Ralph Seltzer. Raynoma initially demurred, because it meant moving with her children from Detroit. Gordy pleaded, and she finally accepted.

Ray's first show with Ross was at Coconut Grove. After the performance, Ray went to the dressing room to congratulate Ross. Before she got a word out, Ross spoke.

"Look," she said softly as she lifted her eyes off her own reflection in the mirror. "I know that tonight was your first. But I do expect that from here on in you will perform to the best of your ability. Also, from now on, I would prefer that you refer to me as 'Miss Ross.' I know that you have known me for some time, but in my position I need to be treated with more respect."

"My reaction was a strong mixture of nausea and pity for her," Ray recalled. "In molding Diana into a superstar, Berry was shaping a monster."

During the coming weeks, Ray oversaw Ross's sixteen-member entourage, arranging everything from her specialized low-calorie menu (prepared by her personal cook) to the order in which the celebrities were allowed to visit in her dressing room. Although Diana relished the celebs who fawned over her, she often said no to requests from ordinary fans. Raynoma almost quit after one show when Ross refused to spend a few minutes with twenty-five blind children who were begging to meet her.

"I'm not going to do it," she screamed to stop Raynoma's repeated entreaties. "I refuse to subject myself to being depressed by seeing a bunch of blind kids!" (Eddie Carroll, Ross's Hollywood hairdresser, remembered a small girl once asking the star for an autograph—the next thing he knew, the child was running from the salon, "sobbing like crazy.")

Raynoma, however, learned to respect, even admire, Ross's drive and ambition, as well as her onstage professionalism. Ross was dependable, stayed far away from drugs, and kept her personal turmoils away from work. Yet her diva attitude made her increasingly unpleasant. She often treated those who worked for her contemptuously. Although she averaged one hundred thousand dollars per week when touring, she complained that Raynoma was overpaid at a weekly salary of $250. "And praise or popularity to anyone other than herself," recalled Raynoma, "amounted to treachery as far as Diana was concerned." When Ross became aggravated with one of her workers, instead of telling them she usually called Gordy and complained.

And while Raynoma saw firsthand Ross's abusive side, there were quiet moments on the road when Ross was lonely and spoke to Raynoma about her personal life. Although she bragged about how great she was in bed and gave details of her many affairs, including ones with Smokey Robinson (an affair that he had adamantly denied to Claudette) and Brian Holland, she seemed obsessed with Gordy.

"Theirs was a love-hate affair," concluded Raynoma. "They needed one another and recognized the other as the fulfillment of their ambitions. She worshiped and reviled him. He'd molded her and her success. For that she loved him, resented him, and was dependent on him."

"Although they surely fell in love," said Smokey Robinson, "theirs was a relationship rooted in business."

Ross tolerated abuse from only one person, and that was Gordy. He sometimes chided her about a costume or the way she sang a song. Harsh words from him could send her running tearfully into her dressing room. But to everyone else, Ross seemed tough. No one talks of her as appearing vulnerable.

It wasn't long before Ross, uncomfortable over her occasional openness with Raynoma, complained to Gordy that Raynoma was not doing a good job. He once again fired his ex-wife.

And while Ross's solo career was off and running, her personal relationship with Gordy was about to end. The two had been lovers for five years. Their professional and personal lives were completely intertwined. Gordy later claimed in his autobiography that Ross broke off their relationship when he refused to marry her. He later told Raynoma that he couldn't have married Ross because he realized "this woman is as selfish as I am. I'm going to have to be kissing her ass all the time. I need somebody to kiss my ass."

What really happened is that Ross at long last discovered that Gordy was having an affair with Chris Clark. Some thought that Gordy was trying to fashion Clark—who had a middling voice—into a white Diana Ross. Many at the label knew of their affair, but Ross was one of the last to learn of it. (On the other hand, Gordy was also one of the last to learn about a brief liaison Ross had had with Philadelphia Eagles player Tim Brown.)

When she confronted Gordy, he denied it. She did not know that one night when she had shown up unexpectedly at his hotel suite, he had hidden Clark in a walk-in closet. Ross spent the night, and Clark slept only feet away. But after too many unexplained missing nights, Ross pried the truth from him. Her pride was too great to see Gordy after that. Ross ended it. Another phase of Motown, this one intensely personal, had also passed into history.

·　　　·　　　·

Gordy was rocked by their breakup. He threw himself into work with a frenzy. As a result, 1970 turned out to be a very good year for the label. He convinced Gladys Knight to record "If I Were Your Woman," a song she did not think right for her image. His instincts were still good, and it was a big hit. "The Tears of a Clown," by Smokey Robinson and the Miracles, had been a moderate success in Britain. Although it was three years old and never intended to be an American single, Gordy decided to rerelease it in the United States. The gamble paid off, as the song went to number one, the first in their long career of hits. And Norman Whitfield and Barrett Strong turned out songs that were not only hits but also reflected some of the era's social upheaval. Out of character for the normally apolitical Motown, "War"—originally written for the Temptations—tackled Vietnam. With Edwin Starr's thundering voice, the song went to number one and became an anthem for a disaffected generation disgusted over an increasingly unpopular war in Southeast Asia. Whitfield and Strong also produced "Ball of

Confusion" for the Temptations, another song that captured the unsettled energy of the times.

Whitfield's frenetic pace in churning out songs matched Gordy's new-found focus on work. For the Temptations, Whitfield turned out "Runaway Child, Running Wild," "I Can't Get Next to You," and "Psychedelic Shack," all of which kept the group on top of the charts. The Tempts mockingly called them "message" songs, because listeners ascribed so much meaning to them, when in fact Whitfield was, according to Otis Williams, just latching on to the popular "psychedelic soul trend."

·   ·   ·

Gordy opened a Los Angeles studio that same year, further consolidating the move west. Located near the company's Sunset Boulevard headquarters, Gordy initially dubbed the new setup Mowest but soon changed it to Hitsville. He picked Guy Costa, the nephew of the noted music arranger Don Costa, as its director.

But spending all his time at Motown enmeshed in music did not assuage Gordy's emptiness about losing Ross. He moved all his family and close friends to Los Angeles. (Only Smokey Robinson, petrified of earthquakes, refused, although he finally gave in two years later.) Although Gordy's sisters Gwen and Anna had been in Los Angeles for a few years, he now relocated his parents (his mother was still one of the two signatories required on Motown's checks), as well as his two brothers, Fuller and Robert. Fuller was in charge of both personnel and purchasing, while Robert ran Jobete, a role he had taken over after Loucye's death.

"And the Jackson Five had become a real part of my family," remembered Gordy. On weekends, the Jacksons competed against the Gordys in a softball game at a local park. At one game, Gordy unexpectedly discovered another diversion from his fretting over the split with Ross. Since Michael Jackson was the smallest player on either team, he invariably played catcher. Gordy noticed on this particular day that every time a ball got past Michael, another youngster ran from the spectator area and grabbed the ball and threw it back into the game before Michael could get it himself. Sensing that his artist was getting frustrated and upstaged by the young stranger, Gordy decided diplomatically to ask the new kid to stop. He did stop and stayed on the sidelines until the game was over. Then he tugged on Gordy's shirt.

"Do you know Ray Singleton?" he asked. Gordy was surprised to hear the name of his former wife.

"Sure I know Ray. She was my wife."

"Well, I'm her son, Kerry."

Gordy recalled standing there stunned for a moment, staring at the youngster's deep green eyes. Then he suddenly reached out, grabbed him, and squeezed him hard. "You are my son, too."

"I know," came the muffled response, as his face was buried in Gordy's shoulder.

Gordy had not seen a picture of Kerry, now ten, in almost six years. Later that day, Gordy discovered that Kerry had wanted to move to Los Angeles to get to know his father. Ray was agreeable. (Their time together was evidently not enough to put Kerry on equal footing with some of the other Gordy children. For instance, that same year, when Gordy called Ray with news about trust funds he was establishing, Kerry got the worst treatment. Hazel Joy, Berry, and Terry, the three children from the marriage with Thelma, were to receive one million dollars each when they turned twenty-one; Kerry was to receive one hundred thousand.)

The contact with Kerry did, however, rekindle an interest in Gordy to learn more about his son Kennedy, who lived in Detroit with Gordy's third ex-wife, Margaret Norton. When he called Norton, she refused to let Kennedy visit. So Gordy offered to move them both to California, and she agreed. According to an account published by Raynoma, Norton, depressed by seeing firsthand Gordy's nonstop conquest of young, beautiful women in Los Angeles, was soon often zoned out on tranquilizers and booze.

His sons, though, weren't Gordy's only new focus. He soon had his attention drawn to his daughter, Hazel, for a most unusual reason. He had received a call from Ewart Abner, then head of ITMI, alerting him that someone impersonating Hazel had written a fan-obsessed letter to Jermaine Jackson.

He showed Hazel the letter and laughed about the writer's overblown prose: "I love you, Jermaine. You are my prince, my dream. I need you, Jermaine. I will love you forever." But Hazel grew sober while her father read the letter. Finally she spoke up, "Daddy, that's personal."

He tried assuring her it was all right. It was only fan mail, he told her, and the stars didn't read any of it themselves.

"But, Daddy, that's still personal. It's none of your business."

Gordy looked carefully at her. Her eyes were filling with tears. Then he suddenly realized she had actually written the note. Gordy could not believe that his fifteen-year-old daughter was infatuated with an image he had created. He certainly did not want her involved with an entertainer, especially not one signed to his company.

Gordy told Hazel that writing a fan letter was not the best way to meet Jermaine, and that if she would wait three months to see if she felt the same, he would impart a secret about how to approach him. He was confident that her crush would end by then.

During the next three months, Hazel was on her best behavior, both at school and at home. She never mentioned Jermaine, and Gordy thought his gambit had worked. Then one evening, at home, she asked to talk to Gordy alone. They went to her room, and he sat next to her on her bed. She seemed excited, and soon he knew why.

"Three months are up," she said.

Gordy asked if she still liked Jermaine.

"Daddy, I love him." Gordy cringed. "I love him more than anything else in the world."

Hazel grabbed her father's hand. "What is the secret?" she asked.

He leaned over and told her simply to be herself. She was crestfallen, thinking he was about to impart much better advice. Gordy assured her that it wasn't a trick, but that one of the most difficult things to understand was that instead of trying to be somebody that she thought Jermaine wanted, she had to trust herself enough to just show who she really was. He told her about how when he was a youngster, he tried to get girls to date him by pretending to be cooler than he really was, and how it never worked.

Finally, she stopped crying and after a long while said she understood and that all she could do was try. The advice was obviously good. Hazel and Jermaine married in 1973, and the two-hundred-thousand-dollar reception Gordy held at the Beverly Hills Hotel was one of the entertainment events of the decade. There were seven thousand white camellias, a storm of fake snow, 175 doves released to a grand musical score, and a towering eight-level wedding cake. The entire ceremony was broadcast on closed-circuit television to the B-list guests who could not fit in the main hall. Smokey Robinson performed "From This Time and Place," a song he wrote for the occasion. On that day, with Hazel wearing a custom-made white dress dripping in pearls and adorned with white mink cuffs and a long mink train, even Gordy felt his initial fears might have been misplaced when it came to Jermaine, one of the most grounded of the Jacksons.

Surprisingly, the one person not happy was Marvin Gaye, who was still in his turbulent relationship with Anna Gordy. "I saw myself being replaced," the increasingly paranoid Gaye later told his friend, journalist David Ritz. "Jermaine was a singer marrying into the family, just the way I had, and just when I was being moved out. It was all part of Berry's plan to get himself a new, younger Marvin Gaye."

"It was clear to everyone except Marvin that Berry loved him," says Ritz. "Gaye wasn't capable of accepting that love."

.   .   .

Suzanne de Passe brought Gordy dismaying news at the end of January 1971: twenty-six-year-old Ross had unexpectedly married Bob Silberstein, a white Jewish record promoter who at the time was managing Chaka Khan and Rufus. (A couple of years earlier, Ross had told a *Look* magazine reporter that mixed marriages were "groovy.") The same day Gordy learned of her marriage, Ross called him.

He was filled with conflicting emotions. He was sad that she had married someone else but also relieved that it meant there was an end to their own tumultuous affair. Gordy could now concentrate just on Ross's career without having emotions get in the way, he thought.

He became more immersed in his affair with Chris Clark, and soon the two were off in the Bahamas, where Gordy enjoyed gambling. Clark was convinced, however, that Gordy was sorting out few of his feelings and that he was still in love with Ross. Although Gordy kept protesting that she was wrong, Clark felt there was no place in his life for her as long as he loved Ross. He could not convince her otherwise, and soon Clark left Gordy to marry a Hollywood screenwriter, Ernest Tidyman.

When Ross soon started to show that she was pregnant, Gordy initially wondered whether the child was his. The two had last had sex—"one for the road" as Gordy dubbed it—only a few months earlier. While he thought it unlikely it was his child, he was protective of Ross, and she used this to her benefit. For instance, in early 1971 she recorded an album of duets with Marvin Gaye. Neither liked the other. At one point, Ross ran into the control room and screamed at Gordy, "Listen, I cannot sing with the man smoking weed. I'm pregnant. I do not want to be around any drugs. I won't go on until you make him stop."

Gordy urged Gaye to stop smoking. "She's going to have a baby, and you don't want the drugs around the baby."

Gaye just smiled. "Fuck Diana Ross. I'm going to smoke this weed or I don't sing."

The two artists ended up recording their duet vocals separately.

"It's hard for me to deal with other prima donnas," Gaye recalled later. "We were like two spoiled kids screaming for the same cookie. It was definitely *not* a duet made in heaven." (After Gaye was murdered in 1984, Ross sensed the commercial potential of a tribute to him and recorded "Missing You," a song written by Lionel Richie.)

In August 1971, Ross gave birth to a girl she named Rhonda. It did not take Gordy long to conclude the child was his. He confronted Ross, and she confirmed he was right. Rhonda and later her two sisters grew up thinking of Gordy only as Uncle BB.

The public did not know that Rhonda was Ross and Gordy's child until Gordy disclosed it in *To Be Loved*. With that disclosure, Ross's marriage to Bob Silberstein finally made sense to many of her friends, who initially could not fathom what had brought them together. When they had married, they barely knew each other and seemed to have little in common. But those who know her say that Ross would never have allowed herself to be an unwed mother at a time when it was still frowned upon by many people. She would have feared that an out-of-wedlock pregnancy would have shattered her wholesome public image.

•   •   •

Gordy's preoccupation with his personal problems during this period in California knocked his usually astute instincts off-kilter. For instance, when Marvin Gaye called in 1971 and said he wanted to do a protest album, Gordy's response was a flippant "Protest about what?" Gaye offered him a small smorgasbord of gripes: "Vietnam, police brutality, social conditions, a lot of stuff."

Gordy told Gaye that he was taking things too far.

Gaye, with his reputation for stubbornness, was not easily dissuaded. "I'm not happy with the world," he told Gordy. "I'm angry. I have to sing about that, I have to protest."

Gordy was not convinced. He urged Gaye to "stick to what works." To Gordy, what worked was what sold. He still had no interest in using his company or the talent of his artists to further social causes.

"If you're gonna do something different," Gordy urged him, "at least make it commercial." He told Gaye that he had worked hard to develop a sexy image that he had to protect at all costs.

Gaye was unimpressed. He told Gordy he was determined to make the album with or without his blessing. With little company support, Gaye went on a cocaine-induced binge and immersed himself in his protest album. It was called *What's Going On* and was a complete break from his previous music, as well as his later sex-themed songs.

"I don't like it," Gordy told Smokey after he had listened to the rough cuts. "I don't think they're going to play it on the radio."

"Look, man," Smokey told Gordy, "all the writers and artists love it. We think it's brilliant—"

"I'm going to talk him out of it," said Gordy.

"That's like trying to talk a bear out of shittin' in the woods. Marvin ain't budging."

Fortunately for Robinson and Gaye, Gordy was not serious about stopping it. Barney Ales also fought hard for the album, telling Gordy that it would be a major error to hold it back. "You could just tell it was going to sell," recalled Ales. When it was released, Ales and Gaye were proved right. Most fans and critics believe that *What's Going On* is the album closest to showing the real Marvin Gaye. "It was the greatest album," said Smokey Robinson, "in my opinion, ever made by anyone."

Not only did *What's Going On* surprise Gordy by going to number one in April 1971, but out of it came three top-ten singles. The album touched on many issues that Gaye found troubling, from the difficulty of ghetto life ("Inner City Blues [Make Me Wanna Holler]") to the environmental crisis ("Mercy Mercy Me [the Ecology]") to the uncertain future of the next generation ("Save the Children") to the moving story of a frustrated Vietnam veteran returning home ("What's Happening Brother"). The album, which was considered radical in 1971, won multiple awards for Gaye and was the largest-selling of his career—although he would stay angry until he died that the Grammys overlooked it completely.

Gordy's instincts were wrong not only about Gaye but also about Stevie Wonder's changing style. In 1970, Gordy privately predicted that "Signed, Sealed, Delivered (I'm Yours)" would be only a moderate success. It was the first single that Wonder had produced, and it turned into a monster hit, one of the biggest of Wonder's career. It won the Grammy Award as best soul song of the year, and it led to Wonder's first appearance at the Copacabana, where he received raves. In September 1970, Stevie, then twenty, married Rita "Syreeta" Wright, a former company secretary and aspiring songwriter who had become a Motown recording artist. She had cowritten some of Wonder's early songs and also had sung backup on a few of his albums. In 1971, with Gordy's blessing, she helped Wonder produce and cowrite the songs for a new album, *Where I'm Coming From*. This time, Gordy thought there were several songs that would be major hits, but the public's reception was lukewarm, and the album did not sell well.

On top of that, Wonder's trust fund, which held all the royalties he had earned as a minor, was finally about to be released to him on his twenty-first birthday, May 21, 1971. It totaled more than one million dollars. Gordy attended Wonder's birthday party in Detroit. The next day, Gordy flew to Los Angeles, and waiting for him in the office there was a letter from Wonder's attorney, threatening to break his contracts. Gordy was furious and called Wonder. It turned out Wonder had not intended to send Gordy that letter. So Wonder fired his attorney and replaced him with a new manager and attorney, Johanan Vigoda, who had previously worked with Jimi Hendrix and Richie Havens. Vigoda, who had a reputation as an eccentric but tough negotiator, was a surprise choice. "It was out of left field," said Phil Jones. But it turned out to be the right choice.

"Vigoda was a godsend to Stevie," Gordy later told *Billboard*'s Adam White. "He was tough, strong, and brilliant, yet sensitive. He cared for Stevie like a father."

With Vigoda backing him, Wonder walked into the office of Ewart Abner. "He came to me," recalled Abner, "and said, 'I'm twenty-one now. I'm not gonna do what you say anymore. Void my contract.' I freaked."

Gordy may not have liked Wonder's hardball tactics, but he knew he could not afford to lose him. Motown finally offered Wonder an unprecedented deal. The contract ran to more than 120 pages, and what was in it was groundbreaking for the label. Gordy not only came up with substantially more money (thirteen million dollars) but relinquished creative control over Wonder's upcoming albums to the artist himself. Also, Gordy ceded half the publishing royalties to Wonder, the first time he had ever done that for an artist. No longer did Gordy and Wonder have a father-son relationship. It was now a more equal partnership. This was a concession Gordy would never have agreed to in earlier years. RCA and CBS were ready if the negotiations failed—Gordy said they would have offered a deal that would have "dwarfed ours." Also, some executives familiar with the negotiations believe that Gordy did not have his heart in the talks.

"He didn't have the fire anymore," recalled Barney Ales. "Anyone could see that. Berry wasn't even listening to the records then, let's be serious. He was going in a new direction. He was all *Lady Sings the Blues* by then."

CHAPTER 27

Lady Sings the Blues

BERRY GORDY WAS IN HIS TWENTIES THE ONLY TIME HE SAW BILLIE Holiday perform, at Detroit's Flame Show Bar. She mesmerized him. After the show, he had his picture taken with her. He realized he had lost the photo when he looked for it a few years later, when he heard she had died.

Gordy forgot about Billie Holiday until 1971, when he was in the midst of his personal turmoil in California. A William Morris talent agent, Joe Schoenfeld, told him about a film project of Holiday's life, with director Sidney Furie and producer Jay Weston. Furie had seen Motown's television special *Diana!* in which Diana Ross had done some scenery-chewing impersonations of W. C. Fields, Harpo Marx, and Charlie Chaplin. He thought she could be right for the film's lead. Gordy quickly met with him. After several hours of intense discussions, they had a handshake deal. Gordy was ecstatic. It fulfilled a long-held ambition to get involved in films—Gordy had told the *Detroit Free Press* as early as 1964 that he wanted Motown to expand into motion pictures—and meant he could move Ross's career to a new level.

Gordy called Ross with the news. He had not heard her so excited since the start of her career. Then, three days after the agreement had been reached, Furie called with bad news. "They don't want Diana Ross," he announced. The project's New York backers—Cinema Center Films—had thought it was foolhardy to cast a singer without any acting experience for the lead of a major motion picture. Gordy was crushed. He barely mustered the courage to tell Ross but did so later that day, and her pride prevented her from revealing how devastated she really was.

A week later, the emotional roller coaster continued when Gordy got another call from Furie. The original deal with Cinema Center had fallen through. "We took the film to Paramount," Furie told him, "and they will accept Diana Ross!"

Gordy was so excited that it took a few minutes for Furie to explain one catch. Paramount wanted Gordy to guarantee the deficit financing, meaning that Gordy was responsible for any costs over two million dollars. Gordy called in Jim White, a number cruncher who was Motown's vice president of business affairs. Gordy gave the green light after White assured him that the budget made sense. For his financial guarantee, Gordy got the rights to have the opening credits read: "Berry Gordy Presents Diana Ross as Billie Holiday in *Lady Sings the Blues*."

Gordy later said that his agreement on *Lady Sings the Blues* was one of the biggest financial miscalculations of his life. But before he discovered what a bad deal it was, he had to first cope with industry predictions of disaster once the word went out that Ross was to play the lead. There was widespread criticism—few thought she could act—and many predicted the project would flop miserably. Besides her few sometimes-painful comedy sketches on Motown-sponsored television shows, she had shown no acting talent and had no professional training. Also, when industry insiders learned about Gordy's financial guarantee, it appeared that he was simply buying his ex-girlfriend a film role. Unless she and the movie proved themselves, there would be little kindness shown in Hollywood to the Motown outsiders.

Ross did not help the situation. She told a reporter that she did not intend to take acting lessons because Doris Day had told her she didn't need them. "If Jim Brown can do it, I can do it, whatever he's doing," she said. And she said she was storing up all her bitter experiences so she would be prepared for Holiday's sad story. When asked what her biggest life trauma had been, she said it was when someone had poisoned her dogs the year before.

But the project's first actual problem had nothing to do with Ross. It came when Gordy, Suzanne de Passe, and Shelly Berger finally saw the script, written by Sidney Furie and screenwriter Terence McCloy. They hated it. At a hastily called meeting with Furie, Gordy told him of his concerns—too many stereotypes and not enough "blackness." Furie was initially defensive, but Gordy convinced Furie to let him hire a black writer for a major rewrite, even though it was only a few months before shooting was scheduled to start.

Gordy did not have to look far—he picked Suzanne de Passe. She said no, however, because she had never before even attempted to write one.

"So what?" he asked her. "You're one of the smartest people I know. And you do know about black people—don't you?"

The middle-class-reared de Passe took the jibing in stride, and it was not very hard to convince her to accept the job—she couldn't resist the chance. Moreover, Gordy himself and Shelly Berger and Chris Clark helped her. Clark, although white, developed such good "black" dialogue that Gordy arranged for her to be hired as an official screenwriter. Billy Davis, Gordy's childhood friend—who shared the same name as Gordy's early songwriting partner—had been hired by Gordy a few years earlier as his man Friday. Davis attended many of the story meetings. He was at his flamboyant best, singing Holiday's songs and reminding the writers about the importance of capturing her dramatic flair.

Gordy kept reminding the creative team they weren't making a documentary. They did not feel constrained to follow Holiday's life exactly. Holiday's sidekick had been the legendary sax player Lester Young, but the writers created a fictional character dubbed "Piano Man" (who would eventually be played to near perfection by Richard Pryor—Gordy knew Pryor, since he had managed his comedy career for many years).

The Holiday estate cooperated, sending the Motown team several boxes of photographs and some letters. In one box, Gordy found the photo of himself next to Holiday at the Flame Show Bar. He considered the reappearance of the photo a good omen.

Early on, Gordy moved with his writers and assistants to a suite of offices inside the sprawling Paramount studios, across town from Motown. Not every role was as easy to cast as Pryor's. The toughest part was Holiday's husband, who in real life had been Louis McKay. One of Gordy's newest assistants, Suzee Ikeda, championed Billy Dee Williams, an actor she insisted had charisma and great looks. Gordy wasn't familiar with him, but after watching a preview tape of the television movie *Brian's Song*, he added him to a growing list of actors who wanted the role. They all read for the part. Gordy and Furie agreed that Williams was the worst. He constantly missed his lines and joked every time he made a mistake. Ross found him amusing, but Gordy and Furie thought he had an attitude and was a "pompous, pretty boy."

Williams grumbled about having to read for the role, finding it demeaning given his track record. Furie told him bluntly that if he didn't, he could leave. After the fiasco, Williams told them he had forgotten his glasses, or otherwise it would have gone smoothly. Giving him the benefit of the doubt, Furie and Gordy called him back as part of a smaller group for a screen test with Ross. His screen test, for which he was prepared, turned out worse than his reading.

Although that should have been the end for him, Gordy had noticed that in both the reading and the screen test, Ross and Williams had great rapport. Gordy wanted to go with him, but the others, including Furie, said no. But Gordy finally convinced them the chemistry was "magic."

In the meantime, Ross immersed herself in Holiday's world. She read books about her and listened to her music. Gordy started calling her "Billie." When Gordy and Furie finally heard the studio recordings that Gil Askey had made of Ross doing some Holiday classics, both found it "spooky" how much she sounded like Holiday. Gordy actually instructed Askey to "pull her back a notch from Billie Holiday and leave a little Diana Ross in there because, 'Her future's got to extend beyond this picture.'" Askey rerecorded all the songs, making them sound less like impersonations.

Principal photography on *Lady Sings the Blues* started in December 1971 in Los Angeles. Gordy discovered immediately that once the cameras started rolling Furie and others viewed him only as the moneyman; they did not want him interfering with the film. Gordy resented that, since he thought he had special insights about Ross and understood the importance of Holiday and how to best tell her story. And he was certain he was needed to ensure the film's "blackness." As a record producer, Gordy controlled every aspect of an album. Now he realized that a Hollywood producer did not have the same control. His inexperience, coupled with Furie's desire to have him stand silently on the side of the set, caused frequent fireworks. Gordy, while trying to downplay the conflict with Furie, has admitted that their battles meant "those next three months of production were tumultuous." One day,

Gordy's incessant interference prompted Furie to storm off the set. He returned only after Gordy pleaded with him overnight.

Unexpected issues became irritants. For instance, two days into the film, Ross saw her wardrobe and called Gordy in tears. She thought the clothes looked terrible. When he tried calming her by explaining that her gowns were authentic period pieces, she exploded: "But they look crappy! I don't want these. I want the best."

"So all the gowns were dumped," Furie recalled. Gordy hired designers Bob Mackie and Ray Aghayan to do a wardrobe that was much glitzier. "The producers felt she was a temperamental bitch," Gordy later said.

While Gordy seemed to be involved in many parts of the production, the one area he neglected was his assigned role of budget manager. He was reminded of it, however, when halfway through filming an assistant unit-production manager had the courage to tell him that the project was running out of money. Gordy did not believe him. When he checked with the film's auditors, though, he was startled to discover that nearly 95 percent of the budget had been spent. Gordy, assured by his friends that all movies go over budget and it was not a problem, immediately set an appointment with the head of Paramount, Frank Yablans. Paramount, at that time, had both *The Godfather* and *Save the Tiger* in production. Gordy was not Yablans's only headache, but he agreed to an early-morning meeting.

The five-foot-five Yablans, bald and cigar smoking, looked like he was straight out of central casting. Wiry and a seeming blur of nervous activity, Yablans started the meeting graciously but without exchanging too many pleasantries.

"How is it going, my friend?" he asked as Gordy entered the large corner suite.

Gordy assured him everything was great, trying to convince himself as much as Yablans. The film was Academy Award caliber, he said, but it was slightly over budget, and he needed to rework his deal with the studio.

Yablans, of course, followed his studio's projects closely. He knew about the turmoil between Gordy and Furie, and was aware that the film was burning cash fast. No one at Paramount had expected the inexperienced Gordy to be a strict enough taskmaster.

Yablans laughed. "What are you talking about?" he gruffly asked Gordy. "Rework the budget? You kidding?"

Gordy tried to be as calm as possible but was nonplussed by Yablans's blunt rejection. Gordy countered that he heard it happened all the time.

"Not with me it don't."

Gordy, now nervous, insisted that the film was a work of art and that Yablans should visit the set.

Yablans stared out the window at the Paramount lot. "The biggest budget for other black films is five hundred thousand, tops. We're giving you two million! You understand what that means, two million bucks for a black film? You should be happy."

That rankled Gordy. "This is not a black film. This is a film with black stars."

Yablans pounced on him again, swiveling around in his large leather chair to face Gordy. "I guess you just don't get the point, do you? Let me see, you're from the ghetto, right? I'll put this in terms you can understand better. You went out and got yourself a case of the clap, and you infected me with it. And now you come back and expect me to pay you to get rid of yours! Does that make it any clearer? . . . If you're out of money, I suggest you end the film right where it's at."

Gordy's voice rose with anger. They were in the middle of the filming, so he asked Yablans how it was possible to stop.

"Easy," Yablans replied calmly. "Just fade to black and put letters on the screen that say T-H-E E-N-D."

Gordy took a few deep breaths and tried to control his temper. Yablans had a reputation for destroying people in confrontations. Gordy decided not to challenge him but instead asked what he could do to save the project.

"Pay everything over two million, and you'll get your money back after deferments, distribution fees, prints, and ads, and everything else. Or," and at this point Yablans grinned broadly, "just bring me a check for the two million, and the film is yours to do whatever you want."

Gordy stood up and walked out.

The next day he showed up at Yablans's office with a check for two million dollars. Yablans was clearly caught off guard. He hesitated before telling Gordy that despite the payment Paramount would still have to distribute the film.

Gordy was not in the mood for Yablans's tactics and reminded him they had a deal.

"I know what I said," Yablans said, waving his hands in dismissal, "but you must have misunderstood me. We took the gamble, investing our money first. Under no circumstances would I have ever suggested that we wouldn't distribute the film."

Gordy disliked Yablans, but had little choice. Paramount kept its control, including ownership and distribution rights. But paying the two million gave Gordy the level of control and creative freedom he wanted. He settled for that.

The filming wrapped in early 1972. Editing had just started when Yablans called Gordy. Paramount's board of directors wanted to see whatever they had in order to judge whether the film might be a hit. Gordy tried to put him off. It was nowhere near ready, without music, montages, and many other critical elements.

Yablans was not dissuaded. "Just grab the reels," he told Gordy, "put them under your arm, come to New York, and let us see them." Gordy protested some more. "Hey," Yablans cut him off. "We're movie people here. We know it's going to be rough. You can narrate the parts that are missing."

Against his better judgment, Gordy relented. In the small New York screening room, filled with studio executives, Gordy played a four-hour rough cut. At different points, the screen merely read "scene to come" or "music to come." Gordy thought, as he watched it, that even with the missing parts it was great and that everybody there would share his enthusiasm. But when the lights came on, most of those in the room stared at the floor, and nobody looked at Gordy.

Yablans spoke up. "Can you meet me in my office?" he asked Gordy, as he walked out without a smile.

Gordy, somewhat puzzled, followed. Yablans actually looked sorry as he turned toward him. "The picture is in trouble, but maybe I can help you. There's a couple of film doctors I know who can probably save it." And Yablans insisted the movie had to be no longer than two hours. Gordy was stunned. He couldn't understand how anybody could fail to see what he did. And he was furious that he had allowed Yablans to talk him into showing the unfinished film. He announced he was returning to Los Angeles to finish the movie.

Back in Los Angeles, Gordy used Yablans's dislike for the film to renegotiate a better deal, lowering his domestic distribution fee and getting better terms in foreign markets. But before Gordy could even start trying to cut the film, he confronted a problem at Motown. Barney Ales, his trusted sales chief, who had been critical in making the label a success, was discontented. Ales had been one of the few executives not to move to Los Angeles—he and his wife, Mitzi, were in no mood to uproot themselves. And Ales considered himself too crucial to Motown for Gordy to let him go. Raynoma Gordy said that Ales had a "power lust—he typified those who'd stop at nothing to receive their thrones, and how he sat high atop his in the kingdom of sales. . . . His kind of mentality was ripping Motown apart." For Gordy, that proved problematic. He needed Ales to help run the company while he worked on *Lady Sings the Blues,* but often when he tried reaching him Ales was unavailable. Tom Noonan made up excuses that Ales was often on the road. "I hated having to cover for Barney," said Noonan, "because Berry knew I was lying, and Barney would make it worse by not calling Berry back for several days. Berry needed Barney but resented how independent he was and how powerful he had become."

"He wanted more autonomy than I wanted to give him," Gordy recalled. "He refused to be subject to the controls I put in place. While I was off in Los Angeles making movies, he refused to report to anyone else. He wanted to do things his way, not my way. I thought perhaps he wanted to go his own way. I made it easy. I told him he was fired."

At the time, Ales told the *Detroit Free Press* that he retired "to devote full time to his investment portfolio." Today, he says that he thought of "Gordy as Caesar, and I was his top general." And he insists he was not fired. "It's just not true. But if that's the way Berry wants to tell it, then fine, I guess. He didn't want to pay me what I wanted, so I left. No hard feelings."

Gordy was sorry to see Ales go. He called Ewart Abner, then running Motown's management division, and informed him he was now in control of sales and marketing. Gordy returned to the film.

•　　　•　　　•

The problem was that there was just too much film. They had shot everything, from great footage to clumsy mistakes. Gordy worked with director Furie and editor Art J. Nelson to cut the footage. He brought in *Life* magazine photographer Lawrence Schiller (later a director and bestselling author in his own right), who convinced Gordy to telescope many scenes into brief montages that powerfully encapsulated parts of the story. Gordy learned the art of editing. Many good scenes had to be cut. After several tough weeks, the team had the film down to two hours and fifteen minutes. Gordy knew they had to cut more before he returned to Yablans.

Finally, he was persuaded that the movie did not need a long scene about the most downtrodden part of Holiday's life, which the crew had dubbed the degradation scene. It was a tough call since Gordy's brother Robert had played the role of a dope dealer in that scene, and removing it meant cutting him out completely. But Gordy became convinced he had no other choice. When he was later about to leave for a preview in Detroit, he realized his family, including Robert, would be there. Gordy scrambled to restore the scene only for that premiere. But after the showing, the audience response was so strong that he decided to keep it in even though it pushed the film back over Yablans's time limit.

The official world premiere for *Lady Sings the Blues* was in New York at the Loews State Theatre in Times Square in October 1972. Diana Ross could not be there, furious that, only a few days from the birth of her second child, her doctor forbade her to fly from Los Angeles. The movie broke the theater's attendance record, previously set by *Love Story.* And while there were critiques of the film's factual inaccuracies, there were many raves, particularly for Ross's powerful acting debut. To capitalize on the great reviews, Gordy directed the Motown publicity department to go into overdrive, scheduling promotional appearances, concerts, and a rush of magazine and television interviews. The film wangled the prestigious closing slot at the Cannes Film Festival, and the first song released from the sound track's double album—"Good Morning Heartache"—quickly climbed the charts. Phil Jones and his staff were not that enthusiastic about the expensive album crammed with old-time tunes, but knowing how dear it was to Gordy, they worked it as hard as any release the company had had in years. "As far as Berry was concerned," recalled Jones, "this might as well have been the only album we had to sell." They made the album the number-one pop record.

Gordy's revenge on Frank Yablans and the rest of the Paramount naysayers came the following February, when *Lady* received five Academy Award nominations, including one for best actress, as well as for best art direction, best costume design, best score and adaptation, and best screenplay. Terence

McCloy, Suzanne de Passe, and Chris Clark shared the last nomination. A month before the awards, Ross won a prestigious Golden Globe. Gordy and Ross and most of their friends thought she was a shoo-in for the Academy Award. Even Liza Minnelli, another nominee, said: "I've got two words to say about the Oscars: Diana Ross." But Gordy rankled many Academy voters with an enormous ad campaign for Ross in the trade papers; he also hosted dinners and sent gifts to the voters. Although many companies now conduct lavish campaigns for their nominees, it was unique at that time, and many complained that he was trying to buy her the award.

The night before the Academy Awards, March 26, Ross threw an extravagant pre-Oscar party at her house. As Gordy later recalled, it was to "celebrate what was certain to be victory, as well as her twenty-ninth birthday." The atmosphere of success in movies had infiltrated Motown—even the stay-at-home Marvin Gaye started plotting how best to break into films. "Diana showed me," he said, "that I could be a movie star."

That night, Gordy, de Passe, and Shelly Berger virtually collapsed on a sofa, exhausted from what had been months of marathon work. Gordy watched that evening in amazement, however, at Ross's energy as she zipped around the room. She was brimming with confidence, certain the award was hers. Gordy's only concern, which he mentioned that night to Berger, was that two black women—the other being Cicely Tyson for *Sounder*—were nominated for the first time ever, and he fretted they might cancel each other out. Berger told him not to worry, that Ross was a cinch. "No way Diana can lose," he assured him.

Gordy smiled. "I know."

The next night at the Dorothy Chandler Pavilion, Ross and Gordy were literally on the edge of their seats when the winner was announced for best actress. The first syllable was *Li* not *Di* as Liza Minnelli was given the award for her role in *Cabaret*. Gordy remembered "shock waves" went through him, and then the next few moments were a blur. "We were heartsick," he recalled. Ross stayed in her seat, as plastic a smile as she has ever flashed frozen on her face. She applauded for Minnelli and then closed her eyes and exhaled deeply. As she left the auditorium, there were tears streaming down her face. Years later, in her autobiography, she wrote falsely, "Although I didn't win, it didn't matter." Those close to her say the unexpected loss sent her into a funk for weeks.

The film was ignored in all categories, and most of Gordy's entourage made only a perfunctory stop after the ceremony at the official post-awards party, the Governor's Ball. Instead, they were anxious to head back to Gordy's house. Despite its five nominations—and that it was a commercial and critical success—Gordy's gathering had the same atmosphere as a losing candidate's campaign headquarters on election night.

CHAPTER 28

"The Beginning of the End"

HEADY WITH THE SUCCESS OF *LADY SINGS THE BLUES*, MOTOWN announced ambitious plans to spend twenty-four million dollars for ten movies and three Broadway shows over the next two years. While the movie division was congratulating itself, Motown's music division was booming again. Marvin Gaye released *Let's Get It On*, an even stronger commercial success than *What's Going On*. The Temptations picked up three Grammys for the previous year's "Papa Was a Rolling Stone" and later released another hit with "Masterpiece." The Temptations had hated "Papa Was a Rolling Stone" when Norman Whitfield presented it to them, and they had recorded it under protest. After it became their fourth number one, sold more than two million copies, and nabbed the Grammys, Otis Williams sheepishly said the song "kind of grew on us."

Stevie Wonder also had success with his album *Innervisions*, released in August 1973, only seven months after he divorced Syreeta Wright, his wife of less than two years. Wonder had been hot again since he had toured as the opening act for the Rolling Stones 1972 tour—his releases that year of "Superstition" and "You Are the Sunshine of My Life" had gone to number one and greatly expanded his appeal to whites.

Fourteen-year-old Michael Jackson released his fourth solo song, the title track to an offbeat movie about a boy whose best friend was a rat. "Ben" was nominated for an Academy Award and became the nation's biggest-selling record, with more than 1.7 million copies. It went number one, his first solo release to do so (one of his earlier singles, "Rockin' Robin," had stalled at number two). "Ben" was another boon to Michael's exploding solo career. Although the five brothers were still recording and getting hits as a group, Michael had been signed to a Motown solo contract in December 1971, and the label was working hard to establish his separate career.

But Gordy's absence from the music side continued to take a toll. Top executives in sales and promotion—such as Phil Jones and Tom Noonan—were getting antsy with the lack of direction. Some, like Noonan, later recounted how drugs had thoroughly corrupted the business. "It had gotten much worse over the years," Noonan recalled. "We once had a small cardboard house with stickers of our records, and we sent it out to the biggest DJs. One of them called me up in a huff and said, 'Tom, I've cut the damn thing up and where the hell is the coke?' "

At a sales-conference meeting, someone whispered to Jones that he heard the police had just raided Casablanca Records, looking for illegal drugs. "I immediately announced, 'No one here better have drugs. If you have them, you better get rid of them.' Everyone got up and ran out of the room."

Many of the old-timers did not like the recent changes. Jones said that "when Gordy went to Los Angeles, he was no longer nearly as hands-on. That hurt us, the business got out of hand. No one was watching the store."

Even Gordy would admit as much years later in a *Playboy* interview: "I would say [moving to Los Angeles] was the beginning of the end."

Barney Ales's departure the year before had also left the sales department without firm guidance. And problems with clashes of ego were also affecting more of Motown's top talent. Norman Whitfield had let his success swell his head. Otis Williams had gone directly to Gordy and complained about the pressure and demands Whitfield had placed on the group. After they finished grueling road tours, Whitfield would cut them little slack, insisting they immediately get back into the studio to record new tracks.

Williams expected Gordy to forcefully resolve the problem, as he always had. Instead, he told a surprised Williams, "I really hope you guys can work it out." And when Gordy did finally talk to Whitfield, he allowed Whitfield to set the rules. "Look, man," Whitfield told Gordy, "I fought too hard for too long to start lowering my standards now. I got to push those cats to get the perfection I know you want and I want. And I ain't changin' my style for nobody."

As Gordy acknowledged years later, that essentially marked the end of Whitfield's collaboration with the Temptations. While Motown shuffled a slew of different producers to the Tempts, even including Gordy himself at one point, none ever delivered the hits that Whitfield had regularly produced.

Gordy started hiring business consultants, who tinkered with Motown's corporate structure. "He had never listened to consultants before," said Phil Jones. "Then all of a sudden he started bringing in people who knew nothing about the music business."

A new umbrella company—Motown Record Corporation—oversaw all the divisions, including Motown Records, Jobete Music Publishing, and the management division, ITMI. Gordy became the chairman. He appointed Suzanne de Passe, still in her twenties, to run the creative division. And for the first time in the company's history, Gordy had recently selected someone else to become president of Motown Records. Ewart Abner had been the chief of ITMI and a vice president of marketing and sales. To many who worked closely with the smooth-talking Abner, he was an unlikely choice. Although very knowledgeable about black music—he had been a partner in the moderately successful Vee-Jay Records—he was not a hard worker and was known for being disorganized and personally abrasive. Motown's next president, Jay Lasker, viewed Abner as "a complete dud."

"He was also a racist," said Phil Jones. "He pretended to be a friend of the white man, but deep down he was a racist." Abner was black, militantly so, and thought that Motown had been diluted by Gordy's reliance on so many white employees. "It's time for a purge," he told a fellow ITMI executive.

Bringing in a black president with militant Afrocentric views might not have been problematic if Motown was a black-owned and -staffed company. However, since Gordy had moved to Los Angeles, the company, which always had had a lot of whites in key positions, had gone even further in that direction. "There were blacks in creative areas," recalled the Supremes' Mary Wilson, "and there had been some black executives back in Detroit, but once we moved to L.A., Motown was white run." Nearly 80 percent of the label's executives were white by now.

Soon, key white employees were being fired, including Phil Jones and Tom Noonan, critical components of the sales department. "I was ready to leave by the time Abner fired me," recalled Jones. "At one meeting, I remember when Abner was in the middle of a sentence about what we should all do when he literally fell over and smashed into the podium, crashed out from being so drunk. We all just shrugged and left the meeting. It was turning into a pretty strange place by 1973."

"He was a heavy drinker," recounted Noonan. "It was obvious to all of us—you smelled the liquor on this breath. And he was a heavy gambler, even more so than Gordy. The alcohol didn't help, and he couldn't afford to lose nearly as much as Gordy could."

Abner even managed to anger the industry's powerful black DJs. When Abner picked up the American Music Awards' Best Vocal Group trophy for the Temptations in 1974, he profusely thanked Dick Clark in his acceptance speech but omitted any reference to the DJs who had regularly played the Temptations throughout their careers. That slight led to a concerted effort to teach Motown a lesson, using the Tempts' "Heavenly," which was then moving up the charts. The DJs simply stopped playing it, and the song nose-dived and disappeared in nine weeks.

And Abner was not the only problem at Motown. In the creative division, while many recognized Suzanne de Passe's innovative thinking, few admired her administrative skills. Production costs ballooned over budget, and release dates slipped. When a group of Motown artists and producers met outside the building to discuss the problems and what to do about them, the company had some security men conspicuously sitting in cars outside their meeting place, jotting down the names of those who attended.

"As the Motown ship began sinking," Mary Wilson later recalled, "the rest of us went down with it."

Gordy was unaware that his selections—particular Abner—were widely considered disastrous. Few called him BG any longer—Motown had grown into a far-flung, larger company, and he was now simply known as the chairman. And Gordy had adopted the trappings of power, tinged with mistrust and suspicion. He often traveled under false names, used disguises sometimes, and had his own growing entourage. He had become, at least in his

own mind, every bit the star that any of his singers were. On more than a
few occasions he considered himself far too busy with movies to get involved in the less glamorous music side of the business.

His interest revived briefly when Marvin Gaye renegotiated a multiyear
deal after the success of *Let's Get It On.* He got a multimillion-dollar package and demanded that Gordy personally sign a one-million-dollar check to
him. Gordy did so, just as he was boarding a flight for Europe, and Gaye was
briefly content, although he soon was scattered among projects in acting,
television, and even an invention to supposedly help people know themselves better.

Gordy's one major concern on the music side came when Stevie Wonder
was in a terrible car accident. Wonder had been riding in a car driven by his
cousin John Harris. They were on the way from Greenville, South Carolina,
to a concert in Raleigh, when their car collided with a trailer truck loaded
with logs. One of the logs smashed the car's windshield and slammed into
Wonder's head, and he was comatose in the local hospital.

"He's not expected to live" was the way that Esther Gordy broke the
news at 3:00 A.M. to her startled brother. It had been eleven years since
Gordy had been woken by a similarly disturbing call in which he had
learned of the serious car wreck involving Beans Bowles and Eddie McFarland.

"I couldn't even recognize him," recalled Ira Tucker, Wonder's publicist,
of when he first saw the performer in the hospital. "His head was swollen
up about five times the normal size." Wonder regained semiconsciousness
in three days, but it took another week before the doctors were certain he
would survive without any neurological damage. His only permanent damage turned out to be his loss of smell. When he was well enough, Gordy
flew him to UCLA Medical Center for rehabilitation. And seven months
after the accident, a period in which he turned increasingly to a fervent religious belief, Wonder had recovered enough to attend the Grammys. Wonder, who has a reputation for being notoriously late for appointments,
recording sessions, and even concerts, made the show on time. He had good
reason for being prompt, as he had been nominated for six Grammys, the
most at that time in the history of the awards. He won five, including one
for album of the year for *Innervisions.* In 1974, Wonder would bag another
five, four of them for his album *Fulfillingness' First Finale.* The following year,

when the Grammy Awards were presented, and Paul Simon won Album of the Year, he thanked Wonder for "not making an album this year."

⋅ ⋅ ⋅

Only years later did Gordy realize how critical a time the mid-1970s were for him. "Being an entrepreneur the way I was," he said, "having a hand in everything at my company, had always worked for me. I can see it was around this time . . . that it started working against me. The executive chain of command was fuzzy since everybody knew only one real boss—me. And their boss had a major preoccupation—making his second movie, *Mahogany.*"

CHAPTER 29

Mahogany

MAHOGANY BECAME DIANA ROSS'S SECOND MOVIE PROJECT AND a time-consuming obsession for Gordy. After the success of *Lady Sings the Blues,* Gordy paid Ross one million dollars per year just to keep her tied exclusively to Motown as an actress while he searched for a new project. Although Ross's Oscar nomination had brought in an early batch of scripts, none seemed right. He suggested to one interviewer that she could become a "black Barbra Streisand." Gordy assigned Rob Cohen, a twenty-three-year-old producer he had hired on a hunch to run Motown Productions, to find a follow-up. Gordy preferred a role where Ross would not sing because he wanted to burnish her credentials as a dramatic actress. And he wanted to team her up again with Billy Dee Williams, since he thought he could create a leading-couple franchise in the mode of Fred Astaire and Ginger Rogers or Spencer Tracy and Katharine Hepburn.

The search ended when Cohen, Shelly Berger, and a writer, Bob Merrill, joined Gordy one day for lunch at his home and told him about a story of a young woman from Chicago's ghettos who dreamed of being, and became, a top fashion designer. At the height of her success, while in Europe, she realized that her happiness was to be found back in her own inner-city neighborhood. Gordy told the trio that the project was "a no-brainer." Ross loved fashion, so he assumed she would be a natural to live out her designer fantasies. There was an almost tailor-made part for Billy Dee Williams as a lover. (For the role of a crazed photographer, *Psycho*'s Anthony Perkins would eventually be cast.) Gordy wanted Tony Richardson, the well-known British director of *Tom Jones*, to shoot the film.

When the proper Englishman first visited Gordy at his Bel Air home, he was fascinated at the extensive security, which included four armed body-guards, surveillance cameras, guard dogs, and a car that followed his up the long driveway. Richardson called them the "Berry Mafia." At that meeting, Richardson noticed that Gordy had a lot of peacocks in his lush gardens. Richardson had peacocks at his St. Tropez home but noticed the ones at Gordy's estate were quiet. When he mentioned that, Gordy answered very matter-of-factly, "That's cause I had their fuckin' voice boxes cut out. I hate the way those little fuckers squawk." Richardson smiled. As he later told a reporter, "I liked the dangerous side of Berry Gordy Jr." It was at that meeting that Richardson also discovered Gordy's favorite line about Ross: "Diana isn't a personality, she's a product." Richardson agreed to direct.

This time, Paramount required he put up only half the money. The studio promised he would still have the control, as the movie's executive producer, to do the film the way he wanted.

Two weeks into production, the crew began filming in Chicago's rough Southside neighborhood. Gordy's mother had flown in to watch, accompanied by Tony Greene, a longtime family friend who acted as her personal assistant. Even with the tall, stout Greene watching over her, Gordy was nervous that his mother had decided to visit such a tough neighborhood. Tony Richardson did not ease Gordy's anxiety. Richardson, wearing a long fur coat, kept barking sharp orders at black residents who occasionally walked into one of the shots. Richardson also seemed to avoid Gordy. Fidgeting for a while on the edge of the set, Gordy finally pulled Rob Cohen aside and asked him to bring Richardson over so he could tell him to tone down his imperious manner. Cohen informed Gordy that Richardson not only did not want to talk to him but did not want anything to do with him. Gordy, whose money was on the line, was angry, but he did not then confront Richardson.

Gordy had started seeing the daily film clips. He felt they were lifeless and that his money was "going down the drain." His frustration finally exploded about 2:00 A.M. one morning at Chicago's Astor Hotel. Gordy was pacing from room to room, with Cohen scurrying to keep up with him. He was fuming that Richardson was ruining his movie. When Gordy indicated he might fire Richardson, Cohen laid out the consequences. The crew could walk off the set, thereby closing the production and causing Paramount to consider the film a troubled one and lose confidence in it. The cost of starting with a new crew and director would be exorbitant. The picture might never be finished.

Gordy agreed to let Cohen have a frank discussion with Richardson to patch things up between them. The next day, Cohen's father unexpectedly died. Before grabbing a flight home, Cohen warned Gordy not to do anything rash while he was gone.

"Stupid I'm not," Gordy had assured him. "I won't even go near him."

The next day, Gordy received a frantic call from Ross on the set. She was excited, and her words rushed out in a torrent. "Black, we got a real problem down here. I need you to come right away. I don't want to get into a fight with Tony."

Richardson was preparing to direct a critical scene in which Ross's character was raped. Ross did not like the actor Richardson had chosen to play the rapist. She preferred another actor, but Richardson did not think he looked the part. When Gordy arrived, Richardson was actually happy to see him, hoping he might calm the furious Ross. Gordy had both actors read for the role. After that, Richardson agreed that the actor Ross wanted was better. The crisis appeared over.

After they started shooting a street scene, Ross again called Gordy. Richardson had only pretended to like the actor she wanted and had reverted to his original choice. Gordy returned to the set and confronted the director. "I thought we agreed on the smaller guy."

"We did," said Richardson in his clipped British accent, glancing up at Gordy. "But I changed my mind."

Gordy was not about to stand down in such a public venue. He said he wanted his choice to play the role. Richardson had dismissed him. Gordy ordered one of his assistants to go and fetch him, and the actor was intercepted before he left the set and brought back to the assembled group. Richardson was not fazed. "Oh, so he's back I see. But I'm not going to use him at all."

Gordy told Richardson again that he wanted him in the scene.

"No."

"OK, Tony," Gordy said, suddenly dropping his voice to a hoarse whisper so Ross and the crew could not hear him, "I'm begging you to please put the man back in as you promised."

Richardson shook his head no.

"OK," Gordy's voice started rising, "then I'm telling you precisely, put the man back in!"

"And I'm telling you precisely, no!"

"You're fired."

Richardson was nonplussed. He turned to his technical staff, composed mostly of fellow Brits with whom he had worked on many projects, and simply announced, "I've just been fired." He then turned back to Gordy. "OK, it's all yours." Then he walked off the set. (Richardson never watched the finished film. Some acquaintances say Richardson so disliked working with Gordy and Ross that he was pleased to get fired, since that entitled him to be paid the two hundred thousand dollars due under his contract. That would not have happened if he had just quit out of his own frustration.)

Gordy stood there in shock. He looked around the street at the giant lights illuminating the area, at the assembled actors, and at the crew. Everyone waited to see what he would do. Gordy decided to direct the rape scene. He used the actor he and Ross wanted. He was so nervous and keyed up about taking on the new role of director that when the scene finished he broke into applause. The crew, not sure what to do, joined him. Only after Shelly Berger whispered in his ear that he should say "Cut" did Gordy issue the command to stop the filming.

The crew helped Gordy set up subsequent shots because he was in the dark about how to do it. Somehow, several scenes got shot that night. And while Gordy was pleased that he handled it, he was also anxious because he knew the next day he had to call Paramount's Barry Diller in New York. Diller, relatively new at Paramount's helm, was the person who had given *Mahogany* the green light, in part because he liked Tony Richardson as director.

Their conversation lasted less than a minute. Although Diller was surprised to learn about Richardson's firing, he also acted pleased that Gordy was directing.

The problem that developed for Gordy in his new role was an unexpected one: friction with Ross. They had fought as a couple, but now over the movie their words seemed more cutting. Gordy had allowed Ross to design her own gowns for the movie, and by the time the crew reached Rome for shooting she was spending so much time on the designs that she was getting little sleep. Irritable and tired, her scenes were frequently flat or had to be reshot. Gordy recalled that she had "become bone thin," but whenever he mentioned that to her she became angry and snapped. And the more he pushed, the more she resented him. At times, he harshly chastised her, often in front of the rest of the cast.

By the beginning of 1975, a couple of months after production had begun, the shooting was seriously behind schedule. As Gordy tried to figure out how to get back on track, he received the news that his mother had suffered a cerebral hemorrhage and was not expected to live. He left Shelly Berger—who had no experience either—in the director's chair and hurried back to Los Angeles.

The Gordy family kept his mother on life support until Berry arrived. After he saw her, the medical equipment was disconnected, and Mother Gordy died. Her death brought Gordy back temporarily from the problems of *Mahogany* to more overwhelming personal ones. Just a year before his mother's death, his father had fallen ill at the age of eighty-five. Although Gordy Sr. had survived his ordeal, complications from diabetes led to the amputation of his left leg above the knee. Now he seemed a broken man. (He lived another five years.) Gordy tried to give him and the rest of the family some support, but he could not long stay away from the film, as his financial independence rode on its success. He made all the arrangements for the funeral and then flew back to Rome. His father and sister Esther followed a few weeks later to watch him direct, and Gordy put them into the film as extras.

Diana Ross had become increasingly difficult, the shooting was still behind schedule, and Gordy was not pleased with many of the takes. A couple of weeks before the shooting ended, Gordy almost lost it. In the middle of a difficult scene, on which he was shooting many takes, Rob Cohen approached him and gently suggested that he "speed it up."

The comment struck Gordy the wrong way. He stood up from the director's chair, told Cohen to direct the film himself, and started walking away.

"Oh, no, wait a minute," Cohen yelled out. "Berry, wait, Berry. . . ." Cohen ran up to Gordy's side and tried calming him. "Exactly what I had done for so many years with other stars," Gordy thought to himself. "Yes, me, I was now a star!"

The film's associate producer, Neil Hartley, ran over and also tried to salve Gordy's bruised ego. Gordy would not budge. Finally, Shelly Berger gently grabbed Gordy by the elbow and calmly took him a few feet away from the others. Then he leaned over and whispered, "Who in the fuck are you kidding? You're not some director working for somebody else who's going to suffer if you walk off and have to kiss your ass to keep you on the film. This is *your* film, *your* money! You're not going anywhere, so why don't you go on up there and get your shit together and finish the movie?"

"Fuck you," Gordy said to him, then turned and walked back to the director's chair to prepare for the next take.

While Rob Cohen's plea had set off Gordy, his real frustration, he later admitted, was Ross. And this brief blowout was only a mild prelude to what soon happened.

As the shooting neared its finish in February 1975, Ross came to the set one day, as Gordy described it, "with her nerves on edge." She was dismissive of whatever Gordy said, whether or not it was complimentary. After shooting a pickup scene—snippets needed to provide continuity—Gordy informed Ross she had to do another take.

For whatever reason, that pushed Ross over the edge. She swiveled to face him. Her large, dark eyes flashed anger. "No we're not. I'm going home!"

Gordy was surprised. The crew became quiet and watched to see what would happen next.

Gordy told her he wanted another take. He had barely finished speaking when one of Ross's hands shot out from her side and caught him with a loud slap across his face. She hit him so hard that his glasses flew across the room. Following that sound, the only noise was the click of Ross's heels as she turned and stormed off. Some members of the crew stood there with their mouths open. A few stifled laughs and smirks. Gordy looked around in embarrassment, and then scurried off after Ross. He refused to believe that she was really going to leave the set. But when he walked inside her trailer, she was furiously throwing her things together.

He began pleading with her. She couldn't do this to him and the movie.

"Don't tell me what I can't do. I'm leaving!" There was rage in her voice.

He needed one more day, he told her.

She just kept packing.

"Diana, listen, it's about principle, too. You don't walk out on any film, but especially this one. My money is in it. I put it up for you. If you walk out now, you know that I can never ever do another movie with you where I put up money."

She did not look at him or say a word. She merely picked up her bag and determinedly walked out of the trailer.

Gordy was stunned. But that night and the following day, he scrambled—mostly in a daze—to finish. Edna Anderson, Gordy's secretary, doubled for Ross's arms and hands in pickup shots. No one noticed in the final film.

The movie may not have been hurt by Ross's late departure, but Gordy was devastated. After years of tumult and repeated published reports that the two had secretly married, she had walked out on him in front of dozens of people. It was the first time in their relationship that he had not made the decision. His friends remember that he was subdued for weeks, his normal spark nowhere to be found.

Actually, during the filming, Gordy had had a new woman in his life, Nancy Leiviska, a beautiful blonde who worked at Motown. Their one-year relationship resulted in Gordy's eighth child, Stefan, born in September 1975. But the strains caused by the film and Gordy's constant bickering with Ross put an end to this affair just as the final editing began on *Mahogany*. Gordy immersed himself in the cutting. He also managed to ignore everything happening at Motown, leaving Ewart Abner to cope with an increasingly dissatisfied staff and roster of artists. The music side of the business meandered without direction or focus.

CHAPTER 30

Hunting Season

GORDY GOT A TELEPHONE CALL WHILE HE WAS CELEBRATING HIS son Terry's high school graduation. It was son-in-law Jermaine Jackson who broke the news that the Jacksons were considering leaving Motown.

A number of their releases—the rhythm and blues "Little Bitty Pretty One," "Lookin' Through the Windows," and "Corner of the Sky"—had had lukewarm receptions. The first two sold a half-million copies each, the poorest Jackson numbers to date. "Corner of the Sky" sold only 380,000.

Joe Jackson showed up at Motown and berated the public-relations and sales staff: "What the hell is going on?" In February 1973, Motown had released "Hallelujah Day," a record it hoped would reverse the Jacksons' sliding fortune. A simple little song, it flopped, selling fewer than 250,000 copies, a new Jacksons low. The next, "Skywriter," sold only 115,000 copies. Not only had single sales dropped precipitously, but the Jacksons' album sales—another measure of their success—had also been sliding. As far as Joe Jackson was concerned, the reason was Motown's failure to promote his sons. Ewart Abner would hear none of it. He made a quick enemy of Joe by suggesting that maybe the group was to blame for its falloff and that its success might have run its course. Gordy, obsessed with *Mahogany*, did not interfere but from afar supported Abner's view that Joe Jackson was well-meaning but off base.

Personal problems complicated the Jacksons' situation. Katherine Jackson had sued for divorce, prompted by Joe's philandering, which had resulted in the pregnancy of his twenty-six-year-old mistress. Michael, meanwhile, was increasingly perturbed at his perception that he was being treated like a mere commodity by both his family and the label. More sensitive than his four brothers, he was tiring of the fifty-city tours and the restrictive security insisted upon by Motown. He was even chastised for taking time out from his rigorous practice schedule to watch Saturday-morning cartoons. And Michael hated the mob scenes that greeted the group when they traveled—at London's Heathrow Airport, for instance, the crowd was so uncontrollable that it surged through police barriers and mobbed the boys before they could get safely inside their limos. Jermaine had chunks of his hair yanked out, and Michael was almost choked when fans started pulling in opposite directions on the scarf around his neck. "You feel as if you're going to suffocate or be dismembered," he later said.

Michael also bristled at the sexual flings his slightly older brothers, just past puberty, were enjoying with young groupies. He resorted, on occasion, to trying to warn away girls. He told one who had been given an address by Jackie Jackson, "My brothers, sometimes they don't treat girls too good. They can be mean. I don't know why they do these things, but they do. Please don't go." His father, who thought fifteen-year-old Michael would be more attractive to his female fans if he gave up his celibacy, locked him in a Las Vegas hotel room with two prostitutes. They failed to arouse him, and his father berated him as a "sissy." Conversely, in Motown, executives fretted that Michael's wonderfully distinctive voice might change—instead of embracing any changes and adapting the music to them, they instead talked callously of administering hormones to him or surgically altering him, as seventeenth-century castrati had been.

When Michael's fourth solo album, *Forever Michael*, was released and stalled at a miserable 101 on the charts—his worst album showing to date—Joe started talking secretly to CBS Records. "That's it!" he had exclaimed. "He's not recording any more solo albums for Gordy. That man's gonna ruin Michael!" Joe had also come to realize that his sons would never make enormous money until they owned the publishing rights to their songs, income that Motown would not share.

Gordy was stunned to learn he might lose the Jacksons. They still had a year on their contract, and, since he hadn't been paying attention, he was unaware of their dissatisfaction.

Now sixteen-year-old Michael met with Gordy before the family made a final decision and courageously told Gordy that he and his brothers resented that they had no freedom to write songs, produce albums, or own publishing rights to the tunes they sang.

"We're all unhappy, Mr. Gordy," Michael told him. "Do you really want us to leave Motown, or what?"

Gordy became defensive. He told Michael that without Motown the group would still be in Gary.

"That doesn't exactly answer my question, Mr. Gordy."

Even after listening to a further litany of complaints that bothered the Jacksons, Gordy was dismissive. He had heard similar gripes from artists for years. If there was a better deal elsewhere, Gordy said he knew the Jacksons would consider it, but that they would stay because Motown was their family. When the meeting finished, Gordy hugged his young star and promised he would not do anything to hurt him or his family.

Michael left feeling that Gordy was not receptive to anything he had said.

CBS made a lucrative bid: a $750,000 signing bonus, a $500,000 recording-fund advance, and $350,000 guaranteed for every album, far more than they received at Motown. It also offered them a 27 percent royalty rate, versus Motown's tiny 2.7 percent rate. The Jacksons agreed to switch labels.

Because of his marriage to Gordy's daughter, Jermaine was torn between his birth family and Motown. In an angry confrontation at the family home, Joe Jackson tried to force Jermaine to stay with his siblings, but Jermaine would not commit. He ran out of the house to avoid his father's anger. The Jacksons were furious with Gordy, suspecting that he was breaking up their act. Finally, one night, just before the group was about to take the stage at the Westbury Music Fair on Long Island, Jermaine announced that he was staying with Motown and walked out. Joe Jackson was emotionally spent from the ordeal.

"It's my blood that flows through Jermaine's veins," Joe said, shaking his head, "not Berry Gordy's."

Joe's other sons were almost pleased to see Jermaine stand up to their bullying father. Even after they had achieved such incredible success and Joe no longer beat them physically, he continued berating them, often in public.

"You all are nuthin', " he would say, or else he would say with a laugh that they were "weird." Criticizing them as overpampered kids, he systematically undermined their self-respect. Yet now that he was in a war with Gordy, none of those sons except for Jermaine had found the courage to leave.

At Gordy and Abner's direction, Mike Roshkind called Joe Jackson to inform him that by contract the company owned the rights to the Jackson 5 name. Roshkind demanded that the Jacksons stop using it. With Jermaine's departure, the baby-faced eleven-year-old Randy had now joined the group, so its original name still fit. Motown and the Jacksons fought over the group's name for the next three years. Finally, Michael persuaded his father to just call the group the Jacksons. And while Roshkind had publicly threatened to cobble together another boys' band and name it the Jackson 5, Motown never did.

Gordy called on the Reverend Jesse Jackson to help him. While at Motown, the group had done several fund-raising performances for Jackson's Rainbow PUSH (People United to Save Humanity) organization. Gordy now asked Jackson to prevent CBS from stealing a black act from a black label. Jackson met with CBS officials but to no avail.

The Noveck brothers convinced Gordy that he had to sue CBS and the Jacksons, if only to let other Motown artists know there was a cost to breaking their contracts. Gordy sued CBS and its subsidiary Epic Records for twenty million dollars and the Jacksons for five million in damages. The Jacksons countersued, claiming that Motown had cheated them out of royalties and that inflated expenses charged against their accounts had defrauded the family. As under its other contracts, Motown charged all recording expenses to the group, even for songs that were never released. During the six years they were at Motown, the Jackson 5 recorded and were charged for 469 songs. Of those, only 174 were released (that was a better ratio than for many other artists at Motown, some of whom had only 10 percent of their recordings released). According to Gordy, the Jacksons still owed the label a half-million dollars in recording expenses for the unreleased songs. Four years later, the Jacksons and Gordy settled, with the Jacksons paying one hundred thousand dollars, less than Gordy's legal costs.

Michael Jackson's debut CBS album, *Off the Wall,* sold more than seven million copies. Released at the close of 1979, it was the biggest album of 1980. And it was far more sophisticated than the bubble gum to which

Gordy had restricted the group. Jackson's follow-up, *Thriller*, is still the biggest-selling album in music history, at more than forty-five million copies.

"At that time," recalled Gordy, "I didn't know the full extent of what losing an act like the J-5 would be. I also did not know that in the industry it was hunting season and Motown was the biggest game in town."

Many Motown executives, however, believed that the Jacksons were lost primarily through the negligence of Ewart Abner. When Joe Jackson had first approached Abner about the contract and asked for considerably more money, Abner not only failed to tell Berry about the overture but then insulted the Jacksons with a lowball offer. By the time Gordy learned of the snafu, the Jacksons were on their way to CBS for three times the money they might have accepted with Motown. There were even suspicions by some inside Motown's promotion and sales department that Abner actually encouraged other music-company honchos to steal some key acts, putting up a feigned fight and in return pocketing bribes for his treachery. Although this is unproved, the fact that key Motown executives talked among themselves about that possibility—and in some cases adamantly believed it—is further indication of how poisonous the atmosphere was in the label's hierarchy.

The few times that Gordy did get involved, he seemed distracted and anxious to return to films. For instance, when the Temptations went through a slump in the mid-1970s, they met with Gordy and pleaded with him to let them form their own publishing company. "Basically, we were grown men and artists," recalled Otis Williams, "and felt that if we did write anything we should have our own publishing." Gordy, accompanied by his brother Robert, ridiculed the idea. "What are you going to do with publishing? Who's going to administer it?" Gordy treated the group as though they were children incapable of doing anything without Motown. And as he talked, he got angrier that the Tempts had even bothered. "We could see spittle forming at the corners of his mouth," recalled Williams. The Tempts left the meeting in a fury. "Damn it," said Williams, "we weren't kids anymore, and the very least he could have done was meet us halfway. . . . It was insulting."

The same thing happened to Smokey Robinson, Gordy's last earnest defender at the label. When Smokey was to meet with Gordy and ask for the rights to form his own publishing company, Gordy showed up late and then kept taking phone calls.

"Berry," Smokey told him, "this is important to me. I want to start keeping my own copyrights."

"I wish you wouldn't bother me with this piddly shit right now, Smoke. I'm in the middle of making a movie and—"

"It's not piddly to me, Berry."

"Look, you can have your publishing, you can have anything you want, but leave me alone 'cause I don't have time for it." Then Gordy stood up and walked out. While they reconciled months later—with Smokey getting his publishing rights—Gordy's dismissive attitude "haunted" Smokey.

It is little wonder, as soul scholar Nelson George wrote, "Since the early 1970s, the magic of Motown was dead. It was now just another record company."

·   ·   ·

Gordy was not showing much better judgment in spotting real troubles on *Mahogany.* He was too close to Diana Ross to have enough perspective to do a tight edit. And since it was largely his money, those working with him feared contradicting his directives, even when they thought he was wrong.

The night before the New York premiere, Paramount executives attended a private screening. Gordy sat in his hotel suite and, with the help of several stiff drinks, tried to convince himself that everything would be fine. Later that night, Roshkind called with the sobering news that the executives had not liked it. Gordy was defensive but spent the rest of the night tossing in bed, unable to understand what everyone—except him, evidently—missed about the film. The next day, at the opening, Gordy was stunned that the theater was only partially filled and that the applause at the end was at best lukewarm. For the first week, the movie drew strong crowds in Los Angeles and New York, but it fell off quickly because of poor word of mouth. While the sound track was climbing to number one, the movie drew ever-dwindling audiences.

Reviews for the film were mostly savage. Gordy thought they were so harsh that they made the bad ones for *Lady Sings the Blues* "sound like love letters."

"Berry panicked after reading the first line of the *Time* magazine critique," recalled Rob Cohen. It chastised him for "squandering one of America's most natural resources: Diana Ross." "Berry was like a raging bull," said Cohen. "He was crazed."

Beyond the financial one, Gordy considered *Mahogany* a personal disaster, since he knew his relationship with Ross would never be the same. The line from the movie, "Success is nothing without someone you love to share it with," hit close to home.

CHAPTER 31

"Problems
All Over the Place"

GORDY WAS HAVING TROUBLE STOPPING MOTOWN'S DECLINE.
Revenues were way down. For a company accustomed to successive chart
hits, far fewer were breaking into the top ten. Gordy seemed overwhelmed
by his problems and kept telling himself, in a surprising bout of defeatism,
that he was inadequate to the challenge of turning Motown around. He
brought in more outside consultants to analyze the company. Based on their
suggestions, he hired new executives who often had little music experience,
hoping they could revitalize the flagging bottom line. But the problems actually worsened, forcing established Motown executives to become more in-
sular and in some cases to refuse to cooperate with the newcomers. Moreover,
Gordy exacerbated the problems by keeping close personal relationships
with a few workers, such as Suzanne de Passe. Whenever de Passe had a
problem with one of the new corporate managers, she appealed directly to
Gordy, who weighed in on her side even when he was not familiar with the
details.

"I wanted to revive the old days," Gordy later recalled. "I wanted a czar-
like character—a screaming, scheming, get-things-done, calculating, demanding kind—to run the company." Gordy was describing the kind of
company chief he had been in his younger days, but somehow he had lost
the zeal and fire.

In 1975, Ewart Abner resigned, under a growing chorus of criticism, as
Motown's president. Gordy reached out to Barney Ales, who had left three

years earlier. He pleaded with Ales to turn the company around. Ales had started his own small Detroit-based independent, Prodigal Records, when he had left Motown. Gordy also asked to buy Prodigal and its tiny roster of artists, hoping that it might revitalize Motown's pop-rock offerings, which were almost dormant on its Rare Earth label.

Ales says "they made me an offer I couldn't refuse," with potential equity if he could work wonders. Ales's children had moved out, his father had passed away, his mother had moved to Houston, and he had completed some other obligations that had split his time between Detroit and Florida, so he was free to relocate to Los Angeles. After discussing it with his wife, Mitzi, he accepted a chance at Motown redux. Ales sold Prodigal to Gordy, and promised to make Motown "the number-one record company again."

Phil Jones—who was back at Motown after Abner's departure—had previously worked for Ales and was a senior vice president in sales and marketing when Gordy reached out to Ales. He tried to talk Gordy out of it. "I told Berry it was a big mistake." Jones told Gordy not to trust Ales, who he believed was looking out for his own interests over those of Motown. "But I make a lot of money with him," said Gordy, "more than I do without him." "Boy, Barney had a bigger ego than Berry. He must have had some real dirt on Berry," joked Jones, "because none of us could figure why Berry found him worth the trouble to get along with."

Suzanne de Passe was also not happy to see Ales return, but she knew it was futile to try to stop his rehiring. She figured that he was so headstrong that eventually he would flame out. Ales openly expressed his disdain for her to his colleagues. Today, he says, "Suzanne de Passe had no creativity. I brought back the creativity when I returned." Some in the company shared his view, and Ales rallied them. Tom Noonan, for instance, said that "Suzanne spent 80 percent of the A&R budget and produced only 20 percent of our income. She lost Thelma Houston [a disco diva with a distinctive quavering, gospel-based delivery], instead wasting her time with a young female singer that she was intrigued by but who went nowhere." But others thought Ales was threatened by de Passe's talent. "Suzanne was very creative and smart," said Phil Jones. "And she had Berry's ear, and that scared the hell out of Barney. Barney was very shrewd and played the political infighting game very well. But he knew Suzanne could not have her feet knocked out from under her."

Initially, Ales did rework some of his old magic. Stevie Wonder's 1976 *Songs in the Key of Life* album entered the pop chart at number one and stayed there for fourteen weeks. The album also won four Grammys for Wonder, including Album of the Year. Everyone was happy for Wonder except for Marvin Gaye, who was increasingly trapped in a web of drugs, prostitutes, and physical and psychological masochism. "Of course I was jealous of Stevie," Gaye said. "How could I not be?"

Ales also worked hard to make a breakthrough with the six-member Commodores, an act Motown had signed in 1971. Ales thought the lead singer, Lionel Richie, also showed tremendous promise as a solo act. Ales's intuition on the Commodores was right, as eventually the group had fourteen top-ten R&B hits, six of which went to number one.

·   ·   ·

But not everything was smooth under Ales. The label continued to suffer artist defections to other labels. These had steadily drained the company for several years but now picked up speed. Some groups had simply broken up (the Marvelettes, for instance, who went on to sue Motown and Gordy for back royalties). The Four Tops went to ABC. "We left Motown," Duke Fakir recalled, "because there was no enthusiasm there. They seemed more interested in making movies than concentrating on their recording acts." The Four Tops also complained about not getting paid, and as for the royalties they did receive, they had often lost them in marathon poker games at Gordy's house.

Gladys Knight and the Pips and Martha and the Vandellas left soon after the Tops. Gordy was upset when Gladys Knight and the Pips went to Buddha Records and immediately had a number-one pop hit with "Midnight Train to Georgia," but he was even more upset when Knight sued him and Motown for $1.7 million in back royalties.

A year after Ales returned, the Miracles left, tempted by a large offer from CBS. (Smokey Robinson, who had already gone solo, stayed at Motown.) The Temptations were next, charging that Motown had failed to promote their recent albums. Further, because of vicious office politics, "it was really time for us to get away from there," said Otis Williams.

Many of the groups might have stayed if they had been handled correctly. The Temptations, for instance, had hired an aggressive local attorney, Abe Somers, to renegotiate their contract. Ales refused to deal with him and demanded that the group fire him. The group refused and appealed to Gordy for help. He never called back. The group decided to leave. When Lee Young Jr., another Motown executive, made a last-ditch effort to find out how much money they wanted, he was surprised to be told they mainly wanted to be treated with respect. That was something Motown no longer provided. Gordy "considered himself above the artists at this point," said Jay Lasker. The Tempts, too, had to fight Motown for the return of their name.

Besides the artists, producers such as Harvey Fuqua, Johnny Bristol, and Nick Ashford and Valerie Simpson fled the chaos of a record label with no direction. Norman Whitfield left to form his own company, Whitfield Records (which folded after seven years of mediocrity). The Motown sales department had been emptied by key departures. Ewart Abner had proven as disastrous a chief executive as many had feared. Gordy, who later said that he felt Abner was responsible for the slide for at least four years, had made little effort to bring him into line.

The unexpected death of former Supreme Flo Ballard in February 1976 worsened the feeling of malaise at the label. Ballard, who tried establishing a solo career after Gordy had dismissed her, had seen her career sputter along in a nonstop series of appearances at honky-tonk bars and dives. With her boyfriend as her hapless manager, she did not take long to exhaust her fifteen-thousand-dollar Motown settlement, which she had agreed to without the benefit of an attorney. When she finally hired lawyers, she was able to get a $160,000 additional payment, though no right to earn royalties from her previous recordings. She later sued Motown for $8.7 million, claiming that the company had secretly conspired with Diana Ross to oust her from the group and failed to accurately report her royalties. Her case was dismissed.

Ballard had given birth to three children since leaving the group. She put on considerable weight and battled depression. In the early 1970s, her house was repossessed. She was broke at twenty-seven. Abandoned by her boyfriend and having pawned all her jewelry, she applied for welfare and moved into public housing in Detroit. There, she was mugged twice. Occasionally, she complained to local reporters of mysterious phone calls and said unknown forces had conspired to humiliate her. When Mary Wilson learned of her plight, she brought her onstage for a final song during one Supremes' show, hoping it might fire her to restart her solo career. But after,

Ballard seemed more depressed than ever. "She just looked up at me," recalled Wilson, "like a child who'd been beaten."

"Mary, leave me alone," Ballard said in a barely audible monotone. "Don't you realize it's over? I don't want to do it anymore. Just leave me alone."

In February 1976, when Ballard's daughter Nicole called some of Ballard's brothers and sisters, worried that her mother was having trouble breathing in the middle of the night, they dismissed it as another attempt to get attention. No one seemed overly concerned that Ballard was already on high-blood-pressure medication and carried nearly two hundred pounds on her small frame. The next day, she was almost comatose, and one day later she was dead, at the age of thirty-two, from cardiac arrest. The medical examiner found both alcohol and an unknown amount of pills in her.

At the Detroit funeral home where Ballard's corpse was taken, large crowds gathered, most of them early Supremes' fans. Anger and grief were the prevailing moods, as many were disgusted at how Ballard's life had ended in poverty and depression. At the New Bethel Baptist Church the following day, where Aretha Franklin's father, the Reverend C. L. Franklin, oversaw the service, thousands of fans lined the streets for blocks around. Extra police did their best to keep the crowds back.

As Mary Wilson drove up to the funeral in a Rolls-Royce, she saw old faces from the projects where the girls grew up. "When Motown had moved to Los Angeles in 1975," said Mary Wilson, "part of Detroit died. Today, though, the city was alive for one more day." Some fans had dressed for the funeral in mink coats and tuxedos, while others were in housecoats or tattered jeans. When Diana Ross arrived, surrounded by four burly bodyguards, the crowd surged forward, hissing and booing. She seemed nervous and pained and then let out a loud sob, stumbling so that her bodyguards almost had to carry her by her arms to a pew. It was a more dramatic moment than any scripted scene from her two movies.

Her large floral arrangement, wrapped in a giant satin banner proclaiming I LOVE YOU, BLONDIE, seemed hypocritical. It would appear even more so when, four months later, Ross told an interviewer, "Florence was always on a totally negative trip. She wanted to be a victim. Then when she left the Supremes and the money stopped coming in, it really messed up her head. She was just one of those people you want to grab and shake and yell, 'Get your fucking life together.'"

As the casket was removed after the ceremony, the crowds became unruly, and some in the church tossed elaborate floral arrangements to the fans to distract them while the hearse made a fast getaway. One frightened attendant actually used the base of one of the arrangements as a weapon to fend off the surging crowd.

Berry Gordy didn't even show up. On that frigid February day, Gordy realized finally how far away he had moved from the fans and citizens of Detroit. No longer was he the street hero who had the magic touch and had created a wondrous label that could do no wrong. Now he was the villain, together with his longtime lover, and he knew that many blamed him for Ballard's lonely death. No one at the time knew that Gordy had paid for the funeral, though he had balked at paying five hundred dollars for a simple grave marker.

• • •

Out of sorts, Gordy invited his second wife, Raynoma, who was working at Jobete once again, to join him in his Bel Air house. For a couple of months, she became his constant social companion, taking time off from work, sharing the same bed with him but not reviving a sexual relationship. Gordy was remarkably nostalgic. He told her he had loved her when they married and bemoaned that now, living in a multimillion-dollar home and attended by waiters and assistants, he might never find a woman who loved just him. "I've gained all these riches," he told her, "but I will never have another woman who will love me for just me and not because I'm Berry Gordy."

After Raynoma returned to her Jobete job, Gordy's brother Robert fired her for having taken so much time off. When she called Gordy for help, explaining it had been to help him, he said, "There's nothing I can do about it—you should have been at work." Gordy, whose judgment had once seemed impeccable, now seemed unable to do the right thing in even simple matters.

"Over the years," Gordy wrote years later in his autobiography, "I noticed that many successful entrepreneurs are driven, self-taught people who have a great desire to be loved and respected. Sometimes they create institutions that outgrow their personal style. I think I fit into that category."

CHAPTER 32

"I Felt Like a Failure"

IN MID-1977, GORDY TEMPORARILY BROKE OUT OF HIS FUNK WHEN Motown acquired the film rights to the hit Broadway musical *The Wiz.* It was an all-black show based on *The Wizard of Oz.* A youngster, Stephanie Mills, had played the Broadway lead. Suzanne de Passe was so impressed that she also gave Mills a recording contract. The original idea was to have Mills play Dorothy in the film and then cast prominent black stars in the other roles for drawing power.

Diana Ross heard about it when she was at de Passe's house for dinner one evening, and she said instantly she was interested in playing Dorothy. She told de Passe that she had seen the Broadway show twice and loved it. The problem was that Ross was almost twenty years too old for the part. De Passe quickly changed the subject.

That night, unable to sleep, Ross watched a video of Judy Garland in *The Wizard of Oz.* Impulsively, she called Gordy and told him she wanted to play Dorothy. He asked her if she had been drinking.

"Of course not," she said. "I've been watching *The Wizard of Oz,* and I had this dream or something about being Dorothy and—"

"Forget it," Gordy interrupted her. "What are you, nuts? You're too old to be any damn Dorothy. Now go to sleep." Then he hung up.

However, the next day, Gordy was surprised to learn from Rob Cohen that Universal was willing to pay one million dollars to have Ross in the role. Ross became more insistent, arguing that Dorothy was "ageless" and that the part "is right for my career." When Gordy's choice as director, John Badham, was told that Ross might play Dorothy, he left the project. (Fortunately for him, the next film he directed was *Saturday Night Fever.*)

Ross's badgering was relentless, and, with the million-dollar inducement from Universal, Gordy reluctantly agreed. The movie project went overnight from a small film to a major star vehicle. The budget zoomed to thirty million, three times the combined production costs of *Lady Sings the Blues* and *Mahogany.* Some directors—Herb Ross, Bob Fosse, and Alan Parker—passed. But ultimately, Sidney Lumet agreed to do it. The screenwriter was Joel Schumacher, and Quincy Jones agreed to do the musical score.

After helping to select the key creative people on the project, Gordy virtually dropped out. He did not get involved in the script, filming, or post-production as he had with the earlier films. He simply did not want several months of feuding with his ex-lover.

Lumet and Schumacher updated the story and made it a modern-day Manhattan fantasy. Dorothy became a twenty-four-year-old Harlem school-teacher. Nineteen-year-old Michael Jackson agreed to play the Scarecrow. ("He kind of idolized me," Ross later said, "and he wanted to sing like me.") Nipsey Russell was cast as the Tinman, Ted Ross as the Lion, Richard Pryor as the Wiz, and Lena Horne (Lumet's mother-in-law at the time) as Glinda the Good Witch.

Schumacher was into est—the California-based New Age motivational course that some charged was a cult—as was Ross. Est's simple principles—that people be responsible for themselves and their own decisions—struck a chord with a woman who had been dependent for so long, personally and professionally, on Berry Gordy. The script was filled with est buzz phrases about knowing "who you are" and "sharing your true self." Later, Ross wrote that "the film proved to be tremendously therapeutic for me."

She put her Beverly Hills home up for sale before the shooting started, and moved into a luxurious apartment in the Sherry-Netherland Hotel on New York's Fifth Avenue. Ross had decided she needed to get the feeling of New York if she was to do an inspired acting job.

The film started a thirteen-week shooting schedule in October 1977. No one remembers Gordy ever being on the set. Without him to control Ross, there was no one who could give her direction if she made up her mind about how a scene was to be shot. The following October, when the film was released, it was thoroughly panned. One critic said that instead of Dorothy killing the Wicked Witch of the East, she should "have aimed for the Wicked Witch of est. [The film] is injected with every self-help jargon of the last fifteen years."

The Wiz had a short run and lost considerable money. It was accompanied in 1978 by two other Motown flops, *Thank God It's Friday*, starring the Commodores and set around a single night at a Los Angeles disco, and *Almost Summer*, a light comedy about high school students.

In a business in which people are judged often by what they did last, the turnaround on Gordy from "genius" to "washed up" was swift. And not only was he chastised for his film farces, he was still technically overseeing a label that was floundering in its core business, music. Like many other music-industry executives, he had missed the early disco fever and even failed to move long after it was a dominant trend.

Smokey Robinson hadn't had a hit in so long that producers joked about him. Known as a teacher's pet because of his friendship with Gordy, Smokey had provoked envy for his success and untroubled life, and many were pleased to see him struggle. In addition, an affair with a Playboy bunny and the pressures it placed on him and Claudette had brought Smokey close to a breakdown. He was now often more passionate about golf—a game he started playing with Marvin Gaye and Berry Gordy back in the mid-1960s—than about being in the recording studio.

Marvin Gaye, too, had fallen flat in record sales; moreover, the mercurial singer had secluded himself in Hawaii. His long-standing resentment of managers, record executives, and lawyers had transformed into a crippling paranoia. Self-hate consumed him, as he damned himself for not standing up to Motown to pursue the career he really wanted as a crooner.

When Smokey Robinson, beset with his own problems, arrived in Honolulu in 1979 for a concert, he visited Gaye, in part to see for himself if the rumors about Gaye "coming unwound" were true. The two had developed a close friendship over the years. Smokey affectionately called Gaye "Dad." When he arrived at Gaye's condo, the door was ajar, and Smokey found a group of men sprawled inside on the floor—"the cats looked strung out." When Smokey finally saw Gaye, at the top of a staircase, dressed only in a robe, "I saw by his eyes that he'd been frying his brain with coke." Gaye admitted he had a "little toot problem" but promised Smokey he could stop "whenever I want." He had been a heavy marijuana user since he was twenty. "I stay high," he used to boast, admitting he liked living "life stoned [rather] than straight," and he had now ventured to other drugs, mainly coke. Often, he needed some coke before going into a recording studio, and he later told journalist David Ritz that he almost always recorded high. His divorce from Anna Gordy after fourteen years had been both violent and melancholy. He had locked himself in an apartment, armed with a pistol, and threatened suicide. It was the first of many such threats. On that occasion, Pops Gordy, Berry's father, had talked him into surrendering the weapon.

Gaye's latest crisis was precipitated by a divorce court that had ordered him to give Anna $305,000 from the advance on his next album and $295,000 of its royalties. He had responded sarcastically with one of his weakest artistic efforts, *Here, My Dear.* Gaye was already behind in taxes, alimony, and child-support payments, as well as in paying his musicians. More than a half-million in debt, he had been forced into bankruptcy. Gaye was also thinking of divorcing his second wife, Janis, whom he had almost killed recently in a frenzied knife attack. They had met when he was recording *Let's Get It On* in 1973, when she was only a sixteen-year-old. She had, he said, "appeared as a gift of God." David Ritz said that Janis became an "obsession [that] would possess him totally, changing his music, altering his life, making all other matters mundane. . . . The woman would inspire, engage, and preoccupy him in a manner bordering on madness."

Suffering from what appears to have been serious clinical depression, Gaye had become increasingly reclusive and often remained in his darkened bedroom for weeks. He was further depressed because Gordy had personally vetoed releasing one of his albums the previous year. It was yet another of his attempts to become a crooner by singing ballads and standards.

When Gaye saw Smokey, he launched into a rambling complaint of the difficulty of being a sex symbol and how weary he was of women "dying to screw me." He had gone on tour, something he viewed as selling out, to raise money. But he had blown most of it on bad investments, such as a Los Angeles recording studio and highly speculative oil deals, as well as drugs. When asked once how much he had spent over the years on cocaine, Gaye laughed. "I don't even want to think about it. To be truthful, I've been careful never to keep track. I don't want to know."

Telling Smokey that he wanted to go to Europe to regroup, he asked for five thousand dollars. Smokey thought it likely would end up in Gaye's nose so he put him off by saying he should call the following week in Los Angeles. When Gaye did call, Smokey finally said no. "OK, man, fuck it!" Gaye screamed and slammed the phone down. The two did not talk again for several years.

. . .

As the personal problems for his stars worsened and the company's music revenue fell again, Gordy had concluded that Barney Ales was not revitalizing the company. Moreover, Suzanne de Passe slowly persuaded Gordy that Ales's only motivation was greed and not the company's best interests. By January 1979, the two again parted company, leaving Gordy in despair as he somewhat desperately started looking for someone else to run the label.

"I burned myself out," said Ales. "I had made a lot of money, but I never really knew what happened. There was a year left on my contract, which they paid me for. We weren't meant to work together anymore."

The word quickly spread in the music industry that Motown was having major difficulties.

By 1980, almost three years since his last album release, Stevie Wonder was the artist on whom Gordy and the rest of the company had pinned most of their hope for a revival. Everyone was waiting for the payoff of Wonder's thirteen-million-dollar contract. What Wonder delivered was an unusual collection of songs titled *Journey Through the Secret Life of Plants.* It consisted mostly of cosmic, meandering instrumentals punctuated by some syrupy lyrics. Gordy said that when he first heard it, "I got a sinking feeling it might not be the smash we so desperately needed." Barney Ales had heard some rough cuts before he left Motown. " 'My God,' I thought," said Ales. " 'How could we do this?' It was so terrible. Roshkind was really running the company then. He was good at public relations, and I told him it should be cut from a double album to just one, and even then it won't sell. Vigoda [Wonder's manager] went nuts, and everyone was afraid to tell Stevie it was pure crap."

Based on Wonder's past sales, the sales department wanted to press two million records. Gordy, nervous about the album's commercial appeal, reduced the number to one million. That turned out to be about nine hundred thousand too many.

It was at this time that Gordy made his fateful three-day jaunt to Caesars Palace in Las Vegas to celebrate his fiftieth birthday. He gambled, drank, and cavorted with the young actress Mira Waters and his assistant, Billy Davis. Immediately after that trip, Gordy received the devastating news from his accountant, Harold Noveck, that Motown was insolvent. Although the Noveck brothers had been urging a drastic reduction in expenses, Gordy's first reaction was to attack them for failing to institute better checks and balances. But he quickly backed off. "I knew the responsibility was mine," he later wrote in his autobiography. "I hadn't been paying attention."

The Noveck news was a wake-up call for Gordy. He was desperate to keep Motown strong enough financially that it would not have to sign a national-distribution deal with a larger record company. That would crimp Motown's independence. It would also mean fewer profits, since any larger company would share the income and some equity in Motown itself. Also, it would mean loss of control over the way records were released, promoted, and distributed. Gordy's concerns were soon heightened when he ran into his friend Jerry Moss, one of the cofounders of A&M Records. Moss and his partner, trumpeter Herb Alpert, had decided that the industrywide decline of independent distributors sounded the death knell for companies such as A&M and Motown. They themselves had inked a national-distribution deal with RCA.

Gordy knew that he had to drastically cut costs. He toyed with selling Jobete, which was a cash cow. (Over a seventeen-year span, eighty-six rerecordings of Jobete songs made the *Billboard* top 100 pop chart, and seventy-seven of those were by non-Motown artists. A dozen were top-ten hits.) When he floated the idea of a sale, he got initial responses as high as forty million dollars. So Gordy talked to Stevie Wonder, who had gained control over the publishing rights of his own songs. He said no. That squelched any possible sale.

The Novecks, meanwhile, urged Gordy to be relentless in making cuts. But Gordy could not bring himself to be so. There were a few dismissals from the bloated staff but not enough to improve the bottom line. Gordy did symbolically cut the salaries for top executives and outside consultants by 15 percent. And he took a bank loan for the first time in his career, although profits from Stevie Wonder's "Send One Your Love" and the Commodores' number-one "Still" helped pay off the loan within a year.

Gordy then brought in Jay Lasker—for a three-year, $675,000 contract—in November 1980. He was a white, tough, cigar-chomping veteran. Lasker had, like Ewart Abner before him, been an executive at the failed Vee-Jay Records. Although Lasker was past his prime, he still knew how to pull some tricks to bring in money, which was then Gordy's primary concern. Lasker specialized as a packager, someone who took a company's hits and rereleased them as compilations and "best of" albums. Lasker also had hints of Mafia associations swirling around him, which helped revive the dormant "Motown is run by the Mob" rumors. Lasker rattled many long-time employees and executives when at his first meeting he told them, "If anybody disagrees with me and goes to Berry Gordy and he agrees with you, that's fine. But if he doesn't, you're fired." Phil Jones was dismayed when he learned Lasker was taking charge. "He had a wide reputation as a crook," said Jones. "If you had given me a list with one hundred names on it, I would never have picked him. No one could ever figure out why he was chosen. He stole a lot of dollars."

Fortunately, early in his tenure, Lasker did produce hits from acts like DeBarge, another family of teenagers, and the self-proclaimed punk-funk king, Rick James, a former staff songwriter who had developed an outrageous touring act that included onstage dope smoking and X-rated lyrics. Despite his wild antics, James, Melvin Franklin's nephew, was critically acknowledged as a substantial talent. He wrote, produced, sang, and played most of the instruments on his albums. James had been personally signed by Gordy, sold a lot of albums, and was one of the last major acts Motown broke.

Most important, however, were the Commodores, led by Lionel Richie. They were a pop-and-funk sextet who signed with Motown in 1971. Suzanne de Passe had brought them to the label to open for the Jackson 5 on one of their European tours. The Commodores, largely on the strength of Richie's songwriting, hit their stride as they changed from a hard funk sound influenced by Sly and the Family Stone to more commercial pop tunes and ballads. The group became Motown's biggest-selling act of the 1970s, and from 1974 to 1980, they averaged two million albums a year in addition to their singles. Their 1978 number-one hit, "Three Times a Lady," became the largest-selling Motown single at the time (more than ten million copies).

Lasker knew how to market acts like Rick James and the Commodores, but he did little to develop new talent to expand the label's roster. And Lasker quickly discovered that Motown was a different company than the one he expected to find. Gordy came to his gigantic suite only once every couple of months. But despite his absence, and lack of involvement, Gordy was extremely protective of his family: among others, Robert, Berry's younger brother, was running Jobete, while Berry's son Berry IV directed A&R. Lasker liked Gordy's relatives but found that they often did not have a clue about what they were doing. Lasker said that the "huge nepotism" that BG built was not only costly, it was a morale-killer to the other employees, because they saw BG's basically "incompetent" relatives sitting around doing nothing.

Lasker's leadership mostly reinforced the perception in the industry that Motown was a company with its best days behind it. The repackaging of songs into compilation albums that were sold at discount outlets across the country and through late-night television infomercials tarnished the reputation that Gordy had built. "With all the repackaging going on," commented Raynoma Gordy, "what Motown had to show for itself was a million different albums with 'Baby Love' and no new talent."

Gordy, himself, did not mind that his products were being sold in merchandise bins at discount outlets. At least Lasker was generating cash. In an effort to reclaim some of Motown's old glory, Gordy personally pleaded with the Temptations, who had released two lackluster albums with Atlantic Records, to return. In a tense meeting at Motown's Los Angeles office, both sides aired their grievances. After they did so, they renegotiated, and Gordy even let the Temptations keep the rights to a music-publishing company they had formed during their absence. In the spring of 1980, they released their first new song with Motown, "Power," a tune Gordy had originally written for DeBarge.

But Gordy had little time to savor the Temptations. In December 1980, he got a visit from a stocky man who described himself as the merchandising manager for the heavy-metal rockers Kiss. It wasn't a complete surprise since Diana Ross, who had divorced Bob Silberstein in 1977, was now dating Kiss's lead singer, Gene Simmons. He had left Cher for Ross, who had recently ended her own high-profile affair with Ryan O'Neal. The stranger told Gordy that Ross had an offer from another record company and that if he wanted her to stay at Motown, he would have to match it—the figure was twenty million dollars. The normally voluble Gordy was stunned and only muttered, "Very interesting."

Gordy had understood that after the fallout over *Mahogany*, his relationship with Ross had permanently changed—but he had never contemplated her leaving Motown. He just assumed they "were linked forever." Ross herself had said as much many times. The previous year, when she wanted to open Diana Ross Enterprises, at Hollywood and Vine, Gordy bankrolled the expensive suite, which was heavily staffed to cater to Ross's personal and public-relations wants. All the employees, on their first day of work, were told to call her only *Miss Ross*, never *Ms. Ross*. Behind her back, the standard way of referring to her was "Miss-Ross-to-You." Two other ironclad rules were that no one could ever mention the words *The Supremes* or play any old Motown music. Gordy ignored her eccentricities, such as requiring all employees to take an est course. After est, Ross went a step further and began visiting a well-known swami named Muktananda Paramahansa.

Ross fired people so frequently that Gordy called on Suzanne de Passe to help out. One Motown employee said, "You never recognized the people answering the phone or doing work for her, it was always someone new the next time you called."

Of course, Gordy and others had tolerated Ross's difficult behavior because she was still bringing in money for Motown. In 1979, she completed a six-week, twenty-eight-city concert tour for her album *The Boss*. Gordy charged the enormous costs for the big-budget spectacle to Ross's new company, so she actually lost money. She felt betrayed when she learned that. It set the groundwork for the stranger who now visited Motown.

Making matters worse for Gordy, only a few months earlier Ross's *Diana* had become the biggest-selling solo album of her career. When Gordy was visited by her Kiss representative, a new passionate ballad, "It's My Turn," was climbing the charts. It was her third top-ten single in 1980. The other two had been "Upside Down," which stayed number one for four weeks, and "I'm Coming Out," which peaked at number five.

Gordy ended the meeting with his uninvited visitor by saying he would make no decision until he spoke to Ross. He was convinced that he could ensure she would stay.

A few weeks later, the Kiss representative arrived again at Gordy's office, this time with Ross. Gordy, who had since learned that RCA was the company pursuing Ross, spoke with both. Jay Lasker joined them. She seemed receptive to his arguments. She even laughed when Gordy took her hand in the middle of the meeting and led her in a slow dance. Shortly after that meeting, however, Ross showed up at Gordy's house. The two retired to his overstuffed, antiques-filled library. Gordy later recalled there was an unusual stiffness between them—"Eyes not connecting. Cups clinking against saucers. Clothes being smoothed that were already smooth."

When Ross started the conversation by calling him Berry instead of her affectionate nickname for him, Black, he knew she was leaving. After she reiterated how much RCA was offering, Gordy tried to deflect her away from thinking about just the money. He told her that she would never find elsewhere what she had at Motown—a family and people who loved her. Gordy also tried to defend Motown's handling of her expenses by reminding her that her recording and promotion costs were exorbitant; also, he said, since not every one of her albums was a big hit, Motown often did not break even. Ross did not buy it.

Gordy did not know that before the meeting she had asked Smokey Robinson, "Do you think I'm crazy to leave Motown?"

"I don't think it's necessarily crazy, baby, but I do think there's something to say for the people who raised you and understand you best."

"What about the money, Smoke?"

Robinson knew Motown would never be able to match RCA's offer and told her so. And when she wondered if she had been too pampered and protected and that it was time for her to head out on her own, he tried to convince her that she was loved at Motown. But finally, after much discussion, she realized she had to go.

"If I don't try to go it alone," she told Robinson, "I'll never know."

By the time Ross met with Gordy, she was determined not to allow him to change her mind. She complained to one employee, "I have a few hundred thousand dollars that I can actually put my hands on. And that's it. After all that work, that's it. I have three kids. I have responsibilities, damn it. I can't believe how Berry has run my money so that it's mostly his money.

How could he do that to me after all of these years? What have I done to deserve this?" (Her complaints closely echoed those of fellow Supreme Mary Wilson from 1971.)

Once Gordy finally realized he was defeated, he halfheartedly congratulated Ross. Neither of them believed he meant it.

In May 1981, Ross signed a seven-year twenty-million-dollar deal with RCA. Gordy was devastated that after twenty-one years she was finally gone. It was a blow to his personal and professional ego. And the more he thought about it, the angrier he became. He was disappointed in her, telling colleagues that he felt she should have known better than to leave just for money.

At other, more introspective moments, he admitted that his love for her was too "protective and demanding" and that he had, in her years at Motown, pushed her "much harder" than other artists. "She got a lot of money, but money wouldn't have mattered if things had been different between us." At one point, Gordy told Lasker, "You know, Jay. I could have gotten her to stay for no money. All I had to do was marry her."

Ross later soft-pedaled her reasons for leaving in her autobiography: "Leaving Motown was a profound experience. The truth is that I did not leave Motown because I was upset or angry or hurt. I left because I was growing as a person and it was time for me to move on."

CHAPTER 33

Motown@25

THE CASH THAT HAD BEGUN FLOWING IN UNDER JAY LASKER SOON dwindled to a trickle. There were only so many ways to repackage early Motown hits and sell them to fans saturated with the same tunes. And the problems were exacerbated when Marvin Gaye, continually in crisis, left for Columbia Records.

Gordy showed little interest as events rocked his label, although he maintained an office at Motown. Immediately after losing Ross, he seemed even more sluggish and appeared to be merely going through the motions. He hardly reacted much when he heard that Georgeanna Dobbins Tillman, an original member of the Marvelettes, had died of sickle-cell amenia. In 1981, Hubert Johnson, formerly of the Contours, killed himself, and Berry again seemed unmoved.

Not even a high-publicity "reunion" tour for the Temptations—bringing back together regular members Melvin Franklin and Otis Williams with David Ruffin and Eddie Kendricks—roused his interest. The group's album *Standing on the Top*, produced by Rick James, received none of Gordy's legendary promotional flair and fell flat. At the close of a five-month tour that finished in Detroit, the artists were bickering as if it were old times. "By the time the fall rolled around," recalled Otis Williams, "I regarded the reunion not as a once-in-a-lifetime dream come true, but an exercise in torture." When the group again broke up, it was Jay Lasker who made a halfhearted attempt to smooth over the differences. Gordy was absent.

The first sign of enthusiasm that anyone noticed in him was when Suzanne de Passe, now running Motown Productions, proposed a twenty-fifth-anniversary television show to celebrate the label's history. Her idea was for the show to be taped before a live audience and then sold as a special to a network. All the profits would go to a charity. By combining altruism and nostalgia, de Passe thought she could convince almost every artist, even those who had left bitterly, to return for one night. Gordy loved the idea.

Not everyone gave an easy yes. Diana Ross did not even return de Passe's calls. During the two years since she left Motown, Ross had become an even bigger diva. She had only moderate success at RCA but relied on an energetic Las Vegas stage act for most of her income. In New York, she had finally become part of fashionable society circles, where she had always longed to be. Fashion designers Halston and Calvin Klein were constant escorts, she had a regular table at the Four Seasons, was frequently at Studio 54, had her three daughters in tony private schools, and spent weekends at the Fairfield, Connecticut, manor she had bought from tobacco heiress Nancy Reynolds. Her *Silk Electric* album cover was a commissioned Andy Warhol original. She employed an extensive personal staff that included housekeepers, chauffeurs, nannies, secretaries, assistants, wardrobe mistresses, and traveling beauticians. When Ross had left Motown, Gordy told colleagues that her ego would ruin her, and, surrounded by only sycophants at RCA, she had indeed launched disastrous ventures like her own cosmetics line, produced her own album, managed herself, and tried to start fashion and merchandising lines.

Finally, when de Passe reached her, Ross demurred. She said she felt awkward about seeing Gordy for the first time in two years at a public show. And she feared if she participated, it might anger her RCA bosses. But de Passe outsmarted Ross. She leaked word to the press that Ross would participate as a "special guest star." Once Ross's fans started clamoring for her to be part of the show, Ross felt it would be worse not to attend. She grudgingly accepted.

Michael Jackson, who had gone on to phenomenal success after leaving Motown, was also not an easy sell. Having established himself as the top pop artist, he was not anxious to retake the stage as part of the Jackson 5 just so Gordy could have good memories. Finally, de Passe asked Gordy to intervene directly. At first, Gordy said he didn't care, but de Passe convinced him that without Jackson, the show would be incomplete. When Gordy asked what might persuade him, she said simply, "Plead." Gordy visited Jackson and discovered that he was willing on one condition: he would perform "Billie Jean," a new song released by CBS that had nothing to do with Motown. How things had changed, Gordy thought, in just over a decade. The youngster from Gary was now in the stronger negotiating position. Reluctantly, Gordy agreed.

With all the stars committed, de Passe was able to get NBC to go ahead with the production. One anxious moment occurred in the rehearsals the day before the show. Diana Ross appeared wearing a floor-length white mink coat, clutching a bottle of Courvoisier, and moaning she had the stomach flu. No one asked her to rehearse, since they feared she might storm out. De Passe worried Ross might use the "flu" as an excuse not to appear at the live show, but everyone was relieved the next day—March 25, 1983—when Ross's limousine arrived at the Pasadena Civic Auditorium shortly before the curtain went up. She entered the pavilion, not talking to anyone but flashing her trademark smile to every photographer there.

The show was taped in front of a packed house. It turned out to be one of the most emotional nights of Gordy's life—a gathering of artists, many of whom he had not seen in years. Diana Ross, who was celebrating her thirty-ninth birthday the next day, sat next to Gordy. He told her she looked great. With Bob Mackie gowns and a small army of hair and makeup helpers, few people could pull themselves together better than Ross. They said little else to each other.

In vintage Motown tradition, there was backstage bickering before the show commenced. Some grumbled that the Marvelettes were not there. David Ruffin and Eddie Kendricks weren't even invited. Ruffin had created bad feelings at Motown with his million-dollar lawsuit seeking unpaid royalties. The duo was still performing, staying in roach-filled motels, constantly falling behind on taxes and large partying bills. And wherever they went, they bad-mouthed Gordy, whom they blamed vociferously for almost everything. Although they had contributed much to the label, and many artists thought they should have been there, it was not a surprise that Motown left the two talented performers off the invite list. (Within a decade, Kendricks died of lung cancer at fifty-two, and Ruffin spent time in jail for tax evasion, lost his house in repossession, and was arrested and convicted several times for drug possession. He had a ferocious crack habit that made him so paranoid that he thought IRA terrorists were chasing him. He died finally in Detroit of a drug overdose in 1991, at the age of fifty, after being dropped off anonymously at a hospital emergency room. His wife, Sandra, filed a lawsuit against Motown in 1995, charging that Ruffin had abandoned his 1968 litigation against the label only because of death threats from company officials. She was unsuccessful.)

There were other complaints. Martha Reeves's song "Heat Wave" had been cut to just a verse and half a chorus. She was steamed. The same with Mary Wells, who had been the label's first big female star. Wells's voice hadn't sounded very good to anyone, and no love was lost for her, since she had been the first to leave the label. (The chain-smoking Wells died in a few years, at forty-nine, from throat cancer.)

But once the show started, there was little reason to complain. Richard Pryor was the MC. After some nostalgic film clips of Motown's early days, the artists began their acts. Smokey Robinson was the first on the stage. He had not performed with the Miracles in more than ten years. The succession of stars was rapid: Martha Reeves, Mary Wells, Stevie Wonder, and Marvin Gaye. The Four Tops and the Temptations were presented in a mock battle, similar to the early Battle of the Stars. The audience loved it. (The groups' managers saw the commercial possibilities, and the two outfits toured together for the next three years.)

Then the Jackson 5 appeared together for the first time since they had left Motown. The audience was frantic. And after the Jacksons performed, twenty-four-year-old Michael Jackson took to the stage alone. Michael had not been on television in years, and to most viewers he seemed thinner, slightly lighter toned in his skin, and more refined in his facial features, the result of extensive plastic surgery. He wore a black sequined jacket, a silver lamé shirt, a black fedora, and short black trousers, set off by white socks and a single white glove studded with 1,200 hand-sewn rhinestones. The glove became one of his trademarks.

When Jackson went into the Moonwalk—a spellbinding routine he had developed by combining dance steps he had seen on *Soul Train* with the spinning techniques he had admired in James Brown and Sammy Davis, as well as Fred Astaire's move of going toward the toes—the audience went crazy.

"It was the most incredible performance I'd ever seen," Gordy said. He sat and marveled at the artist who had once been his. There was a tinge of sadness as he thought of what Motown could have been had it kept talent like Michael Jackson.

Before he could get too melancholy, Diana Ross was onstage, belting out some classics and talking over the audience directly to Gordy. "But Berry's always felt that he's never been appreciated," Ross said as a camera zoomed in on Gordy. (Gordy later recalled, "A little voice in my head shot back— *No Shit.*") Ross continued: "It's not about the people who leave Motown, but it's about the people who come back, and tonight everybody came back." Gordy was smiling for the camera but was thinking, "No, Diana, that doesn't cut it, that doesn't make it OK."

Ross then raised her arm and formed a fist as if in a black-power salute. Some of those gathered behind the stage curtains, including Martha Reeves, Nick Ashford, and Valerie Simpson, rolled their eyes and sighed at her theatrics.

Ross's remarks, however, caused a standing ovation. Mary Wilson and Cindy Birdsong (who had left the business, believing "I was robbed," to become a three-hundred-dollar-per-week medical-lab assistant and was now a born-again Christian) joined Ross, who was singing "Someday We'll Be Together." It was unplanned, and Ross seemed perturbed to see her two colleagues. She kept singing, while glancing occasionally behind to see what the other girls were doing. Every time she moved, Birdsong and Wilson moved with her. Then, suddenly, Ross swung around and pushed Wilson backward. "The audience gasped," recalled Wilson. "In a flash I saw something in her eyes that told me she knew she'd crossed the line." That push was edited out of the show before it aired. (The unused tape was locked away, with only Gordy and Suzanne de Passe having access.)

Smokey Robinson saved the day by rushing onstage, soon followed by other performers including Michael Jackson, Marvin Gaye, Stevie Wonder, and less well known musicians such as Marv Tarplin, the Miracles' great guitarist. Before Ross started singing "Reach Out and Touch (Somebody's Hand)," she shouted for everyone to stand back. "But there were too many of us," recalled Mary Wilson, "and we all pretty much ignored her."

When Mary Wilson grabbed a mike and started to beckon Gordy down from his balcony seat, Ross forced down her hand, pushed the mike away from her mouth, and hissed, "It's been taken care of." That was also cut from the televised show. Wilson made her own, short impromptu speech from the stage, thinking "of all the people, like my dear friend Florence Ballard, who couldn't come back." That, too, was cut from the broadcast.

Then Ross took the microphone and asked Gordy to join everyone. Gordy arrived onstage and stood awkwardly in the middle of those responsible for making Motown famous. Ross hopped up and down like a little girl, waiting for her turn to kiss him. She then walked behind him, pinching his rear as he made his way along the row of stars. Finally, Ross ran to the back of the stage and climbed the orchestra platform so that she was above everyone else. She only left it when a *Life* photographer arrived—then she literally elbowed her way through the group to get to the front, and as the flash went off she grabbed Stevie Wonder and kissed him.

"In the earlier days," recalled Mary Wilson, "Diane would do things like this, but never in public. We were best friends, and I would ignore her antics. But tonight of all nights, why did it have to be this way?"

"Fuckin' Diana," Marvin Gaye muttered to no one in particular, "what's her problem?" A lot of people left the auditorium that night expressing similar sentiments.

The show was televised two months later and received impressive ratings and critical acclaim, which led to a resurgence in Motown sales. In the fall of 1983, the show was nominated for nine Emmys. Its success also led to resentment among some of the artists who had been in it. Although they had donated their services because it was for charity, a video was soon released, off of which Motown was now clearly earning profits. Mary Wilson, for instance, thought that she should be compensated if the money wasn't all going to charity. When Gordy and the label refused, she sued—a lawsuit that would not be settled (with a small payment to her) for another six years.

But not even the grumbling could diminish the luster of the special's critical acclaim and its Emmy nominations. Gordy was at home alone on the night of the awards. When the show won as the Outstanding Variety, Music, or Comedy Program, Suzanne de Passe sprinted to the stage to collect the award. She looked directly at the camera and, with her eyes filling with tears, said, "To a man who changed my life so extraordinarily and so dramatically that I just want to tell him, Berry Gordy, I love you. And this one's for you!"

Gordy started sobbing. A quarter of a century had passed with Motown. He cried that night not only for what he had been through and the nostalgia he felt about it but also because he knew that it was ending. What he had been postponing and ignoring was now at the forefront: it was time to consider a national-distribution link with a major record company.

•　　　•　　　•

In May 1983, a few months before he would savor the Emmy victory, Gordy had walked unannounced into Jay Lasker's office. Lasker was on the phone. A pungent Cuban cigar dangled precariously out of the corner of his mouth, and he was screaming at a distributor, or so Gordy assumed.

"Don't give me that fuckin' 'the check is in the mail' shit," Lasker said in his guttural voice. "If I don't receive that fuckin' check by tomorrow, I'm pulling the fuckin' line." He slammed down the phone.

Gordy managed a weak smile as he slipped into a chair in front of Lasker's cluttered desk. "Just like the old days, huh, Jay?"

"Worse. In the old days at least you had something to look forward to. The independent distributors were getting stronger then. Now it's just the opposite."

Gordy knew it was true. For several months, he had talked with Lasker about possibly hooking up with a major label. Gordy had the latest quarterly accounting from the Novecks. It showed Motown's ills were deep and that its collection problems were accelerating.

"We can't do it anymore," Gordy said somberly to Lasker, who knew without asking what he meant. Lasker just nodded.

That day, Gordy decided to accept a distribution deal that MCA had been dangling. Irving Azoff, the new chief of MCA's record division, sorely wanted a thriving black-music division, and Motown would give him that niche overnight. And for Gordy, who tried to focus only on the benefits of such a partnership, it meant that instead of having to worry about chasing nearly two dozen financially weak distributors, one major company would give Motown a single check each month.

The new partnership got off to a great start when, a few months later, Lionel Richie's *Can't Slow Down* album became a major hit, selling more than ten million copies. Then came "Somebody's Watching Me," a song by an artist named Rockwell, who was really Gordy's son Kennedy. It was his first, and despite an unusual mix of partly sung, partly spoken lyrics cast in a

British accent, the record was a solid hit. Gordy mistakenly thought that these successes meant that Motown's money-crunch problems were over— so much so that he began another film project. This time, he was off to New York to shoot the martial-arts B movie *The Last Dragon* for a new company, Tri-Star Pictures. But it wasn't the actual filming that Gordy remembered years later but rather a single day on the set when Diana Ross unexpectedly showed up.

Ross had done two free performances in New York's Central Park to raise money to build a children's playground. The first night's show had ended with dramatic photos of Ross, wind- and rain-swept, bravely finishing her songs. Those pictures ran on the front pages of the tabloids, the *New York Post* and the *New York Daily News.* The second show, however, ended with marauding gangs of thugs mugging and beating New Yorkers and tourists. Thirty-eight were arrested, and dozens assaulted. But the real public outrage came when city officials discovered how grand Ross's spending habits were. Although she had her own chauffeured Rolls-Royce available, she spent $12,000 on limos, almost $50,000 on catering, $64,000 on first-class airline tickets for staff and assistants, and $56,000 for personal security. Even little bills shocked city officials—$431 to clean a jumpsuit she wore in one show; $260 to do her nails. When all the figures were calculated, the city spent more than $1.8 million on the concerts, and there was no money left for the playground. Finally, she took so much criticism that she hired New York's most heralded public-relations meister, Howard Rubenstein. He convinced her to donate $250,000 to build the playground. She reluctantly agreed.

She finally got her mild revenge in her 1993 autobiography, in which she wrote extensively about the concert and cast herself as a do-gooder who was victimized by an "unpleasant and difficult" mayor, Ed Koch, and an "unkind" parks commissioner, Henry Stern. The book, *Secrets of a Sparrow,* was vintage Ross, a syrupy self-tribute written in a quasi–Hallmark greeting card style full of euphemisms, highlighting her fairy-tale life while emphasizing her vulnerability but bemoaning how she was often misunderstood. There are 148 photos of her, many full-page and some in color. It is filled with personal insights such as: "Having a lot of hair is a huge responsibility, particularly when I'm traveling. It's really quite a job to wash it, brush it, and make sure that I'm not overprocessing it with too much perm or conditioner. In fact, the seemingly simple act of taking care of oneself on the road is actually not simple at all; it is tremendously difficult. There is no time for pampering oneself."

Now Ross had shown up at the movie set where Gordy was because her daughter, twelve-year-old Rhonda Silberstein, had gotten a role as an extra in a dance scene. It was her godmother, Suzanne de Passe, who had arranged the bit part, much to Rhonda's delight. Gordy and Ross had not seen each other in a year since Motown 25.

Ross walked over to Gordy. They did not kiss or hug but stood a few feet apart. "She knows," Ross said softly, nodding her head toward Rhonda. "I told Rhonda you were her father." He reached out and grabbed Ross, giving her an earnest hug.

"What did she say?" he asked.

"Not much. She was surprised and shocked, but she handled it like the champion she is."

"So what do you think?"

"I think she'll be fine. I'm not sure whether she was sad or happy, she took it so well. After all, she's known you as Uncle BB her whole life. I guess that made it a little easier."

Gordy glanced nervously over to Rhonda, who was staring at them. The youngster smiled. In a few minutes, Gordy hugged Rhonda. As he later recalled, they had hugged many times before, but this was different. It was too emotional for either to speak. Ross stood there with an enormous smile. It was the start of a relationship that over the years became increasingly important to Gordy. (Rhonda later became an aspiring jazz singer and actress.)

•   •   •

While Gordy's personal life seemed to be righting itself, his old friend Smokey Robinson, who had long been a model of dependability in an industry filled with egos that flamed out from personal excesses, had run into significant problems. Since the early 1960s, he had smoked marijuana ("gangster," as the Motown artists called it), and by the early 1970s he occasionally used powdered cocaine, as did many of his acquaintances. But Smokey had been one of the most health-conscious singers on the label, bragging in interviews that he didn't smoke even cigarettes, drink alcohol, or eat red meat. In the mid-1980s, however, shortly after the Motown reunion, Smokey had started smoking small bits of crack tucked into the end of cigarettes.

"The best shit I ever had," he recalled later. His habit started with a gram of rock cocaine that lasted for three to four days. Then he began ordering larger amounts and smoking more often. Soon he was partying in all-night binges and lost almost forty pounds off his six-foot frame. He had to pin his pants to hold them up. Friends and family pleaded with him to stop, but he waved them away, denying he had a problem. As he neared bottom, his habit contributed to the breakup of his long marriage to Claudette. (It didn't help that as Claudette made preparations for their twenty-fifth wedding anniversary, she discovered that Smokey had gotten one of his girlfriends pregnant.)

Within eighteen months, Smokey, who had always considered himself blessed for his wonderful life, was waking up in cold sweats, suffering heart palpitations, coughing up greenish phlegm, and fearing his stomach lining had worn away. He felt he "was trapped in hell and couldn't find a way out. . . . Rock cocaine was killing me." He wondered how he had gone from "being a well-respected star to some funky junkie."

At times, he thought back to when he had visited Marvin Gaye in Hawaii. "In Marvin's madness I might have seen a preview of my own paranoia," Smokey later said, "but I wasn't looking."

After Smokey walked out on Claudette, Gordy took him to his Bel Air estate for a week and tried to wean him off drugs with a combination of healthy food and articles filled with scare stories. "I didn't care," recalled Smokey. He told a friend that people were following him, and when his friend said he was hallucinating, Smokey broke away from him, sure he was part of some mysterious plot.

Smokey was the only artist Gordy personally tried to get off dope. They had been such close friends. Smokey had even named his children—son Berry and daughter Tamla—after Gordy and the company. Now Smokey, the one artist that everyone thought would never lose control, needed help. Not even Gordy knew what to do.

At concerts, Smokey sang with none of the fire that was his trademark. "I saw ghosts," he remembered. "Jackie Wilson collapsing on stage, Sam Cooke being shot through the heart. What if my heart gave out? 'He's dead,' I heard imaginary voices say as I walked back to my dressing room. 'The guy's good as dead.' "

James Jamerson, the best of the Funk Brothers in the estimation of most critics, died broke in 1983 from complications from cirrhosis and heart failure due to alcoholism. He was forty-five. Jackie Wilson, Gordy's first star, died in 1984 in a New Jersey nursing home after spending nearly ten years in a coma. Both deaths made Smokey feel mortal and unsettled him. And his unraveling life seemed to mirror Motown's own disintegration.

CHAPTER 34

"Everything Had Changed"

AFTER THE SUCCESS OF MOTOWN 25, THERE WAS A TREMENDOUS
surge of nostalgia about the label. Artists from the Rolling Stones to Sister
Sledge suddenly did Motown cover songs. Motown's music represented a
generation in 1983's *The Big Chill*. (Motown was astute enough to ask for the
film's sound-track rights, and the resulting record went platinum, selling
three million copies in the United States alone.) Michael Bennett's 1981
Broadway hit *Dreamgirls*, with a story line loosely based on the lives of the
Supremes, had an upsurge in ticket sales. (Diana Ross refused to see the
play, in which the underappreciated Flo Ballard character stole the show.)
Groups such as the Temptations and the Four Tops were just as likely to be
seen in guest appearances on popular television shows like *Moonlighting*, *The
Love Boat*, or *The Fall Guy* as they were to be seen onstage singing. Motown's
classic artists and their songs found their way into commercials as jingles,
rankling music purists but bringing the label some needed money in an
otherwise dry creative stretch.

Sometimes groups entered the charts, as the Temptations did with
"Treat Her Like a Lady," but the hits were infrequent. A series of labels—
most notably Rare Earth—created by Motown to tap into the rock and
pop market had ceased operating. The same happened with Motown's effort to get a foothold in country music with the Melodyland and Hitsville
labels. Even Soul Records, established in 1964, had finally folded in a sea of
red ink after fourteen years.

There were still major artists who had helped to create that early magic, but some were losing the battles with their demons. Marvin Gaye had, as David Ritz noted, "another series of crazy crises." In 1980, after the collapse of his second marriage and a flat album, Gaye, chased by incensed creditors and the IRS, fled to England, then to Belgium, taking his son Frankie ("Bubby") with him, something his second wife charged was kidnapping. (His son had no passport, and when Gaye crossed borders in Europe, he hid the boy under blankets.) He almost married a prostitute while in Europe—he had been fascinated by them ever since he lost his virginity to one at fifteen. He floated through a seemingly endless series of one-night stands and ingested ever more drugs. When given the chance for a decent performance, he invariably sabotaged it. He showed up too late to sing at a command performance before Princess Margaret and other royals, and on his way to Manchester, England, for a show he fled through a bathroom window in a London train station and began another drug binge. Most of those around him were hangers-on who wanted only to party on his dwindling money.

David Ritz visited him in Europe, and Gaye launched into a long monologue about how much he liked cocaine, which he used to snort, rub on his gums, and sometimes even eat. "I like the feeling," he said. "No one will ever tell me it's not a good feeling. A clean, fresh high, 'specially early in the morning, will set you free." It was in Europe that he started freebasing, ratcheting up his addiction and paranoia to a new intensity.

His long relationship with Motown had been irreparably damaged when the company, anxious to get some money back from the six hundred thousand per record they had guaranteed him, released *In Our Lifetime* in 1981 without his permission. In an interview in *Blues and Soul* magazine, Gaye infuriated the label when he told the reporter, "As far as I am concerned it is definitely my last album for Motown—even if Berry does not release me from my existing recording obligations and I am, in fact, under obligation to record for the rest of my natural life for Berry. If he refuses to release me, then you'll never hear any more music from Marvin Gaye. . . . I'll never record again." Gaye was now so open about his drug use that he snorted copious amounts of cocaine in front of the interviewer.

When he returned to the United States in 1982, after a nearly three-year exile, he was signed to CBS Records, which had bought out his Motown contract. Late that year, Gaye delivered a smash song for CBS—the moving and deeply erotic "Sexual Healing," his first number-one hit since 1971's "What's Going On?" The song brought him his first ever Grammys in the R&B category for Best Male Vocal and Best Instrumental Performance. In April 1983, he reluctantly agreed to an American concert tour—his first in four years. But he was as erratic as ever, consuming huge amounts of coke, arriving spaced out and late for concerts, and chattering obsessively about the next song he wanted to record, "Sanctified Pussy." (It was later released by CBS as "Sanctified Lady.") At times, he fretted about being assassinated. During some live performances, he surprised audiences by doing a striptease. His confrontational dealings with CBS began to resemble those of his turbulent Motown years.

When Smokey saw him for the first time since 1979, he recognized that Gaye was still stoned. Robinson, battling his own drug problems, tried getting through to him but failed.

On April Fool's Day 1984, the day before Gaye's forty-fifth birthday, his father, a prominent Washington, D.C., Pentecostal preacher, shot him to death. As David Ritz reported, Gaye had been living, high on drugs, in his parents' house for the last six months. "With Marvin high on coke and his father, a few steps down the hallway, drunk on vodka, the atmosphere was poisoned by chemicals, memories, and mutual antagonism." At times, Gaye seemed close to madness, hurling around pistols and telephones and threatening his parents. He locked himself in his bedroom, sending out for coke and watching porn videos. He ranted that a murderer was stalking him. He beat up a Japanese girl and an Englishwoman after having sex with them. "My son, my poor son," said his mother after his death, "turned into a monster."

On the day he was murdered, Gaye and his father had gotten into a screaming match over a misplaced letter from an insurance company. When his father refused to leave his bedroom, Gaye started punching and shoving him. Gaye's mother stopped the scuffle. The senior Gay had warned that if Marvin struck him, he would kill him. In a few minutes, he reappeared and fired a bullet from a .38-caliber revolver into his son's chest. As Gaye slumped to the floor, his father walked over and fired another shot into his chest, point-blank.

After the murder, the transvestite lifestyle of Gaye's flamboyant father soon became public and kicked off a tabloid frenzy over the sordid details of Gaye's life and his family. Stories of how the senior Gay had terrorized his children, beating Marvin repeatedly, also filtered out. Marvin, who had sold an estimated thirty million albums during his career, had four homes, ten cars, and two boats, in addition to a gigantic jewelry collection. Yet he died with only $30,000 cash. He owed more than $4.2 million to the IRS, $300,000 in alimony to Anna and Janis, and hundreds of thousands more to creditors worldwide. Seventeen months after Gaye's murder, his personal property was auctioned at the Los Angeles County Courthouse. Motown successfully bid $46,000 for the film rights to his life.

The senior Gay, meanwhile, pleaded not guilty, claiming he hadn't known the gun was loaded. Before the trial began, a walnut-sized tumor was discovered in his brain and was surgically removed. Still, a court held him competent to stand trial. Persuaded by traces of PCP in Gaye's body (a drug that can induce violent behavior) and the large bruises on Gay Sr., the judge let him plead guilty to involuntary manslaughter, and in November 1984 he walked out with only a five-year probationary sentence. Gay Sr. was free to return home to his own bouts with depression and his fifth of vodka a day. But at least his son's violent struggle with life was over.

"Now I was moving in the same direction [as Marvin Gaye]," recalled Smokey. "Why couldn't I stop myself?" Smokey's drug addiction had worsened. Finally, in 1986, he was taken by a friend to local faith healer Jean Perez, who ran a ministry in a run-down section of Los Angeles. From that night—when she embraced and prayed with him—Smokey, who was not a religious man, abruptly abandoned drugs. "The Lord washed me clean" was how he later described it.

By the late 1980s, Smokey was on a yoga and vitamin regimen. He came no closer to drugs than golf, which he jokingly called "the heroin of sports." He even had a minirevival. Managed by Motown executive Mike Roshkind, he started a worldwide tour, had three hits off a new album, *One Heartbeat*, in 1987, and even won his first Grammy. That same year, a sobbing and emotionally spent Smokey was inducted into the Rock and Roll Hall of Fame and Museum.

But Motown, even with a revived Smokey, was still a shadow of what it had been. "The Motown we knew in the sixties," said Otis Williams, "was a once-in-a-lifetime phenomenon, and everything had changed, even Berry."

At times, it appeared that the label had mostly become famous groups touring the golden-oldies circuit. Since Motown owned the names, it could freely substitute new singers to keep a group going. Martha Reeves had fake Vandellas, Mary Wilson—who had developed her own cocaine problem in the 1980s—sang with substitute Supremes, and the Marvelettes had no original members left but still performed under the group's name. (The Marvelettes had a white promoter who managed their career independent of Motown—rumor had it that he had won them in a high-stakes card game with Gordy.) The Temptations had only two originals, Otis Williams and Melvin Franklin. Over twenty-eight years, the group ran through fourteen different singers. Some ex-members toured as "formerly of the Temptations." The Four Tops were all original members but were gone from the label for eight years before returning in 1983. Songwriting and production teams like HDH and Ashford and Simpson—who had married after leaving Motown—were distant memories.

In 1985, Motown produced another television special, *Motown Returns to the Apollo.* It was supposed to be a tribute to all the acts that had performed there over the years. Bill Cosby emceed, and the old-timers reassembled, including Diana Ross, Martha and the Vandellas, Stevie Wonder, the Four Tops, and Smokey Robinson and the Miracles. Mary Wilson, who had lawsuits against Motown, was not invited, although a friend took her along as his date, and she sat in the front row during the taping. At one point, Bill Cosby dragged her onstage to sing some backup for Smokey and the Four Tops. For the finale, when all the artists gathered for a farewell song, Diana Ross approached her.

"Want to pick a fight tonight, Mary?"

Wilson ignored her. She just said, "Diane, I love you."

Mary Wilson was edited out of the final show.

A few years later, when Mary Wilson attended a Diana Ross solo concert and went backstage to see her, Ross refused to come out until Wilson left. Their break, after years of rivalry and jealousy, was now complete.

CHAPTER 35

The Final Curtain

As record sales floundered, Motown found it increasingly difficult to sign new artists, and it started reducing its staff. The label needed forty million dollars annually just to break even. The tightfisted Lasker did not believe in expensive music videos, just as MTV was revolutionizing the industry. A succession of department chiefs, most without any vision for a turnaround, did not help.

The problem was more than just losing money. Gordy had never considered music work—it was almost an enjoyable hobby. But after thirty years, it had become unpleasant. He had always assumed that building a company was an entrepreneur's most difficult task, but he now discovered that saving one was even tougher. When he started out, he considered what he was doing to be about "90 percent creative and 10 percent business. . . . Now, doing about 98 percent business and 2 percent creative, I was stuck and I hated it."

Over a two-year stretch, Motown had had only two gold albums and one platinum one. But there were some bright spots. The only consistent artist was Lionel Richie, who had left the Commodores for a solo career in 1982. He became the first performer to have an astonishing nine number-one hits in nine consecutive years. In some weeks, Richie's album sales accounted for 90 percent of all records sold by Motown. And in 1985, Stevie Wonder picked up an Oscar for the best song for "I Just Called to Say I Love You," the theme song for the film *The Woman in Red*. (Songwriter Lloyd Chate, who charged that Wonder had stolen his song, sued him, but a decade later a San Francisco appeals courts ruled for Wonder.) The following year, Richie also took home an Oscar for "Say You, Say Me," the theme to the Gregory Hines/Mikhail Baryshnikov movie, *White Nights.*

But Motown was not doing well enough. After missing the disco craze, it had also missed the beginning of the surge in rap and hip-hop. Rumors circulated in the industry press that Motown might be for sale. The company denied it. But actually, Jay Lasker had approached Gordy in 1986 with the news that MCA now wanted to buy the company.

A sale was something that Gordy once considered unthinkable. He had always wanted to keep the business in his family, passing it to his children. He also felt some obligation to the early employees as well as to Motown's legacy and its black heritage. But by 1986, it was on the table. One thing that might have influenced Gordy's decision to sell was something that Billy Davis, his longtime man Friday, told him. Davis had moved into Gordy's mansion to spend his final months when dying of AIDS. One night, as he was near the end, Davis advised Gordy: "You're tired, man. You better enjoy your life. Live. . . . You better get a grip. You got too much shit on your head. You've done it, man. You've done it. Move on. Look at our heroes— Joe Louis, Sugar Ray Robinson—one fight too many. Look at those other cats who didn't know when to stop. You could just be another nigger who made it to the top and died broke." Gordy took it all in.

Through the early fall of 1986, Gordy weighed his options: selling off every company, including Motown and Jobete; selling only one with some stipulations; selling just personal assets; and even auctioning off some masters. Finally, in November, he was leaning toward a sale of just Motown. With Lasker, Harold Noveck, and Lee Young, Gordy had a luncheon at his home for MCA's top executives, Irv Azoff, Sid Sheinberg, and Lew Wasserman. The MCA executives assured Gordy they would protect Motown's integrity while also paying him a top price.

One possible hitch was that Stevie Wonder still had that unusual contractual clause that allowed him to veto any sale. He had already rejected a sale of Jobete a year earlier. Gordy invited Wonder over on Christmas Eve. Wonder, not atypically, was five hours late. He then wanted to start playing some new songs. When Gordy finally got around to explaining the purpose of their meeting, Wonder was initially resistant. He told Gordy, "As long as

you own it, I feel secure—in the hands of strangers it might change drastically." But Gordy was blunt about the company's dire financial problems:
if it was not sold, it might fold. Wonder was uncharacteristically somber
and quiet. Gordy told him that Motown and MCA had arranged a three-
million-dollar bonus for Wonder if the sale went through. The next day,
though, he called and reluctantly gave his approval.

Getting past Wonder was one hurdle, but now Gordy learned that MCA
was not valuing the company as he had expected. They concentrated on
Motown's current financial statements, meaning they did not want to pay
much. And some of the terms of the proposed contract—such as that
Gordy would be forbidden from using his own name in the music business
for five years—rankled him. The contract kept getting shuffled between
lawyers, but as Gordy recalled, "Each time they would return it, it seemed
never to reflect exactly what we had agreed upon. That, I think, bothered me
the most." Also, time was against him. He stood to lose a major tax break if
he did not complete the deal by December 31. MCA knew that, and Gordy
surmised they were dragging out the negotiations in the hope that he might
cave in. They, as had many others in his past, underestimated Gordy. They
were also not aware that prominent black figures, such as Bill Cosby, were
strongly urging him not to sell Motown. Suddenly, the fighter in Gordy
again emerged, and twenty-four hours before the deadline he called Sidney
Noveck and told him to call it off, saying he had a bad feeling about it.

The reaction around Gordy was mixed. Motown insiders feared Gordy
might never sell yet still not get involved enough to rescue the company. It
might just sink with him. Friends and colleagues outside the company, ig-
norant of the desperate situation, were relieved. They sent congratulations,
thinking that his refusal to sell signified his desire for a comeback. "The
outpouring of love and admiration was overwhelming," said Gordy. "It
made me feel like a hero or something just because I didn't sell. I got
psyched."

For the first half of 1987, Gordy was reenergized and focused more on
Motown's recording business than he had in years. He realized how thoroughly Jay Lasker had cheapened Motown's value by selling inexpensive
repackagings in the schlockiest retail stores. The two clashed over Lasker's
failure to aggressively promote Gordy's latest protégé, Carrie McDowell, a
young white singer who was living at Berry's Bel-Air mansion. Gordy finally

fired Lasker in July 1987, after he had run Motown for seven years. "He thinks he's so smart," Lasker groused to a friend, shortly after he was let go. "Let Gordy fuck it up on his own."

Gordy promoted from within, making Skip Miller, the chief of the promotion department, and Lee Young Jr., the company's in-house counsel, copresidents. And Gordy induced Al Bell, who had run rival Stax Records, to head the creative division.

Gordy put the company through a restructuring in which he laid off some well-paid executives, field promotion representatives, sales employees, and promotion and publicity workers. But the efforts were too late.

One afternoon, in early 1988, Smokey Robinson sat in Gordy's office. He could not imagine Motown without Gordy. That day, he told Gordy how much he wanted a hit to help save the company and how much everyone appreciated what Gordy was doing.

Gordy did not react. He just sat there, slumped in his chair. Smokey noticed the dark circles, the clenched jaw, and the eyes that did not seem to focus on anything in particular. His dear friend was a defeated man. Finally, Gordy spoke up softly. He told Smokey that it would take much more than a single success to get the company out of the red. The only way to save it was to sell it.

"I will always remember that look on Smokey's face," Gordy recalled. "His eyes were like saucers. . . . As he sat there stunned, I multiplied his reaction by millions of other people."

"I'm tired, Smoke."

"I know you are. I know you are."

Fay Hale, who had worked at Motown for nearly thirty years, came in a few days later and told Gordy many still thought he shouldn't sell. "They say Motown is too important. It means too much to too many people to sell. It's an institution. How can you sell a way of life?"

Gordy exploded. "*They* say! Who in the fuck is *they?* Do *they* know I'm losing millions? How in the hell can anyone tell me I can't sell something I created, nurtured, and built from nothing?"

·   ·   ·

By June 1988, Gordy had decided to sell to Boston Ventures Management, a group of investors led by a former executive vice president of First National Bank of Boston and MCA, for sixty-one million dollars. As Gordy reflected in his autobiography, "From eight hundred dollars to sixty-one million. I had done it. I had won the poker hand." Boston Ventures now owned 70 percent of the label, while MCA Records held 20 percent and also got a ten-year agreement to distribute Motown's records for a 25 percent fee. At Gordy's insistence, 10 percent of the equity was set aside for future black ownership.

What was sold was the Motown name and record catalog, the masters, and all the artists' recording contracts. Gordy did not sell Jobete Music, which owned the publishing rights to Motown's songs, nor did he sell his film and television company. The following year, that looked like a good move, when Suzanne de Passe and Gordy oversaw Motown's incredibly successful CBS miniseries *Lonesome Dove*, which collected an Emmy, a Golden Globe, and a Peabody. It made up for a series of missteps from television's *Nightlife*, with David Brenner, to films like *The Last Dragon* to the stage's *Satchmo;* in 1991, Gordy withdrew from production and allowed de Passe to take a majority control of their joint company and rename it De Passe Entertainment. "I've made a lot more money for others than for myself," commented de Passe. "I can't retire."

There were immediately critics of Gordy's Motown sale. They thought he either had a duty to hold or that he erred by selling to a white-run conglomerate. Dick Griffey, whose Solar Records was briefly touted as the "Motown of the eighties" was typical: "To see Motown sucked up by corporate America is a sad day for most blacks in this country. The Motown tradition lies in the black experience—their music, their ownership, their history—and I think that's where it should remain." Jesse Jackson had visited Gordy before the sale and also urged him not to sell. Gordy had told him, "I have three choices: sell out, bail out, or fall out. Which do you suggest?"

Jackson gave a small laugh and didn't argue any further. "OK, Brother Berry, do whatever you have to do" were his parting words.

What the new owners bought was a shadow of the company that had been so dynamic in the 1960s. Boston Ventures and MCA selected a successful black music executive, Jheryl Busby, a thirty-nine-year-old MCA music-division president, to run Motown. Busby had come up from the streets of Los Angeles to head MCA's moribund black-music division and in four years transformed it from a money loser into a producer of nearly one hundred million dollars in sales. He received a 10 percent "black-owned" stake in the venture.

The following year, Diana Ross, who had been signed to MCA, agreed to return to Motown. Instead of taking money, she took some MCA stock and a spot on the board of directors. Ross was now living an even more luxurious and pampered lifestyle due to her marriage to a multimillionaire Norwegian shipping magnate, Arne Naess. She traveled between four homes, was a regular on the Concorde, and sternly directed an extensive staff that attended to her wishes. At businesses she visited, even at Motown, and at her own lawyers' offices, workers were now told not only to call her Miss Ross but to "avert their eyes" when she was around. It seemed, more-over, that Ross might very well get the reception she hoped for at the new Motown when Jheryl Busby exclaimed, "It's like the queen returning home." It was not to be. When she finally released a new album—*Workin' Overtime*—it stalled at number 116, and no single cracked the top one hundred. It was her worst-selling album in twenty years.

Within three years of Gordy's sale, a serious dissension had developed between Busby and MCA. Although the new Motown had some hits—Boys, a teen quartet from Compton, California, had two number-one hits on the black singles chart, while Today, a New York quartet, also went number one—Busby generally thought that MCA treated Motown's products as second-class and failed to promote them adequately. MCA in turn had grown frustrated with Busby. Busby was a superb marketer, but he was a disorganized administrator who relied too heavily on an inexperienced staff. Further, Stevie Wonder and Lionel Richie were not delivering long-overdue albums. Other acts could not break out.

Busby announced that MCA had treated Motown "like a Third World country" and tried to get the Dutch-based PolyGram to manufacture and distribute its records. PolyGram offered a thirty-million-dollar line of credit and a promise to hire black-music specialists to promote Motown's music. When MCA ignored the company's complaints, Motown signed with Poly-Gram. It simultaneously sued MCA, seeking ten million dollars in damages, charging "ineptitude and deliberate misconduct," and asked the court to terminate MCA's ten-year distribution deal. MCA countersued two weeks later. It charged Motown and Boston Ventures of conspiring to sell the company to a wealthier suitor while cutting MCA out.

Finally, in 1993, Boston Ventures sold Motown to PolyGram. MCA's lawsuit was settled. The new owners issued ten million shares of stock worth $301 million, and they assumed $24 million in company debts. That price tag netted PolyGram thirty artists, the biggest of which was Boyz II Men, and a catalog of thirty thousand master recordings, dating to the sixties.

Gordy had initially not taken much interest in the MCA-Motown discord. He was consumed by a divorce from his latest wife, Grace Eaton, whom he had married not long after he had sold the company. But now, with PolyGram in charge, he was brought back as the company's chairman emeritus. Jheryl Busby stayed on as president. PolyGram also made a contribution to Gordy's 1987 legacy to Detroit, the not-for-profit Motown Historical Museum, housed in Hitsville's original building on West Grand Boulevard. Michigan declared it a historical landmark the following year.

But the Motown museum seemed small-time compared to PolyGram's ambitious plans to put the Motown name on everything from children's books to theme restaurants, hotels, television shows, videos, films, stereo equipment, clothing, souvenir shops, and even a cable shopping channel. There were suggestions of a Chrysler LeBaron Motown Edition. Jheryl Busby, still at the helm, had a clear vote of confidence for major expansion with the infusion of PolyGram money. Busby was convinced that Motown's problem was that it did not keep up with music trends and did not aggressively try to capitalize on its brand-name value.

"There was a study done by the Harvard Business School," Busby said, "and it found that only three American entertainment trademarks are known around the entire world—Disney, Playboy, and Motown. If Disney has Mickey Mouse and Donald Duck and Goofy . . . then these are our characters, if you will, the licensable names that make Motown come alive for the consumer."

A Motown Café eventually opened in midtown Manhattan but folded after five years, challenging the idea that there was a sustained public demand for memorabilia dished up with overpriced and mediocre food.

By this time, Diana Ross, Stevie Wonder, the Four Tops, and the Temptations were newly signed to lifetime contracts with the label. But Smokey Robinson, the writer of more than four thousand songs, had finally left in 1991 for the small SBK Records label. (He returned in 1999, after SBK folded—his new manager was Suzanne de Passe.) And even though Motown was no longer Gordy's company, lawsuits from the way he had run the firm for thirty years continued to haunt it. In 1993, the same year Poly-Gram bought it, former singer Kim Weston—complaining that she had "never, ever received an artist royalty from Motown"—filed a three-million-dollar lawsuit over royalties back to 1966. PolyGram settled the suit a year later for an undisclosed sum.

In 1995, thirty-four-year-old Andre Harrell, born two years after Gordy founded Hitsville, replaced Busby. Harrell—who received a twenty-million-dollar signing bonus—was called rap's Berry Gordy for the incredible success at his own label, Uptown Records, where he had launched artists such as Mary J. Blige and Jodeci, as well as discovered the nineteen-year-old producer Sean "Puffy" Combs. He moved Motown from Los Angeles to New York, since he thought there were better R&B producers there for the music he believed would revitalize the label. Gordy called Harrell "extremely bright" and believed he was the right person for the job.

Harrell promised to open a satellite office in Detroit but never did. A year into his tenure, he still had not produced a single hit but had made headlines with his lavish spending, much of it on high-profile parties he called "ghetto fabulous," which in his case consisted of a mixture of edgy black attitude with white monied business moguls. He had no management experience with a company the size of Motown, and both hubris and ego led him to make early mistakes. When he moved the company to New York, he let some of his workers rack up twenty-thousand-dollar monthly hotel bills for "temporary quarters," and he hired his personal valet as a member of the A&R department. In Los Angeles, he threw himself a welcome bash at Le Dome restaurant, featuring a bevy of models hired from a local agency. A fountain ran with Cristal Champagne at two hundred dollars per bottle. Then he spent one million dollars on his own promo campaign, plastering posters around New York and Los Angeles that showed him cockily smoking a cigar while sitting in a leather wing-backed chair. FROM UPTOWN TO MOTOWN, the poster announced. Compounding all the excess, in an interview he bragged about his budget-busting spending, how "fly" he had become since taking over Motown. He boasted that the money PolyGram paid him to run the label "was like NBA superstar shit numbers."

The media started taking the company's nonperformance to task.

Newsweek, for instance, did an extensive story titled "Pittsville, U.S.A." Calling the company "hitless and hemorrhaging money," the magazine charged that "Motown is but a shadow of yesteryear, lately known more for unbridled spending and champagne soirees than for its music." PolyGram showed its displeasure by leaking word that it expected to rack up 1996 losses of seventy million dollars and that no profits were expected until 1998. Harrell did not last that long; he was gone twenty-two months after taking over. During his tenure, he had failed to break any major act. Danny Goldberg, president of PolyGram's Mercury Group, assumed overall responsibility for the floundering label and appointed George Jackson, a partner at a television and music-production company, as Motown's new president. (Jackson died in February 2000 at the age of forty-two of complications from a stroke.)

Gordy caught the music world by surprise in December 1997 when he announced he had sold half of Jobete and all of a sister company, Stone Diamond Music, to EMI Music Publishing for $132 million. Those two companies had been bringing in an estimated ten million dollars annually in profits to Gordy. In addition to earning money every time a Motown song played on any commercial radio station, Jobete had licensed the songs for movie and television themes and many international commercials—some, like "I Heard It Through the Grapevine," were used for everything from California Raisins (an incredibly lucrative ten-year campaign) to German cigarettes and Finnish chewing gum. Gordy, sixty-eight years old, and co-owner Esther had decided that it was time to sell a chunk of their prized collection.

"I'm surprised that the catalog was available" was the typical reaction, expressed by Cowen and Company analyst Harold Vogel. But the sale made sense since EMI—the world's largest owner of song catalogs—had handled the international distribution for Jobete for years; with the purchase, it gained domestic rights. Moreover, Gordy felt comfortable with Martin Bandier, the chairman of EMI, saying, "He's part of the family."

EMI was now responsible for administering the publishing catalog's day-to-day operations, freeing Gordy and Berry IV from the constraints of running the remnants of the family business. "Today's business climate is not for me," Gordy told *The New York Times.* "I'm a songwriter, that's what I love. That's the real reason why I'm giving over the songs." Gordy began enjoying semiretirement, spending many days on the golf course with Smokey Robinson or close friends Sidney Poitier and producer David Wolper. He was a regular at Hugh Hefner's Playboy Mansion soirees and on the lunch and party circuit with David Geffen and Barry Diller.

Gordy was conscious that time was passing quickly. Within only a few years, many of his former artists had died. Junior Walker had died of cancer in 1995. That year had also seen the passing of Melvin Franklin, the bottomless-bass Temptations singer, of heart failure at only fifty-two. Choker Campbell, Motown's musical director, died two years before that of cancer at fifty-nine and was so broke that no one claimed the body—he was buried in a public grave. And just after the Jobete sale, the Four Tops' soft-spoken Lawrence Payton died at fifty-nine of liver cancer.

Randy Taraborrelli interrupted Gordy's leisurely life by writing a book about Michael Jackson, in which he alleged that Gordy had cheated his artists out of their royalties. Gordy sued for one hundred million dollars for libel. Gordy had already tried to ensure that his view of Motown's history was preserved when he published his autobiography, *To Be Loved.* It barely had a cross word about anybody. Gordy told friends he had found it cathartic and had exorcised some of his lingering unease about selling the label. Not all who had worked with him were as pleased. To them, Gordy had taken too much credit for the label's success. "There are a lot of inaccuracies in the son of a bitch," said Barney Ales. "When I first read it [in a draft manuscript], it was nine hundred pages long. Somebody edited it way down, and they lost a lot of the *wes.* Now it's all *Is.*"

In June 1998, Motown had its fortieth anniversary in Detroit, and it was cast as a gala charity event for twelve needy organizations. The slide of the company was evident. Smokey Robinson, Diana Ross, Stevie Wonder, and Gladys Knight were no-shows.

Six months later, in December, Seagram bought PolyGram for $10.4 billion and folded PolyGram's music division into its own Universal Music Group, thereby creating the world's largest record company. Seagram executives pledged to save $300 million a year in costs by firing 3,000 employees, dropping 200 bands, and gutting some of the poorest-performing labels. Initially, it seemed as though Motown was about to be sent to its grave. Duke Fakir told a Detroit newspaper, "It's really a sad day. It's really disheartening." He announced he would like to buy the Motown name from Universal and revive the label with a Detroit base. No one from Universal even returned his calls.

•   •   •

But Universal finally decided the recognizable brand name was worth keeping. It renamed a new subsidiary Universal/Motown, with a rejuvenated artist roster that included acts such as Grammy winner Erykah Badu and Chico DeBarge, as well as a New York staff of thirty. Rising R&B executive Kedar Massenburg was appointed to run the operation. Boyz II Men, Motown's biggest act in the 1990s, was moved to the Universal label. Danny Goldberg, who had overseen the operation before the shakeup, got a ten-million-dollar golden parachute. It seemed as though no one had made money off Motown since Gordy had sold it except the executives who had passed through the revolving door at the chairman's office. The only Detroit-era acts still with the new company were Diana Ross, Stevie Wonder, and the Temptations.

In 1998, Suzanne de Passe, in partnership with Berry Gordy, produced a successful television docudrama depicting the lives of the Temptations. It helped briefly to revive interest in the label and its early music. Smokey Robinson composed the film's theme music. De Passe caused some controversy when she filmed the project in Pittsburgh, saying that Detroit "was too burned out" to play itself. Unnoticed by most people, the show also spawned four lawsuits. The heirs of the late David Ruffin and others sued over rights of privacy. One vainly tried to get an injunction to stop the show's airing. The other suits, filed after the show was broadcast, were dismissed. Johnnie Mae Matthews, a former manager of the group, sued for defamation. In true Motown style, the music and entertainment eventually stopped, but the litigation lasts forever.

•   •   •

Sometimes, memories of the early days at a company that is such a part of American music history engender nostalgia, even among artists who have long since fallen out with one another. That happened in 2000, when Diana Ross, Mary Wilson, and Cindy Birdsong decided to do their first concert tour in thirty years. Between the Motown aura and the hunger of baby boomers for a final chance to see the Supremes, the concert promoter, SFX, thought the multicity tour would earn millions. But it played out as anyone familiar with the history of infighting at Motown might have expected. After all three singers agreed to the tour and tickets were sold, there were press leaks that Diana Ross had been guaranteed between fifteen and twenty million dollars. Now separated from her tycoon husband of thirteen years, Arne Naess, she needed a large infusion of money to maintain her grand lifestyle. After they learned about Ross's fee, Wilson and Birdsong also demanded larger guarantees. When more money was not forthcoming, they canceled. Mary Wilson took to television and blasted the tour. Ross ignored the controversy as though it was beneath her and instead hired two backup singers, Lynda Laurence and Scherrie Payne, both of whom had sung in the Supremes three years after she had left the group. Ticket sales were so slow, however, that a few concert dates were postponed, then canceled. Finally, the entire tour was called off after a few lackluster shows—reviews were terrible, and audiences were small. Bob Grossweiner, a concert-industry analyst, said, "There has never been a tour bought by a national promoter that's done as bad as this one and had a clash over money like this one."

In 2002, Ross admitted herself for alcohol and drug rehab at the Promises facility in Malibu, claiming addictions to prescription pills and liquor. Ross's spokesman said the fifty-eight-year-old diva wanted to be ready for another planned summer tour. On August 1, nine days after kicking off a ten-city North American concert tour, Ross abruptly canceled her tour, offering no explanation. Poor ticket sales had again dogged her.

·   ·   ·

Also in 2002, Motown reported its first profits in a decade. It boasted a record fifteen Grammy nominations. And with the label temporarily fashionable again, its president, Kedar Massenburg, relentlessly pursued the same goal that PolyGram had failed to reach ten years earlier: selling the Motown brand name to advertising agencies. Singer Brian McKnight was signed to promote Sears, AT&T, Verizon, and Hanes; the Temptations landed Häagen-Dazs; Erykah Badu got the Gap and Heineken Red; and India.Arie was also placed with the Gap. Massenburg announced that the company had an agreement with Kraft Foods for Black History Month—its female R&B singers were depicted on boxes of macaroni and cheese. A Motown CD sampler became a popular giveaway at T.G.I. Friday's restaurants nation-wide. And Pepsi and Motown were in negotiations to launch a music and soda campaign tentatively called "Neo-Classical Soul."

·　　·　　·

The legacy and achievements of Motown still stand as record holders in the music industry: memories that will last generations; music that never seems out-of-date. But there was also jealousy, power lust, greed, and personal excesses that derailed almost all the major musicians in their primes. To those who loved the music and now read about the latest commercialization of the label, those heady days—when a group of enthusiastic teenagers in the tiny Hitsville studio changed the music world—seem very distant indeed.

Bibliography

BOOKS

(Instances in which a second edition is listed refer to the paperback)

Anderson, Christopher. *Michael Jackson: Unauthorized.* New York: Simon & Schuster, 1994.

Benjaminson, Peter. *The Story of Motown.* New York: Grove Press, 1979.

Betrock, Alan. *Girl Groups: The Story of a Sound.* New York: Delilah Press, 1982.

Bianco, David. *Heat Wave: The Motown Fact Book.* Ann Arbor: Pierian Press, 1988.

Brown, Geoff. *Diana Ross.* New York: St. Martin's Press, 1981.

Dannen, Fredric. *Hit Men: Power Brokers and Fast Money Inside the Music Business.* New York: Times Books, 1990.

David, Saul. *The Industry.* New York: Times Books, 1981.

Davis, Sharon. *I Heard It Through the Grapevine: Marvin Gaye.* Edinburgh: Mainstream, 1991.

Dineen, Catherine. *Michael Jackson: In His Own Words.* London: Omnibus Press, 1993.

Early, Gerald. *One Nation under a Groove: Motown and American Culture.* Hopewell, N.J.: Ecco Press, 1995.

Fong-Torres, Ben. *What's That Sound: The Contemporary Music Scene from the Pages of Rolling Stone.* New York: Anchor, 1976.

George, Nelson. *Top of the Charts.* Piscataway, N.J.: New Century Education Corporation, 1983.

———. *The Michael Jackson Story.* New York: Dell, 1984.

———. *Where Did Our Love Go? The Rise and Fall of the Motown Sound.* New York: St. Martin's Press, 1985.

Goodman, Fred. *The Mansion on the Hill: Dylan, Young, Geffen, Springsteen, and the Head-on Collision of Rock and Commerce.* New York: Times Books, 1997.

Gordy, Berry, Jr. *To Be Loved: The Music, the Magic, the Memories of Motown.* New York: Warner Books, 1994.

Gordy, Berry, Sr. *Movin' Up.* New York: Harper and Row, 1979.

Haskins, James. *The Story of Stevie Wonder.* New York: Lothrop, Lee and Shepard, 1976.

————. *I'm Gonna Make You Love Me: The Story of Diana Ross.* New York: Dell, 1980.

Hirshey, Gerri. *Nowhere to Run: The Story of Soul Music.* New York: Times Books, 1984.

Jackson, La Toya, with Patricia Romanowski. *Growing Up in the Jackson Family.* New York: Dutton, 1991.

Jackson, Michael. *Moonwalk.* New York: Doubleday, 1988.

Kingsley, Abbott. *Calling Out Around the World: A Motown Reader.* London: Helter Skelter Publishing, 2001.

Larkin, Rochelle. *Soul Music.* New York: Lancer Books, 1970.

Lazell, Barry, ed. *Rock Movers and Shakers.* New York: Billboard Publications, 1989.

Licks, Dr. *Standing in the Shadows of Motown: The Life and Music of Legendary Bassist James Jamerson.* Wynnewood, Pa.: Dr. Licks Publishing, 1989.

Miller, Jim, ed. *The Rolling Stone History of Rock and Roll.* New York: Random House, 1976.

Morse, David. *Motown.* New York: Macmillan, 1971.

Motown Album, The. Introduction by Berry Gordy. New York: Sarah Lazin Books, St. Martin's Press, 1990.

Motown Story, The. Foreword by Adam White. London: Orbis, 1981.

Pareles, Jon, and Patricia Romanowski, eds. *The Rolling Stone Encyclopedia of Rock and Roll.* New York: Rolling Stone Press / Summit Books, 1983.

Peterson, Virgil W. *The Mob: 200 Years of Organized Crime in New York.* Ottawa, Ill.: Green Hill, 1983.

Pitts, Leonard, Jr. *Papa Joe's Boys: The Jacksons Story.* Cresskill, N.J.: Starbooks, 1984.

Reeves, Martha, and Mark Bego. *Dancing in the Street: Confessions of a Motown Diva.* New York: Hyperion, 1994.

Report of the National Commission on Civil Disorders. New York: Bantam Books, 1968.

Ritz, David. *Divided Soul: The Life of Marvin Gaye.* New York: McGraw-Hill, 1985; New York: Omnibus Press, 1991.

Robinson, Smokey, with David Ritz. *Smokey: Inside My Life.* London: Headline, 1989.

Ross, Diana. *Secrets of a Sparrow.* New York: Villard, 1993.

Shaw, Arnold. *Black Popular Music in America.* New York: Schirmer Books, 1986.

Singleton, Raynoma Gordy. *Berry, Me, and Motown: The Untold Story.* Chicago: Contemporary Books, 1990.

Stars and Superstars of Black Music, The. Secaucus, N.J.: Chartwell Books, 1977.

Taraborrelli, J. Randy. *Motown—Hot Wax, City Cool, and Solid Gold*. New York: Doubleday, 1986.

———. *Call Her Miss Ross*. New York: Birch Lane Press, 1989.

———. *Michael Jackson: The Magic and the Madness*. New York: Birch Lane Press, 1991.

Turner, Tony, with Barbara Aria. *All That Glittered: My Life with the Supremes*. New York: Dutton, 1990.

———. *Deliver Us from Temptation: The Tragic and Shocking Story of the Temptations and Motown*. New York: Thunder's Mouth Press, 1992.

Waller, Don. *The Motown Story: The Inside Story of America's Most Popular Music*. New York: Charles Scribner's Sons, 1985.

Wenner, Jann, ed. *The Rolling Stone Interviews*, Vol. 2. New York: Warner Books, 1973.

Westbrooks, Logan, and Lance Williams. *The Anatomy of a Record Company*. Los Angeles: Westbrooks, 1981.

Whitall, Susan. *Women of Motown: An Oral History*. New York: Avon Books, 1998.

Williams, Otis, with Patricia Romanowski. *Temptations*. New York: G. P. Putnam's Sons, 1988.

Wilson, Mary, with Patricia Romanowski. *Supreme Faith: Someday We'll Be Together*. New York: HarperCollins, 1990.

Wilson, Randall, and Thomas Ingrassia. *Forever Faithful! A Study of Florence Ballard and the Supremes*. San Francisco: Renaissance Sound and Publications, 1999.

SELECTED ARTICLES

Allen, Bonnie. "Suzanne De Passe: Motown's $10 Million Boss Lady." *Essence*, September 1981.

Alterman, Lorraine. "Supremes, Flo Ballard: It's Said She's Leaving." *Detroit Free Press*, September 1, 1967.

Arrington, Chris Rigby. "DePasse—The Protégé." *California Living*, January 15, 1984.

Ashenfelter, David. "Songwriters Battle Gordy." *Detroit Free Press*, July 21, 1998.

Barrett, Charles. "Motown Industries Growth." *The Hollywood Reporter*, November 1, 1976.

Beier, Elspeth. "Motown's Going Uptown in Boss' Palatial New Digs." *Detroit Free Press*, March 2, 1967.

Benjaminson, Peter. "One of Original Supremes Now Leads Forgotten Life." *Detroit Free Press*, January 17, 1975.

Bennett, Laurie. "Maxine Powell—Style." *Detroit Free Press Magazine*, January 3, 1993.

Brown, Geoffrey. "The Jackson Family Grows More Versatile." *Black Stars*, September 1975.

Brown, Stanley H. "The Motown Sound of Money." *Fortune,* September 1, 1967.

Burrell, Walter Price. "The Accidental Supreme." *Soul,* March 9, 1970.

———. "The Intimate Lives of the J5." *Black Stars,* November 1971.

Cabell, Terry. "Motown Lady—Esther Gordy Edwards." *The Detroit News,* February 2, 1981.

Cain, Pete. "The Motown Mob." *Rock,* July 6, 1970.

Charles, Nick. "The Private Soul of Michael Jackson." *Rock and Soul,* May 1975.

Crenshaw, J. "Jackson 5 Stir Up Some Great Vibrations." *Soul,* October 15, 1973.

"David Ruffin Does His Thing with Talent and Flexibility." *Michigan Chronicle,* June 21, 1969.

Davis, Leah. "Berry Gordy—King of the Mountain." *Soul,* October 6, 1969.

DeLeon, Robert A. "At Home with Jackie Jackson." *Jet,* February 13, 1975.

Dreyfus, Joel. "Motown's $10 Million Gamble." *Black Enterprise,* July 1981.

Dunbar, Ernest. "The Jackson Five." *Look Magazine,* August 25, 1970.

Eldridge, Royston. "Will Stevie Wonder Become Another Sammy Davis?" *Melody Maker,* April 5, 1969.

Everette, Cheryl. "dePasse—The Boss." *New York Daily News,* December 20, 1986.

Feldman, Jim. "Miss Ross to You." *The Village Voice,* August 2, 1983.

Forsythe, William. "Diana Ross Walks Out." *Philadelphia Bulletin,* June 1969.

Galloway, Earl. "Fantastic Jackson 5." *Chicago Defender,* June 12, 1975.

George, Nelson. "Diana Ross on Diana Ross." *Record World,* November 14, 1981.

———. "Standing in the Shadow of Motown." *The Musician,* October 1983.

George, Nelson, with Mark Rowland. "Michael Jackson's Perfect Universe." *Musician,* July 1984.

Gilmore, Mikal. "Motown's Showy, Soulful Anniversary." *Los Angeles Herald Examiner,* March 28, 1983.

Goodman, Fred. "J5's High Energy Keeps Vegas Jumpin'." *Record World,* April 21, 1975.

Graff, Gary. "Renewing Motown." *Detroit Free Press,* August 4, 1993.

———. "Motown Move Was Bad for Music—Gordy 'Wanted to Be in the Movie Business.'" *Detroit Free Press,* November 5, 1994.

Grein, Paul. "Motown Retunes Its Sputtering Hit-Making Record Machine." *Los Angeles Times,* February 10, 1988.

———. "The End of an Era." *Los Angeles Times,* June 6, 1988.

Haber, Joyce. "Berry: The Mentor from Motown." *Los Angeles Times,* January 20, 1975.

Harmetz, Aljean. "How to Win an Oscar Nomination." *The New York Times,* April 3, 1973.

Higgins, Chester. "The Temptations." *Ebony,* April 1971.

Hilburn, Robert. "Motown's Berry Gordy Looks Back." *Los Angeles Times,* March 22, 1983.

Holliday, Barbara. "De-Supremed Supreme Talks." *Detroit,* October 20, 1968.

Holloman, Ricky. "Keeping Up to Date with Jermaine and Hazel." *Right On!,* October 1974.

————. "The Jackson 5—Offstage." *Right On!,* July 1975.

Hunt, Dennis. "Michael Jackson—Hooked on the Spotlight." *Los Angeles Times,* December 17, 1979.

Johnson, Herschel. "Motown: The Sound of Success." *Black Stars,* June 1974.

Johnson, Robert E. "Berry Gordy Tells Why He Allowed His Daughter to Wed." *Jet,* January 3, 1974.

Jolson-Colburn, Jeffrey. "Jackson, EMI Targeting Jobete." *The Hollywood Reporter,* October 6, 1989.

————. "Jobete Says It Has $190 Million Bid." *The Hollywood Reporter,* November 10, 1989.

King, Don. "Joe Jackson on J-5 Split: Never Gave Us an Opportunity." *Soul,* August 18, 1975.

————. "Motown Prexy Says Jermaine Will Stay." *Soul,* August 18, 1975.

————. "Why J-5 Switched to Epic Revealed." *Soul,* August 18, 1975.

————. "Motown Censors Performers." *Good Evening,* April 29, 1976.

————. "Jermaine Jackson: I Just Made My Choice . . . They Made Theirs." *Soul,* November 8, 1976.

Kisner, Ronald. "Ex-Supreme Fights." *Jet,* February 20, 1975.

LaMarre, Linda. "The Motown Mansion." *Detroit News Magazine,* April 11, 1971.

Legge, Beverly. "Jackson 5 at the Centre of the Universe." *Disc,* May 3, 1975.

Lingeman, Richard B. "The Big, Happy, Beating Heart of the Detroit Sound." *The New York Times Magazine,* September 27, 1966.

Lucas, Bob. "Jackson: His Music and His Family Life." *Jet,* November 20, 1976.

McBride, James. "Suzanne dePasse—Wonder Woman." *US,* February 24, 1986.

Madias, Mike. "Motown Owes Early Fame to 'Frantic' DJ in Detroit." *The South End,* January 25, 1990.

Manning, Steve. "Behind the Scenes with the Jackson 5." *Rock and Soul,* July 1975.

————. "The Truth about Michael Jackson." *Black Stars,* January 1978.

Martinez, M. R. "Motown: The Legend Loses Its Luster." *Rhythm and Business,* July 1988.

"Marvin Gaye Turns Actor," *Tan Magazine,* May 1969.

Mazza, Bob. "Jackson 5 Moves to Epic." *The Hollywood Reporter,* July 17, 1975.

Miller, Bill. "Echoes: Motown Origins." *Let It Rock,* November 1974.

Miller, Edwin. "Michael Jackson Digs the Wiz." *Seventeen,* August 1978.

"Motown, The Supremes, and Hitsville USA." *Sepia,* August 1966.

Murphy, Mary. "An Intimate Glimpse of Diana Ross." *Los Angeles Times,* November 1, 1972.

Nickerson, Rhetta. "Hair-Pulling, Choking and Knives." *Soul,* January 15, 1973.

O'Connor, John J. "Motown 25." *The New York Times,* July 8, 1983.

Orth, Maureen. "Boss Lady." *Newsweek,* June 28, 1976.

Oviatt, Ray. "Hitsville, U.S.A." *The Blade,* August 22, 1975.

Peyko, Mark C. "Change Was Motown's Greatest Enemy." *The Ann Arbor News,* July 16, 1988.

Playboy, interview with Berry Gordy, September 1994.

Pomerantz, Susan. "Motown Readies Lawsuits." *The Hollywood Reporter,* June 10, 1975.

Pond, Steve. "Lionel Richie: The Pot of Gold." *Rolling Stone,* March 3, 1983.

Propes, Steve. "Lamont Dozier." *Goldmine,* June 20, 1986.

Roberts, Johnnie L. "Lady Sings the Blues—dePasse." *Newsweek,* November 2, 1998.

Robinson, Louie. "Why Diana Ross Left the Supremes." *Ebony,* February 1970.

Rubine, Namoi. "Papa Jose Reflects on His Talented Sons." *Soul,* July 9, 1973.

"Ruffin Is His Own Man Now." *Michigan Chronicle,* May 19, 1969.

Sauter, Van Gordon. "Motown Is Really Big." *Detroit,* March 21, 1965.

"Special Salute Issue to Motown President Barney Ales, A." *Record World,* July 2, 1977.

Spiegelman, Judy. "David Ruffin Answers the Big Question." *Soul,* May 19, 1969.

———. "What Does the Future Hold for the Jackson Five?" *Soul,* February 14, 1972.

Stassinopolous, Maria. "Diana Ross." *Town and Country,* May 1983.

Stein, Jeannine. "Suzanne dePasse: My Style." *Los Angeles Herald Examiner,* August 26, 1985.

Stevenson, Richard. "Can Motown Be Supreme Again?" *The New York Times,* February 19, 1989.

———. "Putting Motown Back on the Map." *The New York Times,* February 19, 1989.

Talbert, Bob, and Lee Winfrey. "A Talk with Berry Gordy." *Detroit Free Press,* March 23, 1969.

Taraborrelli, Randy. "Hollywood Is Talking about Diana Ross." *Black American,* March 10, 1976.

———. "An Intimate Chat with Martha Reeves." *Right On!,* July 1977.

———. "Richard Pryor—the Wiz." *Soul,* October 30, 1978.

———. " 'Diana' the Untold Story—the Complete Series." *Soul,* winter 1981.

Thurston, Chuck. "Motown Exiting City a Little at a Time." *Detroit Free Press,* June 9, 1972.

Tiegel, Eliot. "Motown Expansion in High Gear with Broadway, TV, Movies." *Billboard,* June 11, 1966.

Townsend, Richard. "Diana Did It Berry's Way." *New York Sunday News,* August 8, 1976.

Turbo, Richard. "The Very Private Lives of the J5." *Sepia,* October 1973.

Werba, Hank. "Motown's Berry Gordy Emerges." *Variety,* January 27, 1975.

White, Adam, ed. and interviewer. *"Billboard* Salutes Berry Gordy—The Man Who Built Motown."*Billboard,* November 5, 1994.

Williams, Michaela. "The Motown Sound." *Chicago Daily News,* September 25, 1965.

Williams, Ted. "The Supremes at N.Y.'s Copa." *Soul,* June 8, 1967.

Willing, Richard. "Motown Feud Strikes Sad Chord." *Detroit News,* February 26, 1995.

Wilson, Jeffrey. "Exclusive Interview with Mary Wilson, Pts. 1 and 2." *California Voice,* July 1983.

Woods, Nadra. "How Motown Made Millions in Music." *Sepia,* July 1971.

Papers and Archival Collections

Motown Records, Universal—New York company archives, including all Motown Record Corporation press releases, promotional materials for record releases, artist fact sheets, and artwork.

Government Publications, Collections, and Documents

Amended articles of incorporation and the certificate of merger and amendments of Motown Record Corporation, April 7, 1976, Wayne County archive.

Forms of the U.S. Patent Office, nos. 965,808 and 965,809, registering in the name of Motown Record Corporation the logo Jackson 5ive and the name Jackson Five (class 107, Int. CI. 41).

Testimony of Berry Gordy Jr., before the Senate Copyright Subcommittee, 92d Cong., 1st sess. *Congressional Record* (April 19, 1971), vol. 117.

Selected Trial Transcripts and Proceedings

Fannie Armstrong v. Gordy Co., Civil Action 91-121906, Wayne County Third Circuit Court.

Florence Ballard v. Leonard A. Blum, Civil Action 166269, Wayne County Third Circuit Court, 1970.

Bromery v. Motown Record Corp., Civil Action 93-329145, Wayne County Third Circuit Court.

Cheryl R. Bromery v. Motown Record Corp., Civil Action 93-329145, Wayne County Third Circuit Court.

Gail Davis v. Diana Ross, U.S. District Court, Southern District of New York, 1984.

Dozier v. Jobete, Civil Action 92-235544, Wayne County Third Circuit Court.

Lamont Dozier v. Jobete Music Co., Civil Action 92-235544, Wayne County Third Circuit Court

Mary Wilson Ferrer v. Motown Record Corporation, before the State of California Labor Commissioner, 1977.

Holland v. Jobete, Civil Action 88-815355 (also 93-300180), Wayne County Third Circuit Court.

Brian Holland v. Jobete Music Co., Civil Action 93-300180, Wayne County Third Circuit Court.

Edward Holland v. Motown Record Corp., Civil Action 92-233992, Wayne County Third Circuit Court.

Holland-Dozier-Holland v. Motown Record Corp., Civil Related Actions 91-132170; 91-826947; 92-235544; 93-300180; 94-404193; 96-625302, Wayne County Third Circuit Court.

Katherine Jackson v. Joe Jackson, Los Angeles Superior Court, Los Angeles County, Case 42680; also a second action in Case D076606.

Michael Jackson et al. v. Motown Record Corporation of California et al., Los Angeles Superior Court, Los Angeles County, Case 139795, 1975; related is *Toriano Jackson, Sigmund Esco Jackson, Marlon Jackson, and Michael Jackson, a minor, by Joseph Jackson, his Guardian, v. Motown Record Corporation of California*, 1977. This case also comprises:

——. Deposition of Joe Jackson, November 18, 1975 (Supplemental Declaration, February 20, 1976; Declaration, March 30, 1976).

——. Depositions of Michael, Jermaine, Tito, Jackie, and Marlon Jackson, January 15, 1976.

——. Sworn Declaration of Michael Jackson, February 20, 1976.

——. Deposition of Berry Gordy, March 4, 1976.

——. Deposition of Suzanne de Passe, March 4, 1976.

——. Sworn Statement of Anthony D. Jones, March 4, 1976.

——. Sworn Declaration of Ralph Seltzer, March 5, 1976; Deposition of Seltzer, March 24, 1976.

Jobete Music v. Edward Holland, Civil Action 91-105618, Wayne County Third Circuit Court.

David Ruffin v. De Passe, Civil Actions 81-120366; 96-651416; 98-826947, Wayne County Third Circuit Court.

David Ruffin v. Motown Record Corporation, Wayne County Third Circuit Court, October 3, 1968.

Schroder v. Jobete, Civil Action 94-40181L, Wayne County Third Circuit Court.

Agatha Weston v. Jobete Music, Civil Action 94-404193, Wayne County Third Circuit Court.

Index

About the Author

GERALD POSNER, a former Wall Street lawyer, is an award-winning author of seven books on subjects ranging from Nazi war criminals to assassinations to the lives and careers of politicians. A regular panelist on the History Channel's *HistoryCENTER*, he has written dozens of articles and editorial pieces for national newspapers and magazines. He lives in New York and Miami with his wife, author Trisha Posner. More info is at www.posner.com.

About the Type

This book was set in Centaur, a typeface designed by the American typographer Bruce Rogers in 1929. Rogers adapted Centaur from the fifteenth-century type of Nicholas Jenson and modified it in 1948 for a cutting by the Monotype Corporation.